LABOR ECONOMICS

Second Edition

LABOR ECONOMICS

Theory, Evidence, and Policy

BELTON M. FLEISHER

Ohio State University

THOMAS J. KNIESNER

University of North Carolina

Prentice-Hall, Inc., Englewood Cliffs, New Jersey 07632

Library of Congress Cataloging in Publication Data

FLEISHER, BELTON M
  Labor economics.

  Includes bibliographies and index.
  1. Labor economics. I. Kniesner, Thomas J.,
joint author. II. Title.
HD4901.F47 1980   331   79-21218
ISBN 0-13-517433-3

Editorial/production supervision
  and interior design by Ann Marie McCarthy
Cover design by Edsal Enterprises
Manufacturing buyer: Edmund W. Leone

Printed in the United States of America

10 9 8 7 6 5 4 3 2 1

PRENTICE-HALL INTERNATIONAL, INC., *London*
PRENTICE-HALL OF AUSTRALIA PTY. LIMITED, *Sydney*
PRENTICE-HALL OF CANADA, LTD., *Toronto*
PRENTICE-HALL OF INDIA PRIVATE LIMITED, *New Delhi*
PRENTICE-HALL OF JAPAN, INC., *Tokyo*
PRENTICE-HALL OF SOUTHEAST ASIA PTE. LTD., *Singapore*
WHITEHALL BOOKS LIMITED, *Wellington, New Zealand*

To
Charlotte and Harry

Contents

PART II

The Labor Market in the Short Run under Competitive Conditions   *45*

CHAPTER 3

The Demand for Labor in Competitive Markets   *47*

The Firm's Labor Demand Curve When Capital Is Fixed.
The Demand Curve for Labor When the Firm Adjusts Capital.
The Demand for Labor by a Competitive Industry.
Evidence on the Demand for Labor.   Frontiers of Labor Demand Analysis.
Conclusion.

CHAPTER 4

Labor Supply: Family Members in the Short Run   *95*

The Utility Function.   Consumption Opportunities: The Budget Constraint.
Utility Maximization: The Decision Whether or Not to Work.
Utility Maximization: Hours of Work.   Evidence on Labor Supply.
Frontiers of Labor Supply Analysis: The New Home Economics.   Conclusion.

CHAPTER 5

The Interaction of Supply and Demand in Competitive Labor Markets   *153*

Equilibrium in a Single Competitive Labor Market.   Multimarket Equilibrium.
Frontiers of Competitive Equilibrium Analysis: The Economics of Industrial Safety.
Conclusion.

PART III

The Labor Market in the Short Run under Conditions that Interfere with Competition   *183*

CHAPTER 6

The Labor Market When Buyers Are Noncompetitive   *185*

Product Market Monopoly.   Monopsony.
Evidence : The Incidence of Monopsony in the United States.
Frontiers of Labor Economics : Pay and Performance in Professional Baseball.
Conclusion.

CHAPTER 7

The Labor Market When Sellers Are Noncompetitive:
The Economics of Unions   *217*

The Formation of Unions.   Union Membership.
Sources and Uses of Union Power.   Measuring the Economic Effects of Unions.
Frontiers of Labor Economics : Public Employee Unionism.   Conclusion.

PART IV

The Labor Market in the Long Run   *267*

CHAPTER 8

Long-Run Labor Supply: Human Capital and the Household   *269*

The Household Investment Framework.
Evidence on the Rate of Return to Investment in Schooling.
Frontiers of Labor Economics : Investment in Children.   Conclusion.

CHAPTER 9

Investment in Human Capital: Firms   *307*

An Overview of Measurement Problems.   Theoretical Analysis.
Measuring OJT Costs and Returns.   Frontiers of OJT Analysis.   Conclusion.

PART V

Some Labor Market Aspects of Economic Welfare   *337*

CHAPTER 10

Wages and Wage Structure   *339*

The Historical Behavior of Real Wage Rates in the United States.
The Distribution of Earning Capacity among Individuals.
Frontiers of Labor Economics: Does Investment in Human Capital Really Affect
    Labor Market Productivity?
Conclusion.

CHAPTER 11

Unemployment   *371*

Unemployment in Labor Markets.
The Varieties of Unemployment and Their Causes.
Distinguishing among Frictional, Structural, and Cyclical Unemployment.
Frontiers of Labor Economics.   Conclusion.

CHAPTER 12

Unemployment, Money Wages, and Inflation   *425*

Search Behavior and Inflation.
Inflation, the Firm's Employment Strategy, and "Waiting."
Evidence on Inflation and Unemployment.   Conclusion.

Preface

This book is an extensive revision of *Labor Economics: Theory and Evidence* by Belton Fleisher. Every chapter has been rewritten to incorporate the explosion of theory and research that has gone on in labor economics over the past ten years and to enlarge coverage of topics which experience tells us were treated too briefly in the first edition. So much of this text is new that it is fair to look upon it as an endeavor equally shared by both authors. Users of the first edition will note the following significant changes and additions:

1. An attempt has been made to show the applications of each important component of labor market theory to social policy.
2. Most chapters now include a section on "Frontiers of Labor Economics." These are especially interesting areas of study into which economists are just beginning to venture. The purpose of these sections is to promote student interest in these areas of research and to present material that is a little more advanced than the remainder of the text.
3. We have greatly increased coverage of the following important topics: labor unions, the labor market under noncompetitive conditions, human capital, and unemployment.
4. We have provided a detailed outline of each chapter as a guide to both instructor and student.
5. Each chapter now concludes with a set of exercises.
6. An instructor's manual contains additional theoretical and empirical material to aid students and instructors who want a more intensive course. It also provides brief answers to the exercises.

In the chapter outlines, we have indicated with an asterisk (*) sections that require a bit more mathematical or quantitative sophistication than others.

They may be omitted at the discretion of the instructor. Some of these sections are included in the "Frontiers" discussions, and others in the main body of the chapters. We have intentionally introduced a certain "unevenness" of difficulty in the book because we want those students who are willing and able to do so to get as clear a feeling and understanding for what scientific labor economics is all about as is possible in an undergraduate text. Obviously, within the space constraint of a usable textbook we have not been able to achieve anything approaching uniform coverage in all areas of current research in the field. Our choices of what material to include in these sections were governed by our judgment as to their value in teaching labor economics.

As with the first edition, the goal we have set for ourselves has been to integrate modern neoclassical labor market theory, policy applications, and evidence in one text. We have aimed for a book that enables the student to develop a set of tools which will be useful *after* the course has been completed. Toward this end, much emphasis has been placed on a problem solving approach—the use of economic analysis to develop sensible views of current issues. The exercises at the ends of the chapters are designed to aid further in the development of these skills. In presenting evidence, we discuss problems of measurement in labor economics, and try to help the student evaluate how well data currently gathered correspond to variables in our theoretical analysis. Chapter 2 is entirely devoted to a survey of measurement problems in economics. It is designed to give the student enough information to read the remainder of the text intelligently, even without previous courses in statistical procedures.

We have organized the second edition into five general parts. In Part I we develop the concept of labor economics as a science. In Part II we consider the labor market in the short run under competitive conditions, and in Part III under conditions that interfere with competition. Part IV presents the material on the labor market in the long run: investment in human capital. Part V deals with some labor market aspects of economic welfare: real wages, unemployment, and inflation.

Within each chapter a basic theoretical framework is first developed, then manipulated to produce implications about behavior. Some of the behavioral implications are important in their own right; others produce a basis for sound economic policy. Finally, the best evidence available concerning the validity of the theory is presented and discussed.

We feel strongly that the approach we have adopted helps to achieve the goal of promoting responsible and informed citizenship through liberal education. We live in an age of great danger to science through politicization of universities and the educational process in general. At the same time, government is increasingly using the advice of social scientists to help design social programs. It is crucial that citizens understand the scientific methods and criteria which can help them choose among alternative outcomes to find the policies that will promote desired social ends most efficiently.

Acknowledgments

Our greatest debt is to the numerous scholars whose attempts to relate economic theory to the world around us have resulted in the articles, dissertations, monographs, and books that provide the basis for much of this text. We are extremely grateful to the reviewers whom Prentice-Hall has asked to comment on all or part of the second edition. Their comments have been of great help. We trust that when we have decided not to follow their advice, our reviewers do not interpret these difficult decisions as reflecting lack of appreciation for the time and effort they have devoted to us. The following is an alphabetical list of the scholars Prentice-Hall asked to help us. The length of the list is an indication of the care our publisher has devoted to ensuring a high level of quality. These reviewers are Daniel S. Hamermesh, Michigan State University; Edward Lazear, University of Chicago; Philip L. Martin, The Brookings Institution; Richard W. Moore, LeMoyne College; Gerald W. Scully, Southern Methodist University; Norman J. Simler, University of Minnesota; Michael L. Wachter, University of Pennsylvania; Bruce Vavrichek, University of Maryland.

We have also been generously advised by friends and colleagues at our respective institutions. These, in alphabetical order, include (at Ohio State) William Dewald, Howard Marvel, and Stephen McCafferty; and (at the University of North Carolina) C. A. Knox Lovell, Solomon W. Polachek, and Helen V. Tauchen.

In addition, we would like to thank Donald Cymrot (Miami University of Ohio), Robert Fearn (North Carolina State University), Roger Feldman (University of Minnesota), Barry Hirsch (University of North Carolina at Greensboro), Randall King (University of Akron), and Marjorie Bechtel McElroy (Duke University) for their helpful comments.

The following students have read all or part of the manuscript at various stages and have helped us immensely to eliminate mistakes and expository difficulties: Gordon Massey at Ohio State and Francis Pampush at the University of North Carolina.

Finally, we want to acknowledge the help of Jeanette White, who typed the manuscript with her usual skill and good cheer.

PART I

Labor Economics
as a Science

CHAPTER 1

Introduction: The Science of Labor Economics

A. Educational Objective: To introduce you to the general way in which economists conceptualize labor issues

B. Labor Economics as a Science
1. Why care about the science of labor economics
   a. Scientific knowledge valuable for own sake
   b. Scientific knowledge serves as a basis for evaluating alternative social policies
      (1) Positive aspects of public policy
      (2) Normative aspects of public policy
2. The science of labor economics as a systematic study leading to the discovery of regular patterns of behavior
   a. Events leading up to such discoveries: hypothesis formulation
   b. Evaluation of a discovery: hypothesis testing

C. Labor as a Factor of Production
1. Labor is an essential ingredient in the production of nearly every commodity
2. An input-output table for society as a conceptual framework for viewing the role of labor as a factor of production

D. Labor as the Human Resource
1. Is it proper to subject labor to a logical quantitative analysis similar to that of markets for money or commodities
2. Labor is a unique factor of production
   a. Physically inseparable from the human being in which it is embodied
   b. Indefinite contracting (slavery) is illegal

3

E. Labor as a Source of Income
1. Sales of labor services account for a majority of the sales of all factors of production
2. Circular flow of income in society
F. The World of Labor: Behavior to Be Explained

Labor Economics as a Science

This is an introduction to the way economists think about labor. By contrast, we might concern ourselves with how employers think about labor, or with how they ought to think about it. Another possibility would be to discuss labor problems from the point of view of employees and other members of the labor force. Each of these approaches has merits, and they are not mutually exclusive. The emphasis of this book, however, is on labor economics as a science.

Positive Analysis and Labor Market Policy

Economists engage in the scientific study of the allocation of scarce resources among alternative uses. Labor, or labor power, is an extremely important resource. It is so important that there have been attempts to found economics on the proposition that labor is the source of all value. While it has turned out to be more useful to consider the production of commodities as dependent upon a variety of resources in addition to labor, such issues as the pricing and allocation of labor are still among the most important in economics.

Why should you care about the science of labor economics? Only a very few readers of this text plan to have careers as economists—practicing social scientists. Scientific knowledge is valuable for its own sake; but more important, it serves as a basis for evaluating alternative social policies. As citizens you will want to be able to develop informed judgments concerning labor market policies. Should you favor lowering minimum wage rates for youth? Should there be more or less "free" education? How big should labor unions be? What restrictions should be placed on them? These and many other questions affecting labor markets are dealt with by government at various levels, and scientific knowledge of labor markets will help you to decide how to answer them. Even if you do not plan to become a professional economist or actively involved in political decision-making, you will at least want to be able to choose intelligently among politicians advocating alternative approaches to these and other economic problems. So, even though we take a *scientific* approach to labor economics, our goal is to help you formulate clear ideas about labor market *policy*.

The economic policies you prefer will depend in part on your *normative* judgment as to what social goals you believe are desirable. This text cannot provide the answers to such normative questions as whether incomes should be more equally distributed or whether those who earn the largest amounts deserve to keep all their income. It will, however, help you to decide which kinds of policy actions will achieve your desired goals most efficiently. What will help improve the well-being of poor people most effectively—a progressive income tax, more schooling, minimum wage legislation, or stronger unions? The answers to these questions involve *positive* judgments based on scientific knowledge.

Normative questions are extremely important, but their discussion is not a part of scientific labor economics. We may discuss a question such as this one: "Does the personal income tax reduce or increase the amount of work people want to do?" This is a *positive* question, since it can be answered on the basis of scientific economic analysis. Everyone with the appropriate analytical training should reach a similar conclusion. However, the answer will not tell us whether an income tax is good or bad, since we may differ in our view of the ethical desirability of basing tax payments on income or wealth. The difference between normative and positive can be viewed as analogous to *equity* versus *efficiency*. While it is scientifically possible to determine whether society is obtaining the maximum output from its set of resources (efficiency), whether those resources are used in a way that is "fair" to the members of society (equity) is a normative question; one person's judgment is no more or less acceptable than another's. It is just as "reasonable" to have the currently existing set of incomes in the United States as it is to take money from you and give it to me (or vice versa).

There are a number of reasons why in this text we direct our attention to *positive* aspects of public policy and labor markets. Most of us have been exposed to much more discussion of the moral issues surrounding labor markets than the positive issues, and our analysis here will partially correct this imbalance. Most important, however, if you wish to make statements as to what governmental policy *should be* concerning labor issues, you must accompany those statements with suggestions for implementation. It is not sufficient to say that government should foster lower unemployment, for example. You must also make a recommendation as to *how* this is to be done. Should unemployment insurance be reduced? Should wage subsidies be paid to employers who hire more labor? In short, positive analysis is necessary for normative analysis. In order to suggest a governmental action, it is necessary to have a "feel for" whether or not that action will have the desired effect. This comes with experience, and the discussion in the next chapter will provide you with practice in analyzing how governmental actions influence labor market behavior.

What, then, does the science of labor economics entail? We use the word "science" to mean a systematic study leading to the discovery of regular patterns of behavior. But what events lead to such discoveries, and how can we know a discovery when we see one? The events leading to discoveries and the criteria for evaluating them are much the same as in other sciences. Consider the science of aeronautics, for example. Aeronautical engineers have rather good ideas about what combinations of metals, design, and power will cause an airplane to fly. By means of analysis, they can plan an airplane in advance and be fairly confident of most of its aeronautical characteristics. When a new design has passed through the final stage of production, its designers have hypothesized that it will fly. The hypothesis is tested by a pilot (usually highly paid, which suggests that the hypotheses of aeronautical engineers are not always true), and if the plane flies, we say the hypothesis is confirmed by observation, or by "the facts." If it crashes, we say the hypothesis is disconfirmed. Of course, before we finally decide to accept the hypothesis as useful for predicting the behavior of the airplane, many test flights are necessary. If the first flight is a failure, a minor modification of design may result in a substantial improvement in the predictive value of the hypothesis that the airplane will fly. On the other hand, even the best-tested airplanes sometimes crash because of factors over which the designers did not have adequate control. Thus, even a widely accepted hypothesis, such as "Under certain conditions a DeHavilland Twin Otter will fly," will occasionally be contrary to observed phenomena. We accept the hypothesis that Twin Otters are airworthy, even though it does not predict perfectly, because it is the best available hypothesis about Twin Otters.

Scientific studies in many fields have led to the formulation of hypotheses whose predictions of observable behavior are accepted with widely varying degrees of certainty. Most of our hypotheses about airplanes probably fall somewhere in the middle of the certainty scale. Near the most certain extreme of the scale is the hypothesis that if a lead ball is dropped from a roof, it will fall to the ground; near the most uncertain extreme lie the attempts of geologists to predict earthquakes and of meteorologists to forecast the weather. In some branches of economics, behavior patterns are rather accurately predicted by existing hypotheses (for example, the hypothesis that the long-run marginal propensity to consume in the United States is 0.9), while in others we have only begun to develop an orderly framework for observing behavior (a good example of unreliable hypotheses pertains to our ability to predict the turning points of business cycles).

How are hypotheses developed? Of course, there is no surefire "recipe" for developing useful hypotheses about economic or any other kind of behavior. Nevertheless, on the basis of experience, two ingredients appear to be necessary. One is intuition—a feeling for what is relevant and interesting, or "the ability to ask the right questions." The second ingredient is the ability to develop an orderly or logical framework or theory, rationalizing what has been seen and suggesting what else will be observed if the theory is a useful one. The implications of a theory about observable phenomena are hypotheses, and the two most important ingredients in formulating useful theories and hypotheses are relevance and logic.

This book explores some of the important hypotheses economists have developed about labor. Not all of them have been thoroughly tested; many of them have hardly been tested at all. Nevertheless, they represent an index of the degree of knowledge we possess about labor and labor markets. Since we are interested in labor market theory because of its importance in evaluating policy alternatives, we will show some of the implications of the hypotheses we discuss for policy. Equally important, we will try to give you an idea of how well these hypotheses fare when compared to "real world" behavior. After all, if they are not "true," then they cannot be of much use in helping to decide on good labor market policy.

Labor as a Factor of Production

Labor is an essential ingredient in the production of nearly every commodity, along with other productive resources such as soil, water, or iron ore. Of course, most productive factors are seldom used in their pure states. By the time they enter the productive processes, they have usually gone through several stages of production or refinement. Soil is graded, fertilized, and contoured; ore has to be discovered, mined, and transported; water must be purified and piped. Labor is a very highly refined resource, and it appears in many varieties. Very few persons enter the labor force before the age of sixteen; by that time, we have all been fed, clothed, educated, doctored, tested, and sometimes psychoanalyzed, repaired, and moved, so that even the most basic labor power is itself the result of an intricate production process.

Nevertheless, as a first approximation let us imagine that there are basic factors which go into the production of the commodities consumed in the various sectors of the economy. This way we can develop a framework for viewing the economic system which helps illustrate some of the basic questions the subject of labor economics is designed to answer. Figure 1–1 is a simple *input-output table* consisting of six numbered or lettered rows and six columns. Each number represents an industry, such as agriculture, steel, or automobiles, which combines factors of production and semifinished commodities in the production of further commodities. The rows lettered L and K represent factors of production, such as labor and capital. The columns labeled C and G represent the sectors of the economy which purchase the goods and services produced by industries 1 through 4 and some of the factor services yielded by L and K. The sectors C and G represent two divisions of the economy, a household and a government sector (we assume for simplicity there is no investment or foreign trade).

Sales or Output →

Purchase or Input ↓

	1	2	3	4	C	G
1	X_{11}	X_{12}	X_{13}	X_{14}	X_{1C}	X_{1G}
2	X_{21}	X_{22}	X_{23}	X_{24}	X_{2C}	X_{2G}
3	X_{31}	X_{32}	X_{33}	X_{34}	X_{3C}	X_{3G}
4	X_{41}	X_{42}	X_{43}	X_{44}	X_{4C}	X_{4G}
L	X_{L1}	X_{L2}	X_{L3}	X_{L4}	X_{LC}	X_{LG}
K	X_{K1}	X_{K2}	X_{K3}	X_{K4}	X_{KC}	X_{KG}

FIGURE 1–1. Input-Output Table

Note: X_{ij} = Sales of industry i to industry j; thus X_{12} represents the *output* of industry 1 sold to industry 2; X_{1C} represents the output of industry 1 sold to households; X_{L1} represents purchases of labor by industry 1. [i = a row, j = a column.]

Each row of the input-output table represents the sales or output of an industry or factor; each column represents input. Thus, going across row 1 from left to right, we observe the amount of industry 1's output used by itself in further production, the amount used by industries 2 through 4, and the amount of 1's output which is finally sold to households as consumption or to the government. Similarly, going down column 1, we observe the input of industry 1 into itself, of industries 2 through 4 into industry 1, and inputs of basic factors L and K. It may seem strange to you that the basic factors are also purchased by households and government, but such purchases merely reflect the use of labor as domestic service in households and as stenographic and other services in government; the use of capital services by households in the form of houses, automobiles, refrigerators, and so on, and in government in the form of buildings, typewriters, airplanes, and the like.

By definition, the output of each industry is equal to its inputs. Thus, the sum of the entries in columns 1 through 4 equals the sum of the entries in each of the corresponding rows. It follows that the sum of the columns C and G must equal the sum of the rows L and K. This is in accordance with our usual procedures of accounting; all inputs are accounted for. It would be very simple to construct your own input-output table, inserting numbers such that the output of each industry equals its input, and thus convince yourself that the sum of columns C and G must equal the sum of rows L and K. In terms of national income accounting, the sum of C and G represents "final sales" and equals gross national product. The sum of L and K represents all the payments to factors of production, and it also equals *gross national product*, (*GNP*), sometimes called gross national income.[1]

The purpose of the input-output table is to provide a conceptual framework for viewing the role of labor as a factor of production. The factors are used in combination as inputs in the productive processes which will eventually turn out final goods and services. The input-output table in Figure 1–1 is very simple. More accurately, we could show labor and other factors themselves being transformed in the productive process. Thus, we might have several entries for each factor, such as L_1, L_2, L_3, with L_1 (for example, eighth-grade graduates) being employed directly in some of the industries but also entering into the production of L_2 (for example, high school graduates), and so on.

Labor as the Human Resource

Some readers may object that labor, being a human resource, cannot properly be subjected to the logical, quantitative analysis appropriate for the investigation of the markets for money, agricultural goods, and other commodities. This objection is based on a misconception of the role of analysis in developing scientific knowledge. The analysis of labor is indeed complicated because it is a human resource. Individuals do not always act as if they were maximizing an easily ascertainable index of money income or profits. Where you work and the nature of your job may be as important as how much you earn. These considerations mean that good labor market theory is difficult to develop, not that it is undesirable. If anything, formal theory becomes even more crucial as organized thinking becomes more difficult. Insights, intuition, and knowledge of the "real world" are indispensable ingredients in developing relevant theory, but they are not substitutes for it. Labor economics has developed as a field of investigation because a great deal of special knowledge is necessary to develop useful hypotheses about labor markets; it would be wrong to say that it has developed because a scientific approach to the study of labor is not a useful one.

Labor is a unique factor of production because it is physically inseparable from the human being in which it is embodied. Thus, nonmoney matters are much more important in decisions about the allocation of labor than of almost anything else. For instance, if you owned a truck rental service, you would not care very much whether the trucks were driven in hot or cold climates, in smoky or clean air, in rain or sun, except insofar as these conditions affected their productivity. Certainly you would not care as much as if

---

[1] We are ignoring such complications as indirect business taxes and capital consumption allowances which cause GNP, as usually measured, to diverge from net national product and/or national income.

you were making a decision about the conditions under which *you* would work. As a rule, you do not have to live or work where your money (non-human assets) does; however, you do have to be in the place where you perform labor services.

One of the most important aspects of the physical inseparability of labor power and human beings is that our social mores have led us to outlaw certain kinds of contracts between sellers and buyers of labor which are perfectly legitimate between sellers and buyers of almost anything else. One cannot, for example, sell or buy the labor of one person indefinitely. Slavery is against the law. This has important implications for labor market processes which take place over long periods of time—notably education and training. In subsequent chapters we will explore the theory of human capital that has grown to accommodate the special nature of labor market processes that take place through time.

Labor as a Source of Income

Although all the factors of production are directly or indirectly owned by persons who constitute part of the household sector, labor is the most widely owned factor. Household sales of labor constitute about 70 percent of the sales of all factors of production—that is, the share of wages, salaries, and the wage component of entrepreneurial income constitute about 70 percent of the national income. In your first economics course, you undoubtedly were introduced to a *circular flow diagram* like that in Figure 1–2. This emphasizes the importance of thinking of labor as a source of income, as well as a factor of production. Part of what determines the allocation of labor among alternative uses is decisions by households regarding the expenditure of the income from the sale of labor and other factors. At the same time, households determine their income (given wage rates and unemployment conditions) by deciding how much labor to sell. Thus income determines, and is determined by, the allocation of labor among alternative uses, including the alternative of employment within the household sector.

At the bottom of the circular flow diagram we see the household sector, which sells factors of production, including labor, to the business sector. The business sector is shown at the top of the diagram. The business sector pays the household sector for the rights to employ the factors. Sales of factors by the household sector to the business sector determine both the amount of market employment and its direction. Each sale of labor is made not only with respect to a specific amount of work, but with respect to the characteristics of the employer, occupation, and industry in which the worker will be employed. Business firms compete among themselves to obtain the services of workers; members of the household sector make decisions about where to sell their services and how much to sell. At the same time, they

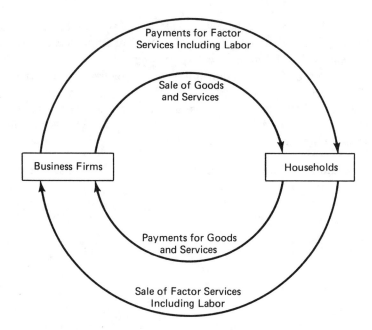

FIGURE 1–2. Circular Flow of Payments and Purchases

determine their command over the output of the business sector. These relationships are crucial in labor economics, although they do not depict the importance of the allocation of labor within the household sector. These within-household decisions, which involve time spent in schooling, child care, and so on, are crucial determinants of future household income.

The World of Labor: Behavior to Be Explained

What follows is a sample list of some topics we will deal with here:

1. How are wage rates determined? Wages reflect the price of labor. Why do some workers command a higher price than others? Why do blacks typically earn less than whites and women less than men? What determines the general level of wage rates and how is the wage level linked to inflation and unemployment?

2. What determines the allocation of workers among jobs? How do individuals decide on the division of their time among market work, schooling, working around the house, and "leisure"? The answers to these questions are related to the answers to those about wage rates and must be considered simultaneously with them.

11

3. How well do labor markets work? Do wages and employment decisions adjust rapidly enough to keep problems of unemployment and unfilled job vacancies at tolerable levels? Why do we have unemployment?

4. What are the effects of labor unions on labor markets and the welfare of all workers? What is the role of labor legislation in labor markets? How do labor markets, unions, and legislation interact to affect the answers to the questions posed in (1) through (3); what are the implications for social and economic welfare?

Finding the answers to these and related questions constitute our task, and yours, in the remainder of this book.

CHAPTER 2

Measurement
in Labor Economics

A. Educational Objectives
   1. Introduce you to important sources of labor market data
   2. Outline some difficulties in measuring theoretical variables, particularly wages, employment, and unemployment, in available data sets
   3. Brief introduction to regression analysis

B. Sources and Interpretation of Labor Market Data
   1. Some important and widely used data sets
   2. Measuring the quantity of labor
      a. Employment
      b. Hours
      c. Quality of labor
      d. Unemployment
   3. Interpreting data on wage rates
      a. Fringe benefits
      b. The time period: permanent and transitory wages

C. Using Economic Data
   1. Exact theories and inexact behavior
   2. Graphical analysis of estimating a labor demand curve
   3. The regression approach
       a. Interpreting linear equations
      *b. Linear transformations
      *c. "Dummy" variables
      *d. An example: estimating a human capital earnings function

---

*Represents more advanced material

13

This chapter is designed to help you understand the chapters that follow—especially the material treating economic "facts" as opposed to theory. Our aim is to provide a minimum background in measuring and using labor market data. Although it is impossible in one brief chapter to provide an exhaustive survey of the sources of data and the quantitative methods used in labor economics, the discussion here should prove helpful.

Sources and Interpretation of Labor Market Data: Overview

In studying the economics of labor markets, terms such as **wage rates**, **quantity of labor**, **employment**, and **unemployment** are crucial variables. We first develop a theory of the relationship among these variables, and then we explore how theory helps us to understand observed behavior. Making the connection between theory and "fact" will be much more rewarding if you understand how these variables are measured and some of the problems involved. It may seem unnecessary to you to dwell on these details—everyone knows what a wage rate is, or an hour of work, you may think. As we go on, however, we believe you will see that it is not always so easy to match the variables of our theories to the data we can obtain.

Many sources of data are used in the study of labor markets. All, however, fall into one of two important categories: One consists of answers to questions asked of households, the other of answers to questions asked of business firms. In the first category are data sources such as the decennial population census of the United States, the *Current Population Surveys* conducted monthly by the U.S. Census Bureau, and many surveys conducted by nongovernment research organizations.[1] In the second cateogry are data sources such as the Census Bureau's *Census of Manufactures* and the monthly *Employment and Earnings* surveys of the U.S. Department of Labor.[2]

---

[1]For a more complete description of U.S. government household surveys, see Bureau of Labor Statistics Report No. 62 and *Current Population Reports*, Series P-23, No. 62, "Concepts and Methods Used in Labor Force Statistics Derived from the Current Population Survey." Three widely used bodies of data produced by nongovernment agencies are the National Longitudinal Surveys of the Center for Human Resource Research at The Ohio State University, the Productive Americans Survey, and the Panel Study of Income Dynamics, both of The University of Michigan Survey Research Center. The first and third are "panel" surveys, in that they follow a particular group of individuals over a number of years. See Herbert S. Parnes et al., *The Pre-Retirement Years: A Longitudinal Study of the Labor Market Experience of Men*, Vol. 1 (Washington, D.C.: U.S. Department of Labor, Manpower Administration, 1970); James N. Morgan et al., *Productive Americans: A Study of How Individuals Contribute to Economic Progress* (Ann Arbor: Survey Research Center, University of Michigan, 1966); and James N. Morgan, ed., *Five Thousand American Families —Patterns of Economic Progress* (Ann Arbor: Survey Research Center, University of Michigan, 1974).

[2]For a description of the establishment surveys (surveys of business firms), see one of the monthly issues of U.S. Department of Labor, Bureau of Labor Statistics, *Employment and Earnings*.

These data sources differ in the kinds of information they provide. Household surveys provide answers to questions about whether household members were working, looking for work, attending school, and so on, during the survey week (the calendar week prior to the date of the survey). Using answers to such questions, we can estimate the size of the labor force (all persons 16 years of age and over who were not working and who were judged by their answers to questions to be seeking work), and the number of persons not in the labor force (the remainder). Household surveys are also used to gather information about dual job holders, earnings and other income of family members, hours worked, family size, and other information important for studying labor force behavior.

Data gathered from firms also provide information about wage rates, and this information is readily obtainable from the firms' financial records. Wage data gathered from firms are likely to be more accurate than those gathered from household surveys, because such hard-to-remember items as paid vacation time, withholding taxes, social security payments, frings benefits, insurance premiums, and the like are recorded there. However, if one wishes to relate wage rates or earnings to the personal and family characteristics of persons receiving them, it is almost impossible to do this on the basis of firms' records alone. Very few studies of labor force behavior have been able to make use of a mix of firm and household surveys in order to combine the best features of both, since the two kinds of surveys are almost always conducted independently. In addition, data gathered from firms provide information about the volume of labor turnover (quits and layoffs), the combinations of labor of different degrees of skill used in production and nonproduction activities, and so on.

It is beyond our scope to evaluate the many data sources used in the study of labor markets, but we will point out some important problems in measuring widely discussed concepts. This we do in the next few paragraphs. In many instances, available data do not conform neatly to the economic concepts we would like to measure. While a well-formulated theory will provide information on the ideal way to measure economic variables, considerations of cost, protection of personal privacy, or political expediency may hinder gathering perfectly appropriate data. Relating the available information to the concepts of economic theory is a difficult and essential branch of what we call *econometrics*, the application of statistical methods to the study of economic data and problems.

Measuring the Quantity of Labor

When studying labor markets, one of our most important tasks will be to specify the quantity of labor and the units in which it is measured. We might speak of *employee-hours*—work units of constant quality. Although we begin our study of the theory of labor markets as if we could easily measure homogeneous employee-hours of labor, in fact such measurement is seldom easy. Let us look at a few of the problems of measuring the quantity of labor in the context of the total size of the labor force.

Most people would agree that the unit *labor force* should measure the amount of labor resources in the economy, much as other units provide information about the amount of coal in inventories or in unmined reserves, iron in ore deposits, and so on. A moment's thought will indicate, however, that even for such readily identifiable resources as coal, a figure representing available resources does not necessarily reflect the quantity of coal remaining to be used. It is common knowledge that our known coal reserves have grown over the years. This is not because the geological rate of formation of coal is outpacing use; it is because we have continually devoted resources to searching for new deposits. Furthermore, the quantity of coal reserves is meaningful only with respect to given standards of the profitability of mining coal of given quality. It is common practice to exclude from measured reserves known deposits which at present are too costly to mine considering their quality. Should we similarly exclude from our measurement of the size of the labor force those individuals who choose not to work because their earning power is not high enough to compensate them for giving up non-labor market activities such as attending school, keeping house, and the like? What about those who would like to work but cannot find jobs? Measuring the economy's labor resources makes sense only in reference to a carefully framed set of rules.

THE AMOUNT OF EMPLOYED LABOR

The advantages of alternative labor force measures can only be understood in the context of a theory of the labor market. Figure 2–1 represents an extremely simple but useful theory. It shows the supply and demand for labor in the economy; the quantity of labor of uniform quality in hours per period of time (employee-hours per time period) is measured on the horizontal axis, and the wage rate for labor of uniform quality is measured on the vertical axis. Later on, we will see why the demand curve has a negative slope, and we will also see that the supply curve may not be upward sloping; but Figure 2–1 as it stands is sufficient to demonstrate some important problems of measuring the quantity of labor resources. In its simplest form, the theory implies that the wage rate and the level of employment are determined at the intersection of the supply and demand curves (L_1 and L_2 correspond to such points of intersection); the employment level so determined is an "equilibrium" value.

In a very important sense, the current official measure of the labor force in the United States corresponds to an equilibrium value of employment such

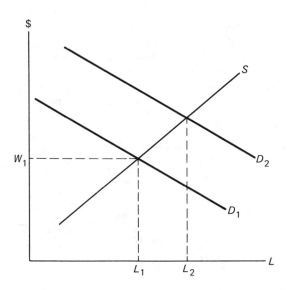

FIGURE 2–1. Labor Demand, Supply, and Employment

as L_1 or L_2 in Figure 2–1. This is because the most important component of the official measure of the labor force is the number of people who are actually working. An important problem of measuring labor resources by a magnitude such as L_1 or L_2 is that it depends on the demand for labor as well as the supply. (We temporarily ignore some other important problems: for example, that reported employment measures *the number of people employed rather than the total hours of employment* and does not measure the quality of heterogeneous workers). There would be no problem if the supply curve of labor were vertical (completely inelastic and insensitive to demand). But in general it is not, and thus the volume of employment does not tell us how much labor could be drawn upon in the case of, say, a war or other national emergency; neither does it tell us how many persons might be put to work if the demand for labor in private industry were to grow.

Employment data for the United States are gathered from household surveys as follows: The total number classified as employed are all persons aged 16 years and over who answer survey questions in such a way as to indicate that they were working or had a job from which they were temporarily absent during the survey week. Table 2–1 shows the actual questions asked monthly of a sample of the United States' population, whose answers are subsequently adjusted according to statistical procedures to yield an estimate of the number that would have been obtained if everyone in the United States had been interviewed. (Not every person about whom answers are obtained is interviewed personally; often questions about several family members are answered by only one respondent.) Persons classified as "employed" are those who answer question 19, that they were "working" most of the prior week, "Yes" to question 20, that they worked at all during the prior week, or who were classified as "with a job but not at work." This last category includes those who answered "Yes" to question 21 and who were absent for reasons 1 through 4 in question 21A. Also included are

TABLE 2–1

Facsimile of Current Labor Force Status Section of Current Population
Survey Standard Questionnaire

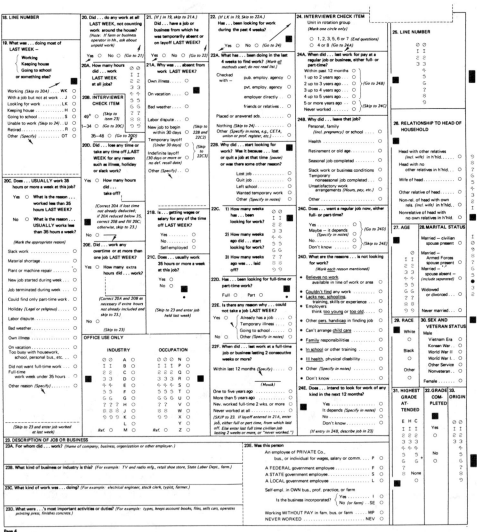

persons who worked 15 hours or more as unpaid workers in a family business or firm.

A simple way out of the problem that measured employment depends on demand conditions might seem to be to measure the total population, rather than L_1 or L_2. But then, should we count the ill, the very young, the aged, and those in school? We probably should not; in fact, we should probably adopt some criterion for measuring labor resources that would exclude certain segments of the population on grounds of our social values or of the economic efficiency of trying to put those of very low productivity to work. We cannot avoid evaluating the population's labor force potential according to some more or less arbitrary criteria, and we may find no better measure of "potential" or "maximum" labor force than to observe the employment behavior of the economy during periods of high labor demand.

HOURS OF EMPLOYMENT

Now we consider the problem of adding the dimension hours to the measurement of employment. Again, economic theory is an invaluable aid. According to economic theory, the number of hours worked depends on labor supply and demand, the number of hours supplied responding either positively or negatively to changes in demand. If we use a market criterion for measuring labor force hours as we do for measuring the number of workers in the labor force, then hours actually worked measures hours in the labor force. But does hours actually worked reflect the number of hours individuals desire to supply? The answer depends on one's view of how labor markets function. Although we all know people who complain about not being able to get enough overtime hours and others who wish they could work a shorter work week, we believe the market criterion represents a reasonable approach to measuring our labor force in terms of hours.

But, given the market criterion, how do we find out how many hours people work? In many cases, we may resort to questioning employers. This is actually done by the government, and one of the principal sources of data on hours worked is provided by the answers to monthly questionnaires sent to employers of a large number of the economy's workers. Monthly surveys of the population also provide information about hours of work, in the answers given by people who worked or by their relatives. Apart from the statistical problems of sampling, which are of a rather technical nature and probably introduce few serious errors into our presently available measures of labor hours, rather important errors may arise simply because of our inability to find out from respondents exactly what their behavior has been, even in the recent past. The problems are serious enough when it is necessary to ask an employee who is paid by the hour how many hours he or she worked in the previous week; the respondent may have worked overtime hours and forgotten, or may neglect to report a temporarily shortened work week. Even worse, interviewers may be forced to ask crucial questions of one family member about the labor force behavior of all persons living in that household. Still worse, the self-employed and many salaried workers probably cannot accurately define when they are working and when they are not. Questions 20A through 20E in Table 2–1 show the painstaking procedure used by interviewers to find out how many hours were worked during the survey week. Notice that it is virtually impossible to discern from the answers whether anyone who worked 35 hours or more was working more or less than he or she desired. It is possible, however, to get some idea of whether respondents who worked less than 35 hours did so voluntarily. Presumably, the ideal measure of employee-hours would reflect the hours workers voluntarily would work under given labor market conditions.

THE QUALITY OF LABOR

The problem of measuring labor quality is so serious that at present there is no official measure of the labor force which allows for quality variation. However, economic theory does suggest ways in which labor quality might be accounted for. If we adopt the view that "labor is what labor does," then labor force members can be weighted by their marginal productivities (see Chapter 3) to calculate aggregate labor force measures. If we knew everyone's marginal product in monetary terms, we could derive a measure of the labor force that reflects variations in quality as well as in the number of workers and hours worked. Lacking such information, we may at least try to account for the variation in labor quality which is associated with underlying conditions generally believed to affect productivity, and which may be more or less easily measured.

One such condition is the educational level of the labor force. If we observe labor force hours declining but the average educational level of workers rising, we have reason to suspect that labor resources are declining less rapidly than the simple hours figure indicates. Other readily observable correlates of labor quality are age and sex; perhaps slightly more difficult to observe is health. Thus, if we observe that since 1900, the proportion of the population in the labor force has remained roughly constant (which happens to be true), while hours worked per week have declined, education has risen, more women relative to men are working, a higher proportion of youth are in school, and a higher proportion of the elderly are retired (although a higher proportion of the population is elderly), may we conclude that labor force quality has risen or fallen? Although there is no easy answer to this question, there is a presumption that it has risen, the principal impetus having been increased educational attainment.

Still another dimension of labor force quality, generally unreported in official statistics but certainly not unnoticed by employers, is the intensity of work effort. As work hours have fallen over the years, it is not unreasonable to suppose that the intensity of work effort has increased, since workers do not tire as much on the job. Surely work effort varies widely among different nations and cultures. While we will have little to say about work effort in this text, it is an interesting and important component of labor force quality, the measurement of which would lend much to our knowledge of the economy's human resources.

THE UNEMPLOYED COMPONENT OF THE LABOR FORCE

We have so far assumed that the labor force might be measured, albeit imprecisely, by counting the number of people at work. However, there are always persons who are on layoff from their jobs, who have lost their jobs and who are looking for work, who have quit their jobs and are looking for new work, and who are entering or reentering the labor force but have not yet found a job. These people constitute the *unemployed*, and the unemployed are by official definition a part of the labor force. All the problems of measuring the employed labor force apply to the unemployed as well. Moreover, the problems associated with inferring from the answers of nonworking respondents whether they are unemployed or out of the labor force merit special attention.

Consider first a simple definition of unemployment suggested by economic theory. In Figure 2–2, we see a diagrammatic description of a labor market in which the wage rate is higher than the level that would equate demand and

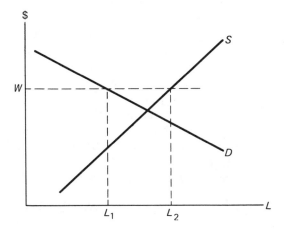

FIGURE 2–2. Labor Demand, Supply, Employment, and Unemployment

supply. Consequently, L_1 units of labor are demanded and $L_2 > L_1$ supplied. $L_2 - L_1$ represents an excess supply of labor (there could just as well be an excess demand if the wage were less than equilibrium). Thus, at the "going wage," W, $L_2 - L_1$ persons are "unemployed." This is a conceivable theoretical definition of unemployment, which, as we will see in Chapters 11 and 12, is much too simple. It associates unemployment with an excess *supply* of labor, whereas information and adjustment costs in labor markets assure that there will always be some workers seeking employment even when supply and demand are in balance. We will not deal here with the difficult question of what level of unemployment is associated with *no* excess demand or supply of labor (the "full employment" level of unemployment). Rather, we will confine ourselves to the equally difficult problem of how we decide when someone who is not working is counted as part of the labor force.

In practice, the measurement of the unemployed component of the labor force relies on two major criteria: (1) An unemployed person must be *available* for work and (2), if not on layoff, be actively seeking work in most cases.[3] Thus, the unemployed must have answered questions 19 and 20 of Table 2–1 that they did not work last week, and questions 21 or 22 affirmatively. For those who are not on layoff, the requirement that an unemployed person be actively seeking work corresponds to a commonsense definition of unemployment. However, the Current Population Survey does not inquire into the conditions under which a respondent would actually accept a job. Perhaps most important, no attempt is made to discover whether a job seeker requires or expects a rate of pay so high that no reasonable employer would offer a job to such a person. Consider a coal miner who is laid off due to mechanization and who cannot find another job as a coal miner. Suppose he had been earning $8.50 per hour, but because of his age, previous training, and so on, the best job he can find now will pay only $4; or perhaps the job would necessitate his moving away from his old home. Now, if the miner does not realize this—after all, a decline in one's market worth is not easy to accept or easy to discover in a short period of time—he may turn down or not look for jobs that pay less than, say, $6 per hour. In fact, if and when he discovers that he can find work only at $4, he may choose to retire from the labor force if he is an older worker—or he may decide to do the best he can with part-time work or welfare. Thus, while the miner would probably be classified as officially unemployed, there would be good reason for classifying him as out of the labor force instead, since if the miner had full information he probably would stop looking for work and would not take a job if he were offered one.

The implication for our measurement of the labor force is clear: To the

---

[3] BLS, *Concepts and Methods Used in Labor Force Statistics*, pp. 3–4.

extent that persons have an incorrect perception of their going wage rates and would change their behavior if they had full information, we probably do not estimate unemployment and the size of the labor force correctly. (This is not to say that persons such as the hypothetical coal miner should not be classified as unemployed for purposes of determining the allocation of unemployment compensation, aid to depressed areas, and so on.) Furthermore, when unemployed workers do stop looking for work and are thus counted as out of the labor force, we should recognize that they might be productive workers and labor force members if they had information about jobs unknown to them, perhaps in other regions of the country.

THE INTERPRETATION OF WAGE RATE DATA

Formally, a *wage rate* is represented by the rate of transformation of a worker's available time into purchasing power over market goods (Chapter 4). That is, it is the value of market goods which can be purchased for an hour's work. The wage rate is an important element in economic theory both because it represents an inducement to work and because it represents the cost to business firms of hiring labor. However, many aspects of the inducement to work and of the cost of hiring labor are not represented by the wage rates recorded in the various sources of wage data.

FRINGE BENEFITS AND COSTS

A substantial proportion of today's jobs involve not only an hourly rate of pay, but also payments into private pension funds, health plans, social security, unemployment insurance schemes, and the like. To what extent do these wage supplements represent additional inducements to workers and additional costs to employers?

From the employer's point of view, a dollar contributed to social security, a private pension fund, or a health insurance program is a cost of production, just the same as a dollar of direct wage payments. Thus, in measuring the relationship between wage rates and production patterns, all the costs associated with hiring labor should be measured, not just the wage rate paid directly to the worker. When measures of the cost of fringe benefits are not available, the question of to what extent the analysis of labor markets is affected arises. This question can only be answered in the context of a particular study, but in general it is probably true that the amount of fringe benefits is positively related to nominal wage rates. Thus, the principal effect would be to understate real wage costs more or less consistently by a fraction. The effect of this error on most studies is probably relatively unimportant. Table 2–2 and Figure 2–3 suggest the relationship between wage rates and wage supplements, or fringe benefits, and also between the size of wage rates and the proportion of supplements in total wages. The former relationship appears to be more consistent than the latter. It is clear that the ratio of fringe benefits to earnings has grown over time.

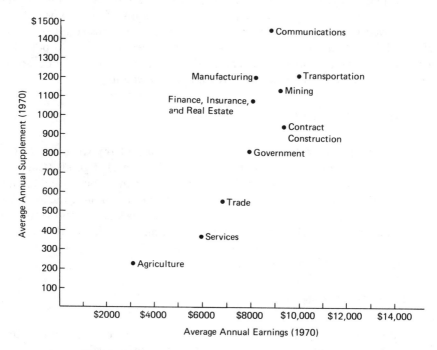

FIGURE 2–3. Annual Wage Supplements and Earnings

If we know their exact amount, wage supplements may be added directly to wage and salary payments to determine the total cost of labor to employers. (However, it is at times important to distinguish between supplemental benefits which depend on the number of hours worked and those which do not, as they will affect employer and employee behavior in different ways.) To what extent may we similarly evaluate the total payment to workers? Consider a case in which workers voluntarily agree to have employers contribute part of their wages to a fund, such as social insurance, health insurance, or the like. They might do this because of certain economies of scale in such financial arrangements. These contributions might then be recorded as wage supplements. Such supplements to wages should no more be considered reductions in the inducement to work than the "deduction" due to worker purchases of food, clothing, or other commodities. That is, workers receive something in return for the withheld supplements which they

TABLE 2–2

Annual Wage Supplements by Major Industry, Various Years, 1929–1970

	(1) Supplement (in dollars)	(2) Earnings	(3)	(4)	(5)
Agriculture, forestry, and fisheries	$ 220	$3,063	0.072	0.3	2.0
Mining	1,140	9,262	0.123	1.6	13.8
Contract construction	948	9,293	0.102	2.3	5.7
Manufacturing	1,202	8,150	0.147	0.9	8.6
Wholesale and retail trade	569	6,886	0.083	0.6	4.4
Finance, insurance, and real estate	1,085	8,026	0.135	2.6	9.3
Transportation	1,203	9,928	0.150	2.0	8.3
Communications and public utilities	1,464	5,946	0.065	2.0	12.7
Services	384	7,965	0.102	0.4	3.0
Government and government enterprises	814			3.5	8.2

(1) Average annual supplements to wages and salaries per full-time employee in 1970. *Source: Historical Statistics of the United States, Colonial Times to 1970*, D 893–904.
(2) Average annual earnings per full-time employee (1970). *Source:* Same as (1) Series D 739–764.
(3) (1) ÷ (2).
(4) Wage supplements as a percentage of wages and salaries (1929). *Source:* H. G. Lewis, *Unionism and Relative Wages in the United States* (Chicago: University of Chicago Press, 1963), pp. 236–37. Reprinted by permission of the University of Chicago Press.
(5) Wage supplements as a percentage of salaries (1958). *Source:* Same as (4).

presumably value at least as highly as any alternative uses to which they might have put the wages had they been paid in the form of cash. Since supplemental benefits are usually not taxable, they may be more valuable to workers than an equal cash payment.

Such plans, however, usually mean that each person must behave in a manner essentially similar to that of his or her co-workers. Social security payments, for example, differ among workers only as wages differ; there is no room for adjustment of the amount paid according to personal wishes. To the extent that workers are bound by institutional arrangements to contribute more of their gross wages than they would prefer, the value of the supplemental benefits received may be less than the amount paid in. (To the extent that more is paid in than would be paid voluntarily, private expenditures of a similar nature may be curtailed; this would in part make up for the difference between the value of benefits received and costs. For instance, as a result of social security payments, some workers may reduce the amount of life insurance they buy.) If the value of supplemental benefits to the worker is less than the amount paid, then net "real" wages should not include the discrepancy. Indeed, observed wage rates should be reduced by the amount of employees' contributions to such programs as social security, if it is thought that the benefits received are viewed as zero by workers.

The Time Period.   So far we have spoken of the wage rate almost as if it were given to each person for all time. However, later on we will learn that time plays an important role in many labor market decisions, and therefore an important role in the measurement of labor market variables. For instance, we will analyze the response of labor supply to wage rates by means of **income** and **substitution** effects (see pp. 113–119). Income is a tricky concept; its value depends on the period of time over which it is measured. To the extent that a change in the wage rate affects income, it must persist for a certain period of time. Thus, it is necessary to specify whether we are measuring a wage rate that is more or less permanent, or "normal," or one that reflects transitory deviations from the normal.

Suppose, for instance, that we want to estimate the labor supply behavior of families of farm workers and that in areas where farm wage rates are persistently relatively high, we expect to observe fewer wives and children of farm workers in the labor force than elsewhere. But, since harvests vary from year to year and from place to place, we should also expect to find that hourly wage rates are unusually high where crops are unusually good, and vice versa. Since an increase in the wage rate that is expected to be temporary will not have a significant effect on a family's view of its normal level of income, when crops are unusually good we should not expect to observe much labor force withdrawal of women and children, and men may work even more than usual, since it pays to supply labor when the wage rate is highest.

Another problem in measuring wage rates that is due to the role of time in economic behavior arises from the importance of certain kinds of on-the-job training (see Chapter 9). In addition to formal and informal training programs, much on-the-job training takes the form of learning by doing. Whatever form on-the-job training takes, it is expected to have the effect of raising future productivity and earnings, so workers are willing to pay for it. That workers are willing to pay is suggested by the relatively low wage rates of apprentices, physicians in residency, and the like. That is, payment is effected in many cases by accepting a wage lower than productivity in order to compensate employers for providing training. Whatever the nature of the training process, investment affects typical age-earnings profiles of many kinds of workers.

Consider the age-earnings profiles of college graduates in 1970, as shown in Table 2–3 and Figure 2–4. Several years after leaving college, college

TABLE 2–3

Age-Income Profile, U.S. Males 14 and Over,
by Years of Education (median income)

Age	Elementary (8 *years*)	4 *Years* High School (12 *years*)	4 *Years* College (16 *years*)
14–15	$ 587	$3,689	—
16–17	706	1,262	—
18–19	2,168	1,853	$ 4,188
20–21	3,222	3,298	2,299
22–24	4,329	5,485	3,728
25–29	5,716	7,721	8,908
30–34	6,469	8,587	11,949
35–44	7,255	9,206	13,950
45–54	7,197	9,437	15,103
55–64	6,439	8,532	13,457
65–74	3,030	4,325	8,159
75–	2,295	2,867	4,682

Source: U.S. Census of Population, 1970. Subject Reports, *Educational Attainment*, Table 7.

graduates earn little more than do high school graduates of similar age. However, early career wage differentials do not reflect the value of on-the-job training typically acquired by college graduates. The amount acquired has been estimated to be substantial, and greater than that acquired by high school graduates. That is, the earnings figures reflect the willingness of workers to accept lower initial wages in return for training and other experiences which are expected to yield higher earning power later in life. The low reported earnings in earlier years therefore understate real earnings because the value of much of the training being acquired is not included. It has been estimated that over an average worker's lifetime, the rate of return to college education and subsequent on-the-job training is in the neighborhood of 10 to 15 percent. The payoffs on these investments are reflected in recorded earnings only later in life. Thus, the age-earnings profile of college graduates is typically steeper than that of high school or grammar school graduates and lies above theirs throughout much of a typical working life.

The point here is not to develop a theory of on-the-job training, but rather to indicate that the relationship between the wage rate and, say, hours worked per week, or any other variable, may be seriously obscured by faulty measurement of the wage rate. If the payment "in kind" that reflects payment for being in a job which allows some kind of training or learning to take place is ignored, the measured wage rate will reflect only money earnings; this will

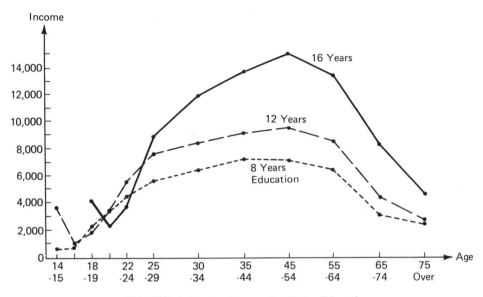

FIGURE 2–4. Age-Income Profile by Education

result in an underestimate of the real wage rate, and the underestimation may be very large for young workers with a great deal of education.

Workers Not Paid by the Hour. In many cases, it is necessary to convert observed payments for labor services to a common time basis. For instance, if the hourly wage rate is the standard measure, the payments made to workers paid by the week, month, or year must be converted to an hourly basis. This is a straightforward procedure if the hours worked per week, month, or year are known. However, measurement errors in estimating hours worked will induce related errors in the calculation of hourly wages. These errors can have an important effect on estimated behavioral relationships. For example, if hours worked are overestimated, the calculated *hourly* rate of pay for a worker paid by the week will be too small. If this hourly rate of pay calculation is used to estimate a labor supply curve, a wage observation that is too low will be matched with an hours observation that is too high, and the resulting estimate of labor supply will be biased. The reverse is also true. If hours of work are underestimated, the corresponding hourly rate of pay calculation will be too large. Such calculations could lead us to believe that when wages rise hours of work decline, even if there were no relationship between these two variables.

The problem is probably most serious in studying the behavior of professional workers and the self-employed. Here it is not only difficult to measure hourly wage rates, but it is not clear that the marginal contribution to income

28

of an hour's extra work is anywhere near equal to average hourly earnings. At this point it is probably best only to point out the problem without suggesting possible solutions.

Using Economic Data to Examine Labor Market Relationships

The kinds of information described above will be used throughout this book and related to economic theory. It is important that the method used to relate data to economic hypotheses be appropriate. Economic theory not only suggests what kinds of economic data to use, but also has implications for the way in which the data should be analyzed.

EXACT THEORIES AND INEXACT BEHAVIOR

An important step in using economic theories and hypotheses to help understand real world events is to make the transition in one's thinking from the exact nature of most theories and hypotheses to the inexact nature of actual human behavior. Everyone is first introduced to economic theory by means of exact relationships such as demand and supply curves, and we develop such relationships for labor markets in this book. When relationships like demand and supply curves are developed theoretically, explicit statements are made regarding which variables are thought to change either independently or in response to other variables (such as price and quantity), and which variables, although they influence the behavior of the dependent variable under investigation, are assumed to be constant for purposes of theoretical analysis. Thus, we often see statements such as this one: *Ceteris paribus* (other things being equal or unchanging), the amount of labor demanded is a negative function of the wage rate. In making such a statement, we do not fail to recognize that changing knowledge of productive techniques, changing prices of other productive factors, deviations from profit-maximizing behavior, the existence of disequilibrium situations, and so on may also influence behavior. However, we recognize that under conditions of unchanging values of these other variables which influence the behavior of labor demand, we can deduce a negative relationship between wage rates and the quantity demanded. The relationship is *exact* because a unique value of the quantity of labor demanded is implied for each wage rate.

We can provide only a brief sketch of ways in which exact economic theory is used in the empirical investigation of inexact behavior; the detailed study of these problems is the subject of econometrics courses. Our discussion is meant to provide enough of an outline so that beginners can follow discussions in this text without too much difficulty. To start, we use the theory of labor demand to illustrate some of the basic problems in relating economic theory to observed behavior.

One of the clearest implications of the theory of labor demand is that the amount of labor demanded by a firm or industry is a negative function of the wage rate or rates of the labor employed. The relationships deduced are exact, but it is often observed that it is difficult to predict the responses of individual employers or industries to particular changes in wage rates. Critics of the hypothesized downward-sloping labor demand curve often dwell on the point that observed behavior is inexact. One may hear the expression "the labor demand curve should be drawn with the broad side of the chalk," meaning that the theoretical implication of a negatively sloped demand relationship is perhaps useful for understanding the effects of very large changes in labor supply or wage rates, but not small changes.

In order to deal with this criticism, it is necessary to recognize the importance of the *ceteris paribus* assumption used in deriving the demand hypothesis. The inexact relationship observed between the quantities of labor demanded and wage rates arise because many variables other than wage rates actually influence demand behavior and are not constant in real world situations. For example, two firms in the same industry, using the same kind of machinery and paying the same wage rates, may differ in that one experiences a fire that destroys one of its plants. To compensate, it may temporarily put on an extra shift in its remaining plants, using more labor than it would ordinarily. The fact of the fire would ordinarily not be known to someone using these data. It would appear, however, that one of the seemingly identical firms was using more labor per plant than the other, although paying the same wage.

Statistical analysis has been developed so that the wage rate paid by these two firms and the quantities of labor they employ can be used in an empirical study of the demand for labor even though we do not possess complete information about the conditions affecting the firms' operations. The statistical procedures used by economists and other social scientists allow us to make use of the *law of averages* in analyzing data. Using the example in the preceding paragraph, we can illustrate what statistical analysis does. Suppose that, in order to study labor demand, we want to relate the quantity of labor demanded by various firms to the wage rates they pay, but that each firm is affected by unknown factors such as a fire. It can be shown, using statistical analysis, that we are justified in relating the *average* quantity of labor employed by firms paying one wage rate to the average quantity employed by firms paying higher and lower rates *if* the following condition holds: *The other variables affecting employment (for example, the fire), which we do not observe, do not vary systematically with wage rates.* In statistical jargon, we say that these "omitted variables" must be *uncorrelated with,* or *randomly related to* the observed variables which are assumed to influence demand (for example, the wage rate).

There are many ways in which the effects of "omitted" random variables may be taken into consideration in studying economic behavior. All of them, however, involve some kind of averaging. Averaging works if the omitted variables (such as the fire that affects one of the firms in our labor demand example) are random, because their influence on the behavior being studied (the quantity of labor demand at various wage rates) averages out to zero—it "cancels out"—over a large number of observations. This is where the law of averages, or to be more precise, the *law of large numbers*, plays a crucial role. One of the most common and best-known applications of the law of large numbers is in the business world: Insurance companies can accurately predict death rates as a simple function of age for large groups of people, even though it is impossible to predict exactly when any individual in good health will die. Another example is the ability of banks to meet their daily demands for cash even though they never have enough on hand to pay off all their depositors at once.

The way averaging would work in a very simple study of labor demand is shown in Figure 2–5. Suppose we have data obtained from observing nine firms, each of whom pays one of three possible wage rates. Each firm can hire all the labor it wants at the wage rate it faces, which is beyond its control. In terms of economic analysis, we say that each firm faces one of three infinitely elastic labor supply curves at wage rate W_1, W_2, or W_3. These firms are found, perhaps, in different geographical areas with different labor mar-

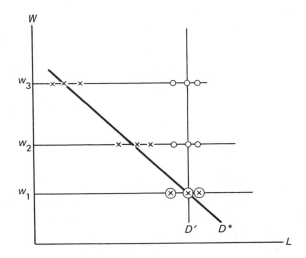

FIGURE 2–5. Estimating a Demand Curve

ket conditions. Nevertheless, they are alike in all other known respects (knowledge of production techniques, market for selling output, and so on), and therefore each firm has the same demand function, which we would like to estimate from the data available. Other variables besides the wage rate do determine the quantity of labor demanded by each firm, but we cannot observe these variables and believe them to be *uncorrelated* (randomly associated) with wage rates. Therefore, we hold the *maintained hypothesis* that the omitted variables in our demand study are uncorrelated with the included independent variable (the wage rate), and we conclude that averaging the quantity of labor the firms demand at each of the three wage rates will provide an *unbiased estimate* of their labor demand curve. The quantities of labor demanded by the nine firms in our study are denoted by the xs in Figure 2–5. Each x represents the quantity of labor demanded by one of the firms at one of the three wage rates. By averaging the three xs at wage rate W_3, the three at wage W_2, and the three at W_1, we determine the average quantity of labor demanded at each of the three wage rates and draw the estimated demand curve D^* through these three points.

The primitive averaging procedure we have described is a legitimate method for estimating a demand curve under very simple conditions. In practice, however, we may have hundreds of observations rather than nine, and we may wish to estimate simultaneously the influence of not only the wage rate, but of other observed conditions, such as the rate of interest, the price of raw materials, the presence of unions, or the existence of "right to work" laws. Fortunately, statisticians, and modern computers, have given us the means to use large numbers of observations and variables in estimated economic relationships. The most common technique for these tasks is **regression analysis**.[4] Regression analysis is a mathematical procedure for estimating a line such as D^*. The procedure possesses desirable mathematical properties, provided that the maintained hypothesis regarding the randomness of omitted variables is correct. If D^* were estimated by means of regression analysis, the following statement would be true: (1) D^* would pass through the mean quantity of labor demanded and the mean of the three wage rates; and (2) the sum of the squared differences (deviations) of each quantity of labor from the estimated demand curve D^* would be as small as possible.

Empirical work using regression analysis is presented frequently throughout this book, and we will give a brief guide to interpreting regression results in this chapter. First, though, we need to describe the pitfalls in using an averaging device such as the procedure described above or the more sophisticated regression analysis when the unobserved or omitted variables are correlated with those whose influence on some form of economic behavior is being investigated. Suppose, in the example above, that the reason some

---

[4]See, for example, the discussion of regression analysis in Jan Kmenta, *Elements of Econometrics* (New York: Macmillan, 1971).

firms must pay higher wage rates than others is that they face unusually strong labor unions. Moreover, suppose that the unions which are strong enough to win especially favorable contracts with employers are also successful in negotiating featherbedding agreements, in which the firms are required to maintain employees they do not want on the payroll. Imagine that these excess quantities of labor are represented in Figure 2–5 by the horizontal distance between the circles, or *o*s, and the *x*s. That is, the circles represent the actual quantities of labor employed by our nine firms, even though they would prefer to hire the quantities represented by the *x*s, given the wage rates they must pay. With the featherbedding agreements, *we do not observe the xs*. Rather, we observe only the *o*s. The labor demand curve of economic theory is represented by the *x*s, however. Now, if we knew about the peculiar nature of the collective bargaining contract for each firm, we could subtract the quantity $o - x$ from the observed employment of each firm and estimate the labor demand curve in which we are interested, D^*. But if we are ignorant of these contracts, we are in a situation in which an omitted variable is *not* randomly correlated with the observed independent variable (the wage rate). You can see in Figure 2–5 that the omitted variable, excess employment, is greatest in those firms paying the highest wage rates.

In other words, the omitted variable in this case is positively correlated with the wage rate. Thus, if we assume randomness when we observe the *o*s instead of the *x*s, our averaging procedure will make us believe that the true demand curve for labor is D' instead of D^*. Since D^* represents the firms' desired quantities of labor, it is an unbiased estimate of the "true" labor demand curve, whereas D' is a *biased* estimate of the true demand curve. If we believed that D' was the true demand curve, and if someone asked us what would happen, say, if a union won an especially large wage increase or if Congress raised the minimum wage by a substantial amount, we would answer that employment would be unchanged. This would be unfortunate, because our prediction of the employment effects of these two events would be based on our ignorance of the fact that featherbedding affected the quantities of labor employed by the firms in our sample. In fact, employment would decline if either of these events took place unless firms were prevented from exerting free choice in hiring their preferred number of workers.

UNDERSTANDING REGRESSION EQUATIONS

Since regression analysis is used so frequently in this text, it would be a good idea to make sure you have a rudimentary understanding of how to interpret the results of estimated regression equations. The basic characteristic of the regression equations we use is that they are all **linear regressions**. (The demand curve in Figure 2–5 is *linear* in that it is a straight line.) Therefore, understanding the properties of linear equations is a necessary step in

understanding the results of estimating regression equations. You may at
first jump to the conclusion that regression analysis is of limited value because
it confines us to demand curves, supply curves, and other economic relationships that are straight lines or their multidimension equivalents (linear
hyperplanes). This is only partly true, however, since regression analysis
allows us to use nonlinear forms which can be *translated* into linear forms,
such as quadratics ("square" terms), logarithms, and more. This will become
clearer to you as we go on.

The demand curve D^* in Figure 2–5 is a simple linear equation involving
two variables, L and W. Therefore, it is a *bivariate* linear equation of the
general form

$$L = \alpha_0 + \alpha_1 W \qquad (2\text{–}1)$$

where L represents the quantity of labor and W the wage rate.[5] α_0 is the
"constant term" and denotes the point at which D^* would intersect the L
axis if it were extended in Figure 2–5. (α_0 is the quantity of labor that would
be demanded if the wage rate were zero.) α_1 is the *slope* of D^* and measures
the rate at which the quantity of labor demanded changes as the wage rate
rises. Since D^* is a *negatively* sloped demand curve, we would expect to
estimate a negative value for α_1 in the example described in the last section.

We may feel that more variables than just the wage rate influence labor
demand—for example, the amount of machinery used by the firm, measured
in terms of the energy required to operate the machinery (horsepower). If
this were so, we might wish to estimate a *multivariate linear demand function*
of the general form

$$L = \alpha_0 + \alpha_1 W + \alpha_2 H \qquad (2\text{–}2)$$

where H represents horsepower. Equation (2–2) cannot be represented in so
simple a fashion as Figure 2–5, since it would require three dimensions
instead of two. The term α_0 is still the "constant term," while α_1 now represents the slope of the relationship between L and W, holding H constant. We
also refer to α_1 as the partial effect of W on L. Put differently, α_1 is the effect
on L of a one unit change in W, given a value of H. Note that we can now
draw a *family* of demand curves D_i^*, corresponding to different values of H.
The point where each of the demand curves crosses the L axis would depend
on the value of H and the estimated magnitude of α_2. Similarly, α_2 represents
the partial effect of H on L (W held constant).

The family of demand relationships described by equation (2–2) is shown

---

[5] Those of you familiar with algebra and calculus may wonder why L is placed on the
left side although it is measured along the horizontal axis, or abscissa, of Figure 2–5. In
estimating a demand or supply equation, quantity would normally be treated as the dependent variable and price as the independent variable. It is the convention used in economics
textbooks of placing price on the vertical axis and quantity on the horizontal axis that is
unusual, rather than the specification of equation (2–1).

in Figure 2–6. Assuming that α_2 is positive, the relationship between L and W lies farther to the right, the greater is H. The L-W demand curves are parallel to each other, with the common slope α_1 (which we assume is a negative number). The L intercept can be solved for by setting $W = 0$ in equation (2–2). Similarly, you should be able to show that the W axis intercepts equal $(-\alpha_0 - \alpha_2 H)/\alpha_1$, which is a positive number so long as H is positive. Why?

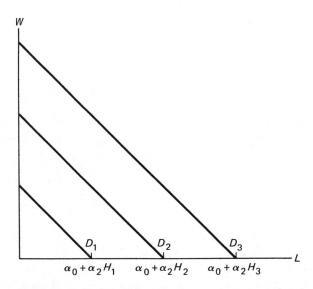

FIGURE 2–6. Diagrammatic Representation of Labor Demand Function (2–2)

Now suppose we are not satisfied with the "straight line" relationships depicted in Figures 2–5 and 2–6. Sometimes we can still use the linear regression approach to estimate our labor demand curve (or whatever), even if we think the appropriate functional form is nonlinear. There are several ways to go about specifying the demand curve in this case, and we will demonstrate one common practice here. Suppose we specify the nonlinear demand curve

$$L = \alpha_0 W^{\alpha_1} \qquad (2\text{--}3)$$

The reason we can estimate (2–3) by means of linear regression analysis is that if we take the logarithm of both sides, we obtain

$$\log L = \log \alpha_0 + \alpha_1 \log W \qquad (2\text{--}3')$$

Equation (2–3) is *linear in its logs,* as equation (2–3') shows. Equation (2–3') is depicted graphically in Figure 2–7a, where the vertical and horizontal axes measure the *logarithms* of W and L, respectively. Its slope equals α_1 and the L intercept equals α_0. Equation (2–3) is shown in Figure 2–7b. Note that the demand curve does not intersect either axis. It cannot, since the logarithm of 0 is undefined. In Figure 2–7a, the logs of W and L equal zero when W and L equal 1, as you know from your mathematics courses.

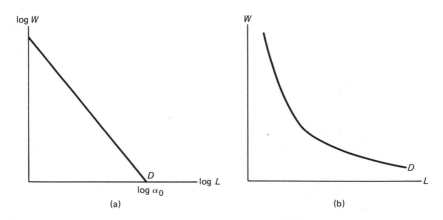

(a)   (b)

FIGURE 2–7. (a) Graph of Equation (2–3′); (b) Graph of Equation (2–3)

The slope, or derivative, of equation (2–3′) has a very useful economic interpretation. Those readers who have taken a course or two in calculus will see this easily; others will have to accept this part of the discussion on faith. The derivative (slope) of (2–3), is

$$\frac{d \log L}{d \log W} = \alpha_1 \qquad\qquad (2\text{–}4)$$

But from our calculus course we know that

$$\frac{d \log L}{d \log W} = \frac{dL}{L} \bigg/ \frac{dW}{W} = \frac{\text{percentage change in } L}{\text{percentage change in } W} \qquad (2\text{–}5)$$

Equation (2–5) has a very familiar interpretation. The derivative of the log of L with respect to the log of W equals the *elasticity of demand* for labor! While the labor demand function represented by equation (2–1) assumes that the change in the quantity of labor demanded changes by the same amount for any equal change in the wage, the demand function represented by equation (2–3) assumes that the corresponding percentage changes are all the same. Equations (2–3) and (2–3′) represent *constant elasticity demand curves.*[6] If we wanted to specify the constant elasticity counterpart of the multivariate demand function (2–2), we could do so by writing

$$L = \alpha_0 W^{\alpha_1} H^{\alpha_2} \qquad (2\text{–}6)$$

or

$$\log L = \log \alpha_0 + \alpha_1 \log W + \alpha_2 \log H \qquad (2\text{–}6')$$

where α_1 is the (constant) elasticity of demand for labor with respect to W and α_2 is the elasticity of demand with respect to horsepower.

Other commonly used nonlinear transformations of the basic linear regression model include the use of the square and higher powers of the variables, use of the reciprocal of one or more variables, and the use of square root or other roots. The interpretation of these transformations will be made as they are used later in the book. Another extremely useful transformation deserves special attention before we go on, however. Some nonlinear relationships we will wish to study are "categorical" in nature, while others can be approximated by the use of categorical transformation of the data. For example, we may be interested in behavioral differences between men and women, northern residents and southern residents, black persons and white persons, or subgroups of three or more categories such as high school dropouts, high school graduates, college dropouts, college graduates, and persons who have received graduate training. The way to deal with categorical differences in behavior is through the use of so-called dummy variables.

Suppose we were interested in the labor demand of firms in two separate industries, and we had information on wage rates paid and number of workers hired by a large number of firms in each industry. Calling one industry A and the other industry B, we can define the dummy variable I_A such that

$I_A = 1$ if a firm is in industry A

$I_A = 0$ if a firm is in industry B (not in industry A).

We could then specify the labor demand function

$$L = \alpha_0 + \alpha_1 W + \alpha_2 I_A \qquad (2\text{–}7)$$

or

$$L = \alpha_0 + \alpha_1 W + \alpha_2 I_A + \alpha_3 W \cdot I_A \qquad (2\text{–}7')$$

---

[6] To prove that (2–3) is also a constant elasticity demand curve, take the derivative of L with respect to W, obtaining $dL/dW = \alpha_0 \alpha_1 W^{\alpha_1 - 1} = \alpha_0 \alpha_1 W^{\alpha_1}/W$. Multiplying both sides by W/L and substituting $\alpha_0 W^{\alpha_1}$ for L on the right side, we obtain

$$\frac{dL}{dW}\frac{W}{L} = \alpha_1, \text{ Q.E.D.}$$

where we hypothesize that α_1 is negative but do not necessarily hypothesize whether α_2 or α_3 are either positive or negative. Equation (2–7) is illustrated in Figure 2–8a. The L intercept of industry A's labor demand curve D_A lies a distance α_2 to the right of industry B's demand curve D_B. If α_2 were negative, then D_A would lie α_2 to the right of D_A. Since equation (2–7) reflects the assumption that D_A and D_B have the same slope, Figure 2–8a shows D_A and

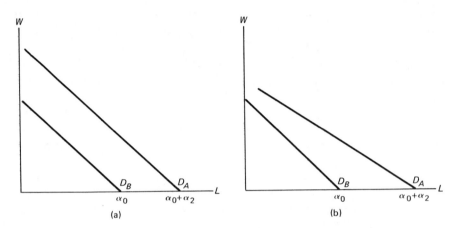

FIGURE 2–8. (a) Graph of Equation (2–7); (b) Graph of Equation (2–7')

D_B parallel to each other, with common slope α_1. Equation (2–7'), on the other hand, is based on the assumption that D_A and D_B not only differ by a constant, α_2, but also that they have different slopes. Figure 2–8b reflects this assumption. With both α_2 and α_3 positive, D_A not only lies to the right, but slopes downward less steeply than D_B. The slope of D_B is α_1 (which we assume is a negative number), while that of D_A is $\alpha_2 + \alpha_3$. If α_2 is positive, then demand curve D_A is steeper than D_B.

An Example. Before concluding our discussion of regression analysis, we will lead you through an example that illustrates the use of nonlinear transformations of the basic linear regression model and that introduces some additional statistical concepts which are part of regression analysis.

One of the most important topics we will investigate in this text is the relationship between schooling and earnings, which is treated in Chapters 8, 9, and 10. The following example of regression analysis is typical of empirical work in this area.[7] We present an estimate of the following equation:

$$\text{Earn} = e^{\alpha_0 + \alpha_1 \text{Educ} + \alpha_2 \text{Exper} + \alpha_3 \text{Exper}^2 + \alpha_4 \text{Mrst} + \alpha_5 \text{Sex} + \alpha_6 \text{Mrstsx}} \qquad (2\text{–}8)$$

[7]We are indebted to Solomon W. Polachek for providing this example.

where

> Earn = an individual's annual earnings in 1969 ($\div$ 100)
> Educ = years of schooling completed
> Exper = potential labor force experience $\equiv$ Age $-$ Educ $-$ 6
> Exper^2 = the square of Exper
> Mrst = a dummy variable ($=$ 1 if an individual is married, spouse present; $=$ 0 otherwise)
> e = the base of natural logarithms
> Sex = a dummy variable ($=$ 1 if the individual is female: $=$ 0 otherwise)

Mrstsx $=$ (Mrst$\cdot$Sex)

Equation (2–8) is clearly nonlinear, but it is linearized by taking the natural log of both sides, obtaining

$$\log \text{Earn} = \alpha_0 + \alpha_1 \text{Educ} + \alpha_2 \text{Exper} + \alpha_3 \text{Exper}^2 + \alpha_4 \text{Mrst}$$
$$+ \alpha_5 \text{Sex} + \alpha_6 \text{Mrstsx} \tag{2–8$'$}$$

For regression analysis of equation (2–8$'$), we estimate the following statistics:

(i) $\hat{\alpha}_0, \hat{\alpha}_1, \ldots, \hat{\alpha}_6$, *estimates* of the "true" values of $\alpha_0, \alpha_1, \ldots, \alpha_6$

(ii) $S_0, S_1, \ldots, S_6$, estimates of the *standard errors* of $\hat{\alpha}_0, \hat{\alpha}_1, \ldots, \hat{\alpha}_6$

(iii) $\bar{R}^2$, the "adjusted coefficient of determination"

Since (ii) and (iii) have not yet been defined and discussed, we will do so now before going on.

The **standard error**, S_i, of an estimated regression coefficient, $\hat{\alpha}_1$, is a measure of the *reliability* with which the "true" value of α_1 has been estimated. The individuals in our sample do not behave exactly in accordance with equation (2–8). Rather, a number of unknown factors cause individuals who have the same schooling, marital status, sex, and age to have different earnings. Thus, if we were to plot points on a graph representing the relationship between log Earn and Educ, for individuals who were all the same age, sex, and marital status, the points would not all fall on the same straight line, just as the xs in Figure 2–5 lie on either side of the estimated demand curve D^*. The greater the distance these points lie from the relationship between log Earn and Educ estimated by regression analysis, the less is our assurance that $\hat{\alpha}_1$ is a good approximation of the "true" α_1 that we could estimate if we only had knowledge of *all* the forces influencing individual earnings. A large estimate of S_1 relative to α_1 tells us that we should not be very confident in the value of α_1 we have estimated. A common way of measuring the size of

S_i relative to α_i is to calculate the ratio $\alpha_i/S_i \equiv t_i$, which is called a **t ratio**. When t_i equals two or more, we can be reasonably confident that $\hat{\alpha}_i$ is "statistically significant"—that is, it is a good estimate. As t_i becomes smaller, we have less confidence in the quality of the information provided by our regression estimates. When t_i is less than 1 (when S_i is larger than $\hat{\alpha}_i$), we have little confidence that there is a relationship between the variables.

The **coefficient of determination**, R^2, and the coefficient of determination adjusted for the number of observations relative to the number of variables in the regression equation, $\bar{R}^2$, is a measure of the overall "explanatory power" of the regression equation. It measures the proportion of the overall variation in the dependent variable that is "explained" by the estimated regression equation. In the simple bivariate case of Figure 2–5,[8] the "unexplained" variation in the dependent variable can be seen as the horizontal distance between the xs and the estimated demand curve D^*. (Actually, R^2 and $\bar{R}^2$ depend on the *square* of these distances.) If all the xs lay exactly on D^*, $\bar{R}^2$ would equal 1. For a very poor "fit," $\bar{R}^2$ and R^2 approach zero.

It cannot be overemphasized that a "low" $\bar{R}^2$ does not mean that the economic theory or hypothesis being investigated is false or useless. It is possible for regression analysis to yield both a low $\bar{R}^2$ and relatively high t ratios at the same time. This is often the case when the sample on which the estimated regression equation is based consists of individual persons, as in our example. What the combination of a low $\bar{R}^2$ and high t ratios tells us is that we have a good idea of how the right-hand, or independent, variables influence the behavior of the left-hand, or dependent, variable, but that behavior is affected by many other forces as well. Thus, although we could not use our estimated regression to predict, say, the earnings of any particular person with a high degree of accuracy, we could use the results to predict what would happen, on the average, to the earnings of a large group of people if each person's schooling were increased by one year. This is not an unimportant accomplishment.

It is equally important to note that it is possible for an estimated regression relationship to be statistically significant but economically untenable. That is, statistically significant relationships may contradict information derived from other investigations we may hold with great certainty. As an example, suppose we gathered data about consumption and income in the United States that showed total consumption expenditures to increase by 20 percent whenever family incomes rose by 100 percent. Since there is reliable evidence already available that the long-run response of consumption to income is much greater than that implied by an elasticity of 0.2, we would under almost no circumstances accept the estimate, even though statistically significant, as a good estimate of the long-run relationship between consumption

---

[8]When the relationship is bivariate, for example, $Y = a + bx$, the square root of R^2 is the correlation coefficient between y and x, usually written as r.

and income. Moreover, a statistically significant relationship may imply an economically insignificant relationship. For example, if it were known with absolute certainty that an additional year of schooling would raise one's earnings by 1 percent, schooling would not be an important determinant of income inequality, and it would be difficult to recommend schooling as an economically important or useful way of raising income levels.

We can now go on to discuss the estimation of equation (2–8′) by means of regression analysis. The results reported here are based on a 1/10,000 subsample of individuals from the U.S. Census of Population, 1970, and consists of all 6,282 individuals in this subsample for whom data were available on all the variables, whose race was white, and who had some earnings in 1969. Here is the regression estimate of equation (2–8′) that was obtained:

$$\text{Log Earn} = 2.04 + .065 \text{ Educ} + .066 \text{ Exper} - .0011 \text{ Exper}^2$$
$$\qquad\qquad (16.5) \qquad (26.8) \qquad\quad (24.2)$$
$$+ .077 \text{ Mrst} - .18 \text{ Sex} - .94 \text{ Mrstsx} \qquad \bar{R}^2 = .38$$
$$\quad (19.9) \qquad (3.8) \qquad (17.4)$$

The t ratios, shown in parentheses below their respective estimated regression coefficients, indicate that each estimated coefficient is "significant"—that is, we can be reasonably confident of the knowledge they provide about the relationship between the dependent variable and the independent variables. The $\bar{R}^2$ tells us that 38 percent of the variation in log Earn can be accounted for by the six variables on the right side of (2–8′) when each is multiplied by its estimated regression coefficient.

What is the economic interpretation of this estimate of (2–8′)? Each regression coefficient provides information about the association between a unit change in a right-hand variable and the natural log of earnings. For example, the coefficient of Educ tells us that, for the average person, an additional year of schooling is associated with greater log earnings of .065. The association with earnings is easy to see if we recognize that for any relationship of the form

$$\log Y = \alpha_0 + \alpha_1 X \qquad\qquad\qquad (2\text{--}9)$$
$$\frac{d \log Y}{dX} = \frac{dY}{dX}\frac{1}{Y} = \alpha_1$$

We can think of α_1 as a "semi-elasticity," denoting the proportionate relationship between X and Y. Thus, an additional year of schooling is associated with 6.5 percent greater earnings.

The association between potential labor market experience and earnings is inferred from the coefficients of Exper and Exper^2. From calculus, we know that

$$\frac{d \log \text{Earn}}{d \text{Exper}} = \alpha_2 - 2\alpha_3 \text{Exper}$$

The association between experience and earnings for the average person varies with the amount of experience, as follows:

$$\frac{d \text{Earn}}{d \text{Exper}} \frac{1}{\text{Earn}} = .066 - .0022 \text{Exper}$$

That is, the association between an additional year of potential experience and earnings is, for the first year of potential experience, 6.4 percent; for the fifth year, 5.5 percent; for the twentieth year, 2.2 percent; and for the fortieth year, -2.2 percent. You should be able to calculate the age at which the association between experience and earnings starts to decline. Does this age depend on the number of years of schooling completed, according to our estimate of equation (2–8′)?

What do the coefficients of the dummy variables Mrst, Sex, and their product Mrstsx tell us? The easiest way to see this is to consider first the values these three variables take on for the four kinds of persons they represent. This is shown in Table 2–4. If we want to know how earnings

TABLE 2–4

Values of Mrst, Sex, and Mrstsx

		Male	*Female*
Married, spouse	Mrst	1	1
present	Sex	0	1
	Mrstsx	0	1
Not married,	Mrst	0	0
spouse present	Sex	0	1
	Mrstsx	0	0

depend on Sex, we need only multiply the appropriate independent variables by their respective regression coefficients. For example, Table 2–4 shows us that for a married woman Mrst = 1, Sex = 1, and Mrstsx = 1. On the other hand, for an unmarried man, Mrst = 0, Sex = 0, and Mrstsx = 0. Multiplying the values of the three variables by their respective coefficients and adding yields, for a married woman, $.077 - .18 - .94 = -1.043$. The corresponding sum for an unmarried man is of course, zero. Now suppose we want to compare the earnings of a married woman to the earnings of an unmarried man of exactly the same age who has exactly the same amount of schooling. We can use the information just calculated to yield

$$\log \text{Earn (woman)} - \log \text{Earn (man)} = -1.043$$

But we also know from our knowledge of the properties of logarithms that the difference between log Earn (woman) and log Earn (man) is identical to the log of the ratio of these two earnings figures. That is,

$$\log \text{Earn (woman)} - \log \text{Earn (man)} \equiv \log \frac{\text{Earn (woman)}}{\text{Earn (man)}} = -1.043$$

The antilog of -1.043 is .35.[9] Therefore, we conclude that, on the average, the earnings of a married woman amount to 35 percent of the earnings of an unmarried man with the same schooling and who is the same age.

Table 2–5 shows the information for all four groups that we need to calculate the proportional difference in earnings among them. From Table 2–5 we can see that the estimated coefficients of Mrst, Sex, and Mrstsx imply that among otherwise identical individuals, unmarried women will have earnings only 84 percent as high as those of unmarried men, while the earnings of married men will exceed those of unmarried men by 8 percent. The earnings of married women will therefore equal $.35 \div 1.08 = 32.4$ percent of the earnings of married men, while the comparison between unmarried women and married men is $.84 \div 1.08 = 77.7$ percent. Why do you think the earnings of married women fall short of the earnings of married men by a greater amount than do those of unmarried women? Does marriage lower a woman's earning power?

TABLE 2–5

Coefficients of Mrst, Sex, and Mrstsx Multiplied by Their Values
(from Table 2–4)

	Male	Female
Married, spouse present	$.077 \times 1 + 0 + 0 = .077$ antilog $.077 = 1.08$	$.077 \times 1 - .18 \times 1 - .94 \times 1$ $= -1.043$ antilog $-1.043 = .35$
Not married, spouse present	0 antilog $0 = 1.0$	$0 - .18 \times 1 + 0 = -.18$ antilog $-.18 = .84$

---

[9]The antilog of -1.043 is equal to $e^{-1.043}$ or $2.718^{-1.043}$.

This concludes our brief discussion of measurement and quantitative methods in labor economics. As you read the remainder of this text, we hope you will try to remember that there is no way to evaluate statistical results without reference to an economic theory which explains how the variables are thought to be related and the kinds of estimates that are acceptable evidence. There is much room for judgment and experience in interpreting the results of empirical investigations, and reasonable and competent economists can and do disagree on whether a given theory or hypothesis has been confirmed or rejected or whether it is useful in helping to understand the real world. At many points we have had to use our best judgment in interpreting empirical studies of labor markets, and other economists may well have wished to use the results of different empirical investigations, or to interpret results differently. The important thing for you will be not so much to read and believe as to read and understand.

PART II

The Labor Market
in the Short Run
under Competitive Conditions

CHAPTER 3

The Demand
for Labor
in Competitive Markets

A. Educational Objectives
  1. Establish the general qualitative relationship between firms' desired amounts of labor and wage rate per unit of labor services
  2. Identify the influence of various environmental disturbances or governmental policies on the quantities of labor firms wish to purchase
  3. Illustrate one technique for verifying and quantifying the expected downward sloping demand curve for labor

B. The Firm's Labor Demand Curve When Its Capital Input Is Fixed
  1. The Production Function
    a. Algebraic representation
    b. Geometric representation: the isoquant map
    c. The average and marginal physical products of labor
  2. The Value of Marginal Product of Labor: The Competitive Firm's Labor Demand Schedule
    a. Factors which disturb the demand for labor
    b. Application of the theory of the demand for labor: the disemployment effects of the winter of 1976

C. The Demand Curve for Labor When the Firm Adjust Its Nonlabor Inputs
  1. Isoexpenditure lines and the firm's optimal (cost minimizing) input combination for a given level of output
  2. The expansion path and the firm's profit maximizing amount of labor
  3. The labor demand curve
    a. The substitution effect
    b. The scale effect
  4. The relationship between the competitive firm's labor demand curves when capital is fixed versus variable
    a. A comparison of the relative slopes
    b. Application: the total cost of unionization

Labor demand is usually referred to as a *derived* demand. That is, it stems from the demand for commodities that labor helps to produce. Have you ever been to a fast-food restaurant like McDonalds, and upon completion of your meal wondered whether you should leave the trash on the table or clean up after yourself? On the one hand you hated the thought of leaving a mess, but on the other you worried about taking away the job of some deserving teenager or senior citizen. If this example "rings a bell," then you are already well on your way to understanding the general principle that the demand for labor depends upon (is derived from) the demand for final output. In the situation above, the more hamburgers sold, the greater the quantity of wrappers left on the tables and the more teenagers hired to clean up.

In this chapter we begin our examination of competitive labor markets by exploring at some length the linkage between the demand for output, the production process, and the demand for labor in the **short run**. We will define the short run as that period of time in which employers hire from a labor force of a particular "quality." Specifically, there is insufficient time for

*Represents more advanced material

a firm to alter its employees' skills through on-the-job training. Although one may choose to supply more or less time to the labor market (including becoming a housewife or a househusband), in the short run one may not get more education or change occupation.

The Firm's Labor Demand Curve
When Capital Is Fixed

The most basic decision-making unit we consider in analyzing labor demand is the firm. To understand how a competitive firm selects a particular quantity of labor services based upon its ability to combine inputs into a marketable product, we must discuss some of the general properties of production. We assume that every firm possesses full knowledge of its **production function**, the technical (engineering) relationship between its inputs and its product.

THE FIRM'S PRODUCTION FUNCTION

Consider a general algebraic expression of a firm's production process

$$Y = F(X, Z) \tag{3-1}$$

where
$$Y \equiv \text{units of output}$$
$$X \equiv \text{units of input } X$$
$$Z \equiv \text{units of input } Z$$

In (3–1), $F(\cdot)$ is a mathematical equation which translates (maps) two inputs, X and Z, into an output, Y, during a given period of time, perhaps a week. Put differently, $F(\cdot)$ tells us that for a particular set of input values, say (X_1, Z_1), a particular amount of output, Y_1, results.[1]

Suppose we are dealing with a firm which uses the services of physical capital (K) and labor (L) to produce widgets (Q).[2] All three are measured as *flows* per unit of time. We assume that the firm in question sells no other products and makes only one model of widget. Moreover, we assume that all labor (capital) is of the same type and quality or that there exists a measurement system which permits the summation of different kinds of labor

---

[1] Two well-known production functions are $Y = \delta X^{\alpha} Z^{\beta}$ and $Y = \gamma[\lambda X^{-\rho} + (1 - \lambda) Z^{-\rho}]^{-\mu/\rho}$, where δ, α, β, λ, ρ, and μ are parameters (constants). The first function is called the Cobb-Douglas production function after its creators, and the second, the constant elasticity of substitution (CES), because of a mathematical property we will discuss shortly. In reality, a firm will use more than two inputs. We choose to discuss the two-input case to simplify the geometric analysis to follow.

[2] Just for fun, see how many of your friends know what a widget is.

(capital). In practice, then, $L(K)$ might represent total weekly employee (machine) hours.

Now let us consider the production of a *given* number of widgets, Q_0. The production function can be rearranged (inverted) to tell us the various combinations of K and L that will result in the level of widget production Q_0

$$K = \tilde{F}(L; Q_0) \qquad\qquad (3\text{--}2)$$

where $\tilde{F}(\cdot) \equiv$ inverted (rearranged) production function.[3] A graph of equation (3–2) is known as an **isoquant** (equal quantity) because it represents combinations of K and L that produce a certain level of output within a given time period. You may be familiar with similar concepts from weather maps, where an isobar is a line that marks places of equal barometric pressure and an isotherm is a line that marks places of equal temperature. The isoquant labeled 100 in Figure 3–1, for example, indicates that a weekly output of 100 widgets may be produced with 6 units of L and 10 units of K (point P) per week or with 11 of L and 6 of K per week (point S). Notice that

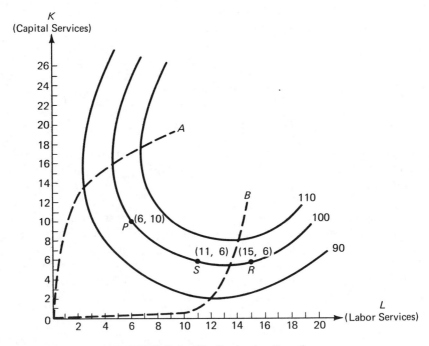

FIGURE 3–1. The Production Function

---

[3] You should be able to show that if the widget production function is Cobb-Douglas ($Q = \delta K^\alpha L^\beta$), then equation (3–2) would look like $K = \left[\dfrac{Q_0}{\delta L^\beta}\right]^{1/\alpha}$.

point R also lies on the isoquant 100. While *technologically* feasible, it will not be chosen by the competitive firm if labor services have a positive price, since R is more expensive than the input combination at point S. To generalize, combinations of K and L along an isoquant above where it becomes vertical or to the right of where it becomes horizontal cost more than another input combination along the same isoquant and may therefore be ignored. The dashed lines OA and OB in Figure 3–1 are called **ridge lines** and delimit the region where production will occur. (In subsequent figures the portions of the isoquants outside the ridge lines are eliminated.) Remember that there are many levels of production possible and that each is represented by a different isoquant, so that Figure 3–1 would be very messy were we to attempt to depict completely the production process for widgets. To keep our example manageable, Figure 3–1 and the geometrical representations of production that follow depict only subsets of isoquants.

A number of properties of isoquants are worth noting. First, a given input combination is associated with only *one* level of output (isoquants do not intersect). The most important characteristics of isoquants, however, are that in general they are *negatively sloped* and *convex* to the origin (as in Figure 3–1). The negative slopes represent the **principle of substitution**, which means that when either factor is reduced by one unit, the other must be increased for output to be held constant. In fact, the slope of an isoquant at a point describes the firm's ability to substitute factors for one another while holding output constant. If the slope were minus 1/3, for example, three units of labor must be added if capital is reduced by one unit. Economists call the absolute value of the slope of an isoquant (at a point) the **marginal rate of technical substitution (MRTS)** between factors. Convexity is the characteristic that, along each isoquant in Figure 3–1, the amount of L necessary to compensate for one less unit of K *grows* as L/K grows.

The production function as illustrated in Figure 3–1 conveys one of the most important ideas in economics: *A given level of output can be produced in alternative ways*. There are numerous examples of this. In heavily populated Asian countries, crops are produced on little land with a great deal of labor. In contrast, in California, where labor is very expensive, similar crops such as rice are produced with relatively large amounts of land and machinery. In business offices, accounting can be done with many bookkeepers working with adding machines or with only a few individuals using sophisticated computers. Thus, the existence of a production function implies that a firm must choose among alternative input blends.[4] How a firm

---

[4]Because this chapter is devoted to the demand for labor by *firms*, we limit our discussions of production to that context. The concept of a production function, though, describes any individual's or group's ability to transform inputs into output. In Chapter 4 we discuss the household's production of commodities such as meals with the inputs of goods purchased in the market and time of family members. A recent article, Solomon W. Polachek, Thomas J. Kniesner, and Henrick J. Harwood, "Educational Production Func-

makes such choices determines its demand for labor. To move intellectually from the firm's production function (an *engineering* concept) to its demand for labor (an *economic* concept), however, we must first know its input purchase options.

THE COMPETITIVE FIRM'S INPUT PURCHASE OPTIONS

In competition, the prices a firm must pay for its inputs are established by forces outside its control—the interaction of supply and demand in the factor markets.[5] Each competitive firm feels (correctly) that it may purchase as many units of K or L as it wants without affecting their respective prices. Under competitive conditions, then, the supply curve of L (or K) to the firm is horizontal (perfectly elastic) at the market price. Such a labor supply curve is depicted in Figure 3–2. The vertical axis measures the dollar price of one hour of labor services, and the horizontal axis measures employee-hours per week. The labor supply schedule is parallel to the horizontal axis, indicating that the firm will obtain no labor if it offers a wage less than $\bar{w}$, but can purchase as much as it wants at $\bar{w}$. The supply curves of other inputs would be drawn similarly.

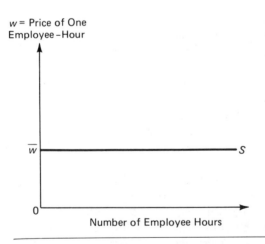

FIGURE 3–2. The Supply Curve of Labor to the Competitive Firm

---

tions," *The Journal of Educational Statistics*, 3, 3 (autumn 1978), 209–31, presents estimates of the mathematical relation between an individual student's study time, class attendance, college board score, and grade on a midterm exam in a macro principles of economics course. For the mathematically trained reader, we offer the following activity: Take the estimates presented in the above article and offer to sell some first-year macro principles students estimates of the amount of time each of them must study in order to achieve grades of A on their first midterm, given intended class attendance and college board score. Ten percent of all profits from this activity must be paid as royalties to Polachek, Kniesner, and Harwood, who accept no responsibility for poor predictions.
[5]The concept of a labor market is formally developed in Chapter 5.

We are now in a position to establish a competitive firm's demand curve for labor when its capital input is fixed. There is good reason to believe that a firm will generally be quite cautious in adjusting its capital input. Generally, investment in new plant and equipment is a relatively expensive undertaking. This fact is underscored by the following description of the paper shortage experienced by magazines in 1978:

> *Paper shortage hits magazines: sharp growth in advertising eats up pages.*
> Publishers of the "slicks," magazines so-called because of their use of coated paper, say supplies of that paper are tight and getting tighter. Jerry Thornton, a vice president of Meredith Corp., publisher of *Better Homes & Gardens* and other magazines, says, "We're buying more and more paper in Europe and even that's getting tight now." International Paper, a major coated-paper maker, says magazines are asking for more tonnage, "but we simply can't give it to them."
> *Main reason for the shortage: Magazine advertising pages are increasing while coated-paper capacity isn't. Paper producers say they're waiting to see if demand holds up before committing millions of dollars to new machinery.* Helping to account for the surge in magazine advertising are the soaring costs of television commercials. As TV time becomes more expensive, more and more major advertisers turn to the slicks.
> Despite the heavy demand, prices for coated papers haven't soared. One publisher estimates they've risen only 5% to 7% in the past year.[6]

Consequently, we expect a firm to adjust its labor input initially by more than its capital input in response to a wage rate change, especially since it may have good reason for suspecting the wage change to be only temporary, perhaps the result of cyclical movements in the economy. As a reasonable first attempt at understanding its demand for labor, then, we will examine the situation in which a competitive firm's input of physical capital is fixed.

When the input of capital services (K) is fixed, we may ignore its supply conditions. The firm in Figure 3–3 is producing an output of 100 units per week with 6 units of K and 7 of L (point R). Suppose the wage rate falls due to an influx of cheap labor. This reduces the firm's cost of production, providing an incentive to expand output. But by how much? As you know, the firm will increase its profit if it expands output whenever the value of additional production is greater than its cost. The value to the firm of additional production is equal to the extra output multiplied by its price. Since the price of output is also beyond the control of a competitive firm, the crucial determinant of its demand for labor will be the behavior of output as additional labor is added to its fixed capital input. Economists call the addition to output that stems from a small increase in labor services (capital

---

[6]*The Wall Street Journal*, January 26, 1978, p. 1 (italics added). Reprinted by permission of *The Wall Street Journal*, © Dow Jones & Company, Inc., 1978. All rights reserved.

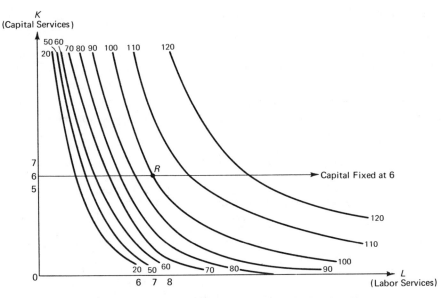

FIGURE 3–3. The Production Function (*K* fixed at 6)

fixed), the **marginal physical product of labor** (*MPP*). We can see labor's marginal physical product by examining the isoquants in Figure 3–3 along a straight line extending from 6 on the *K* axis parallel to the *L* axis. Points on this line represent the levels of output that correspond to various inputs of *L, K* fixed at 6 horsepower-hours per week. Notice that as we move outward along the ray (increase *L/K*), progressively larger inputs of *L* must be added in order to raise production by an equal amount. This is called **diminishing marginal (physical) productivity**.

Let us put aside temporarily the hypothetical firm of Figure 3–3 and make sure we understand the concept of (eventually) diminishing marginal physical productivity of labor. Consider a farmer with 100 acres of land. If he tries to do all the farming, he will be handicapped by the fact that he can be in only one place at a time. But if he hires a helper, the output of the farm may more than double, because some specialization will be possible. Moreover, if there is a hole in the fence at the same time there is a leak in the roof of the barn, both emergencies can be taken care of at once; the resources of the farm will be employed more flexibly. This increasing efficiency of labor may continue as our farmer hires a second, third, or even a fourth helper. As the number of workers on the farm grows, however, the marginal physical product of labor must eventually fall. At some point, the farmer will have so many helpers that an additional one will be idle most of the time waiting for supervision or to use machinery, as well as getting in the way of other workers. The marginal physical product of labor for our hypothetical firm is depicted in Figure 3–4. Units of labor are measured on the horizontal axis. The curve labeled *MPP* is drawn by plotting the *changes* in output (differences between the isoquants) along the horizontal line in Figure 3–3 against the corresponding (initial) amounts of labor. Also depicted is the firm's **average physical product of labor** (*APP*), which is drawn by plotting output per unit of labor along the same line in Figure 3–3 against the corresponding *L*.

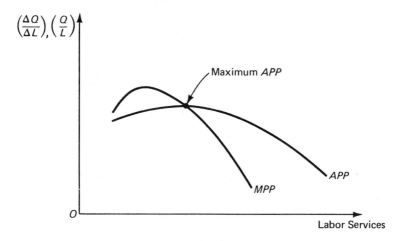

FIGURE 3–4. Marginal Physical Product of Labor and Average Physical Product of Labor

It will simplify analysis to convert these relationships into value terms, since we wish to discover how much labor the firm will hire (at a given wage) in order of maximize its profit, and profit is generally measured in units of money. Remember that ultimately we wish a plot of the firm's profit-maximizing quantities of labor for various values of the wage, its **labor demand schedule.** Because the competitive firm can sell as much output as it wishes at the going price, on which its own actions have a negligible influence, it is a simple task to convert the relations in Figure 3–4 into value terms. We need only multiply the firm's *MPP* and *APP* schedules by the equilibrium price of output to find the **value of marginal product of labor** (*VMP*) and the **value of average product of labor** (*VAP*). Since we are multiplying by a constant, the *VMP* and *VAP* schedules have the same general shapes as *MPP* and *APP*, respectively; this is shown in Figure 3–5.

How much labor will the firm hire when the wage rate is $6 (supply curve *S*)? Remember that a firm maximizes its profit by producing up to the point where marginal cost (*MC*) equals marginal revenue (*MR*), and that in competition marginal revenue equals product price (*P*). Expressed algebraically,

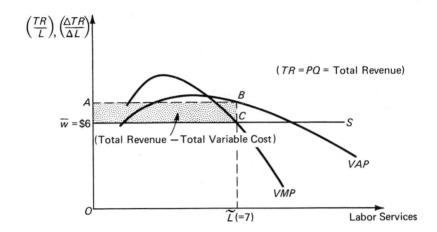

FIGURE 3–5. Value of Marginal Product of Labor and Value of Average Product of Labor

the firm's profit-maximizing output decision is to find the level of production where

$$P = MC \qquad (3\text{–}3)$$

Similarly, the firm will hire labor, the only variable factor of production in this example, until the marginal cost of labor (the wage rate) is equal to the marginal revenue it creates (VMP). Expressed algebraically, the firm's profit-maximizing hiring policy is to find the level of labor where

$$w = VMP \qquad (3\text{–}4)$$

This occurs in Figure 3–5 at point C. At a wage of $6, profit is maximized by hiring 7 units of labor.

It is easy to demonstrate that the firm's profit-maximizing output policy is equivalent to its profit-maximizing hiring policy. A simple example shows that (3–3) and (3–4) are equivalent. Suppose the marginal physical product of labor is 3. This means it would take approximately 1/3 additional unit of labor to produce one more unit of output. That is to say, the marginal cost of output *in terms of labor* is 1/MPP. For convenience, we shall call 1/MPP a **marginal input of labor**. It follows that a marginal input of labor multiplied by the wage rate is the cost *in dollars* of one more unit of output. Thus, all we must do to relate MC to MPP in terms of dollars is to multiply 1/MPP by w, obtaining $w/MPP = MC$. We may then rewrite (3–4) as

$$P = w/MPP \qquad (3\text{–}5)$$

Equation (3–5), which is equivalent to (3–3), can be transformed into (3–4) by multiplying both sides by *MPP* and recognizing that $P \cdot MPP \equiv VMP$. Thus, when K is fixed, the condition under which a firm will maximize its profit in the hiring of labor is identical to that under which it will maximize its profit in the production of output. In what sense, then, is a firm's *VMP schedule* its demand curve for labor when capital is fixed? A labor demand curve answers the question of how much labor the firm will wish to hire at various wage rates. We will see that over most of its range, the *VMP* curve answers this question.

Remember from basic economics that a firm will stay in business (when capital is fixed) so long as total revenue does not fall below total variable cost. In Figure 3–5, the firm hires $\tilde{L}$ units of labor at wage rate $\bar{w}$. The value of average product of labor is A, and the total revenue is, by definition, $(A \times \tilde{L})$, or the area of the rectangle $OAB\tilde{L}$. (Can you explain why?) Similarly, total variable cost is $(\tilde{L} \times \bar{w})$, or the area of the rectangle $O\bar{w}C\tilde{L}$. The amount by which total revenue exceeds total variable cost when the firm maximizes its profit for wage $\bar{w}$ is represented, then, by $\bar{w}ABC$. It is possible to construct such a rectangle for any profit-maximizing output *greater* than the output corresponding to maximum *VAP*. When the wage rate equals maximum *VAP*, however, the rectangle representing the excess of total revenue over total variable cost vanishes. Thus, when the wage rate is less than or equal to maximum *VAP*, the firm will maximize its profit (minimize its loss) by hiring labor up to the point where $w = VMP$.[7] Should the wage rate rise above *VAP*, however, the firm will lose the least by not producing at all. Hence, the *VMP* curve where it lies below maximum *VAP* is the firm's demand for labor schedule when capital is fixed.

It should prove useful at this point to summarize the key results just developed. First, when capital is held constant, the firm's demand curve for labor is downward-sloping. Due to diminishing marginal physical productivity, the profit-maximizing firm will purchase additional labor if and only if the wage rate falls, all other things being equal. Second, underlying the inverse relationship between the wage and the competitive firm's demand for labor services are (1) a particular level of capital services, (2) a given price of final output, and (3) the "state of technology" (the production function) represented in the isoquant map. A change in *any* of these three will disturb *VMP* and *VAP* and, therefore, the firm's labor demand curve. The interrelationship between technology and labor usage is what underlies most popular arguments concerning the labor market effects of "automation." The effect of a change in product price on the demand for labor by a competitive firm will

---

[7]Remember that profit (π) is the difference between total revenue (*TR*) and total cost (*TC*), and that *TC* has two components: $w \cdot L$ plus payments to other (fixed) factors. Even if $TR - w \cdot L$ is positive, profit may still be negative (the firm is losing money). The firm will continue to produce when π is negative so long as its losses are reduced by the act of production ($TR - w \cdot L > 0$).

become obvious in our subsequent analysis of the demand for labor by a competitive *industry*. Let us now examine the effect of an exogenous change in K on the demand for labor.

THE FIRM'S DEMAND FOR LABOR WHEN CAPITAL IS FIXED: APPLICATION

The winter of 1976–77 was very severe in the eastern United States. Unusually cold temperatures led to natural gas shortages and substantial cutbacks in gas available for industrial use. The result was an increase in unemployment in the areas affected. Let us examine this phenomenon with the analytical framework just developed.

In our two-dimensional representation of production, inputs other than labor services are called services of physical capital. Natural gas used to heat an industrial plant or to operate a blast furnace would be an example of such a nonlabor input. In Figure 3–6 the curves labeled $VMP(K_1)$ and $VAP(K_1)$ are drawn for the level of natural gas (K_1) that a plant would have available during a "normal" winter. Since the cutbacks of natural gas were short-lived and unexpected (the result of temperatures far below normal), this situation

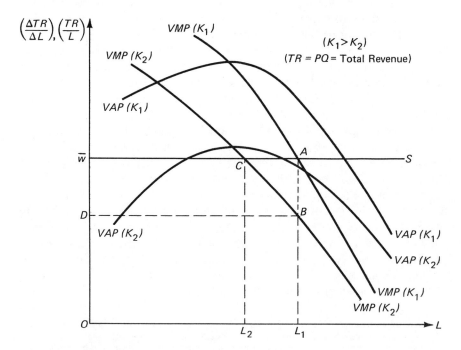

FIGURE 3–6. The Effect of an Exogenous Change in K on the Demand for Labor

may be interpreted as an exogenous decrease in the firm's input of physical capital. In those firms affected by the cutback, the result is a shift to $VMP(K_2)$ and $VAP(K_2)$. The value of marginal product and value of average product of labor schedules shift downward with a decrease in K because labor's marginal and average *physical* products decline when there is less of other factors per worker. In this case, cold temperatures lower productivity by making workers uncomfortable and slowing their movements. In addition to lowering thermostats, firms slowed or shut down machinery requiring gas fuel, further lowering workers' output on the average and at the margin.

Given the fixed wage rate confronting the competitive firm in Figure 3–6 ($\bar{w}$), the profit-maximizing amount of labor in a normal winter is L_1. The downward shift in VMP induces the firm to cut back to L_2, reducing its labor input by $(L_1 - L_2)$. If L is measured by employees, then the unemployment caused by the excessively cold winter is roughly $(L_1 - L_2)$ times the number of firms involved. Alternatively, $(L_1 - L_2)$ may be thought of as each firm's reduction in employee hours. In some firms, the cutback in natural gas was so severe that $VMP(K_2)$ was intersected by S *above* the point where $VMP(K_2)$ $= VAP(K_2)$. (What was the profit-maximizing L in those firms?)

Perhaps you understand the geometry, but the reasoning behind the decline in employment is still somewhat unclear. It will be helpful to think of the situation in two parts: first the environmental disturbance, then the response of the firm. These correspond to a shift in the VMP schedule followed by a movement along the new schedule.

Consider the moment at which K suddenly drops from K_1 to K_2, the firm not yet having adjusted L. When the value of marginal product schedule is $VMP(K_1)$, L_1 units of labor are hired at $\bar{w}$ (point A) because the competitive firm maximizes profit by hiring the amount of L that (at the margin) is "worth" $\bar{w}$. Decreased K lowers labor's value of marginal product schedule, and, in particular, lowers the marginal value of L_1 units to OD dollars (point B). Since the competitive firm cannot affect the wage it must pay, L_1 units of labor now have a marginal value which is less than the wage, and we know that profit is greatest when $\bar{w} = VMP$. In essence, the firm responds to this change in its environment (the decrease in K) by sliding along $VMP(K_2)$ from point B to point C, raising the marginal value of labor to $\bar{w}$ through a reduction in its labor input from L_1 to L_2. Remember that diminishing returns works both ways; given K_2, marginal physical productivity rises as less labor is employed. So, L_2 is the amount of labor that maximizes profit for wage $\bar{w}$ and $VMP(K_2)$ in Figure 3–6.[8]

---

[8] On the lighter side of the topic of labor's marginal physical productivity and its relation to the level of "capital" is a recent study showing that subjects lost muscular strength when exposed to background music which was rock music. Apparently the rock beat is a stress signal that interferes with brainwave rhythms relative to "easy listening," classical, or country music. See *The Wall Street Journal*, January 24, 1978, p. 1.

The Demand Curve for Labor
When the Firm Adjusts Capital[9]

THE FIRM'S INPUT PURCHASE OPTIONS

We now examine the demand for labor by a competitive firm when a wage change is considered sufficiently permanent to warrant adjustment of labor and capital services. The initial step is to represent the firm's input purchase options on the same graph as the production function. In the production diagram, we measure physical quantities of factors along the axes; at first glance there appears to be no place to represent the inputs in monetary terms. However, if we know the dollar prices of machinery and labor, we have the necessary information.

Suppose that the price (wage rate) of a unit of labor services is $1 and the price of a unit of machine services is $2; then the relative price of labor is

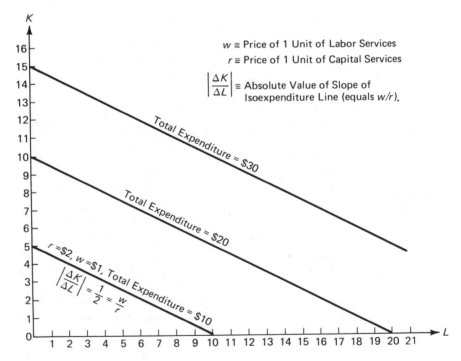

FIGURE 3–7. A Family of Isoexpenditure Lines

---

[9]The analysis of this section is primarily geometric. For a concise analytical derivation, see James M. Henderson and Richard E. Quandt, *Microeconomic Theory* (New York: McGraw-Hill, 1971), pp. 69–70.

1/2. That is, if the firm decides not to purchase some additional L but to purchase instead more K, it can get 1/2 unit of machine services for every unit of labor services it "gives up." In general, the relative price of labor tells us how the firm can implicitly trade L for K when purchasing these two inputs. Note that if the dollar prices of labor and capital do not depend on how much of either factor the firm buys, as in competition, the relative price of labor is independent of input purchases as well.

Three sets of purchase options when the relative price of labor is 1/2 are represented in Figure 3–7. The line nearest the origin is a locus of all combinations of K and L that can be obtained for $10, such as $8L$ and $1K$, $6L$ and $2K$, or $4L$ and $3K$. Note that the absolute value of the slope of this line, $\left|\dfrac{\Delta K}{\Delta L}\right|$, is equal to the relative price of labor. Since each line represents a fixed number of dollars spent on the two factor inputs, they are called **isoexpenditure lines**. Isoexpenditure lines are straight and parallel, since the relative price of labor is beyond the control of a competitive firm.[10] (What would the family of isoexpenditure lines in Figure 3–7 look like if the price of labor were to rise to $2 and the price of capital to remain unchanged?)

COST MINIMIZATION

In the case of only one variable factor, cost minimization does not require special attention. There is only one possible way to produce each level of output. When all points on an isoquant are feasible production methods, the firm must minimize the cost of production (whatever level of output is selected) if it is to maximize its profits. To see how a firm minimizes cost by comparing input purchase options with production possibilities, an isoquant and isoexpenditure lines have been brought together in Figure 3–8. Suppose the firm attempts to produce 100 units of output with the combination of K and L at point T which represents an expenditure of $12. The competitive firm will not select point T, however, if it can produce these 100 units for less. The firm can reduce production cost by substituting L for K until it reaches point R, where the isoquant and isoexpenditure line $10 are tangent (just touch). There is no other combination of K and L that produces 100 units and costs less than $10.[11] In general, the firm minimizes the cost of a given level

---

[10]The relative price of labor is really the rate of exchange between the two factors. While this rate of exchange is similar to the rate of substitution represented by the slopes of the isoquants, it refers to substitution in purchases, as opposed to substitution in the production process. In contrast to the variable substitutability in production represented by convex isoquants is the constant substitutability in input purchases represented by straight isoexpenditure lines.

[11]Notice that 100 is also the highest level of output that can be achieved by spending $10 on factors of production.

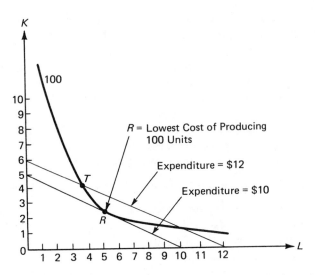

FIGURE 3–8. The Least-Cost Method of Producing 100 Units

of output by producing at a point where an isoexpenditure line is *tangent* to an isoquant.[12]

Let us now look at the nature of the tangency least-cost position more formally. Consider the two isoquants in Figure 3–9. Point B on isoquant 100 lies directly above point A on isoquant 99. They differ by one unit of output and by just enough $K(\Delta K)$ to account for the difference in production (L is the same in both cases). Now compare points A and C. They differ by just enough $L(\Delta L)$ to account for one extra (less) unit of output. The line segment $\overline{AB}$ represents a concept already encountered, marginal input of $L(MI_L)$ (see page 56). Analagously, $\overline{AC}$ is a marginal input of $K(MI_K)$. Thus, we may think of the absolute value of the slope of isoquant 100 as MI_K/MI_L.[13] To generalize, the slope of an isoquant is the ratio of the marginal inputs of the factors, or

$$\Delta K/\Delta L \text{ (isoquant)} = MI_K/MI_L \qquad (3\text{--}6)$$

We have also noted (page 56) that the marginal input of a factor is the

---

[12]There is of course, an exception: the case where an isoquant and isoexpenditure line intersect at one of the axes. You should be able to show that when this occurs, the least-cost method of production uses only one of the two inputs. This case, called a "corner solution," is possible only if the isoquants intersect an axis. Corner solutions are precluded if some small amount of each factor is required in production.

[13]For the remainder of this chapter, reference to the slope of either an isoquant or an isoexpenditure line is to the *absolute value* of the slope.

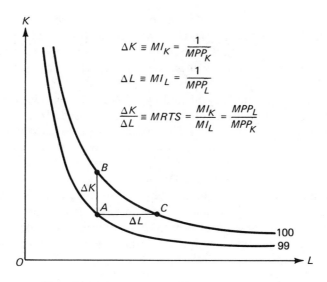

FIGURE 3–9. Definitions of *MRTS*, *MI*, and *MPP*

reciprocal of its marginal product. Therefore,

$$MI_K/MI_L = MPP_L/MPP_K \qquad (3\text{--}7)$$

and

$$\Delta K/\Delta L \text{ (isoquant)} = MPP_L/MPP_K \qquad (3\text{--}8)$$

Equations (3–7) and (3–8) tell us that the marginal rate of technical substitution may be thought of as either the ratio of marginal inputs or the ratio of marginal physical products. Recall, however, that the slope of an isoexpenditure line is the relative price of labor

$$\Delta K/\Delta L \text{ (isoexpenditure line)} = w/r \qquad (3\text{--}9)$$

Since at a point of tangency between an isoexpenditure line and an isoquant their slopes are equal, equations (3–8) and (3–9) yield as the condition for cost minimization

$$w/r = MPP_L/MPP_K \qquad (3\text{--}10)$$

With a slight amount of manipulation, the economic "sense" of (3–10) will become apparent. Divide both sides of the equation by w and multiply both sides by MPP_K, yielding as an equivalent expression

$$\frac{1}{r} \cdot MPP_K = \frac{1}{w} \cdot MPP_L \qquad (3\text{--}11)$$

The term $(1/r)$ represents the amount of K that can be purchased by an expenditure of \$1. Similarly, $(1/w)$ is the amount of L that can be purchased for \$1. Equation (3–11) indicates, then, that when cost is minimized, the last dollar spent on K must increase output by the same amount as the last dollar spent on L. If, as in Figure 3–8, point T, $MPP_K/r < MPP_L/w$, the firm can reduce its expenditure on K by \$1 and spend *less* than an additional dollar on L, while maintaining output at 100. As more L is used, MPP_L falls and as less K is used, MPP_K rises (why?). The firm continues to substitute L for K, reducing the cost of production, until the changes in MPP_K and MPP_L create (3–11).

Finally, one caveat is necessary. Do not confuse cost minimization with profit maximization! While equation (3–10) describes what is required to minimize the cost of any *particular* output, there are many possible levels of production. At only *one* level of output will the firm also maximize profit! Cost minimization is necessary but not sufficient for profit maximization.

THE EXPANSION PATH

In order to relate cost minimization to labor demand when labor *and* capital are variable, we must introduce still another concept—*the expansion path*. Figure 3–10 illustrates a set of isoquants and two possible sets of isoexpenditure lines tangent to them. The sets of isoexpenditure lines represent two possible relative prices of labor. The flatter set represents the same price of physical capital (in terms of dollars) as the steeper set, but a lower

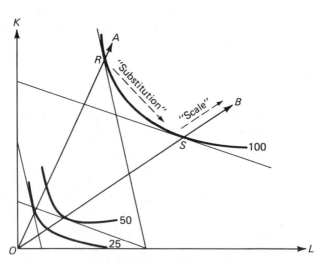

FIGURE 3–10. The Firm's Expansion Paths—The Substitution and Scale Effects

price of labor.[14] Notice that the locus of tangency points between the iso-quants and a set of isoexpenditure lines forms a ray extending outward from the origin. Along each of the two rays in Figure 3–10 we observe the least-cost combinations of factors associated with the various levels of output, given the relative price of labor. Economists call these rays **expansion paths** or **scale lines**.[15] (What does the expansion path look like in the fixed capital situation examined earlier?) The expansion path is an extremely important economic concept. Among other things, it describes how the firm's use of labor will expand and contract over the course of the business cycle. Remember that there is a different expansion path for each set of relative prices (isoexpenditure lines). As the relative price of labor falls, for example, the expansion path moves in a clockwise direction, implying that the cost-minimizing input combination involves a higher proportion of labor.

THE LABOR DEMAND CURVE

Suppose the firm is in equilibrium at point R, on expansion path $\overline{OA}$ (which represents the higher relative price of labor). There it is maximizing profit by equating marginal cost of production with marginal revenue and, as we will see, the value of marginal product of each factor with that factor's price. What will happen to the amount of labor used if the wage falls, generating the expansion path $\overline{OB}$? Two adjustments take place. First, each level of output can now be produced most cheaply with a higher proportion of labor. To see this, think of the firm as moving along isoquant 100 from R to S, where expansion path $\overline{OB}$ crosses the 100 isoquant. This hypothetical movement, which holds output constant but changes the proportions in which the factors are used, is called the **substitution effect** of a change in the relative price of L. The substitution effect implies that even if a firm did not change its output, a change in relative input prices would lead it to change

---

[14]Although a set of relative price lines may be derived from the dollar prices of factors, the dollar prices may not be inferred from the relative prices. This is important because it illustrates that a change in the slope of an isoexpenditure line could come about from either a decline in the price of machinery or an increase in the price of labor. These two changes have the same effect on the relative price of labor, but they have an opposite effect on the cost of production.

[15]For simplicity we have drawn the expansion paths as positively-sloped straight lines. The upward slope means that increases in output require increases in both factors of production. Along a linear expansion path K/L is constant. The linearity means that the production function is such that the slopes of the isoquants depend only on the *ratio* of the inputs (are independent of *level* of output). The Cobb-Douglas function introduced in footnote 1 is an example of a production function with a linear expansion path. For mathematical elaboration, see William J. Baumol, *Economic Theory and Operations Analysis* (Englewood Cliffs, N.J.: Prentice-Hall, 1977), pp. 267–96. The expansion path need be neither upward-sloping nor linear to generate our ultimate result that the demand for labor is inversely related to the wage.

its input *mix* so as to increase (decrease) L and decrease (increase) K whenever w/r decreases (increases).[16,17]

However, since the relative price of labor has fallen because its dollar price declined while the dollar price of K remained constant, the cost of production in general is reduced. Since the cost of production has fallen but the price of output is the same, the competitive firm can increase profit by expanding output. Consequently, it proceeds northeast along expansion path $\overline{OB}$ until marginal cost of production once again equals marginal revenue.[18] The movement from S along expansion path $\overline{OB}$ is called the **scale effect** of the change in the wage.

In our analysis of the demand for labor with fixed K, we demonstrated that the profit-maximizing competitive firm hires labor up to the point where VMP equals w. When all inputs are adjusted, profit maximization requires that the value of marginal product of each factor equal that factor's price. This can be shown with a little algebra. By definition, the cost-minimization condition in equation (3–10) is the same as

$$w/r = MI_K/MI_L \tag{3-12}$$

Cross-multiplication of this equation yields

$$w \cdot MI_L = r \cdot MI_K \tag{3-13}$$

Equation (3–13) provides an important additional interpretation of equation (3–10): When cost is minimized, a one-unit increase in output is equally expensive, whether a marginal input of L or K is used. In other words, when the firm is minimizing the cost of a given output

$$MC = w \cdot MI_L \tag{3-14}$$

---

[16]A standardized measure of the substitution effect is known as the elasticity of substitution (σ), which is defined as the percent change in (K/L) due to a 1 percent change in the slope of an isoquant (marginal rate of technical substitution), which in equilibrium equals the slope of an isoexpenditure line (w/r). In Figure 3–10, σ is the percentage difference in the slopes of rays $\overline{OA}$ and $\overline{OB}$, divided by the percentage difference in the slopes of isoquant 100 at points R and S. Simply put, σ reflects the curvature of an isoquant. The easier it is to substitute labor (capital) for capital (labor), the greater is the value of σ and the more like a downward-sloping straight line is the isoquant. "Perfect" substitution is said to exist when the elasticity of substitution "goes to" infinity. At the other end of the spectrum is a production function whose isoquants are right angles ($\sigma = 0$), indicating that capital and labor must be used in fixed proportions if waste is to be avoided. One way of classifying production functions is according to whether σ varies or is a constant. In the Cobb-Douglas production function (see footnote 1), $\sigma = 1$ and in the CES production function, $\sigma = [1/(1 + \rho)]$. Chapter 7 contains a discussion of the relationship between σ and the elasticity of demand for labor by a competitive industry.

[17]It should be obvious that the substitution effect plays a pivotal role in the demand for labor by a regulated firm whose output is fixed by some government agency and whose input adjustments to wage changes are limited to movements along a single isoquant.

[18]Can you explain how the firm's marginal cost is related to (derived from) the expansion path?

and

$$MC = r \cdot MI_K \qquad (3\text{-}15)$$

Since we know from (3–4) that the profit-maximizing competitive firm chooses output so that marginal cost equals product price, equations (3–14) and (3–15) are equivalent to

$$P = w \cdot MI_L \qquad (3\text{-}16)$$

and

$$P = r \cdot MI_K \qquad (3\text{-}17)$$

respectively. Finally, divide both sides of (3–16) by MI_L and both sides of (3–17) by MI_K, yielding

$$w = (P/MI_L) \equiv P \cdot MPP_L \equiv VMP_L \qquad (3\text{-}18)$$

and

$$r = (P/MI_K) \equiv P \cdot MPP_K \equiv VMP_K \qquad (3\text{-}19)$$

We now have all the information necessary to diagram the competitive firm's demand for labor. As you should expect, VMP_L again plays a crucial role. As the firm now responds to a wage-rate change by adjusting K, we must discuss the interrelationship between K and $MPP_L(VMP_L)$.

In Figure 3–11 the firm, confronted with wage w_1, maximizes profit at

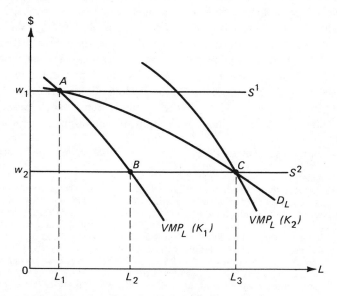

FIGURE 3–11. The Demand for Labor by a Competitive Firm When It Adjusts Capital

point A on $VMP_L(K_1)$.[19] The combination of labor and capital (L_1, K_1) satisfies equations (3–18) and (3–19).[20] What happens to L if the wage rate falls, say to w_2? The firm may initially expand output by using more labor only, moving along $VMP_L(K_1)$ to point B, but eventually it will also adjust K. Remember that $VMP_L(K_1)$ is valid *only* for K_1. When the firm alters capital, as depicted in Figure 3–10, MPP_L and VMP_L shift.

In general, the VMP_L schedule for the new level of capital $VMP_L(K_2)$ lies to the *right* of $VMP_L(K_1)$. To see this, first suppose that the firm increases K as w falls. The greater the amount of capital per worker, the greater the firm's increase in output when an additional worker is hired. In our earlier example of farming, the *increase* in production from an additional helper would be greater the more land, fertilizer, and tractors there were on the farm. However, $VMP_L(K_2)$ lies to the right of $VMP_L(K_1)$ in Figure 3–11 *regardless* of whether at the new profit-maximizing output the firm is using more or less capital. Return to Figure 3–10. Notice that the substitution and scale effects work in *opposite* directions on the utilization of capital. When w declines, less K is used to produce each unit of output, but more units of output are produced. Economic theory does not offer us a prediction as to whether the scale effect or the substitution effect will have a greater influence on K. The amount of K used will decrease if the substitution effect predominates, while it will increase if the scale effect is stronger. It can be shown mathematically that when L and K are the only factors of production, $VMP_L(K_2)$ will lie to the right of $VMP_L(K_1)$ even if $K_2 < K_1$—that is, even if the substitution effect dominates. Thus, the labor demand curve when the firm adjusts K connects points A and C; it is downward-sloping and flatter than the demand curve for labor when K is fixed at K_1 $[VMP_L(K_1)]$.[21]

One final thought is important concerning the difference between the demand for labor by the competitive firm when it adjusts K versus when K is held constant. When K is fixed, VMP_L and the labor demand schedule coincide, so the demand curve for labor is defined for a specific level of capital. When D_L (Figure 3–11) is the demand curve, each point passes through a different VMP_L schedule, though at every point on the demand

---

[19]We draw only the parts of the VMP_L's that lie below the maximum points of the associated VAP_L's.

[20]For convenience, we do not depict (3–19).

[21]Here is a "proof" that when the firm adjusts K, its quantity of labor demanded is more sensitive to wage changes than when K is fixed. In the accompanying diagram, suppose the firm's capital input is initially fixed at K_1 and that the firm is maximizing its profits at point M, using L_1 units of labor. Its cost-minimizing inputs of K and L when both are variable are shown by expansion path $\overline{OA}$. Let the wage fall from w_1 to w_2. With K held constant, the firm adjusts its input of labor by moving to the right along $\overline{K_1MN}$, increasing output to 200 and its labor input to L_2. Eventually, the firm takes advantage of the opportunity to increase profits further by substituting L for K, moving to expansion path $\overline{OB}$. Point R corresponds to a smaller input of K than K_1 and an input of L exactly equal to that at N. If point R corresponded to the firm's new profit-maximizing position we would be very much surprised, because output is smaller at R than at N, even though substitution of L for K lowered the firm's production costs! Since we expect output to increase relative

curve the wage rate is equal to the value of marginal product of labor. The capital input is different at each point along D_L. In this case, the demand curve for labor holds constant the price of capital (r) but not the level of capital used. In general, when we refer to the demand for labor we will be thinking of the latter case, the labor demand curve that is drawn with respect to a given r (and output price). Expressed algebraically, the general labor demand curve when the firm adjusts capital is

$$L = L(w, r, p) \tag{3-20}$$

which says that the number of units of labor services a competitive firm wishes to purchase at any given wage depends also upon the prices of other inputs and final output. The latter two variables provide additional avenues through which government policy can influence employment and earnings.[22] In summary, whether or not a change in w is viewed as sufficiently permanent to warrant adjusting K, or whether a great deal or only a little substitution between factors is possible, *the demand curve for labor by a competitive firm slopes downward with respect to w.*[23] This is one of the most important conclusions we draw in this book.

---

to that at N, the input of labor should also be greater. (Output at point R would equal that at N only if isoquant 200 were vertical, contrary to our basic assumption that the isoquants have a negative slope.)

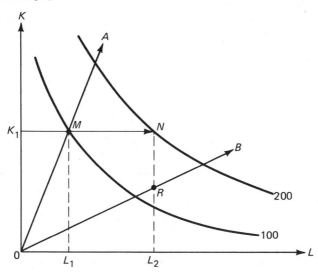

[22]Of course, the firm's demand for other inputs (capital services) also depends on the same variables on the right-hand side of (3-20). For a rigorous presentation of the general theory of factor demand, see C. E. Ferguson, *The Neoclassical Theory of Production and Distribution* (Cambridge, Eng.: Cambridge University Press, 1969), Chaps. 6 and 9.

[23]In Chapter 4 we see that the family may be thought of as a firm which purchases the nonmarket (leisure) time of its members. You should take note of the similarities between the firm and the demand for nonmarket time by a "family" firm.

Assume the competitive firm in Figure 3–12 is faced with wage w_1 and maximizes profit by hiring L_1 units of labor at point A on $VMP_L(K_1)$. Suppose a union leader visits the firm and promises workers that if they unionize, the wage rate will become w_2 (exactly *how* this may occur is examined in Chapter 7). What facts will workers consider in making their decision whether or not to unionize? Among other things, they will evaluate the *economic* benefits and costs of union membership. The most basic benefit will be the increase in the wage rate of $(w_2 - w_1)$ per worker. What is the cost of union membership? Obviously there will be union dues. In addition, since the quantity of labor demanded varies inversely with the wage, lost employment must be considered a cost of unionization. Perhaps you feel that as a serious student of labor economics you realize this, but that the average worker does not. Remember, though, that if past experience does not remind workers of the downward-sloping demand curve, management surely will. Moreover, union leaders are not unaware of the downward-sloping labor demand curve. For example, the late John L. Lewis, long-time head of the United Mine Workers, once said: "It is better to have half a million men working at good wages and high standards of living than to have a million working in poverty."[24]

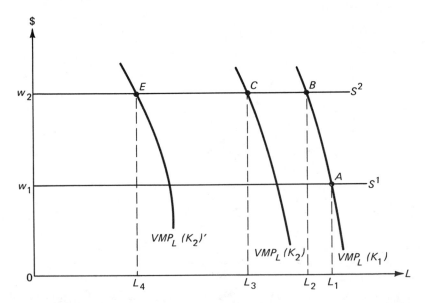

FIGURE 3–12. Possible Initial and Ultimate Responses by a Competitive Firm to a Wage Increase

[24]Roger Leroy Miller, *American Economic Life: Yesterday and Today* (San Francisco: Canfield Press, 1974), p. 186.

The severity of the employment loss due to unionization depends on a number of factors already known to us. The firm will initially respond to the increase in w by moving along $VMP_L(K_1)$ to point B, reducing employment by a relatively small amount, $(L_1 - L_2)$. This reduction in L will be more or less severe depending upon how quickly the marginal physical product of labor increases as the quantity of labor is reduced (the slope of VMP_L). In Figure 3–12, $VMP_L(K_1)$ is drawn such that a relatively small initial reduction in L is necessary to equate $VMP_L(K_1)$ to w_2. If the situation ended here, workers might consider the employment loss, $(L_1 - L_2)$, to be a reasonable price to pay for unionization, since the number of workers dismissed will be small compared to the number of workers who will still be employed at the higher union wage. We know, however, that the story is not over, since once the firm is convinced of the viability of the union, it will adjust K. Suppose that after the wage rate rises to w_2, the firm adjusts its capital to K_2, and that its value of marginal product of labor becomes $VMP_L(K_2)$. (Remember that the conclusion in footnote 21 "works both ways." If the wage *rises*, the value of marginal product of labor shifts to the *left* as the firm adjusts its capital input.) If $VMP_L(K_2)$ lies close to $VMP_L(K_1)$, workers may still view the employment loss $(L_1 - L_3)$ as "worth" the increase in w. If, however, the value of the marginal product of labor schedule shifts rather substantially to the left (to something like $VMP_L(K_2)'$), the employment loss may represent a cost of unionization greater than workers would be willing to pay.

The purpose of this example is twofold. First, it points out the fact that a key aspect of the initial cost (employment loss) of a union may be quite small relative to the ultimate cost. Although a union may at first be able to increase wages quite substantially with little loss of employment, the eventual decline in L may be very large. There are numerous examples of industries (bituminous coal, cotton textiles in the Northeast, agricultural workers in California) or occupations (elevator operator) where this has been the case. Second, the example underscores the importance of the demand for labor in a real situation. Specifically, unions have been relatively quick to form and remain viable in firms where the quantity of labor demanded is relatively insensitive to wage increases.

The Demand for Labor
by a Competitive Industry

A **competitive industry** is a collection of firms, each of which is too small to have any noticeable effect on the prices of output and factors of production. In deriving an industry's demand for labor schedule, we are tempted simply to "add up" the firms' demand curves. In order to examine the issue of what happens to the desired amount of labor services by an industry as the wage changes, first think of what would happen if labor supply conditions changed for an entire industry. If, for example, there were a decline in the wage rate, we know that each firm will use more labor per unit of machinery (substitution effect), and expand production (scale effect) because it will pay to produce more at the going price of output. But will the selling price of output remain unchanged? NO! Although each competitive firm faces a fixed price for its output, an industry does not. As all firms simultaneously attempt to sell more output due to the decline in the price of labor, they (as a group) will be able to do so only if the price of output falls, inducing consumers to purchase greater quantities. The decline in product price will disturb the individual firms' demand curves for labor because their value of marginal product of labor schedules will shift downward. (Why?) As a result, the labor demand schedule of a competitive industry will generally be steeper than the sum of the demand curves of the individual firms. The truth and importance of this fact will become clearer as we develop a numerical example in Figure 3–13.

Assume that we have a competitive industry composed of five identical firms. Figure 3–13a depicts one of the firms. At output price p_1, each will hire the amount of labor that equates the value of marginal product of labor $VMP_L(p_1)$ with w.[25] If, for example, the wage rate were \$5, each firm would hire 10 workers. Industry demand is point B in panel Figure 3–13b, 50 workers. What would happen if the wage falls to \$2.50? If product price

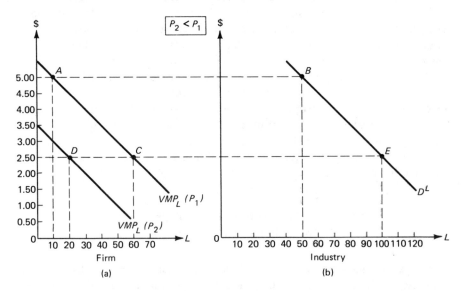

FIGURE 3–13. Derivation of the Demand for Labor by a Competitive Industry with Five Firms

---

[25]For simplicity, the schedules in Figure 3–13 are linear. Remember that VMP_L depends upon p, since $VMP_L \equiv (MPP_L \cdot p)$.

remained unchanged at p_1 when all firms simultaneously expand output, industry demand for labor would be 300 workers, or five times the number of workers demanded by each firm at point C on $VMP_L(p_1)$. Instead, product price falls to p_2 as the industry increases production, and each firm's value of marginal product of labor schedule shifts downward to $VMP_L(p_2)$. At a wage of \$2.50, each firm ultimately purchases 20 units of L and the industry 100 units (point E in Figure 3–13b). Instead of an increase in labor demanded from 50 to 300 workers as the wage rate falls from \$5 to \$2.50 (which would be the case if industry demand were simply the sum of firms' demands), industry demand increases to only 100 workers. Due to the feedback effect of a decline in product price, the quantity of labor demanded by the *industry* doubles rather than increases by a factor of 6. Thus, when the number of firms is fixed, the industry labor demand schedule is made up of points like B and E and the quantity of labor demanded is less responsive to wage changes than the sum of labor demanded by each competitive firm, all other things being equal.

THE ROLE OF INDUSTRY COMPOSITION

The circumstances surrounding production by an industry may be quite different from those for a firm. Essentially, the firm's demand curve for a productive factor must slope downward for the same reason that competitive firms must remain small relative to the size of the industry—diseconomies of scale. Once the firm moves to a new expansion path, the value of marginal product is eventually made equal to marginal factor cost for each input (marginal cost is brought to equality with marginal revenue) as the firm moves northeastward along the path, because we assume that some factor (entrepreneurship?) is fixed in amount for each firm and ultimately limits size. As a result, if there were a change in the labor supply curve to a particular firm, it would be prevented from expanding to take over the entire industry by inherent limits to its size, limits that act primarily to lower the marginal productivities of all variable factors as the firm expands. An industry, however, may expand output in two ways: (1) Initially, each firm may expand its output. (2) Eventually, new firms may enter the industry if existing firms earn positive economic profits. If the new firms that enter as demand grows are as efficient as the old firms, the only factors limiting industry growth are demand for output and supplies of variable inputs. If the industry is small, or does not use highly specialized inputs, demand is the only limiting factor.

Thus, the demand for final output limits the size of a competitive industry and its demand for inputs, while diseconomies of scale limit size and input demand of firms making up the industry. In contrast to the situation where the number of firms in the industry is fixed, when the number of firms in the industry is variable, it is ambiguous, *a priori*, whether the industry's demand for labor is more or less sensitive to wage changes than each of its component firms. The most important aspect of our analysis of the competitive industry's demand for labor, however, is that in general it is negatively sloped. In Chapter 7 we examine in detail the importance of this for trade unions. Now we can see that the inverse relationship between wages and employment also has important implications for economic policy.

THE DEMAND FOR LABOR BY A COMPETITIVE INDUSTRY: APPLICATION

Consider Figure 3–14, which represents a recessionary period in which the wage is $\bar{w}$ and employment (L_1) is below "full" employment. What is the expected effect on employment of a government antirecessionary program that takes the form of a wage subsidy? Since we are interested in the immediate impact of such a public policy, we will confine our analysis to movements *along* the industry labor demand curve, D^L. In particular, we will ignore feedback effects from industries not directly affected by the wage subsidy program as well as any eventual change in the market wage rate due to the imposition of the subsidy.

Let the wage subsidy paid by the government to employers be equal to S dollars.[26] This means that while workers still receive a payment of $\bar{w}$,

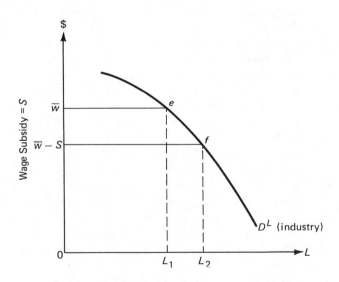

FIGURE 3–14. The Effect of a Wage Subsidy on Employment

---

[26]In an interesting article, Daniel S. Hamermesh, "Econometric Studies of Labor Demand and Their Application to Policy Analysis," *Journal of Human Resources*, 11, 4

employers in reality pay out only $\bar{w} - S$. This decline in the *effective* wage paid by employers leads to an increase in the quantity of labor demanded of $(L_2 - L_1)$. The size of the increase in employment due to the wage subsidy depends upon the elasticity of demand for labor (ϵ), which is a standardized numerical measure of the sensitivity of the quantity of labor demanded to wage rate changes.[27] We can formalize this by first noting that

$$\epsilon \equiv \frac{\Delta L}{L} \bigg/ \frac{\Delta w}{w} \tag{3-21}$$

Multiplying both sides of (3–19) by $\Delta w/w$, the percentage change in the wage, yields

$$\Delta L/L = \epsilon \cdot \frac{\Delta w}{w} \tag{3-22}$$

Thus, the percentage increase (decrease) in employment induced by a v percent decrease (increase) in the wage is equal to the elasticity of demand for labor times v. In the case of the subsidy considered above

$$v \equiv \frac{\Delta w}{w} = \frac{(\bar{w} - S) - \bar{w}}{\bar{w}} = \frac{-S}{\bar{w}} \tag{3-23}$$

Equations (3–22) and (3–23) tell us that, given knowledge of the magnitude of the elasticity of demand for labor (ϵ), the expected increase in employment due to the wage subsidy is $[\epsilon \cdot (-S/\bar{w})]$.[28] (Remember that ϵ is a negative number, since the demand curve for labor is downward-sloping.) Alternatively, we may derive the wage subsidy required to increase employment by a certain percentage(S^*). If the policy-maker's goal is an increase in industry employment of k percent, you should be able to show that the required wage subsidy is[29]

$$S^* = -\bar{w}\left(\frac{k}{\epsilon}\right) \tag{3-24}$$

Having seen the importance of the properties of the labor demand curve for economic policy and other purposes, we now turn our attention to an

---

(fall 1976), 507–25, examines the expected economywide employment impacts of two government wage subsidy programs discussed during the early 1970s: a one percentage point cut in the employer's share of social security taxes and an employment tax credit of $4 per employee-day on each employee-day worked in excess of the previous year's employment.

[27] See Chapter 7 for a discussion of some reasons as to why ϵ may differ across industries.

[28] As an exercise, pretend that the president has asked for your advice in choosing those industries in which wages will be subsidized. He wants to obtain the largest employment increase from a *fixed* amount of government expenditures. What information do you require to fulfill the president's request?

[29] Try working through the general equations in this section with some specific numerical values for ϵ, k, s, w, and L.

empirical analysis of those properties. In particular, we discuss the estimation of the sign and magnitude of the slope of the demand curve for labor.

omit pp 76-83

Evidence on the Demand for Labor

The demand curve for labor can be examined empirically in a variety of ways. One of the best is to estimate simultaneously demand functions for labor and other inputs along with the production functions of the relevant economic units (firms, industries, and so on).[30] This is a good method because one may explicitly inquire the extent to which firms or industries hire that level of labor which equates the value of marginal product of labor to the wage rate. It is also a difficult method, since the quality of nonlabor inputs in the production process must be specified. It would be inconsistent with the technical level of our analysis to examine evidence on the demand for labor from such procedures, however.[31]

Fortunately, we are not completely at a loss. We shall fall back on the less precise procedure of testing the hypothesis that the demand curve for labor by a competitive industry is downward-sloping. We must be aware, though, that should we observe a downward-sloping labor demand schedule, this does not shed much light on whether that demand curve stems from competitive or noncompetitive firms or industries. Even though we may feel the firms or industries that empirically generate a negatively inclined labor demand curve are competitive, we cannot *infer* competition from the sign of the slope, since (as we will see in Chapter 6) noncompetitive market structures also have negatively sloped labor demand schedules. In order to distinguish between competitive and noncompetitive firms or industries, we would have to decide just how steep a labor demand curve would be if it were generated by a firm with monopoly power in the sale of its output, compared to the demand curve for a firm or group of firms without such power. The information we obtain by testing any hypothesis is limited by the reasoning we put into relating the hypothesis to the underlying theory and to the data bearing on it. For the remainder of this chapter, we deal with the very simple hypothesis, derivable from competitive and some noncompetitive theories, that the amount of labor demanded is a negative function of the wage rate. Our purpose is to demonstrate how this hypothesis can be tested, and to discuss in detail the results of one specific test.

---

[30]A basic description of estimating the demand for labor in this way is found in George H. Hilderbrand and Ta-chung Liu, *Manufacturing Production Functions in the United States, 1957* (Ithaca, N.Y.: The New York State School of Industrial and Labor Relations, 1965), especially pp. 53–57.

[31]Hamermesh, "Econometric Studies of Labor Demand," is an excellent survey of this material.

A TEST OF THE THEORY OF LABOR DEMAND:
THE EMPLOYMENT EFFECTS OF MINIMUM WAGE
LEGISLATION IN PUERTO RICO

In order to examine the slope of the labor demand curve, we will look at a study of the response of employment to minimum wage legislation. This has the advantage of enabling us to observe the response of the quantity of labor demanded to an exogenous change in the wage rate (caused by the legislation). Figure 3–15 depicts a competitive labor market before and after the imposition of an effective minimum wage statute. Before the legislation, the industry's equilibrium wage is $\bar{w}$ and its equilibrium level of employment is $\bar{L}$. When legislation establishes a wage floor w_{min} which is higher than the wage that would have prevailed in its absence ($\bar{w}$), the theory of the demand for labor in competition implies that firms respond by reducing employment to $\tilde{L}$. Effective minimum wage legislation means that the wage floor exceeds the competitive equilibrium wage so that industry employment depends on the position and elasticity of the labor demand curve.

In one test, Reynolds and Gregory examined the employment effects of minimum wage legislation in Puerto Rico.[32] The Puerto Rican case has certain advantages from the point of view of testing the hypothesis that the labor demand curve is negatively sloped: (1) Unlike mainland United States,

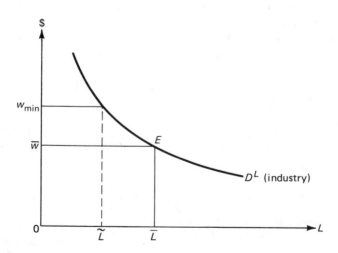

FIGURE 3–15. A Competitive Labor Market before and after the Imposition of an Effective Minimum Wage Law

[32]Lloyd G. Reynolds and Peter Gregory, *Wages, Productivity, and Industrialization in Puerto Rico* (Homewood, Ill.: Irwin, 1965), pp. 41–103. The labor market effects of minimum wage legislation in the U.S. are discussed in Chapter 5.

different minimum wage rates for each industry are adjusted frequently, thus providing a relatively substantial amount of data. (2) Unlike the mainland, wage minimums are quite high relative to average wage rates in covered industries, such that minimum wage rates are the principal factors behind the wage rate increases during the period examined.[33]

Figure 3–16a characterizes the relationship between wage rates and employment in Puerto Rico. w_A, w_B, and w_C are the minimum wage rates in representative industries A, B, and C, respectively. L_A, L_B, and L_C are the respective quantities of labor employed in the three industries at these wage rates. After a period of time, perhaps four years, the minimums are raised, and we observe data such as those depicted in Figure 3–16b, where the dark lines correspond to the demand curves in (a) (the first year) and the dashed lines are for the terminal year of the time period.[34] The subscripts 1 and 2 associated with the wage rates and quantities demanded correspond to magnitudes in the first and last years of the period, respectively. Because the minimum wage rates are raised by different amounts in different industries, and because there is no reason to believe that these wage rate increases are related in any way to interindustry differences in changes in the prices of nonhuman inputs, we are in a position to estimate the average net effects on the amounts of labor demanded. Specifically, we can make use of our knowledge of the frequency with which minimum wage rates are changed in Puerto Rico, the different amounts by which they are changed, and the fact that the minimums are quite high relative to the competitive wage rates to conduct a simple test of the hypothesis that labor demand curves slope downward. Figure 3–16 shows a method of estimating, on the average, the effect of wage increases on the quantities of labor demanded in a large group of industries.

Reynolds and Gregory studied the relationship between wage rates and employment in narrowly defined (3- or 4-digit) manufacturing industries.[35] Data were available for a group of between 37 and 50 such industries. A very important (and probably not unrealistic) assumption underlying their empirical analysis is that the production functions for the industries studied are **homogeneous of degree 1**. This means that for a given set of input prices, an

---

[33]A third, more subtle, advantage of these data is that the unemployment rate in Puerto Rico exceeded 10 percent for the years studied. For many, and perhaps most of the firms, then, it is not unreasonable to think of a horizontal labor supply curve at the "going" wage rate. Moreover, since the individual manufacturing industries were relatively small, the "plentiful" supply of labor at the going wage also implies that single-equation regressions employed by Reynolds and Gregory identify industry elasticities of demand for labor. For elaboration on this latter point, refer back to the discussion of the "identification problem" in Chapter 2.

[34]We assume that over time the demand for output has increased due to reasons unrelated to the minimum wage legislation itself.

[35]For an explanation of 3- or 4-digit Standard Industrial Classification (SIC) codes, see U.S. Office of Management and Budget, *Standard Industrial Classification Manual*.

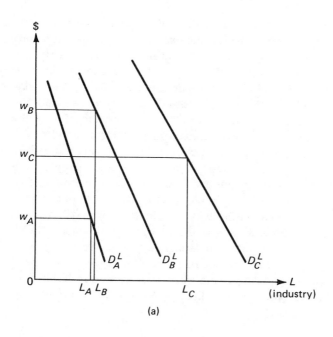

(a)

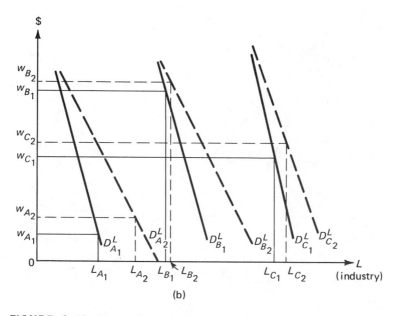

(b)

FIGURE 3–16. Reynolds and Gregory's Method of Estimating the Employment Effect of Minimum Wage Rates Using the Linear Homogeneity Assumption

79

industry's (L/K) is the same at all levels of output, and that a given percentage change in output generates equivalent percentage changes in L and K. For the kinds of manufacturing industries found in Puerto Rico at the time the data were collected (footwear, clothing, light durable goods), the assumption of homogeneity of degree 1 is not unreasonable and, as we will soon see, extremely useful. Examine Figure 3–16b, where we see that for the three representative industries (A, B, and C), employment is influenced by changes over time in market wage rates and shifts in labor demand schedules. Since we are interested in the average net effect of wage rate increases in different industries over time, we require a method of controlling for the effect of output growth on the amounts of labor demanded in each industry. Stated differently, we wish to ignore the impact of the minimum wage on industry output, and to estimate either what employment would have been in year 2 at the wage rates prevailing in year 1 or what employment would have been in year 1 at the wage rates prevailing in year 2. So, we will examine the effect on the amount of labor demanded that comes from changing factor proportions in response to rising wage rates at a given level of output.

The estimation procedure utilized by Reynolds and Gregory is illustrated

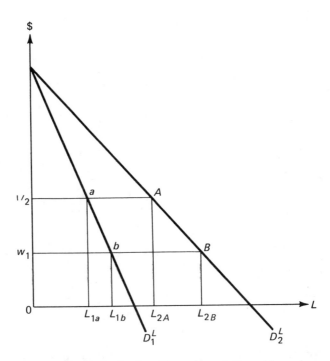

FIGURE 3–17. Further Illustration of Reynolds and Gregory's Method

in Figure 3–17, which represents the demand curves for labor in years 1 and 2 for one of the industries depicted in Figure 3–16b. In year 1 we observe wage rate w_1 and employment L_{1b}. In year 2, we observe wage rate w_2 and employment L_{2A}. In order to estimate the employment effect of the wage increase from w_1 to w_2, we must estimate either L_{1a} (the employment that would have occurred in year 1 at w_2) or L_{2B} (the employment that would have occurred in year 2 at w_1). Given the assumption of homogeneous of degree 1 industry production functions, which implies [output (year 2)/output (year 1)] $= (L_{2B}/L_{1b})$, both of these are easily estimated. The product of L_{1b} and the ratio of output in year 2 to output in year 1 provides an estimate of L_{2B}. By similar reasoning, the product of L_{2A} and the ratio of output in year 1 to output in year 2 provides an estimate of L_{1a}. This is done for every industry in the sample studied; the change in the quantity of labor demanded can then be measured along either demand curve 1 or demand curve 2.

This procedure does not provide a measure of the impact of wage rate changes on the amount of labor demanded via the effect on industry output. It is probably true that some firms did not open plants in Puerto Rico and that others closed down or failed to expand operations because of rising labor costs. To some extent, then, Reynolds's and Gregory's analysis understates the total response of the amount of labor demanded to wage rate changes. Alternatively, there may be an element of overestimation if neglected economies of scale or exogenous increases in efficiency (perhaps due to "learning by doing") would in any event have caused labor inputs to rise less than in equal proportion to output. Two samples of industries were examined to estimate the average effect of wage increases. One includes 37 industries for the period 1949–54 and the other, 50 industries for the period 1954–58. For each of the samples, output is measured by **value added**,[36] and the amount of labor demanded by the employment of production workers in each industry. (Hours of work vary only slightly during the periods studied.) Employment in the first year of each period is "inflated" by the proportionate change in value added for each industry, so the labor demand elasticity estimated is the average response along curves like D_2 in Figure 3–17.

To summarize, L_{1b} (Figure 3–17) for each industry is multiplied by the ratio of value added during the second year of observation to that during the first year, in order to estimate L_{2B}; that is, $L_{2B} = L_{1b}(X_2/X_1)$, where X_1 is value added in either 1949 or 1954, and X_2 is value added in either 1954 or 1958, depending upon the data set under consideration. This estimate of L_{2B} is used with observed values of employment in the second year (L_{2A}) to calculate the average response of the quantity of labor demanded to wage

---

[36]Value added is the total sales of an industry less purchases of partially processed goods and depreciation allowances. It essentially measures the input of all productive factors plus profit. For the period 1949–54, value added in each industry is deflated by the appropriate price indexes; for 1954–58, output prices change little, and no deflation is performed.

rate changes. This is done with separate regression equations for the periods
1949–54 and 1954–58 of the form

$$\left[\frac{(L_{2B} - L_{2A})}{\frac{1}{2}(L_B + L_A)}\right] = a + b\left[\frac{(w_2 - w_1)}{\frac{1}{2}(w_2 + w_1)}\right] \tag{3-25}$$

Notice that the left-hand term of (3–25) is a measure of the proportionate
change in the quantity of labor demanded between points A and B along
demand curve D_2 for each industry, and that the right-hand term is a measure
of the proportionate change in the wage rate for each industry either between
1949 and 1954 or between 1954 and 1958 according to the sample utilized.
Dividing both sides of (3–25) by $\frac{(w_2 - w_1)}{\frac{1}{2}(w_1 + w_2)}$ yields

$$\left[\frac{(L_{2B} - L_{2A})}{\frac{1}{2}(L_{2B} + L_{2A})}\right] \middle/ \left[\frac{(w_2 - w_1)}{\frac{1}{2}(w_2 + w_1)}\right] = \frac{a}{\left[\frac{(w_2 - w_1)}{\frac{1}{2}(w_1 + w_2)}\right]} + b \tag{3-26}$$

which is the elasticity of demand for labor.[37] This may be seen more clearly
if we rewrite (3–26) as

$$\left(\frac{\Delta L}{L^*}\middle/\frac{\Delta w}{w^*}\right)_{a=0} = b \tag{3-27}$$

where* denotes average value and a is temporarily set equal to zero. Thus,
when the estimated value of a is statistically indistinguishable from zero, the
slope coefficient (b) in a regression of the form (3–25) is an estimate of the
so-called arc elasticity of labor demand. If, however, a is significantly different
from zero, the elasticity must be evaluated at particular values of w_1 and w_2,
according to (3–26).

Regression estimates of (3–25) indicate that in both 1949–54 and 1954–58
the constant terms (the as) are not significantly different from zero. Moreover,
the estimated labor demand elasticities are -1.1 (with a standard error of
.2) and $-.92$ (with a standard error of .2), respectively, which suggests that
the estimates of the bs are reliable.[38,39] To obtain some idea of the possible
magnitude of the effect of wage increases on employment in Puerto Rico,
Reynolds and Gregory calculate that had wage rates not risen from 1954 to

---

[37]Notice the difference between how percentage changes are calculated in equation
(3–26) versus equation (3–23). In equation (3–23) they are calculated with respect to the
initial point on the demand curve (point e in Figure 3–14). In (3–26), percentage changes
are calculated with respect to a point which is the average of (midway between) two points
on the demand curve (A and B on D_2 in Figure 3–17). When the points on the demand
curve being compared are close together, the two calculations will produce approximately
the same value for the elasticity.

[38]These elasticity estimates were supplied by Professor Gregory and represent a corrected
version of the results originally reported in the work cited in note 32 (p. 145).

[39]As a point of reference, Hamermesh, "Econometric Studies," reports a range of (output constant) labor demand elasticities for the U.S. of -0.05 to -0.35.

1958, actual employment of production workers in manufacturing would have been greater by 29,000 workers, which is about one-half the actual employment of production workers in manufacturing in 1958.[40] The Reynolds and Gregory study provides evidence consistent with the hypothesis that the amount of labor demanded is a negative function of the wage rate. Moreover, their analysis yields an estimate of the value of the elasticity of demand for labor in Puerto Rican manufacturing from 1949 to 1958. In discussing this study, we have demonstrated a simple method of testing economic theory's most important hypothesis concerning labor demand curves.

Frontiers of Labor Demand Analysis

Although the basic analytical framework of the demand for labor in competition is an extremely flexible tool that is useful in the study of a wide variety of problems, it can be enriched through a more complete representation of the labor input (L). Until now, we have been deliberately vague concerning the mix of employees and hours of work per employee when discussing the quantity of labor demanded. By expanding the basic framework to incorporate these aspects of the labor input, economists have recently been able to examine a number of interesting and important new issues. Of course, this additional knowledge is not free. Even though we will simplify whenever possible, the expanded theoretical analysis is more complicated and difficult to work with.

FIXED LABOR COSTS AND THE EMPLOYMENT-HOURS MIX

In the basic model of the demand for labor, the fact that we do not distinguish between hours of work per worker (H) and the number of workers (N) amounts to an implicit assumption that firms are indifferent between changing H and changing N when more or less labor is desired. We now wish to explore the desirability of this assumption and the implications of relaxing it. Passed in 1938 and amended numerous times, the federal Fair Labor Standards Act (FLSA) establishes a legal minimum wage rate for covered workers, and regulates their hours of work by requiring a wage premium (1.5 times the regular wage) for all hours of work in excess of a standard work week. Since 1940, the standard work week has been 40 hours. Moreover, as of January 1, 1977, twenty-seven states had laws requiring premium wages for hours in excess of a certain number per day or per week, and most union

---

[40]Reynolds and Gregory, *Wages*, p. 101. Care should be taken in interpreting these results. For instance, to the extent that the characteristics of the unemployed, such as education, age, health, reliability, are less desirable to employers than those of the employed, a given reduction in wage rate would have a smaller impact on employment.

contracts also contained such provisions.[41] In light of the "penalty" the vast majority of employers must pay, why do we ever observe employees working overtime? The answer lies in the realization that employers are not always indifferent between more H and more N when more labor services are desired.

In the first part of this chapter we noted that employers will be hesitant to alter the capital input in response to changes in the environment that may be short-lived. Similarly, the various fixed costs of employing new workers make it cheaper to pay premium wages to existing workers than to expand N when temporary increases in production are expected. What are some examples of fixed costs of employment? Whenever a worker is hired, there are costs of recruitment, screening, and initial training. Time spent "learning the ropes" has an opportunity cost. In addition to these one-time expenses, which are incurred whenever a worker is hired, there are costs that, although spread over the employee's length of service, are not fully related to his or her hours of work. Included in this latter category are fringe benefits or taxes paid on a per-employee basis. Payroll taxes that have an earnings level after which employers' contributions cease (social security) have an element of fixed costs involved (why?).[42] Data concerning firms' costs of adding an employee are extremely scarce; however, calculations by the R. G. Barry Corporation for 1969 presented in Table 3–1 indicate that additional workers can be extremely expensive.[43] Given these considerations, we now proceed

TABLE 3–1

Amount of Money Invested per Employee,
R. G. Barry Corporation, 1969

Skill Level	Investment by Firm
Least skilled (i.e., materials handler)	$ 273
Semi-skilled (i.e., maintenance mechanic)	1,712
First-line supervisor	4,000
Middle manager	16,000
Top-level manager	34,500

Sources: "The Roving Kind, Penchant of Americans for Job Hopping Vexes Companies Increasingly," *The Wall Street Journal*, March 25, 1970, p. 1; and "R. G. Barry Includes Its Employees' Value on Its Balance Sheet," *The Wall Street Journal*, April 3, 1970, p. 14.

---

[41]Gordon T. Bloom and Herbert R. Northrup, *Economics of Labor Relations* (Homewood, Ill.: Irwin, 1977), pp. 497–502, report that of the approximately 64.3 million nonsupervisory employees in the civilian labor force in July 1976, about 49.8 million were covered by FLSA and 5 million more by similar state legislation.

[42]Are fringe benefits paid on the basis of a constant amount per hour of work a fixed cost?

[43]For older (1951), but more disaggregated, data concerning the cost of a new employee, see Walter W. Oi, "Labor as a Quasi-Fixed Factor," *Journal of Political Economy*, 70, 6 (December 1962), 546.

to a formal analysis of a competitive firm's optimal mix of employees and hours of work per employee. To simplify the problem at hand, we will examine how a competitive firm minimizes the cost of a given level of output when its capital input is fixed and one skill class of labor is used in production. If output is predetermined, cost minimization is also profit maximization. In any event, remember that cost minimization is necessary for profit maximization.

The existence of a premium rate for overtime means that if a competitive firm purchases an hour of work in excess of the standard work week ($\bar{H}$), it must pay a wage which is αw, where w is the constant straight-time hourly wage rate and α is a number greater than 1 (typically 1.5).[44] Finally, let the firm's given capital input be denoted by $\bar{K}$, and its fixed cost of hiring an additional employee be denoted by f. Expressed algebraically, the firm's expenditures on inputs are

$$wHN + fN + r\bar{K}, \text{ if } H \leq \bar{H} \tag{3-28}$$

and

$$w\bar{H}N + \alpha wN(H - \bar{H}) + fN + r\bar{K}, \text{ if } H > \bar{H} \tag{3-29}$$

With a little manipulation, we can create an isoexpenditure curve from equations (3–28) and (3–29). This will permit a graphical analysis of the firm's optimal (cost-minimizing) (H, N) combination. Consider a particular amount of spending on resources, $\bar{C}$. An isoexpenditure curve indicates combinations of H and N that can be purchased for $\bar{C}$ dollars (given w, α, r, $\bar{K}$, $\bar{H}$, and f). To obtain the expression for an isoexpenditure curve when the work week is at or below the standard work week, we set equation (3–28) equal to $\bar{C}$ and solve it for N, yielding

$$\text{(isoexpenditure curve when } H \leq \bar{H}) \quad N = \frac{\bar{C} - r\bar{K}}{(f + wH)} \tag{3-30}$$

Since all variables but N and H are given to the firm, equation (3–30) indicates how many employees it can hire working H hours per week when it spends $\bar{C}$. Analogously, combinations of N and H that the firm may purchase for $\bar{C}$ when hours of work per employee exceed the standard work week are given by the expression

$$\text{(isoexpenditure curve when } H > \bar{H}) \ N = \frac{\bar{C} - r\bar{K}}{(f + wH + \alpha w(H - \bar{H}))} \tag{3-31}$$

Unlike Figure 3–7, neither segment of the firm's isoexpenditure curve is

---

[44]The fact that workers are assumed to be homogeneous means that they will each work the same number of hours per period. For convenience, we assume that the period under consideration is a week.

linear.[45] The isoexpenditure curve expressed in equations (3–30) and (3–31) is illustrated in Figure 3–18. Notice that there is a kink at $\bar{H}$.[46] The steeper slope immediately to the right of $\bar{H}$ is due to the overtime wage premium. Specifically, the premium wage rate that must be paid when the work week is increased from $\bar{H}$ to $(\bar{H} + 1)$ means that if expenditures are to be held constant at $\bar{C}$, the firm must "give up" more employees than when it increases the workweek from $(\bar{H} - 1)$ to $\bar{H}$.

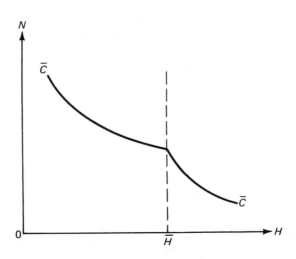

FIGURE 3–18. An Isoexpenditure Curve for Combinations of Employees and Hours of Work Per Employee

Before we can examine the cost-minimizing hours-employment mix, however, we must mention the firm's production possibilities, with special reference to L, the total labor input. Since output depends on the utilization of labor and capital, and K is fixed at $\bar{K}$ in the problem at hand, the firm's level of L is dictated by its production function (technology) and the predetermined level of output, which we will denote by $\bar{Q}$. To see this, we write the firm's production function in its general form

$$Q = F(K, L) \tag{3–32}$$

Since Q and K are fixed at $\bar{Q}$ and $\bar{K}$ respectively, the production function

---

[45]The general equation for the isoexpenditure curves in Figure 3–7 is $K = (\bar{C}/r) - (w/r)L$, which is a straight line since $\bar{C}$, r, and w are constants. Can you explain the economics of the nonlinearity of equations (3–30) and (3–31)?

[46]As an exercise, select values for α, w, r, $\bar{K}$, $\bar{C}$, f, and $\bar{H}$, and plot the associated isoexpenditure curve. It should have the same basic shape as the one in Figure 3–18.

tells the firm what particular level of L it must choose.[47] What is L, though?

Our first inclination might be to say that the answer is obvious: the labor input is simply the product of number of employees and hours of work per employee $(N \cdot H)$. Consider the figures in Table 3–2, where the number of

TABLE 3–2

Employees, Hours of Work per Employee,
and Total Employee Hours

N	H	$(N \cdot H)$	$\Delta(N \cdot H)$
100	0	0	
100	1	100	100
100	31	3,100	
100	32	3,200	100
100	167	16,700	
100	168	16,800	100

employees is held at 100. Compare what happens to total employee hours as the average work week is increased from 0 to 1 hours, from 30 to 31 hours, and from 167 to 168 hours. In each of the three cases, total employee hours increases by 100. If we measure the labor input in the production function by $(H \cdot N)$, then we are implicitly saying that the firm will obtain the *same* increment in L when the average work week is increased by 1 hour *no matter what the average work week is to begin with*! There are various reasons why this is probably not reasonable. Suppose it takes a worker one hour each day to set up. This includes time necessary to reach the work station, prepare tools and equipment, and receive supervision. Were the firm to have a work week of 1 hour, its effective labor input would be zero! Moreover, it is unreasonable to expect that workers never become fatigued. To take an extreme example, if the work week really were 167 hours, the marginal effect on L of an increase in the work week to 168 hours would probably be zero or even negative. Workers may become so fatigued that an increase in the work week would cause them to make so many mistakes, for example, that output would decrease.[48] What we are saying is that the firm's labor input, L, may be

---

[47]Consider the case where the firm has a Cobb-Douglas type production function, $Q = \alpha K^{\beta} L^{\gamma}$. If Q is fixed at $\bar{Q}$, and K is fixed at $\bar{K}$, then Q and K are treated as parameters (constants) and the production function solved for the level of L that satisfies the firm's technology, given preselected values of output and capital. In this case, $L = \left[\dfrac{\bar{Q}}{\alpha} \dfrac{1}{\bar{K}^{\beta}} \right]^{1/\gamma}$.

[48]See Ronald G. Ehrenberg, *Fringe Benefits and Overtime Behavior* (Lexington, Mass.: Heath, 1971), p. 9; Martin Feldstein, "Specification of the Labor Input in the Aggregate Production Function," *Review of Economic Studies*, 34, 4 (October 1968), 337; and Sherwin Rosen, "Short-Run Employment Variation on Class-I Railroads in the U.S., 1947–1963," *Econometrica*, 36, 3–4 (July–August 1968), 515.

thought of as a function of hours of work per employee and number of employees

$$L = G(H, N) \qquad (3\text{--}33)$$

and that this transformation of H and N into L *does not* have the specific form, $L = N \cdot H$.[49] In what follows we shall assume that the labor services function (3–33) has the properties that the marginal contributions of H and N to the firm's labor input are usually positive, but that after a certain level of H, an additional hour of work per worker decreases L.

Since the properties of the labor services function are similar to those of the production function (Figure 3–1), we can easily express equation (3–31) geometrically. Figure 3–19 illustrates an iso-L curve, labeled $\bar{L}\bar{L}$. It is a locus of combinations of H and N that are associated with the level of labor services ($\bar{L}$) necessary to produce the firm's given amount of output ($\bar{Q}$).[50] It is convex and downward-sloping (over most of its range), indicating that the firm is able to trade off N for H (at a decreasing rate) while maintaining a fixed labor input. Notice that the iso-L curve begins to turn upward at H_0. At this point enough fatigue has set in that an additional hour of work per employee lowers the firm's labor input, so that more employees are necessary to hold L constant.

Also included in Figure 3–19 are two isoexpenditure curves. Each repre-

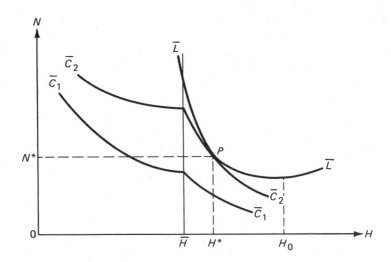

FIGURE 3–19. The Firm's Cost-Minimizing H-N Mix

---

[49]For a technical discussion of the specific mathematical forms the labor services function can take, see Ehrenberg, *Fringe Benefits*, pp. 9, 16, and 114–15.

[50]Remember that the production function (3–32) tells us $\bar{L}$, and that the labor services function (3–33) tells us possible N-H combinations associated with any L.

sents a given amount of total spending on inputs, and $\bar{C}_2\bar{C}_2$ depicts more total spending than $\bar{C}_1\bar{C}_1$. The firm's optimal (cost-minimizing) combination of employees and hours of work per employee occurs at point P, where $\bar{L}\bar{L}$ is tangent to $\bar{C}_2\bar{C}_2$. Combinations of H and N along $\bar{C}_1\bar{C}_1$ are cheaper than (H^*, N^*), but do not yield the necessary labor input. Other combinations of H and N along $\bar{L}\bar{L}$ also provide the required labor input, but are more expensive (lie on a higher isoexpenditure curve) than the combination of employees and hours of work per employee at point P. Notice that the firm in Figure 3–19 has a cost-minimizing work week which exceeds the standard work week. The economic interpretation of the tangency point in Figure 3–19 is analogous to the cost-minimizing combination of capital and labor discussed earlier and illustrated in Figure 3–9. When the firm has found the mix of N and H that is the cheapest way to achieve its required labor input, the last dollar spent on N must increase labor services by the same amount as the last dollar spent on H. Were this not true, the firm could spend one less dollar on $N(H)$, and have to spend less than an additional dollar on $H(N)$, to obtain the required labor input, $\bar{L}$. It would continue to reallocate its spending until it found the H-N combination at point P.

Although we have attempted to simplify whenever possible, it is obvious that the theory of the demand for labor by a competitive firm becomes complex when the labor input is specified more completely, and fixed costs of employment and a premium wage rate for hours in excess of a standard work week are introduced. What are the benefits that made this greater complexity worth it? In general, the answer is that we can examine important new issues.

THE EFFECTS OF AN INCREASE
IN THE PENALTY RATE: APPLICATION[51]

The competitive firm in Figure 3–20 is initially in equilibrium at point R where iso-L curve $\bar{L}\bar{L}$ is tangent to isoexpenditure curve $\bar{C}_2\bar{C}_2$. If federal or state laws were amended to increase the premium rate (α) for hours of work in excess of $\bar{H}$, what would happen to the number of employees and the average work week? An increase in α means that for any work week in excess of the standard, the firm can purchase less N for a given amount of total spending on factors of production. This can be seen from equation (3–31), where the denominator of the expression for the isoexpenditure curve is made larger with an increase in α. Expressed graphically, the increase in α generates a downward rotation in the portion of the isoexpenditure curves to the right of $\bar{H}$. Combinations of H and N that the firm can purchase for $\bar{C}_2$ dollars are

---

[51]In the interest of space, we discuss only one possible application of the model outlined in this section. Others include the effects of changes in $\bar{H}$ or the various components of f on firms' employment-hours mix. (Can you cite an example, of a public policy that would increase f?) See Ehrenberg, *Fringe Benefits*, and Rosen, "Class-I Railroads."

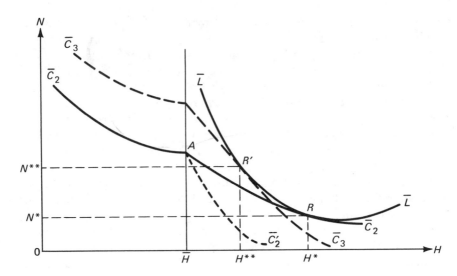

FIGURE 3–20. The Effects on an Increase in the Overtime Penalty Rate on H and N

now denoted by $\bar{C}_2 A \bar{C}_2'$. Since the increase in α makes it more expensive to purchase hours of work, the firm in Figure 3–20 must increase its total expenditures on labor (to C_3 dollars) in order to maintain its output at the required level (remain on iso-L curve $\bar{L}\bar{L}$). (Put differently, the increase in α means that (H^*, N^*) can no longer be purchased for C_2 dollars). As before, cost is minimized at a point of tangency (R'), and due to the convexity of the iso-L curve, the firm now hires more employees (N^{**}) and reduces the work week to H^{**}. By raising the cost of hours of work relative to number of workers, the increase in the penalty rate for overtime leads the firm to substitute N for H in production.

Conclusion

In this chapter we have examined the linkage between the demand for output, the production process, and the demand for labor under competitive conditions in the short run. We began our analysis by considering the situation in which a single competitive firm, facing fixed prices for its inputs and output, can adjust production only through purchases of labor services. In this case, the firm maximizes its profit by hiring the quantity of labor that equates the wage rate to the value of the marginal product of labor. More important, the value of the marginal product of labor schedule serves as the firm's labor demand curve and is downward-sloping due to the diminishing marginal physical productivity of labor. Finally, we saw that exogenous changes in the firm's amount of capital, price of output, or technology will disturb its labor demand schedule in predictable ways.

Next, we analyzed the demand for labor by a competitive firm when it is able to adjust its inputs of labor *and* capital services. This means that a given level of output can be produced in a variety of ways, and that to maximize its profit, the competitive firm must first establish the cost-minimizing combination of inputs for its various possible levels of production. The firm's cost-minimizing input combinations are summarized by its *expansion path*. To choose the optimal (profit-maximizing) amount of labor, the firm locates that point on its expansion path where marginal cost of production equals marginal revenue. The result of this is that, having experienced a wage-rate change, the profit-maximizing firm first moves to a new expansion path, which is known as the *substitution effect* of a wage change, and then moves along the new expansion path until marginal revenue again equals marginal cost, which is known as the *scale effect* of a wage change. Although the analysis of the effect of a wage change on the quantity of labor demanded is more complex when capital is variable, in general the firm hires less labor at higher wage rates and the demand schedule is more elastic (flatter) than in the case where labor is the only variable input. This difference has important implications for the total cost of union-induced wage increases, for example.

An extremely important conclusion developed in this chapter is that the demand for labor by a competitive *industry*, while downward-sloping, is more complicated than the simple sum of the individual firms' demand schedules due to feedback effects of price changes in the market for final output as industry production expands or contracts. Another important result concerning a competitive industry's labor demand elasticity is that it depends on whether the number of firms in the industry is fixed or variable. As a result of this, we cannot reach a general conclusion as to whether the industry demand for labor is more or less elastic than the demand curves of its component firms, although the key result that industry demand for labor is inversely related to the wage rate is preserved. Finally, we examined the important role played by the industry demand for labor in public policies designed to influence employment during times of recession.

Although there are a variety of statistical techniques for examining the hypothesis that firms desire less labor at higher wages, one of the most inventive is utilized by Lloyd Reynolds and Peter Gregory in a study of the effect of minimum wage legislation on employment in Puerto Rican manufacturing during the 1950s. With the working assumption that the manufacturing industry had a production function exhibiting the property of homogeneity of degree 1, they identify an (output constant) elasticity of demand for labor of approximately -1.0.

Finally, we examined a recent extension of the theory of demand for labor which takes into account the firm's distribution of its labor input into hours of work per employee versus number of employees, the possibility of premium wages for overtime, and costs of hiring and maintaining an employment slot. The framework we develop expands greatly the set of questions that can be examined with respect to the effects of public policy. For example, we are able to analyze how legislated increases in the premium wage for overtime work or the requirement of more extensive employment screening tests influence firms' optimal number of employees as opposed to hours of work per employee. In particular, we found that when the firm's output is fixed (regulated), an increase in the premium wage rate for overtime work should increase employment while causing workers to be put on "short hours."

Exercises

1. The Pretty Puppy Palace of Providence, (4P) grooms dogs. The 4P has a fixed capital input and uses only one variable input, labor. Moreover, 4P sells its output and purchases labor under competitive conditions. You are given the following information about 4P's operation.

L	D	MPP	VMP
0	0	—	—
1	10	10	5
2		15	
3	45		10
4	60		
5	72		6
6		10	
7	90		
8			
9	100	4	
10	102	2	1

where

$$L \equiv \text{units of labor}$$
$$D \equiv \text{number of dogs groomed (output)}$$
$$MPP \equiv \text{marginal physical product of labor}$$
$$VMP \equiv \text{value of marginal product of labor}$$

(a) How many dogs are groomed when 6 units of labor are employed?
(b) What is the marginal physical product of the seventh unit of labor?
(c) What is the price of having a dog grommed in Providence?
(d) What is the value of marginal product of the eighth unit of labor? Suppose that the competitive wage in Providence is $6.

(e) How many units of labor will be employed by the 4P?

(f) What will the total (wage) income of 4P's workers be?

(g) What will the gross profit (total revenue minus total labor costs) of the 4P be?

2. The Walla Walla Widget Works (4W) is a competitive firm that can purchase as much labor as it wants at a constant wage rate (w) of $5 and as much capital as it wants at a constant rental rate (r) of $20. Given below are combinations of capital (K) and labor (L), each of which will produce 10 widgets. Given also are the marginal physical products of capital (MPP_K) and the marginal physical products of labor (MPP_L) associated with their respective K-L combinations.

K	L	MPP_K	MPP_L
100	1	.05	5.00
50	2	.10	2.50
25	4	.20	1.25
20	5	.25	1.00
10	10	.50	.50
5	20	1.00	.25
4	25	1.25	.20
2	50	2.50	.10
1	100	5.00	.05

(a) If 4W wishes to produce 10 widgets at minimum cost, what K-L combination should it choose? Explain briefly and depict graphically.

(b) What fraction of 4W's total cost of production is labor?

*3. Return to the discussion of the effect of an increase in the overtime premium rate (α) on the firm's optimal employment hours mix (pp. 89–90). Suppose that the firm's initial cost-minimizing work week were *less* than $\bar{H}$. In this case, what effect would an increase in α have on N and H? Explain carefully and depict graphically.

References

BAUMOL, WILLIAM J., *Economic Theory and Operations Analysis*. Englewood Cliffs, N.J.: Prentice Hall, 1977, pp. 267–96.

BLOOM, GORDON F., and HERBERT R. NORTHRUP, *Economics of Labor Relations*. Homewood, Ill.: Irwin, 1977, pp. 497–502.

EHRENBERG, RONALD G., *Fringe Benefits and Overtime Behavior*. Lexington, Mass.: Heath, 1971, pp. 5–22.

FELDSTEIN, MARTIN, "Specification of the Labor Input in the Aggregate Production Function." *Review of Economic Studies*, 34, 4 (October 1967), 375–86.

*Indicates more difficult exercises

FERGUSON, C. E., *The Neoclassical Theory of Production and Distribution.* Cambridge, Eng.: Cambridge University Press, 1969, Chaps. 6, 9.

HAMERMESH, DANIEL S., "Econometric Studies of Labor Demand and Their Application to Policy Analysis." *Journal of Human Resources,* 11, 4 (fall 1976), 507–25.

HENDERSON, JAMES M., and RICHARD E. QUANDT, *Microeconomic Theory.* New York: McGraw Hill, 1971, pp. 69–70.

HILDEBRAND, GEORGE H., and TA-CHUNG LIU, *Manufacturing Production Functions in the United States, 1957.* Ithaca, N.Y.: The New York State School of Industrial and Labor Relations, 1965, pp. 53–57.

MILLER, ROGER LEROY, *American Economic Life: Yesterday and Today.* San Francisco: Canfield Press, 1974, p. 186.

OI, WALTER W., "Labor as a Quasi-Fixed Factor." *Journal of Political Economy,* 70, 6 (December 1962), 538–55.

POLACHEK, SOLOMON W., THOMAS J. KNIESNER, and HENRICK J. HARWOOD, "Educational Production Functions." *Journal of Educational Statistics,* 3, 3 (autumn 1978), 209–31.

REYNOLDS, LLOYD G., and PETER GREGORY, *Wages, Productivity, and Industrialization in Puerto Rico.* Homewood, Ill.: Irwin, 1965, pp. 41–103, p. 145.

ROSEN, SHERWIN, "Short-Run Employment Variation on Class-I Railroads in the U.S., 1947–1963." *Econometrica,* 36, 3–4 (July–October 1968), 511–29.

The Wall Street Journal, January 24, 1978, p. 1.

The Wall Street Journal, January 26, 1978, p. 1.

CHAPTER 4

Labor Supply:
Family Members
in the Short Run

A. Educational Objectives
  1. Establish the qualitative relationships between the individual family member's desired quantity of market work and the hourly wage rate and nonemployment income
  2. Identify the influence of various environmental disturbances or government policies on the desired amount of market work
  3. Discuss evidence bearing on labor force participation and hours of work

B. Utility Maximization—The Decision Whether or Not to Work
  1. The utility function—graphical representation
     a. Indifference curves between "leisure" and market goods
     b. The marginal rate of substitution or "home wage rate"
  2. Consumption opportunities: the budget constraint
     a. Nonemployment income
     b. The market wage rate
  3. Labor force participation and the reservation wage rate
     a. The effect of changes in wage rates and nonemployment income
     b. The effect of income maintenance laws on labor force participation
     c. The influence of young children on labor force participation

C. Utility Maximization—Hours of Work
  1. The utility-maximizing work hours decision
  2. The supply of hours of work
     a. The influence of a change in nonemployment income
     b. The effects of a change in the market wage: substitution and income effects
     c. The effect of Social Security on hours of work

D. Evidence on Short-Run Labor Supply
  1. Experimental data: The New Jersey Experiment

In the study of labor supply the family plays a pivotal role, not unlike that of a firm, deciding how to use its limited resources in the best way to achieve its goals. The decision we focus on when analyzing labor supply is how the family allocates the time available between the market and other uses. When time is "sold" to the market in exchange for income, we say that labor is supplied, or that market work is performed. On the other hand, the family uses some of its time in a wide variety of nonmarket activities including child care, personal health maintenance, and amusements; in addition time may be spent in activities such as schooling which, although yielding no money income at the moment, may influence the amount that can be earned in the future.

The process by which individual family members decide how much of their time to supply to the market is doubtless very complex. That is, a husband may consider his wife's wage rate, the nonlabor income of the family,[1] his expected duties in the home, and the attitudes of the community, his wife, and his children in deciding when, where, and how much to work in the labor force. We may think of the wife, children, and other family members as behaving similarly. While it is important to emphasize that each family member's labor market decision is reached via a simultaneous process in which all members' decisions are made, to incorporate all the important variables in a first approach to the theory of labor supply would make the analysis unnecessarily complicated. Therefore, we will assume that one

---

　*Represents more advanced material

　[1] That is, income due to rent, dividends, interest, capital gains or, in general, the family's income from nonhuman assets, as well as payments from public and private welfare agencies.

family member assumes the role of decision-maker for each individual, taking into consideration each person's attitude, wage, health, and so on.[2]

The Utility Function

The decision-maker presumably decides how much, if any, of each family member's time to supply to the market to achieve the greatest possible satisfaction from the family's limited resources. Basically, these resources are defined by the amount of time available, the value of time when sold or supplied to the market, and the family's ability to purchase market goods and services even if no one works. The ways in which the family's resources can be combined to provide satisfaction are formally represented by a **utility function.**

From what has been said so far, it should be easy to see that the only reason time is supplied to the labor market is in order to obtain wages, or employment income, to buy market goods. Unfortunately, when time is traded for income it can no longer be used for other purposes. Therefore, the decision-maker has to balance the family's desire for goods against its wishes to use time in nonmarket activities. The utility function tells us how economic well-being ("utility") is related to various combinations of market goods (or the equivalent real income) and time used by the family in nonmarket activities. For convenience, we will often refer to all the nonmarket uses of time as "leisure," even though it is perfectly obvious that many, if not most, of the things family members do other than work at market jobs, such as caring for children, cooking, fixing up the house, and so on, are not always "fun."

We can write the utility function in a form analogous to the production function, equation (3–1), as follows:

$$U = u(G, H) \qquad (4\text{--}1)$$

where

$U \equiv$ the level of "utility" or economic well-being,

$G \equiv$ units of market goods,

and

$H \equiv$ hours of "leisure."

In equation (4–1), $u(\cdot)$ is a mathematical relationship that translates (maps) flows of two commodities, goods and hours of leisure, into utility per period of time. Figure 4–1 shows a typical utility function relating economic well-being to the levels of market goods and leisure used by a representative

---

[2]See Gary S. Becker, "A Theory of Social Interactions," *Journal of Political Economy*, 82, 6 (November–December 1974), 1063–94.

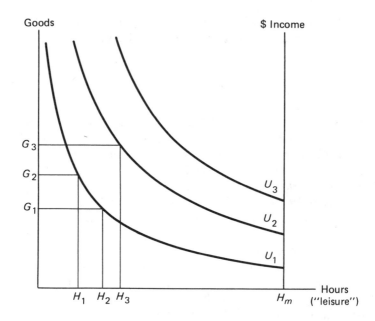

FIGURE 4–1. A Utility Function

family member. The horizontal axis measures the number of hours in a given period of time used in nonmarket activities, while the vertical axis measures the flow of market goods per time period. The number of hours per period of time is strictly limited; there are, for example, 168 hours in a week. This maximum is denoted in Figure 4–1 by the amount H_m on the horizontal axis. The quantity of market goods is measured along the vertical axis. Assuming that the prices of various goods do not change over the time period, we can also measure the amount of goods in terms of dollars, or income. This equivalent monetary measure of market goods is shown on the vertical line on the right-hand side of Figure 4–1, going through H_m. You should be careful to note that the amount of work gets smaller as the amount measured on the horizontal axis gets larger. The number of hours of labor supplied to the market is equal to H_m minus the amount of nonmarket time used by the family. An increase in the use, or "consumption," of goods and nonmarket time is assumed to result in an increase in the family's utility.

The utility function consists of a family of negatively sloped, convex lines called **indifference curves**, such as U_1, U_2, and U_3 in Figure 4–1.[3] Each indif-

---

[3]The numbers attached to indifference curves are important only for ranking the curves in order. By contrast, the numbers attached to the isoquants in Chapter 3 have *cardinal* significance; they can be added together across firms. Note that each indifference curve in Figure 4–1 is numbered, with the numbers increasing as we move outward from the origin toward the northeast, implying higher levels of satisfaction as consumption increases. However, the numbers attached to the indifference curves are not unique; we may use any

ference curve represents a constant level of utility, or satisfaction, with the curves lying farther from the origin representing higher levels of utility. Along each indifference curve, the different combinations of consumption of hours and goods all yield the same satisfaction; that is, the consumer is "indifferent" between the consumption of commodity combinations denoted by any two points along a particular curve. Thus, we might have named the indifference curves *iso-utility curves*. The meaning of the statement that the family is indifferent to consuming any of the alternative combinations of commodities along a given indifference curve is illustrated in Figure 4–1. The consumption of commodity combination G_1 and H_2 is defined to yield satisfaction equal to the consumption of the combination G_2 and H_1; however, consuming a combination of G_3 and H_3 yields more satisfaction than either of the first two combinations.

The most important characteristics of the indifference curves are their slope and their shape. Their negative slope implies that it is possible to hold the level of utility constant while substituting hours for goods in consumption; thus, the negative slope implies the condition of substitutability in consumption between hours and goods. A term often applied to the slope of an indifference curve is the **marginal rate of substitution** (MRS) between the two commodities; the term "marginal" denotes the rate at which a small amount of hours can be substituted for a small amount of goods, holding utility constant. The convex shape of the indifference curves implies imperfect substitutability between hours and goods. If hours and goods were perfect substitutes, then the MRS would be the same, no matter what combination of hours and goods was being consumed; the indifference curves would be straight lines. The principle of imperfect substitutability implies that though the family can maintain a constant level of utility by trading time for goods, and vice versa, the greater the proportion of time consumed to goods consumed, the greater the marginal (additional) amount of hours required to compensate for giving up a marginal amount of goods. Clearly, this relationship works in the opposite direction too: the greater the proportion of goods consumed to hours consumed, the greater the marginal amount of goods required to compensate the family for giving up a marginal amount of hours.

The family's decision-maker can choose to forego market income, or dollars, in return for using more of a family member's time in nonmarket

---

set of numbers which fulfills the condition that as we move toward the northeast, the numbers get larger. We are indifferent as to whether we measure successively higher utility levels as 1, 2, 3; 1.1, 1.2, 1.3; 100, 200, 300, and so on. The reason is that we wish to avoid the implication that the amount of satisfaction achieved by a consumer in one family can be compared with, or added to, the amount achieved by a consumer in another. Therefore, we are willing only to rank the indifference curves. More precisely, we adopt an ordinal rather than a cardinal utility index. We measure utility similarly to the way we measure the events at a horse race—"1st," "2nd," and so on, with the ordering of the events being the only important characteristic of the measurement. This does not in any way limit our ability to describe labor supply decisions as arising from the utility-maximizing behavior of the family's decision-maker.

activities. The MRS measures the decision-maker's willingness to do so. Thus, it is often useful to think of the MRS as a kind of wage rate. The market wage rate, after all, is the price at which a unit of time can be sold to the labor market—it represents the additional dollar amount of goods the family can obtain if it foregoes one hour of leisure. The MRS, on the other hand, represents the dollar amount of market goods the decision-maker is willing to give up, or "pay," in order to avoid selling an hour of time to the market. Thus, it represents the value, in terms of goods or equivalent dollars, placed on using a small additional amount of time in nonmarket activities. For this reason, we shall often refer to the MRS, the slope of an indifference curve, as the **home wage rate**. The MRS at the point where an indifference curve intersects the vertical line through H_m is of particular interest. Since it is impossible for the decision-maker to allocate more than H_m hours to nonmarket activities, the home wage at a point such as the intersection of U_1, U_2, or U_3 with H_m tells us how much the family decision-maker would be willing to pay in order to buy an additional hour of time, if it could be obtained.

Consumption Opportunities:
The Budget Constraint

Obviously, if utility increases with the consumption of time and goods, utility maximization implies proceeding indefinitely far upward and to the right (northeast) of the utility map—consuming an infinite amount of goods and hours. There are, however, constraints that prohibit the family from consuming infinite quantities of these commodities. First, time is strictly limited to 168 hours per week: this is a basic constraint. Second, family members cannot dictate the terms at which their labor services are sold to the market. We assume family members sell their time as labor services in a competitive market. Thus, there is a fixed, market-determined wage rate at which their time can be exchanged for dollars. Finally, while the family's nonlabor sources of income such as interest, dividends, rent, government welfare payments, and the like may permit the purchase of some market goods even if no work is performed, the amount of such nonemployment income is surely limited.

Family members are prevented from consuming unlimited quantities of goods and hours because only limited amounts of hours and income are available to them. These limitations are summarized in the *budget constraint* which defines the family's *consumption opportunities*. Figure 4–2 shows the budget constraint pertaining to one family member. As in Figure 4–1, goods are measured along the vertical axis and hours consumed (not worked or sold) are measured along the horizontal axis. The line parallel to the vertical axis and intersecting point H_m measures the dollar equivalent of market

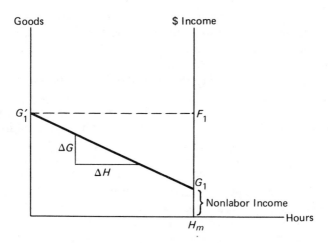

FIGURE 4–2. The Budget Constraint

goods, or income. Given the level of nonemployment income G_1 and the amount of market goods which can be bought with the pay for an hour's work, ΔG, the budget constraint is the line connecting G_1' and G_1. If this were the only family member to do market work, G_1' would be the amount of goods that could be obtained if all available hours were sold in the market. (We ignore here the issue of proper sleep, food, and recreation; alternatively, H_m can be viewed as total available time less the number of hours required to maintain productivity.) Economists sometimes refer to the quantity G_i or F_1 as **full income.**

The absolute value of the slope of the budget constraint is $\Delta G/\Delta H = (G_1' - G_1)/H_m$ and represents the **market wage rate.** The market wage rate is constant and independent of the number of hours worked because we have assumed that individual workers have no direct control over the rate of exchange between market goods and time.

Utility Maximization: The Decision Whether or Not to Work

We assume that the family decision-maker chooses an amount of work that provides the greatest amount of utility, given the budget constraint. We will analyze the decision-maker's problem of constrained utility maximization in two steps. First, we look at the decision whether or not to work at all. Later on, we look at the number of hours of work chosen, given that the decision has been made to sell some time to the market.

The decision-maker's problem is to get to the highest indifference curve allowed by the budget constraint. In analyzing the decision whether or not to work at all, focus on the point G_1 in Figure 4–3, where the budget constraint and indifference curve U_2 intersect at H_m hours of nonmarket time. Point G_1 is obviously a possible choice of the decision-maker, as is point g, since both lie on the budget constraint and thus do not exceed the set of available opportunities. Given the way in which the indifference curves have been drawn, it should be apparent that the greatest level of utility will be attained if *no market work is performed*—that is, if this family member does not participate in the labor market. Point g, while attainable, lies on indifference curve U_1, which indicates lower economic well-being than U_2, the indifference curve through G_1. Clearly, the closer a point lies to G'_1, the lower would be the indifference curve going through the budget constraint at that point. *Figure 4–3 shows that if the indifference curve which intersects the budget constraint at the point indicating zero hours of market work (H_m) is steeper than the budget constraint at that point, then the greatest level of economic well-being is achieved by not participating in market work at all.*

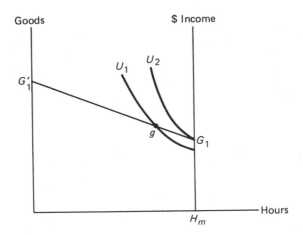

FIGURE 4–3. Utility Maximization: No Work

The preceding paragraph has demonstrated that given the assumed shape of the budget constraint and indifference curves, the necessary and sufficient condition for no hours to be sold to the labor market is that the MRS between market goods and time exceed the market wage rate when no market work is performed. Perhaps this crucial aspect of the decision whether to work or not will be more meaningful if we recall that the MRS is also called the *home wage rate*. The condition that the MRS be greater than the market wage is the same thing as saying that the home wage exceed the market wage. This means that the amount of income the decision-maker would be willing to sacrifice if only one more hour of time could be obtained exceeds the amount of income which can be obtained if one hour of time is given up to the market. That is to say, the family's valuation of an additional hour of time (when the maximum amount is being consumed) is greater than the market's evaluation. Under these circumstances, since more time would be bought if that were possible, it makes obvious sense for the decision-maker not to sell any.

In Figure 4–4, the indifference curves are drawn in such a way as to show the situation when the decision to work in the market will enable the family

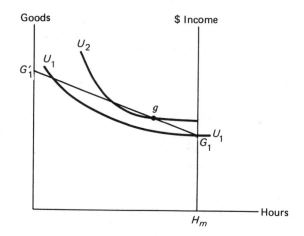

FIGURE 4–4. Utility Maximization: Work

to reach a higher level of utility than the decision not to work. Again, both points G_1 and g represent feasible situations, since both lie on the budget constraint. Now, however, if g is chosen, the level of economic well-being will be represented by indifference curve U_2, which lies above the indifference curve associated with a decision to do no work at all, U_1. Figure 4–4 shows the converse of Figure 4–3: *If the indifference curve passing through the budget constraint at H_m is less steep than the budget constraint at that point, then the greatest level of economic well-being is achieved by selling some time to the labor market.* The decision-maker chooses to sell some time to the labor market when the MRS between market goods and nonmarket time (at zero hours of work) is less than the market wage. In other words, if the home wage rate is less than the market wage rate, the family's value of time (when no work is performed) is less than that of the market, and it pays to sell time in return for the amount of income that can be obtained.

Those individuals who perform some market work in our economy (or who are actively seeking work) are called **labor force participants,** and the proportion of labor force participants in the total population is called the **labor force participation rate.** Economists and policy-makers are often interested in the labor force participation rate and its determinants, because labor force participation is necessary in order to obtain sufficient market income for most persons to lead a comfortable life. Moreover, the labor force participation rates of various subsets of the population—married women, older persons, and teenagers—provides information about how men and women specialize in obtaining market income, performing child care and other kinds of work in the home, how older persons fare in providing for their material desires, and how youth allocate their time between current market work and preparation for future economic well-being through formal education. Therefore, we will spend some time analyzing how changes in the budget constraint affect the labor force participation decision, given the family's utility function.

Participation and the Market Wage Rate. Let us reexamine Figures 4–3 and 4–4, and recall that a family member will participate in the labor force if, and only if, the home wage is less than the market wage at the point on the budget constraint corresponding to an allocation of H_m hours to nonmarket activity. This relationship between the home and market wage rates is recapitulated in Figure 4–5. Note that since we have assumed the budget constraints are straight lines, the market wage along constraint $G_1 G_1'$

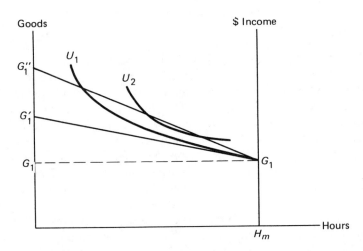

FIGURE 4–5. The Effect of a Wage Change on Labor Force Participation

is measured by $(G_1' - G_1)/H_m$, and that along $G_1 G_1''$ is $(G_1'' - G_1)/H_m$, which is clearly greater, since $(G_1'' - G_1)/H_m - (G_1' - G_1)/H_m = (G_1'' - G_1')/H_m > 0$. The MRS along indifference curve U_1 at point G_1 is greater than $(G_1' - G_1)/H_m$ but less than $(G_1'' - G_1)/H_m$. Thus, at the lower wage the family member depicted in Figure 4–5 performs no market work. An increase in the wage rate to $(G_1'' - G_1)/H_m$ will cause the family member to enter the labor force, however. For any nonlabor force participant, as the market wage increases, it will eventually reach a value where the individual is indifferent between working and devoting H_m hours to nonmarket activity. At this value, called the **reservation wage rate**, the budget constraint is tangent to the indifference curve at H_m hours. Clearly, *a sufficiently large increase in the market wage, holding nonemployment income constant at some level such as G_1, will make the market wage exceed the home wage. At this point, a family member who had been allocating all available hours to nonmarket activities will enter the labor force.*

It should be apparent that no increase in the market wage, all other things being equal, can cause someone who is selling some hours to the labor market to leave the labor force. Why? The condition for labor force participation is that the market wage exceed the reservation wage at G_1. If the market wage is greater than the reservation wage at G_1, further increases in the market wage can only widen this inequality, never reduce it. To summarize, our theory implies that labor force participation and the market wage rate rise and fall together.

Participation and Nonemployment Income. The budget constraint is determined not only by the market wage rate (its slope), but also by the level of nonemployment income, which is measured by the height at which the constraint intersects the vertical line through H_m. Thus, we need to examine the effect of changes in nonemployment income on labor force participation, holding the market wage rate constant. Such a shift in the budget constraint is depicted in Figure 4–6, where an increase in nonemployment income from G_1 to G_2 is shown. The wage remains constant at $(G_1' - G_1)/H_m = (G_2' - G_2)/H_m$.

In order to analyze the effect of changes in nonemployment income, we need to make a further assumption about the utility function. We need to know what happens to the value of hours in terms of market goods as utility increases, holding the consumption of hours unchanged. We will assume that hours of nonmarket time is a **normal commodity**, meaning that the amount of income (goods) the family is willing to give up in order to consume an additional hour of time in nonmarket activities rises as utility increases, the consumption of hours remaining unchanged. An increase in utility, holding constant the consumption of hours, can be traced out along the vertical "income" line through H_m; and the normality assumption is reflected by the increasing steepness of the indifference curves at H_m hours, as the level of

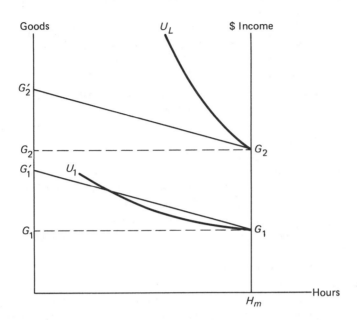

FIGURE 4–6. The Effect of a Change in Nonemployment Income on Labor Force Participation

utility rises. Thus, indifference curve U_2 is steeper at point G_2 than is indifference curve U_1 at G_1. In other words, the assumption that nonmarket hours is a normal commodity means that the reservation wage rate rises as utility increases. *If we assume that nonmarket hours is a normal commodity, then a sufficiently large increase in nonemployment income will cause a working individual to leave the labor force.* Thus, in Figure 4–6, the family member is a labor force participant at market wage $(G_1' - G_1)/H_m$ and nonemployment income G_1; an increase in nonemployment income from G_1 to G_2, however, causes the family member to become a nonparticipant. As nonemployment income rises, the value of the reservation wage rate rises, while the market wage obtainable remains unchanged. Eventually, the reservation wage exceeds the obtainable market wage, and the greatest economic well-being is attained by performing no market work.

Two changes in the budget constraint, both of which affect economic well-being in the same direction, have opposite effects on labor force participation. An increase in the market wage rate and an increase in nonemployment income both make it possible to consume more market goods and (for labor force participants) to allocate more hours to nonmarket activities. When the market wage rises, however, it becomes more lucrative to sell hours to the labor market in exchange for income, and thus labor force participation becomes more likely. Alternatively, as utility rises, the reservation wage rate increases, and therefore labor force participation becomes less likely when nonemployment income grows, other things equal.

LABOR FORCE PARTICIPATION: APPLICATIONS

Numerous applications of the analysis of labor force participation have implications for labor market policy as well as for our understanding of labor force behavior patterns. We shall illustrate two of them in this section. The first application deals with the effect of "welfare" laws such as Aid to the Families of Dependent Children, the Federal Food Stamp Program, and the like on labor force participation. The laws constituting the set of income-maintenance programs in the United States vary considerably among states and localities, but it is fair to characterize them in simple terms using the concept of the budget constraint. Essentially, these laws guarantee a minimum level of income or its equivalent in food stamps, subsidized housing, medical care, and so on for the family, depending on its size and composition. However, the nonemployment income guaranteed to the family is reduced by a substantial amount for each dollar earned through market work. This *implicit tax* on market earnings is sometimes dollar for dollar or more—actually exceeding 100 percent in some cases.

Let us see how an income-maintenance program with a substantial tax on employment income can be characterized in terms of a budget constraint. In Figure 4–7 there is no source of nonemployment income from sources other than government support. In the absence of an income-maintenance program,

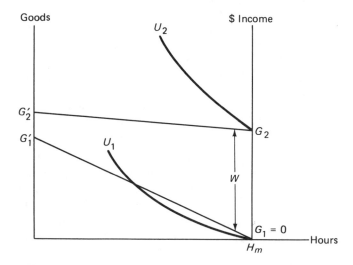

FIGURE 4–7. A Budget Constraint Representation of Income-Maintenance Laws

the budget constraint is $G_1 G_1'$, the level of nonemployment income, G_1, being zero and the market wage being $(G_1' - G_1)/H_m$. Since the slope of indifference curve U_1 at point G_1 is less than the slope of the budget constraint through G_1, the actual market wage rate exceeds the reservation wage rate, and the individual represented in Figure 4–7 performs some market work.

The introduction of an income maintenance program as described above shifts the budget constraint from $G_1 G_1'$ to a position such as $G_2 G_2'$. The basic welfare payment (W) if no market work is performed, and hence no employment income received, is G_2. As work and employment income increase, the welfare payment is reduced. This reduction is indicated by the declining distance between $G_1 G_1'$ and $G_2 G_2'$, as one moves toward the left. For every dollar increase in earnings, W is reduced by $\$t$, the implicit tax rate $\times \$1$. Thus the effective market wage along the constraint $G_2 G_2'$ is only $(1 - t)$ as large as along $G_1 G_1'$. For example, if W is reduced by $\$.30$ for every $\$1$ increase in labor income, the implicit tax (t) is 0.7. Since the reservation wage is higher at G_2 than at G_1, both the increase in nonemployment income (W) and the reduction in the effective wage rate tend to reduce labor force participation. In Figure 4–7, the individual who sells some hours to the labor market in the absence of the income-maintenance program leaves the labor force entirely when the program is introduced.

The major problem facing policy-makers in designing income-maintenace programs is to achieve a sufficiently high level of nonemployment income to help the "deserving poor" maintain an acceptable standard of living, to reduce the effective market wage by as little as possible in order to maintain work incentives, and to keep the cost of the program within reasonable bounds. Unfortunately, these goals conflict. One way to keep welfare expenditures low is to remove recipients from the program when they earn sufficient income; this, however, reduces work incentives, thus causing otherwise able workers to remain out of the labor force and on the welfare roles. Achieving a "humane" level of income maintenance implies a relatively high level of welfare payments, W, for those with low total incomes. Maintaining a high W for those who are least able to work is costly, and again program designers are tempted to reduce W as rapidly as possible when employment incomes rises, thus inducing severe work disincentives that are likely to be counter productive in terms of maintaining program costs at acceptable levels.

A second application of the analysis of labor force participation sheds light on the effects of commuting costs and the presence of young children on labor force participation.[4] Figure 4–8 depicts the situation of, say, a married woman who has young children to care for. If she accepts a market job, we assume that the children will be cared for "free" by their grandmother, but delivering them and picking them up every day from the grandmother's

---

[4]This application is taken from John Cogan, "Labor Supply with Time and Money Costs of Participation" (Santa Monica, Calif.: Rand Corporation, 1976).

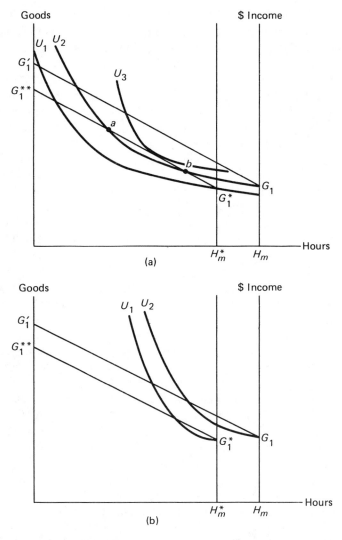

FIGURE 4–8. The Effect of Commuting or Child Care Time on Labor Force Participation

house requires a substantial chunk of time that can neither be sold to the labor market for employment income nor used in nonmarket activities. From the married woman's point of view, therefore, her available "useful" time is H_m hours if she does not work, but only H_m^* if she enters the labor force. Similarly, if working in the marketplace requires commuting to work, available useful hours are reduced by an amount dependent on the distance traveled, traffic congestion, and available means of transportation. The question is, what is the effect of child care (or commuting) problems on the wife's labor force participation decision? Common sense suggests that these extra time costs associated with market work reduce the likelihood that the wife will participate in the labor force, and that is what our theory of labor force participation confirms.

In Figure 4–8, the wife would clearly sell some time to the labor market in return for employment income if there were no "lost" time associated with market work, since the slope of the indifference curve intersecting point G_1 is less than the slope of the budget constraint. The reservation wage is less than the market wage. When time must be taken away from nonmarket activities that cannot be used to earn market income, the effective amount of available time becomes H_m^* if the wife works in the market. $H_m - H_m^*$ hours are required to deliver the children to their grandmother and pick them up for every week of market work. Thus, the effective budget constraint becomes $G_1^* G_1^{**}$ instead of $G_1 G_1'$ as soon as the wife takes a job. The market wage rate and nonemployment income remain the same, but the effective number of hours is reduced by $H_m - H_m^*$. Note that real full income (measured along the goods axis) is reduced by $G_1' G_1^{**}$, which equals the market wage multiplied by loss of effective time. Whether the wife will participate in the labor force in the presence of this time cost of market work depends solely on the shape of the indifference curves, given the market wage and nonemployment income. In Figure 4–8a, the indifference curves are rather flat, indicating that the "decision-maker" is willing to exchange a relatively large quantity of the wife's time for market goods. In Figure 4–8b, on the other hand, the steepness of the indifference curves implies that a relatively high value is placed on using the wife's time in nonmarket pursuits. In Figure 4–8a, the indifference curves are so flat that the wife will participate in the labor force even though labor force participation involves the loss of $H_m - H_m^*$ hours of effective time. Utility is higher if she works than if she does not participate in the labor force. This can be seen by noting that part of the effective budget constraint $G_1^* G_1^{**}$ lies above indifference curve U_2, which represents the utility associated with performing no market work (U_2 passes through point G_1). Any of the hours-income combinations between points a and b on $G_1^* G_1^{**}$ are feasible choices involving some market work and would yield a higher level of utility (such as U_3) than U_2. In Figure 4–8b, if the wife works, no part of the effective budget constraint lies above the indifference curve associated with nonparticipation. Therefore, the best that can be done is to allocate H_m hours to nonemployment activities, even though some market work would be undertaken if there were no loss of effective time resulting from the need to provide for child care or commuting time.

The preceding analysis shows why the presence of preschool-age children is likely to reduce the labor force participation of married women. It also suggests that women who intend to participate in the labor force for most of their lives have an incentive to have few children and to space them fairly close together so as to reduce the time required for child care while offspring are very young. From an economic policy point of view, the interrelationship between child care costs and labor force participation lends insight into problems of wage inequality between men and women. As we shall see in Chapter 10, there is considerable concern over the cause of the discrepancy between the market wage rates of men and women. In Chapters 9 and 10 we will focus on the determinants of market wage rates for individuals: One of the important forces at work is experience, which of course can only be acquired while a labor force participant. Since mothers typically devote more time to child care than fathers, children raise the cost and thus reduce the extent of mothers' labor force participation, they also have an influence on the future earning power of their mothers. Thus part of the difference between male and female wage rates can be attributed to the influence of children on the labor force participation decision.

Utility Maximization: Hours of Work

In this section we analyze the number of market work hours chosen, assuming that the decision to work at all has already been made. Analyzing the hours of work decision requires a somewhat more precise understanding of the relationship between the indifference curves and the budget constraint implied by utility maximization. In order to see how the decision-maker maximizes utility given the budget constraint, start at G_1' in Figure 4–9 and proceed

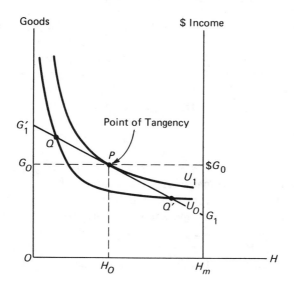

FIGURE 4–9. Utility Maximization and Hours of Work

toward G_1 until the highest indifference curve is reached. This will be at point P, where utility is maximized by consuming H_o hours and G_o goods such that the budget constraint is tangent to an indifference curve. If the price of each "good" is \$1, then point P also represents a choice of \$$G$ income, $G - G_1$ of which represents wage income. Hours of work equal $H_m - H_o$. It follows from the assumed shape of the budget constraint and the indifference curves that there is one, and only one, point such as P. Suppose the decision-maker decided on a combination of goods and nonmarket hours corresponding to point Q, which does not represent a point of tangency between $G_1'G_1$ and an indifference curve. The indifference curve passing through Q is U_0, representing a lower level of utility than U_1, the curve which passes through P. It is clear that at Q consumption possibilities are such that by giving up some goods and consuming more hours, the decision-maker can increase utility. This will be true until the consumption combination represented by point P is obtained. Obviously, the same argument would apply in reverse if the initial point chosen were Q', where "too many" hours and "too few" goods would be consumed.

Formally, we can express the condition of utility maximization as follows: Recall that the absolute value of the slope of the budget constraint is the market wage rate which we now represent by the symbol W_m. Thus, along a budget constraint

$$\Delta G/\Delta H = W_m \qquad (4\text{--}2)$$

The slope of the indifference curves, on the other hand, represents the home wage rate, W_h. Thus, along an indifference curve

$$\text{slope of indifference curve (absolute value)} = MRS = W_h \qquad (4\text{--}3)$$

The tangency condition of utility maximization can therefore be expressed symbolically as follows: Utility is maximized when the slope of the budget constraint is equal to the slope of an indifference curve having a point in common with the budget constraint. At this point[5]

$$W_m = W_h \qquad (4\text{--}3)$$

At a point like Q in Figure 4–9, $W_h > W_m$. That is to say, the value the family places on an additional hour of time allocated to leisure exceeds the income that must be sacrificed if one less hour is devoted to market work. Thus Q represents too much market work and too little time devoted to nonmarket activities from the point of view of utility maximization. Similarly, at Q', $W_m > W_h$; the home wage is less than the market wage. Since the amount of income the family is willing to sacrifice in order to use one

---

[5]As we have seen, for nonparticipants, $W_m < W_h$ when utility is maximized.

more hour in the home is less than the labor income which can be earned by selling the hour to the labor market, utility maximization requires increasing the number of hours of market work.

THE SUPPLY OF HOURS OF WORK

We have seen that once the decision has been made to participate in the labor force, the number of hours of work is chosen to achieve the greatest level of economic well-being consistent with the time and income constraints faced by the family. The *supply schedule* of hours of work tells us how this optimal number of hours is affected by changes in the wage rate and non-employment income. Ultimately we will concentrate on the relationship between hours of work and the market wage rate. First, however we analyze the influence of a change in nonemployment income, holding the market wage constant.

In order to analyze the effect of a change in nonemployment income on hours of work, we proceed in the same way as we did in studying the influence of nonemployment income on labor force participation. We assume that leisure is a normal commodity, meaning that the amount of income (goods) the family is willing to give up in order to consume an additional hour of time in nonmarket activities rises with utility, the consumption of hours remaining unchanged. In other words, the home wage rises as utility increases. For example, in Figure 4–10, if nonemployment income is G_1 and the market wage is $(G_1' - G_1)/H_m$, utility maximization implies choosing to work $H_m - H_o$ hours in return for $\$(G_o - G_1)$ market income. Now, suppose nonemploy-

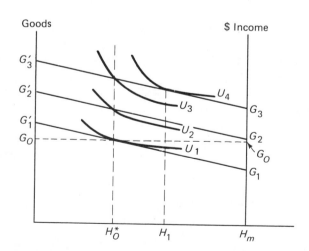

FIGURE 4–10. The Effect of Income Change on Hours of Work

ment income rises to G_2, or still higher to G_3, but the market wage remains unchanged. Along budget constraints $G_2 G_2'$ and $G_3 G_3'$, it is still clearly possible to choose to consume H_o hours. However, the indifference curves, U_2 and U_3, passing through H_o hours along these higher constraints, are steeper than U_1 at H_o hours. Clearly, along constraints $G_2 G_2'$ and $G_3 G_3'$, neither U_2 nor U_3 is the highest indifference curve attainable. When nonemployment income is G_3 and $H_m - H_o$ hours of work are chosen, the home wage rate exceeds the market wage rate; fewer hours should be worked and more devoted to nonmarket activity. $H_m - H_1$ represents the utility-maximizing number of market work hours after nonemployment income has risen to G_3, the wage rate $(G_3' - G_3)/H_m$ remaining equal to $(G_1' - G_1)/H_m$. Thus the assumption that nonmarket time is a normal commodity also implies that hours of work fall when nonemployment income rises and the market wage rate remains the same.

The way Figure 4–10 is drawn, *both* goods (income) and nonmarket hours are normal commodities. Successively higher levels of nonlabor income raise the maximum utility attainable, and the points of tangency between the indifference curves and budget constraints rise upward and to the right (northeast). The consumption of both hours and goods increases. Although we have assumed that the consumption of both hours and goods increases as utility rises, there is nothing in economic theory compelling us to do so. Nevertheless, the assumption of a forward-sloping utility-consumption path for the family member has intuitive appeal. One can imagine cases in which either goods or hours would be an "inferior commodity."[6] If goods were an inferior commodity, the utility-consumption path would slope toward the southeast; if hours were inferior, toward the northwest. However, with broad commodity groups, the assumption of a northeasterly sloping utility-consumption path seems reasonable.

The aspect of the supply of hours of work on which we want to focus most attention is the relationship between hours of work and the market wage rate. The effect of a change in the market wage on hours of work chosen is shown in Figures 4–11 and 4–12. A change in the wage rate is represented by a change in the slope of the budget constraint. We now wish to examine the effect of a change in the wage rate with nonlabor income unchanged, so we rotate a budget constraint about a single point on the vertical line going through H_m. As the budget constraint is rotated clockwise, the wage rate increases. Figures 4–11 and 4–12 show two budget constraints, each depicting a different wage rate, but the same nonlabor income.[7] The wage rate is lower along the constraint $H_m G_1'$ than along $H_m G_2'$. The point of utility maximization is P along $H_m G_1'$ and Q along $H_m G_2'$. Note that Q may lie either to the right or to the left of P. We cannot predict from economic theory whether an

---

[6]No study known to the authors has suggested that such a case has been observed.
[7]Nonlabor income is set equal to zero for convenience in Figures 4–11 and 4–12.

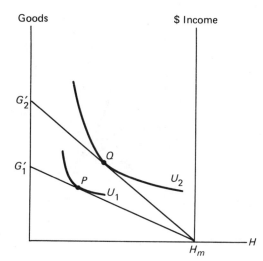

FIGURE 4–11. Reduced Labor
Supply with Increased Wage Rate

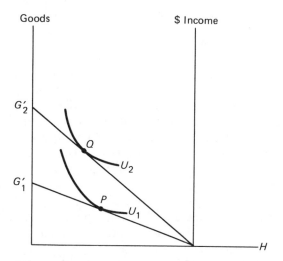

FIGURE 4–12. Increased Labor Supply with a
Rise in the Wage Rate

increase in the wage rate will result in a larger or a smaller amount of labor being supplied by the family! The case of a reduced amount supplied is shown in Figure 4–11, while the case of an increased amount is shown in Figure 4–12. (Recall that an increase in the wage rate can never reduce labor force participation to zero hours.)

What lies behind the ambiguity concerning the effect of a change in the wage rate on the change in the amount of labor supplied? We see more

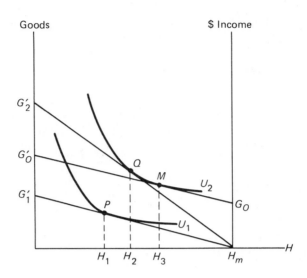

FIGURE 4–13. The Substitution and Income Effects of a Wage Change on Hours of Work

clearly in Figure 4–13. Note that by increasing the wage rate, the family is moved to a higher indifference curve; that is, when the wage rate increases, the family is better off. In Figure 4–13, we note that indifference curve U_2, the highest achievable after the budget constraint rotates from H_mG_1' to H_mG_2', lies above U_1, the previously highest attainable indifference curve. (We assume that Q lies to the northeast of P.) Now, we could also increase the family's welfare to U_2 without increasing the wage rate by increasing nonlabor income just enough to compensate not having the wage increased. In other words, imagine placing the family on budget constraint G_oG_o', which is parallel to H_mG_1', but tangent to indifference curve U_2 (at M). G_o represents just enough nonlabor income to compensate the family for not receiving an increase in his wage rate; note that since G_oG_o' is parallel to H_mG_1', the wage rates along the two constraints are the same.

But what would be the difference in behavior if the budget constraint were G_oG_o' rather than H_mG_1' or H_mG_2'? We see that along H_mG_2', $H_m - H_2$ hours are worked and H_2 hours consumed, whereas along G_oG_o', only $H_m - H_3$ hours would be worked, while H_3 hours would be consumed. The implication is that if we were to raise the family to U_2 by increasing nonlabor income rather than the wage rate, the incentive to work is decreased. In other words, keeping the family on an indifference curve (U_2) while changing the budget constraint will cause hours of work to change in the same direction that the wage rate is changed. Theoretically this must happen because of the negative slope of the indifference curve. The difference in the number of hours worked along U_2 between the two different wage rates, $H_2 - H_3$, is called the **sub-**

116

stitution effect of a change in the budget constraint from $H_m G'_1$ to $H_m G'_2$. Alternatively, we could lower the wage rate from $H_m G'_2$ to $H_m G'_1$ and measure the substitution effect on U_1. (For small changes in the budget constraint, there is a negligible difference in these two ways of measuring the substitution effect.) When the family moved from U_1 to U_2 by means of a change in nonlabor income only, consumption of hours rises from H_1 to H_3, and hours worked falls by $H_3 - H_1$. This is called the **income effect** of the change in the budget constraint from $H_m G'_1$ to $H_m G'_2$.

The initial change in the budget constraint from $H_m G'_1$ to $H_m G'_2$ causes the family to change the consumption of hours from H_1 to H_2. Because an increase in the wage rate is in one respect similar to an increase in nonlabor income, the change from H_1 to H_2 can be broken down into two components: (1) $H_2 - H_3$, the change due to the change in the wage rate, holding the level of utility constant, called the substitution effect; (2) $H_3 - H_1$, the change due to the change in the level of utility, holding the wage rate constant, called the income effect. To summarize, *the substitution effect says that the family will buy less (more) leisure as it becomes relatively more (less) expensive due to a wage increase (decrease); the income effect says that a wage increase (decrease) makes the family richer (poorer) so that it buys more (less) of a normal good.* Thus, the gross effect on consumption of hours of a change in the wage rate is $(H_2 - H_3) + (H_3 - H_1) = H_2 - H_1$. Since we have assumed that leisure is a normal commodity, the income effect is to raise hours consumed and reduce hours worked, when the wage rate rises. On the other hand, the substitution effect always causes hours worked to rise so long as the indifference curves are negatively sloped. It can now be seen that the income and substitution effects have opposite impacts on hours worked when leisure is a normal commodity. Thus, economic theory implies that hours worked may either rise or fall as the result of an increase in the wage rate, and the issue may be resolved only by empirical investigation. The separation of the effect of a wage change on hours of work into substitution and income effects will help us to understand several of the applications of labor supply theory to policy issues discussed later in the text.

What, then, does the supply curve of work hours look like? Many economists agree that the labor supply curve of family members looks something like that in Figure 4–14. Over a low range of wage rates, the substitution effect dominates the income effect, and the supply curve slopes upward with respect to the wage rate. Beyond this, the income effect dominates, and the labor supply curve is "backward bending," implying that market work declines as the wage rate rises. The supply curve in Figure 4–14 is drawn with respect to a given level of nonlabor income. If nonlabor income were to increase, the assumption that leisure is normal means that S would shift to the left, with fewer work hours offered at each wage rate.

Note that when the labor supply curve is negatively sloped with respect to the wage rate, there is no implication that as wage rates increase, earned

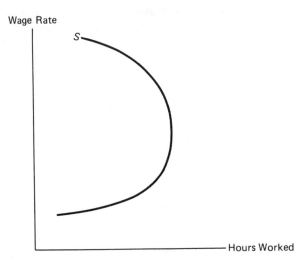

FIGURE 4–14. The Supply of Hours of Work

income declines. Whether earned income rises or falls with respect to wage rate increases depends on the elasticity of the supply curve; if the elasticity of the labor supply curve is algebraically greater than −1, then income rises as the wage rate rises. Another point to remember when using the theory of labor supply to help understand real-world behavior is that we have been treating the income effects of changes in nonlabor income and of changes in wage rates as though they were commensurable. They are, in theory, if wage rate changes are thought to be of long duration, or permanent. To help understand this point, consider the following example: If a worker is offered the opportunity of working overtime hours for a few weeks, the effect on normal income is relatively small. Even though weekly income may rise considerably, the increase has to be treated in the context of normal income in the absence of overtime work (and in the context of whatever nonlabor income may accrue to him or her). Thus, the income effect of a wage rate change that is expected to be temporary—that is, what economists often call a transitory change in the wage rate—is theoretically much smaller than the income effect of a permanent or persistent wage rate change. On the other hand, the effect of such a change in the wage rate on the price of hours relative to market goods is independent of whether the change in the wage rate is permanent or transitory. Thus, for transitory wage rate changes, the substitution effect is much more likely to dominate the income effect than it is for permanent changes. An example of the application of this point is that if we accept the existence of a backward-bending labor supply curve as the principal explanation of the long-term decline in hours of work per week (this is discussed on pp. 132–36), we may be troubled by the fact that over short

118

periods of time (such as the period of a business cycle) workers tend to work longer when unemployment is low, and wage rates, including overtime premiums, are high, than at other times. The difference between the effects of permanent and transistory wage rate changes should help account for this.

THE SUPPLY OF HOURS OF WORK: APPLICATION

One of many interesting applications of the theory of the supply of hours of work has to do with the effect of social security legislation on the labor supply of older people. The federal Old Age, Survivors, Disability, and Health Insurance program (OASDHI) provides that most workers and their employers are required to pay a tax on their earnings to the federal government, in return for which they are eligible to receive pension benefits after they turn 62 years of age. There is a provision to this program, however; as of 1978, until the age of 72, benefits are reduced by $.50 per dollar of earnings in excess of $4,000 per year. The effect of this provision on the amount of market work can be analyzed with the theory of labor supply we have developed.

The provision of social security benefits subject to receiving no more than $4,000 in annual earnings influences hours of work through its effect on the budget constraint. This is illustrated in Figures 4–15a and b, which depicts the situation of someone who is eligible to receive social security benefits of $3,600 per year and whose market wage rate is $8 per hour. Suppose this individual had been working 40 hours per week—2,000 hours per year—and that nonemployment income (including the implicit rent on a completely paid-off home) is $3,600 per year. Thus the budget constraint in the absence of social security starts at $3,600 per year if no market work is performed and slopes upward at the rate of $8 per hour. By working 2,000 hours per year, the individual chooses to consume 6,760 hours of leisure and $19,600 of income. To keep our example simple, we ignore federal, state, and local income taxes.

Access to social security benefits results in a significant change in the budget constraint. If no work is performed, it is now possible to consume $7,200 worth of market goods each year. The constraint rises at a rate of $8 per hour, but a kink occurs at 500 hours of work (8,260 hours of leisure) because if more work is performed, the $4,000 limit on wage income becomes effective. After 500 hours are worked each year, social security benefits are reduced by $.50 for each additional dollar of earnings until no benefits are received at all. This means that the budget constraint is not as steep over the range between 500 hours of work (8,260 hours of leisure) and 1,400 hours of work (7,360 hours of leisure). That is, after working 500 hours in a year, the next 900 hours of work (at $8 per hour) increase income by only $3,600 ($4 per hour) because the $3,600 in social security benefit is being reduced by

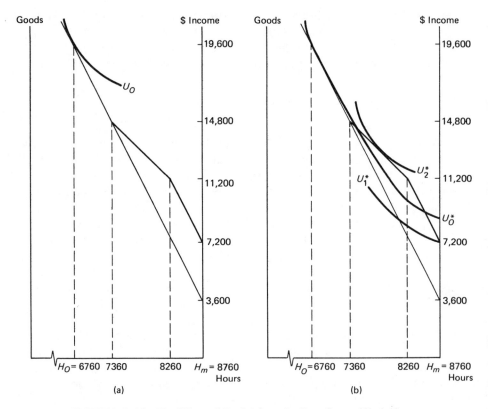

FIGURE 4–15. The Effect of Social Security Benefits on Work Hours

$.50 for each $1 in wages. An individual who works 1,400 hours receives wage income of $14,800—the $3,600 social security benefit has been entirely replaced by $3,600 in earnings over and above the $4,000 in wage income allowed before benefits are reduced. For market work exceeding 1,400 hours per year, income once again rises at the market wage rate of $8 per hour, so there is a second kink in the budget constraint at 7,360 hours of leisure.

The labor supply effect of social security legislation on hours of work depends on the provisions of the program (for example, maximum benefits and maximum allowable labor income before benefits are reduced), the market wage rate, and preferences for goods vs. leisure as reflected in the utility function. Given the nature of the program and the market wage rate as specified in the example outlined above, individual differences in preferences will determine what happens to hours of work. In Figure 4–15a, the indifference curve (U_o) tangent to the budget constraint at 2,000 hours of work lies completely above the budget constraint as determined by social security legislation. This is because the home wage falls rapidly as fewer hours are worked and more allocated to nonmarket activities. Therefore, there will be no change in hours of work as a result of the availability of social security benefits. The worker depicted in Figure 4–15a will neither want to retire nor reduce work hours. You should be able to see, however, that if maximum allowable labor income were increased, then the kinked portion of the post-social security budget constraint would lie at a higher level of income, possibly rising above indifference curve U_o. Then the individual depicted in Figure 4–15a will respond to the availability of benefits by working fewer hours.

In Figure 4–15b, the indifference curve (U_o^*) tangent to the budget constraint at 2,000 hours of work falls below the budget constraint as determined by social security legislation. Its steepness indicates that as more time is allocated to leisure, the home wage does not decline rapidly. Therefore, the availability of social security benefits makes a sharp reduction in work hours relatively attractive. U_2^* represents the higher level of utility achievable by taking advantage of social security benefits and working less. However, it may not be feasible for a worker to reduce hours of work so severely and still keep a job. Employers may be reluctant to allow part of their work force to spend, say, only 15 hours a week on the job while other employees work 40 hours. (Certain aspects of employers' preferences in determining work hours are treated in Chapter 3.) Therefore, the worker who desires to take advantage of social security benefits may be forced to make an all or nothing decision: either quit to retire (or possibly find a new part-time job), or forego social security. In Figure 4–15b the indifference curve U_1^* passing through $7,200 income and zero work hours (retirement), is lower than U_o^*. Therefore this worker will not retire if the employer will not allow individual employees arbitrarily to reduce the number of hours worked per week. (You should be able to draw the indifference curves to demonstrate the case in which the worker will retire.)

One policy implication of the analysis of the effect of current social security legislation on hours of work is similar to that discussed previously with respect to income-maintenance programs. Insofar as we are concerned with the well-being of older individuals in society, it may be good to consider the impact on mental and physical health of complete withdrawal from the labor force. Current legislation, through the ceiling on maximum monthly labor income (but not on income from nonlabor sources), reduces the effective market wage rate over a broad range of work hours for many members of the labor force, thus inducing retirement among many who would prefer to remain on the job if they could increase their incomes sufficiently by doing so. Modification of the social security system to reduce the implicit tax on labor earnings would increase work incentives for these people. Although such modification would increase the amount of social security benefits paid to workers who remain on the job, the increases would be offset (perhaps completely) by a reduction in the number of retirees who receive the maximum benefit for which they are eligible.

Evidence on Labor Supply

The short-run theory of the labor supply is one of the most widely tested and applied parts of the economic theory of labor markets. Recall that short-run labor supply theory does not deal with decisions about the accumulation of human capital—education, training, and so on—which are treated later in this book. Rather, it refers to decisions made about when and how much to work, given the quality of labor. Of course, decisions about when and how much to work cannot be separated completely from decisions about the accumulation of human capital, because choosing the age at which market work begins in earnest is connected with decisions about education and training (both formal and on the job). Nevertheless, since it generally pays to acquire education and training early in life, most decisions about hours of work, temporary withdrawal from the labor force, and retirement are made after decisions about education and training. These work decisions are, of course, influenced by prior schooling and training choices, which are reflected in the budget constraint through the wage rate and nonlabor income.

Experimental Data: The New Jersey Experiment.   Labor supply is one of the few kinds of economic behavior that have been subjected to "experimental" studies. As we mentioned in Chapter 2, most of the social sciences as well as many of the natural sciences must rely on nonexperimental information. In an experimental situation, considerable effort is devoted to hold constant all influences on the form of behavior to be studied except that of the variable whose effect we may be interested in. This is difficult enough to accomplish in a laboratory situation, but it is extremely costly and perhaps impossible to achieve when the individuals studied are free to conduct their lives as they see fit without unusual restraint on their freedom of action.

One of the best-known and most widely studied experiments in economic research, which illustrates the inherent difficulties in such attempts, was The New Jersey negative income tax experiment.[8] Since the New Jersey experiment bears on the application of labor supply theory to income-maintenance

---

[8]More detailed summaries of the New Jersey experiment are contained in "Symposium Articles—The Graduated Work Incentive Experiment," *Journal of Human Resources*, 9 (spring 1974), and Joseph A. Pechman and P. Michael Timpane, *Work Incentives and Income Guarantees: The New Jersey Negative Income Tax Experiment* (Washington, D.C.: The Brookings Institution, 1975). For a critical review of earlier studies and new estimates, see John F. Cogan, *Negative Income Taxation and Labor Supply: New Evidence from the New Jersey–Pennsylvania Experiment* (Santa Monica, Calif.: Rand Corporation, 1978), R2155-HEW.

schemes as well as being an example of an attempted social experiment, it is worth discussing at some length before we go on to look at nonexperimental evidence. A *negative income tax* is a plan whereby the federal government would guarantee every family a minimum income (say $4,500) dependent on family size, but independent of whether anyone in the family works or is capable of working. Income from any other source, however, would be "taxed" at some rate. For example, for every dollar of wage income received above the guarantee level of $4,500, the amount of income received from the government would fall by $.50—an implicit tax of 50 percent.

The New Jersey negative income tax experiment involved 1,300 families who were assigned either to experimental or control groups. Those in the experimental group were guaranteed (over roughly a three-year period beginning in 1968) various minimum income levels and subjected to a tax on income from all other sources ranging from 30 to 70 percent. The control group received nothing. The purpose of the experiment was to discover whether cash allowances whose net benefits decline as work income increases have an appreciable effect on work effort. In principle, the answer to this question can also be inferred from nonexperimental data, since it is possible to observe the work behavior of families who differ in wage rates and non-employment income. These differences shift the budget constraint in the same way as a negative income tax, and the response of work hours and labor force participation to differences in market wage rates and nonemploy ment income levels therefore ought to be the same as to comparable manipulation of tax rates and minimum benefit levels in a negative income tax program. Unfortunately, the results of numerous studies of nonexperimental data do not all agree as to what the disincentive effects of a negative income tax on working people would be. Therefore, the New Jersey experiment was attempted.

Experience with the experiment points up the difficulty in achieving sufficient control over unwanted influences even in experimental situations. It would have been morally objectionable to restrain the freedom of participants in the experiment other than to require that as a condition of participating, they report income and work behavior truthfully and regularly. Thus, participants were free to take advantage of alternative income-maintenance programs offered by the State of New Jersey. While potential participants were not eligible for New Jersey aid initially, an unforeseen change in state legislation made it attractive for some program participants to opt for state aid. Employed fathers who previously had been ineligible for state aid became eligible under certain circumstances. This created difficulties in evaluating the experimental results that have not been resolved. There is another difficulty with the New Jersey experiment of a more fundamental sort. The experiment lasted a much shorter period of time than would have been desired to test the effects on work incentives of an income-maintenance scheme expected by participants to last indefinitely. Participants were aware that at the end of three years they would face a different effective wage rate and access to nonemployment income. The effect of this knowledge on behavior is uncertain, but it is likely that workers who had a firm commitment to labor force activity would be reluctant to give up good jobs in order to take advantage of their new opportunities during the experiment, because they might find it difficult to regain equivalent jobs when the experiment was over. Alternatively, other workers, less firmly attached to the labor market, might find it attractive to withdraw from market work during the period their effective wage rates were temporarily low because of the experimental negative income tax.

Partly because of these difficulties, the results of the New Jersey experiment did not provide clear-cut evidence on the work-disincentive effects of a negative income tax. Among white families, there was a slight tendency for husbands to reduce their market work and a greater tendency for wives to do so. However, there were puzzling differences in responses to the various plans (income guarantee–tax rate combinations) within the experiment and among ethnic groups (white, black, and Spanish-speaking families). Therefore, the experiment cannot be said to have provided a definitive test of labor supply theory or of its implications for the work disincentives of alternative income-maintenance programs. Before leaving this topic, one further aspect of the experiment should be emphasized. The experiment was designed to measure only the *disincentive* effects of a negative income tax income-maintenance program on families whose heads were not already taking advantage of income support. As we saw above, one application of labor supply theory implies that a negative income tax with a relatively modest tax rate (say 50 percent) would encourage market work among those who currently participate in a plan or group of plans that tax income at rates near 100 percent. Thus, the total effect of a negative income tax plan would consist of the *reduction* in work effort of families who would not have been supported by some income-maintenance program otherwise and the *additional* market work of families whose effective tax on earnings is reduced by replacing present welfare schemes with the negative income tax.

Nonexperimental Data.   Much greater effort has been devoted to studying labor supply behavior by means of nonexperimental data—information available from surveys and censuses of the normal activities of business firms and households. As we have said, the way in which nonexperimental data are used is to compare labor supply behavior among individuals or groups of individuals who have different wage rates, nonemployment income, and different values of other variables that affect labor supply. The trick in drawing valid conclusions based on nonexperimental data is to make sure that all the intercorrelated influences on the behavior to be studied have been accounted for (see Chapter 2). For example, differences in labor supply among individuals or groups may be studied either over time or among individuals or groups at a moment of time. Both kinds of observations are

subject to the problem that a major correlate of wage rate and income differences is differences in the amount of education and other forms of human
capital. Thus, it is an open question whether we can legitimately claim to be
testing a short-run theory of labor supply, the response of the amount worked
to wage and income changes, when the amount of human capital per person
is also variable. In some studies attempts have been made to estimate the
effects of wage rates and incomes holding education (but not explicitly other
forms of human capital) constant; in others, this has not been done. Therefore, the reader should bear in mind that the estimated effects of wage rates
and incomes on the amount of labor supplied must be interpreted with
caution as evidence bearing on the short-run theory of labor supply responses
to permanent wage and income levels. (The importance of measuring permanent changes in wage rates is discussed on pp. 26–27 of Chapter 2.)

LABOR FORCE PARTICIPATION

The concept of labor force participation deals with the labor supply in a
categorical sense; that is, in discussing labor force participation, we treat the
question of whether an individual offers any hours at all to the labor market.
By official definition, any individual who worked at least one hour or was
unemployed during the survey week is considered to participate in the labor
force. The proportion of a group who participate in the labor force at any
moment of time is the labor force participation rate. As Table 4–1 shows, the

TABLE 4–1

Labor Force Participation Rates, 1900–1970

Year	Total Civilian Labor Force*	Males 65 and Over	Married Women
1900	50.2%	63.1%	05.6%
1920	50.3	56.6	09.0
1930	49.5	54.0	11.7
1940	52.9	41.2	15.6
1950	54.1	41.4	23.0
1960	56.1	31.5	31.7
1970	59.0	24.8	40.2
1977	62.3	20.1	46.6

*1900–30, persons 10 years old and over; 1940–60, 14 years old and over; 1970, persons
16 years old and over.

Source: Historical Statistics of the United States, Colonial Times to 1970, Part 1, Series D11,
D35, D60. Figures for 1977 are from the Employment and Training Report of the President 1978,
Tables A–1 and A–4. They are not based on the same data as the decennial census figures and are
not strictly comparable with them.

relatively stable proportion of the population performing some market work masks marked changes in labor force composition that have taken place over the years. For example, while the overall labor force participation rate of the civilian population has risen moderately, that of married women has risen by 600 percent and that of men 65 years of age and older has fallen by 60 percent. In the next few pages, we will explore the forces impinging on the labor force participation of married women in some detail.

The most striking change in labor force participation during this century has been that of married women. The increase once seemed paradoxical because it occurred in the presence of rising income levels. This seemed to contradict the observation that among families at a moment in time, the labor force participation rate of married women is lower, the higher the income received by husbands. The relationship between wives' labor force participation and husband's income is shown as it existed in 1960 in Table 4–2. It stands out most clearly when women 20 to 44 years old are studied separately, since the low-income groups among all wives tend also to have a large proportion of the elderly, who have low labor force participation for reasons discussed above. Table 4–2 also shows how children affect the labor force participation of married women. The theory of labor force participation suggests that by reducing the effective amount of time available when mothers work in the labor market, the presence of young children reduces participation. The loss of effective time results in an increase in the home wage

TABLE 4–2

Labor Force Participation Rates of Married Women, Husband Present, March 1960, by Presence and Age of Children and Income of Husband in 1959 (Percent)

		Wives 20–44 Years Old			
Income of Husband	All Wives 14 Years Old and Older	Total	No Children under 18 Years	Children 6 to 17 Years Old Only	Children under 6 Years
Total	30%	32%	59%	40%	19%
Under $2,000	30	41	54	53	29
$2,000–$2,999	32	37	64	48	24
$3,000–$4,999	36	37	63	49	22
$5,000–$6,999	30	29	60	38	17
$7,000–$9,999	25	21	51	32	9
$10,000 and over	16	15	*	19	8

*The number of observations is less than the minimum required for sampling reliability.

Source: Glen G. Cain, *Married Women in the Labor Force* (Chicago: University of Chicago Press, 1966), p. 3. Reprinted by permission of The University of Chicago Press.

rate, so that at given market wage rates women are less likely to participate in the labor force when young children are at home.[9]

A major breakthrough in understanding the determinants of the labor force participation of married women occurred when Jacob Mincer noted that while family income levels have surely risen, market wage rates received by married women have grown, too, and this has tended to draw wives into the labor market.[10] Mincer found that the positive effect of rising wage rates has been larger than the negative effect of rising family income levels. Following Mincer's study, Glen Cain, and William Bowen and T. Aldrich Finegan explored the determinants of the labor force participation of married women in great depth.[11] Both studies confirmed the essential features of Mincer's findings—that the *net* effect of rising wage rates and family income levels has been to increase the labor force participation rate of married women.

Some representative results of Cain's study are shown in the top half of Table 4–3. In Cain's study, the effects of wage rates and income on labor force participation are reflected in the coefficients of the income of wives who worked 50 to 52 weeks in 1949 (w) and of husbands' incomes (y), respectively. If we examine Cain's regression reported in Table 4–3, which contains only the variables representing wives' and husbands' income, we find that the estimated effect of a $100 increase in husbands' incomes is to reduce the labor force participation of wives by the regression coefficient of husbands' income—0.3 percentage points. The estimated wage effect of a $100 increase in the income of women who worked 50 to 52 weeks, holding husbands' income constant, is to raise the labor force participation rate of married women by about 1.3 percentage points.

Table 4–3 also shows regression results that represent an attempt to estimate the influence of additional variables influencing the labor force participation of married women. If the influence of such variables is not estimated simultaneously with that of income and earning power, the estimated effects of incomes and earning power may reflect these other influences as well, because the variables affecting labor force participation are rather highly intercorrelated. The additional variables used in Cain's study are the median years of schooling completed by females aged 25 years and older, the unem-

---

[9]Of course, family decisions to have children are not independent of the decision on how much market work the wife will perform. These are simultaneous decisions in the long run. See, for example, R. J. Willis, "A New Approach to the Economic Theory of Fertility Behavior," *Journal of Political Economy* (March–April 1973); and Belton M. Fleisher and George F. Rhodes, Jr., "Fertility, Women's Wage Rates, and Labor Supply," *American Economic Review*, 69, 1 (March 1979).

[10]Jacob Mincer, "Labor Force Participation of Married Women," in *Aspects of Labor Economics* (Princeton, N.J.: Princeton University Press, 1962).

[11]Glen G. Cain, *Married Women in the Labor Force* (Chicago: University of Chicago Press, 1966); William G. Bowen and T. Aldrich Finegan, *The Economics of Labor Force Participation* (Princeton, N.J.: Princeton University Press, 1969).

TABLE 4–3

Regression Results: Labor Force Participation
of Married Women in 1950 and 1970

	y	w	e	u	c	R^2
1950						
Regression coefficient	−0.84	1.48	0.95	−0.56	−0.53	0.56
Elasticity at means	−1.31	1.49				
Standard error	(0.31)	(0.35)	(0.45)	(0.26)	(0.16)	
Regression coefficient	−0.30	1.29				0.38
Elasticity at means	−0.47	1.26				
Standard error	(0.29)	(0.31)				
1970						
Regression coefficient	−0.17	0.39	0.31	−1.7	−0.32	0.43
Elasticity at means	−0.34	0.43				
Standard error	(0.063)	(0.12)	(0.081)	(0.25)	(0.15)	
Regression coefficient	−0.20	0.40				
Elasticity at means	−0.40	0.45				0.072
Standard error	(1.077)	(0.13)				

Definitions:
1950
y: Median income (in hundreds of dollars) in 1949 of male family heads, wife present.
w: Median income (in hundreds of dollars) in 1949 of females who worked 50 to 52 weeks.
e: Median years of schooling completed by females ages 25 years and older.
u: Male unemployment rate (in percentage).
Dependent Variable: Labor force participation rate (in percentages) of married women living with their husbands for standard metropolitan areas in the North with populations 250,000 and over.

Source: Glen G. Cain, *Married Women in the Labor Force* (Chicago: University of Chicago Press, 1966), p. 23. Reprinted by Permission of The University of Chicago Press.

1970
y: Median earnings (in hundreds of dollars) of married men ages 14 and over who worked 50 to 52 weeks in 1969.
w: Median earnings (in hundreds of dollars) of women ages 14 and over who worked 50 to 52 weeks in 1969.
e: Percentage of women over 25 years of age with more than 12 years' schooling in 1970.
c: Percent of married women ages 16 to 59 who have children under 6 years old living at home.
u: Civilian unemployment rate, census week 1970 (percentage).
Dependent variable: Labor force Participation rate (in percentages) of married women living with their husbands, ages 16–59, for 99 SMSAS with population 250,000 and over.

Source: *U.S. Census of Population*, 1970.

ployment rate of males, and the fraction of husband-wife families with at least one child under 6 years of age. Education is presumed to reflect the tendency of highly educated people to be employed in jobs with relatively high nonmonetary benefits; other things being equal, such benefits are hypothesized to raise the amount of labor supplied.[12] The coefficient of education—0.95—implies that an increase by one year in the median level of schooling of females aged 25 years and over increases labor force participation by 0.95 percentage points.

The coefficient of the unemployment rate sheds light on the important issue of whether fluctuations in the demand for labor induce, on balance, net increases or decreases in the size of the labor force. The unemployment rate is supposed to represent the general state of demand for labor, which varies from city to city because areas are affected differently by occasional fluctuations in the general level of business activity and by the rises and declines of different industries. Unfortunately, differences among cities in labor *supply* conditions may also affect the unemployment rate, and this simultaneous equation problem (see Chapter 11) makes it extremely difficult to interpret the regression coefficient of unemployment in regressions like those of Table 4–3. An increase in unemployment has a direct effect on family income: it reduces the income of the family temporarily below its normal level. In order to maintain consumption at a level consistent with normal income, families experiencing unemployment may resort to drawing on savings, or to borrowing if their credit is good. Family members (specifically wives in the studies represented in Table 4–3) who typically do not hold jobs may attempt to find them. This is called *the added worker effect* of unemployment. However, increases in the level of unemployment also result in increased difficulty in finding work. This in turn influences the amount of labor supplied in the same way as a wage rate reduction, because an increase in the difficulty of finding work at any wage rate reduces the attractiveness of seeking employment. The impact of increased difficulty is called the *discouraged worker effect*, and it reduces the likelihood of a person's being in the labor force. Therefore, when unemployment rates are high, the added worker effect operates to force more wives than usual into the labor force, while the discouraged worker effect pushes in the opposite direction, inducing some wives who would like jobs to give up the search and no longer be counted as labor force participants.

The regression coefficient of unemployment in Cain's study is −0.56, implying that the discouraged worker effect outweighs the added worker effect for wives living with their husbands. A 1 percentage point difference in the unemployment rate is associated on the average with a 0.56 percentage

---

[12]Moreover, individuals who plan to perform a relatively large amount of market work will find it to their advantage to acquire more schooling. Therefore, schooling may also reflect a greater tendency to work in the market, all other things being equal.

point difference in the participation rate in the opposite direction. The dominance of the discouraged worker effect over the added worker effect is borne out in other studies of the labor force behavior of married women, and it is also probably typical of the behavior of fringe or marginal labor force groups, such as youth and the elderly. There is considerable disagreement, however, regarding the amount by which the discouraged worker effect outweighs the income effect and the overall importance of the effect of unemployment on labor force participation.[13]

We have already discussed the effect of young children on the labor force participation of married women. The coefficient of the variable representing the presence of children under 6 years of age is negative, as hypothesized, implying that a 1 percentage point increase in the fraction of such families is associated on the average with a 0.53 percentage point reduction in the labor force participation rate of married women. When Cain's 1950 study is repeated using 1970 data, once again the signs of all regression coefficients remain unchanged, but substantial differences in magnitudes occur. When the additional variables are included, not only is the wife's wage effect much smaller than in 1950, but the effect of husband's income is also much smaller. Indeed, all the 1970 coefficients are smaller than their 1950 counterparts, with the exception of the coefficient of unemployment, which is much larger.[14] The explanatory power of both 1970 regressions as measured by R^2 is smaller than that of the 1950 regressions, especially when husband's income and wife's earning power are the only explanatory variables. Evidently, the influence of the wage rate and family income on the labor force participation of married women has fallen over the years, while that of other variables has risen. Why this should be so is a topic worthy of further research.

How valid are the results of these cross-sectional studies? Do they provide reliable information on the causes of variation in the participation of married women? One way to answer this question is to see how well the regression coefficients can account for the phenomenal increase in the labor force participation of married women over time when they are multiplied by the change over time in their respective variables. In conducting this test of validity, we will use the results of the regressions in which only y and w are

---

[13]When the effect of unemployment on labor force participation is estimated using data that varies over time for the entire economy, such as quarterly (three-month) averages of labor force participation and unemployment, the resulting estimates are much smaller. See, for instance, Jacob Mincer, "Labor Force Participation and Unemployment: A Review of Recent Evidence," in R. A. and M. S. Gordon, eds., *Prosperity and Unemployment* (New York: Wiley, 1966), pp. 91–98; Bowen and Finegan, *The Economics of Labor Force Participation*, Chap. 16; and Belton M. Fleisher and George F. Rhodes, Jr., "Labor Force Participation of Married Men and Women: A Simultaneous Model," *Review of Economics and Statistics*, 58 (November 1976), 398–406.

[14]A similar change over time based on a study using a somewhat larger set of variables is reported by Judith M. Fields in a note entitled "A Comparison of Intercity Differences in the Labor Force Participation Rates of Married Women in 1970 and 1940, 1950, and 1960," *Journal of Human Resources*, 11 (fall 1976), 568–77.

the independent variables. There are two principal reasons for this: (1) As we have mentioned, variables such as number of children, unemployment, and desired schooling levels may themselves be affected by labor force participation decisions; causality may run in both directions with these variables; (2) the theory of labor supply is more precisely and simply developed in terms of wages and income levels than when other variables must be considered. It is therefore worth knowing whether such a simple theory can actually explain observed behavior.

Cain performed the test of "explaining" the change in labor force participation rates between 1939 and 1957 with the 1950 regression coefficients he obtained for y and w for white and black married women separately.[15] For white women, the actual increase in the labor force participation rate was 15 percentage points, while the "predicted" change obtained by multiplying the change in y and w between 1939 and 1957 by their respective regression coefficients is 10 percentage points. The actual change for black women over this period was 10 percentage points, while the predicted change was either 7 or 5.6 percentage points, depending on which of two alternative wife's earnings measures is used. Thus, between 56 and 70 percent of the increase in the labor force participation of married women over the period can be attributed to the combined influence of wife's wage and husband's income, when the effects of these variables are measured by Cain's 1950 regression results. When these same results are applied to the increase in the labor force participation of all women over 14 years of age over a later time period—1948 to 1965—similar degree of explanation is achieved.[16]

Unfortunately, the 1970 regression results reported in Table 4–3 cast some doubt on our ability to explain labor force participation. The problem is that the 1970 regression results indicate a much smaller effect on wife's wage rate relative to husband's income than do those based on 1950 data. Thus, when the 1970 regression coefficients are applied to the change over time in their respective variables, the predicted rise in the labor force participation rate of married women is negligible. The labor force participation rate of married women did not stop growing in 1965. It rose about 6 percentage points between 1965 and 1970 and another 3.6 percentage points by March 1975.[17] The 1970 wage and income coefficients fall far short of being able to account for the increase in labor force participation during the periods we have already examined and for the continued increase during these most recent periods as well. Economists have not yet come to grips with this challenge. The question that needs to be answered is this: "Has there been a change over the past twenty years in the forces at work driving up the labor force

---

[15]Cain, *Married Women*, pp. 86–87.

[16]The income and wage data are contained in Bowen and Finegan, *The Economics of Labor Force Participation*, p. 583, while the labor force participation data are from *The Manpower Report of the President*, 1975, Table B-2.

[17]*Employment and Training Report of the President 1976*, Table B-2.

participation of married women, or are the forces the same but revealed more clearly in the 1950 regressions than in the 1970 regressions?"

HOURS OF WORK

Once the choice to perform some market work has been made, the labor supply decision involves choosing the desired number of hours. In theory this choice is influenced by the worker's market wage rate, the wages that can be earned by other family members, and income from nonemployment sources. As we have seen, when there is an increase in the worker's own wage rate, it is theoretically uncertain whether desired hours of work will rise or fall. In contrast to its effects on labor force participation, an increase in the market wage influences hours of work through an income effect as well as a substitution effect. Since the income effect on hours of market work is likely to be negative, the overall influence of a wage increase on desired work hours may also be negative if the income effect is large enough to offset the theoretically positive substitution effect. The question we ask in this section is whether the theory of labor supply helps us understand the behavior of hours of work in the United States. In particular, we focus on what we call the "full-time" work week—weekly hours worked by family members who are the principal sources of market earnings for their families.

Before going on to answer this question, we should consider some possible objections to viewing hours of work simply as a labor supply phenomenon. To what extent is it reasonable to suppose that observed work hours represent only the equilibrium choices of individuals responding to their opportunities (wage rates), given their other economic circumstances, tastes, and attitudes? After all, is it not likely that these data also represent employer preferences, technological constraints, collective bargaining, and wage and hours legislation? To be sure, employer preferences and technological constraints may be important in some occupations, and it would certainly be inefficient for employers to have work forces composed of personnel who at any moment of time work different numbers of hours per week at their own discretion and who change the number of hours worked at will. Employers are not likely to ignore the extra hiring and training costs that result when more workers are required to offset a declining work week. Thus, labor *demand* as well as *supply* may influence observed hours of work. As we will see, employers' interests may well have influenced the length of the average full-time work week in the second half of this century. As far as wages and hours legislation is concerned, the federal Fair Labor Standards Act (FLSA), requiring an overtime premium for work hours exceeding 40 per week, became effective in 1938. Hours of work in most industries fell substantially throughout the early part of this century and cannot therefore be attributed to FLSA. A similar argument applies to the effects of trade unions, which did not cover an important proportion of the labor force (and then never much more than half of all production workers, as we shall see later on) until after most of this century's decline in the length of the work week had already occurred.

When hours of work data are examined, it becomes clear that the decline in weekly hours of work is one of the most dramatic economic changes of this century. Table 4–4 shows average weekly hours in three important and representative industries—manufacturing, building trades, and retail trade.[18] It also shows the economywide data on the "standard" (full-time) work week constructed by Clarence Long for the years 1890–1950. All these series confirm a substantial decline in average weekly hours of work through 1940. This decline has been interpreted as a supply response to rising wage rates and income levels,[19] an interpretation with which we are inclined to agree. But in order to have confidence in this view, we need to explain why, in 1940 or thereabouts, the decline in weekly hours of work seems abruptly to have ceased.

The task of solving the puzzle of the halt in the decline of the full-time work week has been undertaken by Thomas Kniesner.[20] Kniesner's solution demonstrates the importance of distinguishing between short-run and long-run labor supply decisions. As we pointed out earlier, the labor supply theory presented in this chapter is essentially a short-run theory, explaining the response of labor force participation and hours of work to changes in the market wage rate. By distinguishing between short run and long run, we mean that wage changes caused by worker decisions to acquire additional schooling or training influence work-leisure choices in a different way than do wage changes caused by other forces (such as an increase in the demand for labor of a given quality).[21] Why should this be so? One reason is that individuals who increase their market earning power through further schooling are already expressing a commitment to market work. This should lead us to expect that for a given wage rate, workers with greater schooling will probably work longer hours than other workers. Moreover, those jobs to which

---

[18]In 1960, these industries accounted for the following proportions of production workers in nonagricultural industries of the United States: manufacturing, 31 percent; building trades as represented by contract construction, 5.3 percent; retail trade, 15.5 percent. *Statistical Abstract of the United States, 1967*, pp. 227–28.

[19]See, for example, H. G. Lewis, "Hours of Work and Hours of Leisure, *Proceedings of the Ninth Annual Winter Meeting, the Industrial Relations Research Association* (December 1956), 196–206.

[20]"The Full-Time Workweek in the United States, 1900–1970," *Industrial and Labor Relations Review*, October 1976.

[21]Please bear in mind that the long-run–short-run distinction does not necessarily denote a distinction between long and short periods of time. A long-run decision does indeed involve a choice affecting an individual over a longer, rather than a shorter, time period. Thus, the decision to complete high school will affect the course of someone's entire life. On the other hand, rising wage rates over a long period of time, such as thirty years, may or may not have anything to do with decisions workers have made in the past to acquire schooling or training, although such wage increases will probably affect short-run decisions on desired hours of work and labor force participation.

TABLE 4–4

Average Weekly Hours in Manufacturing and Selected
Nonmanufacturing Industries, 1890–1975*

	(1) Manufacturing		(2) Building Trades and Building Construction		(3) Retail Trade	(4) Hours in Standard Work Week
Year	(a)	(b)	(a)	(b)		
1890	62.2	—	51.3	—	—	—
1895	62.3	—	50.3	—	—	66
1896	62.1	—	—	—	—	—
1897	61.9	—	—	—	—	—
1898	62.2	—	—	—	—	—
1899	62.1	—	—	—	—	—
1900	62.1	—	48.3	—	—	62
1905	61.1	—	46.1	—	—	—
1910	53.5	—	45.2	—	—	57
1915	58.2	—	44.8	—	—	—
1920	53.5	47.4	43.8	—	—	53
1925	52.2	44.5	43.9	—	—	—
1930	—	42.1	—	—	—	52
1935	—	36.6	—	30.1	—	—
1940	—	38.1	—	33.1	43.2	43
1945	—	43.4	—	39.0	40.9	—
1946	—	40.4	—	38.1	41.6	—
1950	—	40.5	—	37.4	40.0	41
1955	—	40.7	—	37.1	39.0	—
1959	—	40.3	—	37.0	38.2	—
1960	—	39.7	—	36.7	38.0	—
1967	—	—	—	37.7	35.3	—
1968	—	—	—	37.4	34.7	—
1969	—	—	—	—	34.2	—
1970	—	39.2	—	37.4	33.8	—
1975	—	39.4	—	36.6	32.4	—

*1975 data from *Monthly Labor Review*, January 1977, p. 86.

Source: Historical Statistics of the United States, Colonial Times to 1970. (1a) Series D 769 (data from employer payrolls). (1b) Series D 803 (production workers). This series may be understated because large firms are oversampled. (2a) Series D 774 (union hours). (2b) Series D 78 (non-supervisory workers, building construction). (3) Series D-884. (4) Clarence D. Long, *The Labor Force under Changing Income and Employment* (Princeton, N.J.: Princeton University Press, 1958), p. 272.

comparatively well-educated workers have access are traditionally relatively pleasant, in that working conditions are better, the tasks more interesting, and so on. This factor also would increase hours of market work, all other things being equal.

Still another force differently influencing the long-run and the short-run relationship between wage rates and work hours operates from the demand side of the labor market. As we mentioned above, employers may not view a reduction in hours of work per employee as costless, because in order to obtain the same number of total work hours, more workers must be employed. As we shall see in Chapter 9, employers tend to invest more money in searching for and training better-educated workers. Therefore, as schooling increases, so does employers' resistance to a reduced work week. This means that as workers acquire more years of schooling, they are likely to find they are offered higher wage rates, but they will also find that these higher rates of pay are more readily obtained if they are willing to put in more rather than fewer hours of work per week.

Thus, when wage rate increases are due to rising schooling levels, we should expect there to be a different association with hours of work than when the increases are attributable to other forces. Kniesner found that the long-run–short-run distinction is indeed important in accounting for the leveling off in the length of the work week after 1940, and that the major force modifying the effect of wage rates on hours of work has been the rising level of education of the population. Between 1910 and 1940, median years of schooling completed by persons age 25 and over rose from 8.1 to 8.6. This represents a rate of increase of about 0.2 percent per year in level of schooling. The median level of schooling soared to 12 years by 1970, an annual rate of increase of 1.1 percent. At the same time, the rate of growth of wage rates (corrected for price level changes) also accelerated, but not by nearly as much. Between 1910 and 1940, the average real hourly wage rate in manufacturing rose by about 2.6 percent annually, while between 1940 and 1960 the annual rate of growth was about 3.0 percent.[22] Thus, the relative influence of schooling on hours of work may well have increased over the years. When the influences of schooling, wife's earning power, and unemployment rates on hours of work are held constant, Kniesner estimates a relationship between weekly hours of work and real hourly earnings in manufacturing of -0.5 in elasticity terms; this relationship holds for years both before and after 1940. Since an additional year of schooling is estimated to increase the average work week by one hour, the approximately 3.5-year increase in median years of schooling since 1940 has had a substantial offsetting effect to rising hourly wage rates. If there had not been the acceleration in years of schooling com-

---

[22]Thomas J. Kniesner, "Recent Behavior of the 'Full-Time' Workweek in the U.S." (Unpublished Ph.D. dissertation, The Ohio State University, 1974), Appendix A.

pleted among members of the labor ,force, the full-time work week would probably have continued to decline after 1940 about as rapidly, in percentage terms, as it did before.

It is most interesting to speculate on the causes of the acceleration in educational attainment of the labor force after 1940. Although we cannot offer an explanation of this trend, we can account for much of it by examining what happened in the economy twenty years earlier. According to Easterlin, in the 1920s and 1930s there was an expansion of secondary (high school) education in the United States that surpassed any advances made in the preceding hundred years.[23] Moreover, European migration was largely curtailed in the mid-1920s by legislation, and by the time the increasingly well-educated young people of the twenties and thirties entered the labor force, they were the principal source of labor force growth in the United States.

LABOR SUPPLY FUNCTIONS DERIVED

What happens to the quantity of labor supplied when there is an increase in wage rates? The answer to this question tells us what the labor supply curve looks like. As we have seen, derivation of the labor supply curve depends upon what other variables are being held constant when the wage rate changes and in which population group we are interested. The labor supply curve also depends on whether we are examining the effect of economywide variation in wage rates or changes in only one industry or local labor market. Here, we will summarize briefly what theory and evidence on the short-run labor supply tell us about the relationship between market wage rates and the quantity of market work offered by households.

The Economywide Labor Supply.   When there is a change in the economy-wide average rate of pay for market work, two types of labor supply responses are elicited: There will be changes in decisions regarding whether to engage in any market work at all, and those individuals already participating in the labor force may wish to adjust their work hours. The major source of variation in labor force participation has come from married women, who have substantially increased their labor force participation in response to historically rising wage rates. However, rising wage rates also imply higher levels of family income, and in response to this change, the participation of older workers has declined. The net effect of rising wage rates on the labor force participation of all groups has been a significant increase in the proportion of the population engaged in labor market activity. Between 1870 and 1970,

---

[23]Richard A. Easterlin, *Population, Labor Force, and Long Swings in Economic Growth* (New York and London: National Bureau of Economic Research, 1968), p. 64.

the total labor force participation rate in the United States has risen from 44.3 percent to 59.0 percent.

At the same time, average work hours of "full time" workers have declined, offsetting the rising participation rate. The net change in the supply of market labor is the outcome of these two opposite trends, along with what has happened to the work hours of "part time" workers. We do not have the space to evaluate fully the overall response of the quantity of labor supplied to rising wage rates, but it appears that the economy's labor supply curve is not as elastic as the behavior of hours of work or labor force participation suggest taken by themselves.

The Labor Supply to Industries and Local Labor Markets. The labor supply response to a change in the average wage rate in a single industry or labor market is theoretically not the same as that in the economy as a whole. The principal reason for this difference lies in what variables are being held constant when analyzing the labor supply decision. In the case of the economywide labor supply, we focus on variation in the price of leisure while assuming no change in the relative attractiveness of employment in alternative industries or locations. Now we focus on what happens when the wage rate in a single industry or location changes, wages elsewhere in the economy remaining unchanged. The labor supply decision in this case involved choosing where to work much more than whether or how much. Assuming equality of working conditions (other than rate of pay), it is clearly in a worker's interest to obtain the highest possible wage rate. Therefore, the labor supply curve to an industry or local labor market should be positively related to the wage rate. Since changing jobs from one industry or local market to another involves costs that may be substantial, the supply of labor to industries and localities has a significant long-run aspect. The importance of the long-run–short-run distinction in comparing the labor supply of local labor markets with that of the economy will be touched on in a further discussion of evidence on the participation of married women in Chapter 5. That discussion underscores the importance of using the utmost care in applying labor supply theory to labor supply behavior.

Frontiers of Labor Supply Analysis:
The New Home Economics

Throughout this chapter, we have approached labor supply as the choice between market work and "leisure," recognizing that this distinction, although useful as a first approximation, hides much of economic interest. Recently, economists have begun to look beneath the surface of the leisure concept and explore how nonmarket activities contribute to economic well-being. One might say that the emphasis on the role of time out of the labor force constitutes an invasion by economists into the realm of home economics—and so, in a sense, it is. The essence of this "new home economics" is to place the family as an economic entity on a par with the firm, whereas traditionally the family is viewed as deriving utility from the consumption of time and market goods. The new approach recognizes that "hours" are never consumed by themselves, nor are market goods. Hours are not enjoyable without goods, and all goods require time to consume. Thus, the household is viewed as a firm that combines time and goods inputs into "commodities" which it both produces and consumes.[24] Time is required both as an input in the commodity production process and to trade in the labor market for the other essential input—market goods. Labor supply is therefore determined as the outcome of decisions on which commodities to produce, how many to produce, and how to produce them.

Although it may seem contrived at first to view the household as a firm, once you think about it, it is not really strange at all. Food (raw materials) and time are combined by the household to produce home-cooked meals or, in a more complex process, food, shopping time, preparation time, and mealtime are combined in the household to produce "nutrition." Time and market goods (tickets) are combined to yield the commodity, attending a baseball game. Numerous parental uses of time are combined with market goods such as clothing, food, schooling, medical services, and the time of children to produce "child quality." Young adults use their time and schooling to enhance their future earning power by producing "human capital" (see Chapter 8). It is intuitively appealing, then, to view the family as deriving utility from the commodities produced in the home with time and market goods inputs. The quantity of labor supplied by the family is still viewed as the complement to the quantity demanded for use in the household. The advantage of the household production approach over the simpler theory of labor supply developed earlier in this chapter is that it facilitates the systematic study of a wide variety of household activities and labor supply. Since economists feel that it is possible to understand production technology better than "tastes," the production approach allows us to explain a wide spectrum of behavior (including aspects of labor supply) with fewer special assumptions about tastes than is possible without it.

Unfortunately, the gain in understanding the intricate relationship among consumption, production, and labor supply activities is not achieved without cost. That cost is a somewhat more complex theory than when household

---

[24]Three names closely associated with the "new home economics" are Gary S. Becker, Kelvin J. Lancaster, and Robert T. Michael. See Becker's "A Theory of the Allocation of Time," *The Economic Journal*, 75 (1965), 493–517; Lancaster's "A New Approach to Consumer Theory," *Journal of Political Economy*, 74, (1966) 132–57; and Michael and Becker, "On the New Theory of Consumer Behavior," *The Swedish Journal of Economics*, 75 (1973), 378–96.

consumption activities and labor supply are viewed as unconnected processes. Thus, the outline of some of the basic features of the household production approach will not be as extensive as we would like it to be. In the next few paragraphs, we will develop some interesting topics dealt with in the study of household production and relate it to family labor supply decisions.

THE HOUSEHOLD AS A FIRM

The household production approach makes use of the analysis of the firm's demand for labor developed in Chapter 3 and integrates it with the theory of household behavior developed in this chapter. On the production side, the household is viewed as using various inputs to produce the commodities that yield satisfaction, or utility. For simplicity, we divide these inputs into two groups: time and market goods. The household's constraint, therefore, rests in the fundamentally limited amount of time available, the market wage rate, the family's nonlabor sources of market income, and the family's technology and efficiency, or productivity, in combining inputs in home production.[25]

The technology the family uses to produce commodities is described in the same way as that of a firm, by a production function relating inputs and output. Any production used to describe firm behavior may also be used to describe household behavior. To avoid making our discussion overly complicated, we will retain the essence of the household production framework but assume that household production functions are of the *fixed proportion* variety. This means that market goods and time must be used in a given proportion in the production of each commodity. The isoquants for any particular commodity then look like those in Figure 4–16.[26] To produce output level Q_1 of some commodity, goods (G) and time (T) are required. Additional units of goods cannot be substituted for time, and vice versa. Similarly, to produce output Q_2, G_2 goods and T_2 units of time are required. The ratio is $G_1/T_1 = G_2/T_2$. Since scarcity prevails, the family will minimize its production costs and will never use more goods or time than are needed

---

[25]Interfamily differences in efficiency in home production is a much neglected area of economic research, although an issue of fundamental importance in understading such serious social problems as economic and social mobility. Not all social scientists have ignored this issue, however, and the household production approach has stimulated new interest in it. Earlier studies emphasizing the importance of efficiency in household production include Wesley C. Mitchell, "The Backward Art of Spending Money," *American Economic Review*, 2, 2 (June 1912), 269–81; and Margaret G. Reid, *Economics of Household Production* (New York: Wiley, 1934).

[26]The fixed proportion production function yields the right-angle isoquants illustrated in Figure 4–16, because to produce a particular level of output, such as Q_1, it is uneconomical to use more than G_1 units of goods or T_1 units of time, since they cannot be substituted for each other. The isoquants could therefore be equally well represented simply by the points such as a and b, which represent the unique efficient input combinations for each level of output. For further information, consult C. E. Ferguson and J. P. Gould, *Microeconomic Theory*, 4th ed. (Homewood, Ill.: Irwin, 1975), pp. 150–54.

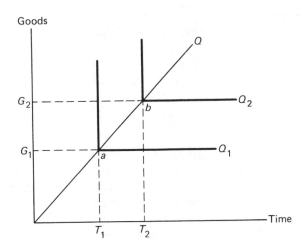

FIGURE 4–16. Household Production with Fixed Proportions

to obtain any given level of output. The only relevant points on each isoquant are therefore the minimum cost points *a* and *b*, which lie on the expansion path $0Q$.

Since with fixed proportions, changes in the relative cost of time and goods do not induce substitution between the factors of production, goods and time, the entire production process can be adequately described simply by the expansion path $0Q$, whose slope $G_1/T_1 = G_2/T_2$ denotes the factor proportions characterizing the production of this commodity. Even though factor proportions are fixed for each commodity, commodities differ in the relative amounts of goods and time used. This means, as we shall see, that a change in the wage rate, which alters the relative price of time and goods, affects relative commodity prices, consumption of the commodities, and labor supply. In Figure 4–17, two expansion paths characterizing two production functions are shown. Commodity *a*, whose production function is described by expansion path Q_a, is relatively time-intensive, with slope G_a/T_a, while the slope of expansion path Q_b, describing the production function of commodity *b*, is G_a/T_b, implying that commodity *b* is relatively goods-intensive.

HOUSEHOLD AS FIRM: A NUMERICAL EXAMPLE

A simple numerical example will show how the household production approach works. Again, we have to make fairly restrictive assumptions in order to keep the example from becoming too complex. Therefore, we assume a two-person (husband-wife) family in which the husband works "full time"

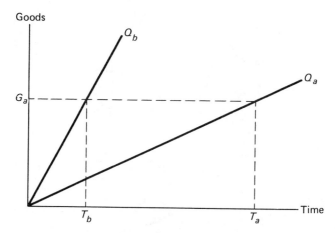

Goods

Q_b

Q_a

G_a

T_b T_a Time

FIGURE 4–17. Household Production for Two Commodities Differing in Relative Time Intensiveness

and performs no household tasks, while the wife divides her time between home production and market work. We can thus lump the husband's earnings and the family's nonemployment income together and treat it as income available to the family if the wife performs no market work. The constraint facing the household is specified by the conditions given in Table 4–5. The family's goal, similar to that in the labor supply analysis presented earlier in this chapter, is to allocate its full income ($52,300) between the relatively time-intensive commodity A and the relatively goods-intensive commodity B. The wife's labor supply decision is determined simultaneously. These interrelated decisions can be described in two steps. First, in Figure 4–18 we diagram the alternatives faced by the family in choosing how much to produce of A and B.

TABLE 4–5

Family Production: A Numerical Example

Annual income available if wife does not work	(Y)	$8,500
Wife's hourly market wage	(W)	5.00
Total time to be allocated by wife between household production and market work	(T)	8,760 hours/year
Hours required to produce one unit of commodity	$\begin{cases} A \equiv \beta_L = 4 \\ B \equiv \gamma_L = 2 \end{cases}$	
Market goods required to produce one unit of commodity	$\begin{cases} A \equiv \beta_G = \$10 \\ B \equiv \gamma_G = \$10 \end{cases}$	
Full income $= Y + WT$		$52,300

141

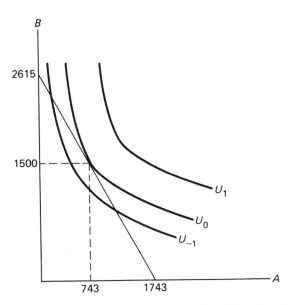

FIGURE 4–18. Household Production Possibility Frontier

Figure 4–18 shows the household's production possibility frontier for commodities A and B, based on the information given in Table 4–5. The marginal and average cost of producing one unit of A (π_A) is $\$5 \times \beta_L + \beta_G = \$5 \times 4 + \$10 = \$30$, while the marginal and average cost of B (π_B) is $\$5 \times \gamma_L + \gamma_G = \$4 \times 2 + \$10 = \$20$. If the household's full income were "spent" on B, it would be possible to obtain approximately 2,615 units of B, while only 1,743 units of A could be obtained if no B were produced, since it is more costly in terms of goods and time. The cost of A in terms of B (the slope of the production possibility frontier) is equal to the ratio of the marginal costs $\pi_A/\pi_B = 30/20 = 2615/1743 = 1.5$. For every unit of commodity A produced, 1.5 units of B must be foregone. The household's tastes for A and B are given by a family of indifference curves, one of which, U_0, is tangent to the production possibility frontier. Thus, the household maximizes its satisfaction by choosing to produce (and consume) 1,500 units of B and 743 units of A. (Note that this combination exhausts full income, since $1500 \times \$20 + 743 \times \$30 \simeq \$52,300$.) The wife ends up devoting $\beta_L \times 743 + \gamma_L \times 1500 = 5972$ hours to home production and allocating the remainder of her time $(8760 - 5972 = 2988$ hours) to market work. Her earnings, $\$5 \times 2788 = \$14,940$, plus other family income ($\$8,500$), equal $\$22,440$. Allowing for rounding errors in our example, $\$22,440$ is just the amount of money needed to purchase $\$7,430$ worth of goods to go into production of commodity A and $\$15,000$ required for commodity B.

All the variables that influence the supply of labor in the traditional approach have a similar impact in the household production framework. Furthermore, as we shall see, the household production approach provides a convenient means to analyze the influence of forces affecting commodity consumption and labor supply that are more awkward to deal with in traditional consumer and labor supply theory.

First of all, consider the effects of changes in family income and the wife's market wage rate. Suppose the husband receives a wage raise so that in Table 4–5, income available if the wife doesn't work (Y) rises to $12,500 and full income ($Y + WT$) increases to $56,300. Since there has been no change in β_L, β_G, γ_L, γ_G, W, or the price of a unit of market goods, the marginal and average costs of A and B (π_A and π_B) remain unchanged, as does the slope of the production possibility frontier. However, the increased full income is represented by a parallel outward shift of the production possibility frontier as shown in Figure 4–19. Now, a maximum of 2,815 units of B or approximately 1,877 units of A can be produced. (Note that the increase in the maximum output of B would cost $200 \times \$20 = \$4000$, and that of A would cost about $134 \times \$30 \simeq \$4000$.)

If both A and B are normal commodities—that is, if the consumption of each commodity rises with a parallel outward shift in the production possibility frontier—then the household will produce (and consume) more of both of them. Suppose for example, there is an equi-proportional increase

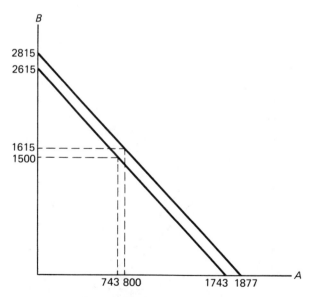

FIGURE 4–19. Effect of Increase in Y on Household Production Possibility Frontier and on Consumption of A and B

in the household's demand for A and B, so that consumption rises to 1,615 units of B and 800 units of A. The quantity of home time needed to produce the commodities rises to 6,430 from 5,972, and time devoted to market work falls from 2,788 to 2,330 hours. Thus, when both commodities are normal, hours of labor supply decline when there is an increase in the amount of income available when no work is performed. This is similar, in the traditional approach, to the effect of an increase in nonemployment income on labor supply when leisure is a normal commodity. You should be able to see that even if either A or B were inferior (consumption falls when Y rises), hours of market work would not fall unless the time intensity of the inferior commodity were sufficiently large relative to the other commodity. (The relative time intensity of commodity A is the ratio β_L/γ_L.)

When the wife's wage changes, there occur both an income effect, as outlined in the preceding paragraphs, and a substitution effect on both commodity consumption and, indirectly, hours of work. Suppose the wife receives an increase in her wage rate (W) from $5 to $8 per hour. Full income ($Y + WT$) thus increases to $78,580 from $52,300. π_A grows from $30 to $8 \times 4 + $10 = $42, while π_B grows from $20 to $8 \times 2 + $10 = $26. These changes are depicted in Figure 4–20. There is a greater proportional increase in the household's capacity to produce B than A, which is reflected in a clockwise rotation of the production possibility curve. The relative price of B in terms of A has fallen. This change in relative price is due to the relative time inten-

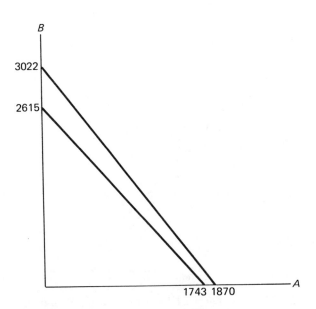

FIGURE 4–20. The Effect of an Increase in W on the Household Production Possibility Frontier

sity of A. Since A uses more of the wife's time for every dollar of market goods in production, the 60 percent increase in the wife's wage has caused π_A to rise by 40 percent, but π_B to rise by only 30 percent. Whereas at the initial wage of $5 per hour, 1.5 units of B had to be given up if one more unit of A were produced, the cost of A is now a little more than 1.6 units of B.[27]

Since the new A-B production possibilities frontier lies above the old one, the household is clearly better off as a result of the increase in the wife's wage rate. If A and B are both normal commodities, there will be an income effect of the wage raise inducing greater production of both A and B, increasing the amount of time devoted to household production, and reducing labor supplied to the market. On the other hand, the increased relative cost of A will induce a substitution effect toward greater production of the less time-intensive commodity B, increasing hours of market work. Whether the quantity of market work rises or falls as a result of the wage increase depends on the relative magnitudes of the income and substitution effects, as in the traditional approach.

SOME APPLICATIONS

Human Fertility. The household production framework has provided valuable insights into many kinds of economic and social behavior. Moreover, it has drawn attention to the interconnection between labor supply and other household economic decisions. One important application has been in the study of human fertility. Historically, family size has declined in countries where per capita income has increased, and at a moment in time, U.S. Census data suggest a tendency for families with high income levels to desire fewer children. These relationships vary in size and direction from time to time and place to place, and according to which additional variables are

---

[27]An interesting implication of this analysis bears on the true cost of living. Official cost of living indexes, such as the Consumer Price Index (CPI) reflect the dollar cost of purchasing goods, not the full cost of producing commodities. With the CPI, an increase in measured family income due to a rise in Y has the same effect on economic welfare as an equal increase in family income due to a rise in W. In the household production approach, an increase in W results not only in an increase in economic welfare as indicated by full income, but also an increase in the cost of living which partially offsets the increase in full income. Thus in Figure 4–19, the household's capacity to produce (and consume) both commodities A and B increases by approximately 7.7 percent, equal to the increase in full income. On the other hand, in Figure 4–20 the capacity to produce A and B rises by approximately 7.3 percent and 15.6 percent, respectively, even though full income has risen by 50.2 *percent*! Similarly, national income statistics, which measure only market production, cannot capture changes in economic well-being attributable to home production, which is a broader concept. Increases in income due to, say, dividend or interest payments, have the same effect on measured national income as equal increases in wages. Moreover, when women enter the labor force in increasing numbers, national income statistics measure the full increase in earnings (production of goods), but do not reflect concomitant reductions in household production because of reduced home time that partially offsets the increased production of market goods and services.

held constant. Consequently, economists and demographers have not reached any general agreement regarding whether desired family size rises or declines with family income levels.[28]

Recently, advances have been achieved in our understanding of fertility behavior in conjunction with the labor supply behavior of married women by means of the household production approach. In the household production approach, children have been viewed as relatively (mother's) time-intensive with respect to all commodities produced and consumed in the household. In Figure 4–21, the production possibility frontier $C_1 Y_1$ describes the choices available with respect to consumption of children (C) and all other commodities lumped together (Y). An increase in family income from sources other than the wife's market wage rate will push the frontier outward parallel fashion, as in Figure 4–19, leaving the price of children in terms of other commodities unaffected. Thus, if children are a normal commodity, desired family size would rise with income rather than decline, as has often been observed. However, when there is an increase in the wife's wage rate, although the frontier shifts rightward, it also becomes steeper, reflecting an increase in the relative cost of children in terms of other commodities. This is depicted in Figure 4–21. Since wage rates of husbands and wives tend to rise together

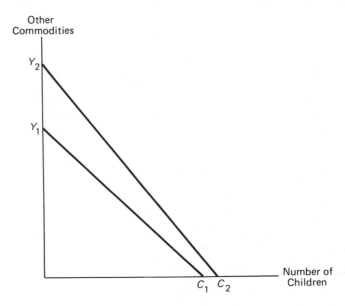

FIGURE 4–21. The Household Production Approach to Fertility

---

[28]See, for example, papers in *Demographic and Economic Change in Developed Countries*, Universities–National Bureau Conference Series 11 (Princeton, N.J.: Princeton University Press, 1960); "New Economic Approaches to Fertility," *Journal of Political Economy*, 81, 2, part II (March–April 1973); and H. Leibenstein, "On the Economic Theory of Fertility," *Journal of Economic Literature*, 12, 2 (June 1974), 457–87.

over time and to be positively correlated across households at a moment in time, the simple relationship observed between family size and family income is due to the effect of relative prices as well as income. This may help to explain the irregularities and inconsistencies which have been noted in the family size-income relationship.

The household production approach emphasizes the importance of price and income effects in determining the number of children families desire. Moreover, attention is drawn to the interconnection between factors determining the labor force participation of married women and family size (we alluded to this interconnection between labor supply and family size above). In the household production framework, it becomes apparent that it may not be correct to say that women with large families tend to work less "because" they have a lot of children. Rather, labor supply and family size are viewed as subject to common underlying causes.

The "economic" approach to fertility has proved useful and has stimulated much empirical work. There is some evidence that although children do represent a normal commodity, the tendency for the number of children to increase with family income is much weaker than for the amount families spend on their children (schooling, medical care, and so on). Moreover, there is also a relatively strong negative influence of mother's wage rates on the desired number of children. The negative forces tend to dominate the positive forces determining desired number of children when the simple relationship between family size and income is examined.

Private vs. Public Transportation. Because of increasing congestion of our urban streets and freeways, air pollution, and energy considerations, public policy in recent years has been oriented toward encouraging use of public mass transportation systems (and car pools). Nevertheless, the traditional American one person per car commuting pattern has proved difficult to alter despite rising gasoline prices, subsidized bus and subway systems, and exhortations by political leaders. In the household production framework, the reason for this lack of success may not be hard to find. When commuting is viewed as a *commodity* produced with inputs not only of market goods (automobile, fuel, or commuter ticket), but also the worker's time, then the importance of time spent waiting for the bus or train, or coordinating a car pool, becomes apparent. The full cost of "cheap" public transportation is seen to be considerably higher than the price of the fare alone. As wages and incomes rise, the importance to consumers of economizing on their time in commuting and other forms of travel increases. The persistence of seemingly "wasteful" forms of commuting to work is difficult to understand only if we ignore the full cost of producing the commodity "transportation."[29]

---

[29]For an application of this approach to the demand for transportation, see Reuben Gronau, "The Value of Time in Passenger Transportation: The Demand for Air Travel," Occasional Paper No. 109 (New York: National Bureau of Economic Research, 1970).

Restaurant Meals.   Does the rapid growth of moderately priced restaurant chains and inexpensive "fast food" purveyors reflect a decline in traditional family values and attitudes toward home cooking? In the household production framework, the preparation and consumption of home-cooked meals is a relatively time-intensive method of obtaining the commodity "nutrition." Moreover, when the wife works in the labor market, not only is there less of her time available for household tasks, but coordinating her working hours with the desired mealtimes of other family members may be more difficult. As wage rates increase, the cost of home-cooked meals relative to restaurant meals increases, thus shifting consumption patterns toward the latter as well as inducing greater labor force participation of married women. Thus, we do not need to rely on speculation about changes in attitudes toward traditional patterns of consumption and family behavior to understand the growth in expenditures on meals consumed outside the home.

Conclusion

In this chapter we presented the theory of labor supply in two parts: labor force participation and hours of work. In focusing on the most notable single change in the labor force since World War II, the increased participation of married women, we found that economists have had a moderate degree of success in explaining this trend in the labor supply. Recently, however, some research has failed to replicate earlier results. It is an important challenge for students of labor supply to reconcile recent studies of the labor force participation of married women with those based on data pertaining to the 1950s and 1960s.

Another major change in labor force behavior has been the decline in average hours worked by "full-time" labor force participants, although the major part of the reduction in work hours took place during the first half of this century. We showed how the theory of labor force participation can be extended to encompass the behavior of hours of work as well. Recent research has offered persuasive evidence on the reasons for the halt in the reduction of weekly hours of work that occurred sometime in the 1940s.

Finally, we briefly discussed a new approach to the theory of the labor supply based on a view of the household as a producing unit not unlike a firm. The household production approach emphasizes the interrelationship between labor supply and other family economic decisions. This approach makes it possible to introduce variables reflecting efficiency in consumption activities directly into the study of various forms of household behavior, in addition to the traditional wage and income variables. Moreover, it emphasizes the interrelationships between labor supply and many other decisions, such as number of children, within a single analytical framework.

In this chapter, we have considered labor supply behavior in the short run only, taking as given such variables as basic skills and schooling. Long-run labor supply analysis, which is treated in Chapters 9 and 10, deals with these topics. There we recognize that within constraints, we are able to make choices among alternatives which determine our future wage rates via schooling, training, migration, health, and other investments in human capital.

Exercises

1. Brutus Buckeye is unmarried and has a utility function depicted by the indifference curve map below.

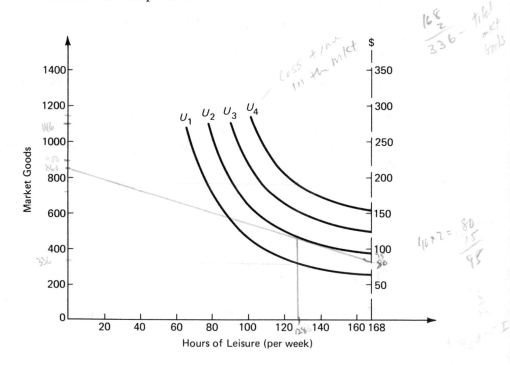

Brutus is unskilled and faces a constant hourly wage rate of $2. In addition to any earnings, Brutus' parents send him a check for $15 every week. Brutus wants to maximize his utility.

a. How many hours should Brutus supply to the labor market? 40 hrs

b. What will Brutus' total income be? $40×40 per yr   or $95 a week

2. In order to raise revenue, the government of Echidna is considering levying either (a) a lump-sum head tax or (b) a proportional (fixed rate) tax on earnings. The government is worried, however, that people may

work less in response to the tax they choose. Which of the two taxes will lead a utility-maximizing worker to supply less time to the labor market? Explain carefully and depict graphically.

3. Consider the following excerpt from a recent article, "Workaholics Fidget Away Vacations."

The lawyer who takes up woodworking as a hobby, and then works at it compulsively, his electric saw still running in the dawn hours.

"This type of person is a work freak, a 'workaholic'," says [psychiatrist Francis L.] Clark. "Work is his whole life and he can't seem to enjoy anything else. He can no more give up work than an alcoholic can give up booze."

Georgetown's Dr. Clark has these suggestions: "If you are under a lot of pressure in your work, make it a point to take all your vacation time. Don't let it accrue. *In fact, companies should require their employees to take time off.*" (*The National Observer*, June 30, 1973, Dow Jones & Company, Inc.)

a. Using the basic labor-leisure diagram learned in this chapter, depict the indifference curve budget constraint configuration for a workaholic.

b. With this geometric tool, evaluate the potential success of Dr. Clark's prescription for curing workaholism. Specifically, if companies require employees to take time off, will this reduce the incidence of workaholism? Be as complete as possible in your answer.

References

BECKER, GARY S., "A Theory of the Allocation of Time." *Economic Journal*, 75, 3 (September 1965), 493–517.

———, "A Theory of Social Interactions." *Journal of Political Economy*, 82, 6 (November-December 1974), 1063–94.

BOSKIN, MICHAEL J., "Social Security and Retirement Decisions." *Economic Inquiry*, 15, 1 (January 1977), 1–25.

BOWEN, WILLIAM G., and T. ALDRICH FINEGAN, *The Economics of Labor Force Participation*. Princeton, N.J.: Princeton University Press, 1969.

CAIN, GLEN G., *Married Women in the Labor Force*. Chicago: University of Chicago Press, 1966.

COGAN, JOHN F., *Labor Supply with Time and Money Costs of Participation*. R-2044-HEW. Santa Monica, Calif.: Rand Corporation, 1976.

———, *Negative Income Taxation and Labor Supply: New Evidence from the New Jersey–Pennsylvania Experiment*. R2155-HEW. Santa Monica, Calif.: Rand Corporation, 1978.

Demographic and Economic Change in Developed Countries. Universities-National Bureau Conference Series 11. Princeton, N.J.: Princeton University Press, 1960.

EASTERLIN, RICHARD A., *Population, Labor Force, and Long Swings in Economic Growth.* New York and London: National Bureau of Economic Research, 1968, p. 64.

FERGUSON, C. E. and J. P. GOULD, *Microeconomic Theory, 4th ed.* Homewood, Ill.: Irwin, 1975.

FIELDS, JUDITH M., "A Comparison of Intercity Differences in the Labor Force Participation Rates of Married Women in 1970 and 1940, 1950, and 1960," *Journal of Human Resources*, 11, 4 (fall 1976), 568–77.

FLEISHER, BELTON M., and GEORGE F. RHODES, JR., "Labor Force Participation of Married Men and Women: A Simultaneous Model," *Review of Economics and Statistics*, 58, 4 (November 1976), 398–406.

———, "Fertility, Women's Wage Rates, and Labor Supply." *American Economic Review*, 69, 1 (March 1979).

GRONAU, REUBEN, "The Value of Time in Passenger Transportation: The Demand for Air Travel." Occasional Paper No. 109, National Bureau of Economic Research, New York, 1970.

KNIESNER, THOMAS J., "Recent Behavior of the 'Full-Time' Workweek in the U.S." Unpublished Ph.D. dissertation, The Ohio State University, 1974, Appendix A.

———, "The Full-Time Workweek in the United States, 1900–1970." *Industrial and Labor Relations Review*, 30, 1 (October 1976), 3–15.

LANCASTER, KELVIN J., "A New Approach to Consumer Theory." *Journal of Political Economy*, 74, 2 (April 1966), 132–57.

LEIBENSTEIN, H., "On the Economic Theory of Fertility." *Journal of Economic Literature*, 12, 2 (June 1974), 457–87.

LEWIS, H. G., "Hours of Work and Hours of Leisure." *Proceedings of the Ninth Annual Winter Meeting, the Industrial Relations Research Association*, December 1956, pp. 196–206.

LONG, CLARENCE, *The Labor Force under Changing Income and Employment.* Princeton, N.J.: Princeton University Press, 1958.

MICHAEL, ROBERT T., and GARY S. BECKER, "On The New Theory of Consumer Behavior." *The Swedish Journal of Economics*, 75, 4 (December 1973), 378–96.

MINCER, JACOB, "Labor Force Participation of Married Women," in *Aspects of Labor Economics.* Princeton, N.J.: Princeton University Press, 1962.

———, "Labor Force Participation and Unemployment: A Review of Recent Evidence." In Robert A. Gordon and Margaret S. Gordon, eds., *Prosperity and Unemployment.* New York: Wiley, 1966, pp. 91–98, 73–112.

MITCHELL, WESLEY C., "The Backward Art of Spending Money." *American Economic Review*, 2, 2 (June 1912), 269–81.

"New Economic Approaches to Fertility," *Journal of Political Economy*, 81, 2, Part II (March–April 1973).

PECHMAN, JOSEPH A., and P. MICHAEL TIMPANE, *Work Incentives and Income Guarantees: The New Jersey Negative Income Tax Experiment.* Washington, D.C.: The Brookings Institution, 1975.

REID, MARGARET G., *Economics of Household Production.* New York: Wiley, 1934.

"Symposium Articles—The Graduated Work Incentive Experiment," *Journal of Human Resources*, 9, 2 (spring 1974).

U.S. Department of Commerce, Bureau of the Census, *Historical Statistics of the United States, Colonial Times to 1970.* Part 1, Series D11, D35, D60, D182-232, G372-415, p. 71.

U.S. Department of Commerce, Bureau of the Census, *Statistical Abstract of the United States, 1967*, pp. 227–28.

U.S. Department of Health, Education and Welfare, Social Security Administration, *Social Security Bulletin: Annual Statistical Supplement, 1965*, p. 41.

U.S. Department of Labor and U.S. Department of Health, Education and Welfare, *Employment and Training Report of the President, 1976*, Table B-2.

U.S. Department of Labor, *The Manpower Report of the President, 1975*, Table B-2.

WENTWORTH, EDNA C., "Income of Old-Age and Survivors Insurance Beneficiaries, 1941 and 1949," *Social Security Bulletin*, 13, 5 (May 1950), 3–10.

WILLIS, R. J., "A New Approach to the Economic Theory of Fertility Behavior." *Journal of Political Economy* (March–April 1973).

CHAPTER 5

The Interaction of Supply and Demand in Competitive Labor Markets

A. Educational Objectives
   1. Analysis of how the forces of labor supply and demand interact in competitive labor markets to determine workers' economic welfare
   2. Determination of how exogenous changes in the variables which underlie labor supply and demand schedules disturb wages, employment, and working conditions

B. The Concept of a Labor Market

C. Equilibrium in a Single Competitive Labor Market
   1. Definition of equilibrium
   2. Comparative statics analysis
      a. Exogenous events which shift labor supply or demand schedules
      b. Qualitative effects of supply and demand shifts on equilibrium wages and employment
      c. Application: who pays for social security

D. Multimarket Equilibrium
   1. Forces promoting multimarket equilibrium
   2. Economic efficiency
      a. Definition
      b. A reasonable social objective
   3. Application: equity and efficiency effects of minimum wage legislation with incomplete coverage
   4. Application: the labor force participation of married women revisited

E. Frontiers of Competitive Equilibrium Analysis: the Economics of Industrial Safety
   1. Background
   2. The determination of the rate of industrial injuries in competition

3. The effect of workers' compensation on the level of industrial safety: the role of workers' perceptions of injury risk
4. The effect of OSHA on the level of industrial safety; the roles of financial penalties for noncompliance and the probability of plant safety inspections

In this chapter we apply the knowledge gained in Chapters 3 and 4 to analyze how the forces of supply and demand interact in competitive labor markets to determine wages, employment, and "working conditions." Moreover, we are interested in understanding how exogenous changes in factors that underlie labor supply and demand disturb these schedules and thus workers' economic welfare, especially since many such disturbances are the result of government policy. Before we can proceed, however, it is important to elaborate briefly on the somewhat nebulous concept of a labor market, given the central role it plays in the analysis to follow.

It probably seems odd at first to think about a market for *labor*. Most of us have seen pictures of the New York Stock Exchange in action, but who has been to a slave auction? Fortunately, this does not mean that the concept of a labor market produces a misleading impression of how economic factors affect workers' economic welfare. It is best to think of a market as a convenient abstraction that economists use to organize ideas. We do something similar in casual conversation when we refer to such intangibles as "the civil rights movement," "women's liberation," or "the democratic process." The point here is that a labor market is really the "place" in economic theory where supply and demand interact. As a result, a market is an extremely flexible analytical tool to have at our disposal, and economists have used it to study regions (the labor market of Chicago), industries (the labor market for production workers in manufacturing), and occupations (the labor market for lawyers). So, the criterion we will use to evaluate the scientific value of the concept of a labor market is not how well it represents an observable economic institution, but whether it helps us to formulate an economic analysis that provides us with reasonably accurate and useful insights into phenomena we seek to understand.

Equilibrium in a Single Competitive Labor Market

In order to understand how the forces of supply and demand determine wage rates and employment, we will discuss a single competitive labor market in which the number of workers and the number of firms is fixed. Premium wage rates for overtime work will be ignored. Moreover, firms will be assumed to be indifferent to the number of employees versus hours of work per employee, so that the quantity of labor they desire to hire (and workers wish to supply) may be represented simply by total employee hours. Our hypothetical labor market is depicted in Figure 5–1 by a labor supply curve

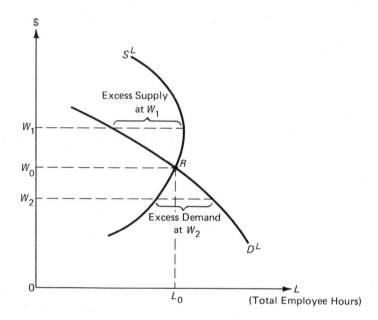

FIGURE 5–1. Labor Market Equilibrium

(S^L) and a labor demand curve (D^L). Remember that in a competitive labor market there are numerous firms and individuals. The labor demand curve represents the total number of labor hours firms desire to purchase at various wage rates, allowing for feedback effects from the market for final output. D is downward-sloping for the reasons discussed in Chapter 3. The supply curve of labor indicates the total number of hours workers wish to sell at each wage rate. For the set of workers pictured in Figure 5–1, rising income levels are eventually accompanied by an increased desire to spend time in home production (leisure) so that the labor supply curve bends backward.[1]

Where S^L and D^L intersect (point R) denotes the **market-clearing** or **equilibrium** combination of W and L. The labor market is said to be cleared at wage rate W_0 because the amount of labor workers desire to sell matches the amount employers desire to purchase. At a wage rate higher than W_0, say W_1, workers are "frustrated" in the sense that they wish to sell more labor

---

[1] If we were to measure the quantity of labor by the *number* of workers, could S^L be backward-bending?

than firms are willing to buy. At a wage rate below W_0, say W_2, firms are frustrated in their attempts to purchase labor. The intersection of supply and demand is a labor market equilibrium because it represents a satisfactory transaction for both groups.

COMPARATIVE STATICS ANALYSIS OF A LABOR MARKET

Probably the most important use of a supply and demand model is to generate predictions of how exogenous events influence wages and employment. Suppose that the supply of labor increases and demand remains unchanged. What do we expect to happen to the market wage rate and the quantity of labor services firms hire? Economists answer this question by comparing the initial labor market equilibrium point with the equilibrium point after supply has shifted. Such a comparison is known as **comparative statics analysis**.

In general, changes in the environment surrounding the "actors" in a labor market are responsible for shifts in supply or demand curves. For example, we know from Chapter 4 that a market labor supply function indicates workers' desired hours of work at various wage rates, *given their nonemployment income*. Were some to receive windfalls, say from winning lottery tickets, they would very likely spend part of that newly acquired income on leisure, and the market labor supply function would shift to the left. Alternatively, the market demand curve for labor is a sum of the value of marginal product schedules of individual firms. If technology suddenly changed so as to make workers more productive, the resulting increase in firms' marginal physical productivity schedules would lead to a rightward shift in market labor demand. Table 5–1 lists some events that shift supply or demand schedules.[2]

Having identified some factors that disturb labor supply and demand curves, it is relatively simple to link these events to their effects on equilibrium wage and quantity of labor. To do so, we assume that the market for labor is initially in equilibrium and will achieve equilibrium following the environmental shifts under examination. The predicted impact of a set of events, then, is obtained by comparing the labor market equilibrium point before and after their occurrence. You should be able to show, for example, that an increase in the marginal physical productivity of labor will increase both W and L if labor supply is upward-sloping. The predicted labor market impacts of various combinations of supply and demand shifts when the supply curve is upward-sloping are summarized in Table 5–2. Notice that when only one of the two curves is displaced, we obtain unambiguous qualitative predictions for the changes in W and L. If exogenous events disturb both S^L and D^L, how-

---

[2]As an exercise, construct a table of how S^L and D^L shift in response to changes in the factors listed in Table 5–1. For example, does an increase in household productivity shift the supply of labor to the right or to the left?

TABLE 5–1

Events That Shift Labor Supply or Demand Curves

Events That Shift an Individual's Labor Supply Curve

1. Change in nonlabor income
2. Change in wage or earnings of other family members
3. Change in household productivity
4. Change in distaste for market work

Events That Shift a Firm's Labor Demand Curve

1. Change in technology
2. Change in the price of final output
3. Change in price (quantity) of other productive factors

TABLE 5–2

The Qualitative Effects of Market Supply and Demand
Curve Shifts on Labor Market Equilibrium*

	Supply Increases	Supply Decreases	Supply Unchanged
Demand Increases	$\Delta W \gtreqless 0$ $\Delta L > 0$	$\Delta W > 0$ $\Delta L \gtreqless 0$	$\Delta W > 0$ $\Delta L > 0$
Demand Decreases	$\Delta W < 0$ $\Delta L \gtreqless 0$	$\Delta W \gtreqless 0$ $\Delta L < 0$	$\Delta W < 0$ $\Delta L < 0$
Demand Unchanged	$\Delta W < 0$ $\Delta L > 0$	$\Delta W > 0$ $\Delta L < 0$	$\Delta W = 0$ $\Delta L = 0$

*The labor supply curve is assumed to be upward-sloping.

ever, we can predict the change in only one of the two variables without information as to the relative magnitudes of the shifts. Which of the entries in Table 5–2 will be different if the labor supply curve is backward-bending? Which will differ if S^L is vertical?

APPLICATION: WHO PAYS FOR SOCIAL SECURITY?

The relatively simple tool of comparative statics analysis is useful in examining the labor market impact of a wide variety of governmental programs. In 1977, Congress carefully considered legislation aimed at maintaining the solvency of the social security system. The concern arose from falling birth rates and increasing life expectancy. In particular, the proportion of the United States population over 65 is expected to grow over the next fifty years or so, while the proportion in the prime working age group declines. Either social security benefits must be lowered within the next few decades, or some way must be found to finance the anticipated increase in benefit payments. The latter solution requires a transfer of funds from general tax revenues or an increase in the payroll tax which is currently the source of revenue for social security retirement benefits. Although Congress decided to increase taxes, there was considerable disagreement about whether the increased taxes should be levied on employers or workers. The arguments in favor of levying the tax on employers rest on the belief that they can better afford it. Alternatively, arguments in favor of levying the tax (or part of it) on employees rest on the feeling that the eventual recipients of social security benefits should bear the financial responsibility. You may be surprised to learn that the theory of supply and demand in competitive labor markets implies that Congress has very little power over the incidence of, or who actually pays, the taxes that finance social security benefits. No matter who "writes the checks," employers or employees, the true tax burden is dependent on the forces of supply and demand.

To see why this is so, examine Figure 5–2, which depicts the situation in which the economy's labor supply schedule is negatively inclined in the relevant range. The demand curve reflects employers' view of the value of the marginal product of their employees (VMP_L). If there were no tax, employers would maximize their profits by hiring L_0 units of labor at an equilibrium wage of W_0. Figure 5–2a describes what happens to equilibrium if a tax of t

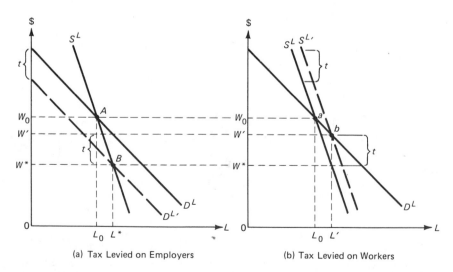

(a) Tax Levied on Employers   (b) Tax Levied on Workers

FIGURE 5–2. The Supply and Demand for Labor and the Incidence of a Specific Tax

dollars per unit of labor is levied on employers.[3] From the point of view of employers, the tax reduces the benefit of hiring an additional unit of labor from VMP_L to $(VMP_L - t)$. Even though the extra L "brings in" VMP_L, the tax must be subtracted to calculate employers' *net* benefit. This produces a downward shift of the labor demand schedule in Figure 5–2a to $D^{L'}$. The result is an excess supply of labor at wage rate W_0 that leads to a decline in the wage to W^* and an increase in employment to L^*, where the labor market is again cleared. At the new equilibrium point B, the full cost of a unit of labor to employers is $(W^* + t) = W'$. More important, the decline in the equilibrium wage from W_0 to W^* exceeds the tax, t. Put differently, employees really "pay" more than the tax, because the new equilibrium wage is less than the initial wage minus the tax $(W_0 - t)$! Despite Congress' intent that employers pay for social security retirement benefits, employees are the actual payers. They are required by market forces to accept a wage lower than before the tax was imposed on employers. As we will see shortly, the fact that $W_0 - W^*$ exceeds t results from the negative slope of the supply curve. First, though, we will show that the result above is independent of upon whom Congress levies the tax.

In Figure 5–2b workers know that their paychecks reflect a rate of pay W_0, but that a tax of $\$t$ per unit of work will be deducted in the future. Since their take-home pay determines their labor supply, the effective labor supply curve shifts upward by t to $S^{L'}$. This leads to a decline in the equilibrium wage (and the value of the marginal product of labor) to W', and to a reduction in workers' take-home pay to $(W' - t) = W^*$. So we see that the tax actually paid by workers $(W_0 - W^*)$ is the same no matter who Congress intended to bear the burden of the social security tax.

The result that the market wage declines by more than t, the amount of the tax, follows from the negatively sloped labor supply curve. When the labor supply schedule has either zero or positive elasticity, the incidence of the tax is somewhat different. Figure 5–3 illustrates the case in which Congress imposes the tax on employers. In (a), the supply curve is vertical; in (b), it is upward-sloping.[4] Once again, when employers realize they must pay a tax of $\$t$ per unit of labor in addition to the wage, the labor demand curve shifts downward by distance t. When the quantity of labor supplied is independent of the wage (Figure 5–3a), employers continue to pay W_0 per unit of labor, but the net wage received by workers falls to $W^* = (W_0 - t)$. Thus, when the labor supply schedule exhibits zero elasticity, the tax is paid entirely by workers. In Figure 5–3b, the decline in the market wage leads to a reduc-

---

[3]In reality, the tax imposed by Congress is not a specific (fixed dollar per unit of labor) tax, but rather proportional to wages paid, with a ceiling on total payments. To take these facts into account would complicate the analysis significantly while leaving the basic conclusion unchanged.

[4]We leave as an exercise the case in which supply has a nonnegative slope and the tax is levied on workers.

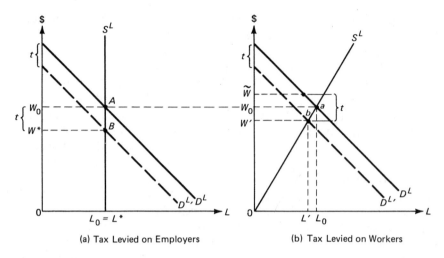

FIGURE 5–3. The Incidence of a Specific Tax When Labor Supply Has a Nonnegative Slope

tion in employment as the result of the positively sloped labor supply curve, and the equilibrium wage declines by less than in the preceding examples. A unit of labor now costs employers W', but they must pay t per unit to the government to support the social security system, so that the full wage is $\widetilde{W} = (W' + t)$. Thus, when the labor supply curve is upward-sloping and the tax is levied on employers, the tendency for the wage to fall is offset by the reduction in employment from L_0 to L' and the resulting increase in the value of the marginal product of labor to $\widetilde{W}$. Since $(W_0 - W')$ is less than t, the tax in this case is borne by *both* employers and employees. As before, workers pay all or part of a tax meant by Congress for employers alone.

Multimarket Equilibrium

From our analysis of a single competitive market for labor, we know that an equilibrium wage rate will persist so long as there is no economic incentive for firms or individuals to alter their behavior. For example, in the labor market represented by Figure 5–1, if W_0 is such that employers can increase their profits by purchasing labor elsewhere (equilibrium wages in other markets are lower than W_0), or if workers can increase their economic welfare by seeking employment elsewhere (equilibrium wages in other markets exceed W_0), then W_0 will not be the long-term equilibrium. Suppose we ignore for simplicity the fact that search by employers or employees can be quite time-consuming and costly. In this case, all labor markets will be in equilibrium, or there will be **multimarket equilibrium**, when the wage rate of a given type

160

of labor is the same in all alternative employments of given (nonwage) characteristics. When there is wage inequality among labor markets, excess supplies
will occur in markets where wages are high and excess demands in those
where wages are low. The resulting frustrations on the parts of buyers and
sellers of labor will cause wage rates to move toward their long-term, multimarket equilibrium values.

In order that we may see more clearly how the forces of supply and
demand lead to equal wage rates across labor markets, let us consider the
example of an economy composed of two competitive labor markets (for
example, geographical regions). The curves labeled D_I and D_{II} in Figure
5–4 represent the demand schedules for labor by firms in markets I and II,
respectively. Our sample economy has a total labor force of six identical
(equally productive) workers, and jobs are alike in both regions in the sense
that each employer offers the same work week, fringe benefits, and working
conditions. Finally, we will assume that there is insufficient time for firms to
build or rent new plants, so that only workers may move between regions,
and that wage information is readily available and migration costless.

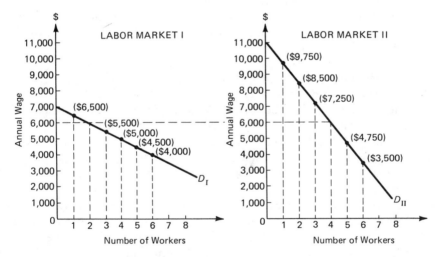

FIGURE 5–4. Multimarket Equilibrium

Suppose five individuals are initially located in market I and one in market
II. This distribution of workers generates temporary market clearing wages
of $4,500 in I and $9,750 in II. Remember, however, that all five workers in
market I are just as talented as the one in market II and that news of the
higher wages in market II will eventually spread. As soon as one of the
workers in market I realizes that his or her economic welfare can be improved
through relocation, the distribution of workers becomes two in market II

and four in market I. The increased quantity of labor in II and the decreased quantity of labor in I narrows the equilibrium wage gap to $8,500 versus $5,000. Workers will continue to migrate from market I to market II as long as they can gain from the move. The flow stops when market I has a labor force of two workers and market II a labor force of four workers. At this point, multimarket equilibrium occurs as both markets clear at an annual wage of $6,000, and there is no economic incentive for any worker to relocate.[5,6]

Speed of Adjustment. Labor markets typically do not adjust to changing supply and demand schedules as rapidly as markets for commodities and other factors of production. Consider the markets for financial assets. Since information about alternatives is widespread and transaction costs small, prices adjust rapidly to disturbances, and interregional and interasset differences in price behavior are rare. Markets for grain, beef, pork, and cotton also behave this way. By comparison, the adjustment of labor markets is sluggish indeed. However, in evaluating the adjustment of labor markets to equilibrium, it is necessary to examine the causes of sluggish adjustment as well as the nature of alternative methods for eliminating them. (The roles played by labor market adjustments to changing demand and supply conditions in the determination of unemployment and inflation rates are treated in Chapters 11 and 12.)

Economic Efficiency. When competitive multimarket equilibrium is achieved, the value of the marginal product of labor is equal to its wage rate, and the wage rate for labor of a given quality is the same in each market.[7] Therefore, the value of the marginal product of labor is the same everywhere. This equality of VMP_L in alternative employments leads to what is called **economic efficiency,** which means that society obtains the largest possible output (national income) from its available quantities of resources.

To understand how multimarket equilibrium in a competitive economy generates economic efficiency, let us return to our fictional economy of Figure 5–4. When there were five workers in market I and one worker in market II, VMP_L was $4,500 in I and $9,750 in II. The ensuing relocation of one worker lowered output in market I and increased output in market II such that society's total value of production (income) increased by approximately $4,000. (Can you explain why?) You should verify the results that total production increases until multimarket equilibrium is achieved and that any

---

[5]It should be noted that "overshooting" may also occur. Too many workers may move to market II at first, so that multimarket equilibrium requires some to return to market I. Can you cite a real world example of such return migration?

[6]A formal analysis of the individual's decision to migrate is presented in Chapter 9.

[7]Multimarket equilibrium will produce "equalizing" wage differences for workers of a given quality if job characteristics differ. Once such difference, the likelihood of being injured at work, is the topic of the last section of this chapter.

distribution of workers other than two in market I and four in market II is associated with a lower total income for society. Similarly, if in the United States, labor's *VMP* in the manufacture of autos were to exceed labor's *VMP* in the manufacture of pants, say, the movement of labor "from autos to pants" would increase national income. Migration of workers would continue, and total output would increase, until the *VMP* discrepancy was eliminated. This fact is important because it means that barriers to the mobility of workers between labor markets, such as discrimination, trade unions, or license requirements, impose a cost on society in the form of reduced aggregate income.

Other things being the same, including the distribution of income, most of us would agree that economic efficiency is desirable. However, forces that interfere with competition and prevent economic efficiency usually also change the income distribution. As a result, we cannot conclude that such interferences are "bad" unless we believe the income distribution that accompanies them is "no better than" the one associated with competitive equilibrium. It may help to think of society's total income as a pie. Given technology and the apportionment of productive resources among individuals, a competitive economy creates the largest pie possible. Competitive equilibrium also cuts the pie into slices, each slice representing someone's income. Suppose a trade union restricts the movement of workers between labor markets and thus reduces the size of society's income pie. If *everyone's* slice were made smaller in the process, we would be justified in concluding that this interference with competition is undesirable, since everyone loses. Suppose, however, that when the pie is shrunk it is also *recut,* so that those who previously had the largest slices now have their pieces reduced and those who previously had the smallest slices now have theirs increased. In this case, some individuals are better off than they were before, and we cannot categorically infer that inefficiency is undesirable unless we are also willing to say that greater equality of incomes is of no social value. During the course of our study of labor economics, we will identify and discuss numerous institutions that preclude economic efficiency. We now examine one frequently controversial interference with competitive equilibrium, minimum wage legislation.

APPLICATION: MINIMUM WAGE LEGISLATION IN THE UNITED STATES

Social concern over low pay and poor working conditions in some industries during the late nineteenth and early twentieth centuries provided the foundation for minimum wage legislation in the United States. In 1912, Massachusetts passed a law with the purpose of persuading employers to pay "standard" wage rates established by a state wage board. Employers who paid substandard wages had their names publicized.[8] Eight additional states passed minimum wage laws the next year; in seven of these states the wage floors were mandatory, but they applied only to women and minors.[9]

Passage of the National Industrial Recovery Act (NIRA) in 1933 brought with it the first federal minimum wage statute. NIRA established a floor on wages of between 30 cents and 40 cents per hour. NIRA was declared unconstitutional in 1937, however, and in 1938 the Fair Labor Standards Act (FLSA) was passed to regulate hours of work and wage rates. FLSA has continued to be the basis for national floors on wage rates.[10] The 1938 minimum wage of 25 cents has been revised approximately every five years since then to bring the minimum to around 50 percent of the average hourly wage rate in manufacturing.

An important feature of minimum wage legislation in the United States is its coverage, which is incomplete and depends upon industry, product line, and firm size. During the twenty-three years following the passage of FLSA, wage floors applied mainly to the more capital-intensive industries. Table 5–3 summarizes the industrial distribution of workers affected by the

TABLE 5–3

Percentage of Employed Persons in Firms Covered by Minimum Wage Legislation by Industry and for the Aggregate, Selected Years

	Year		
Industry	*1947*	*1962*	*1968*
Mining	99%	99%	99%
Construction	44	80	99
Manufacturing	95	95	97
Transportation and communications	88	95	98
Wholesale trade	67	69	76
Retail trade	3	33	58
Finance, insurance, and real estate	74	74	74
Services	19	22	67
Aggregate (excludes farming and government)	56	61	79

Source: Finis Welch, "Minimum Wage Legislation in the United States," in Orley Ashenfelter and James Blum, eds., *Evaluating the Labor-Market Effects of Social Programs* (Princeton, N.J.: Industrial Relations Section, Princeton University, 1976), p. 2.

---

[8]Roger Le Roy Miller and Raburn M. Williams, *The Economics of National Issues* (San Francisco: Canfield Press, 1972), p. 65.

[9]Ibid., p. 66.

[10]Finis Welch, "Minimum Wage Legislation in the United States," in Orley Ashenfelter and James Blum, eds., *Evaluating the Labor Market Effects of Social Programs*, (Princeton, N.J.: Industrial Relations Section, Department of Economics, Princeton University, 1976), pp. 1–38.

federal minimums in recent years. Approximately half of nonagricultural nongovernmental employment was in covered firms until 1961, when extensions raised aggregate coverage to just over 60 percent. By 1968, the number had risen to almost 80 percent. Of the industries listed in Table 5–3, the most dramatic increases occurred in services and retail trade. In March 1974, minimum wages were required of 7 million additional workers. Among them were 5 million federal, state, and local government employees; 1.3 million domestic workers (maids, and so on); 654,000 employees of chain stores where a previously existing $250,000 annual sales exemption was phased out; and 100,000 workers in various small firms where exemptions were eliminated.[11] As a result, coverage in the private nonfarm sector increased to almost 83 percent, with retail sales (coverage increased to 63 percent) and services (coverage increased to 83 percent) again the industries most affected.[12,13]

Let us draw on our knowledge of the concept of multimarket equilibrium to determine some of the economic effects of a minimum wage law with incomplete coverage. Consider an economy composed of two sectors (C and U), each of which demands the labor services of unskilled workers. To simplify our discussion, assume that labor demand schedules indicate the number of unskilled workers industries wish to hire at various wage rates (hours of work per employee are fixed), that jobs for the unskilled are equally attractive in the two industries, and that the unskilled always want to work (their supply of labor is fixed). We know that in this situation, multimarket equilibrium will occur when the arrangement of unskilled workers and firms between the two sectors is such that wages are the same in the two sectors. This takes place in Figure 5–5 at a wage rate of $\bar{W}$, with $\bar{E}_c$ the equilibrium employment in industry C and $\bar{E}_u$ the equilibrium employment in industry U. A wage floor of $W_{\min}$ is now imposed on firms in sector C; since the law leaves workers' marginal productivity schedules unaffected, employment declines there to E'_c.[14] Remember that all unskilled workers desire jobs, so that the quantity of labor they offer to firms in the uncovered sector increases

[11]Ibid., pp. 3–5.

[12]Ibid. The 1974 legislation also increased the wage floor to $2 in May 1974, $2.10 in January 1975, and $2.30 in January 1977. For a discussion of the 1977 FLSA amendment, see 1977 *Minimum Wage Law, Fair Labor Standards Act with* 1977 *Amendments* (Washington, D.C.: The Bureau of National Affairs, 1977).

[13]Remember that FLSA is not the only legislation establishing wage minimums. The U.S. Department of Agriculture has enforced a wage floor for sugar workers since 1934, and forty states plus the District of Columbia had minimum wage laws in 1976. See ibid., p. 4, and Gordon T. Bloom and Herbert R. Northrup, *Economics of Labor Relations* (Homewood, Ill.: Irwin, 1977), pp. 500–02.

[14]We are assuming that all firms obey the law. The Fair Labor Standards Act contains mechanisms for enforcement of minimum wage provisions and incentives for compliance by employers. Jacob Mincer, "Unemployment Effects of Minimum Wages," *Journal of Political Economy*, 84, 4, part 2 (August 1976), S99, discusses recent unpublished research which suggests a high degree of compliance by firms in the United States.

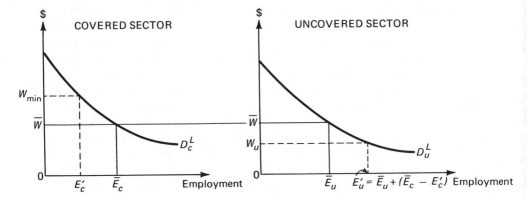

FIGURE 5–5. Multimarket Equilibrium before and after Minimum Wage Legislation with Incomplete Coverage

by the number of persons displaced by the minimum wage legislation ($\bar{E}_c -$ E'_c). Ultimately, the increased supply of labor to the uncovered sector bids down wages there to W_u, and both labor markets are again cleared.

Notice that the economic effects of the minimum wage are similar to those of a taxation program which redistributes income from workers in the uncovered sector to workers in the covered sector. In the above example, the two sectors employ approximately an equal number of workers before the legislation. Moreover, the minimum wage is such that half the workers initially employed in the covered sector (one-fourth of the total labor force) are displaced. As a result, 75 percent of the unskilled work force suffers an economic welfare loss.[15] In general, the number of "winners" versus "losers" depends upon the relative size of the covered sector, the elasticity of demand for unskilled labor in the covered sector, and the minimum wage relative to the competitive multimarket equilibrium wage. The size of the implicit per capita tax paid by the "losers" ($\bar{W} - W_u$), depends upon all these plus the elasticity of demand for unskilled labor in the uncovered sector.[16]

APPLICATION: THE LABOR FORCE PARTICIPATION OF MARRIED WOMEN REVISITED

Our analysis of labor supply in Chapter 4 examined aggregate cross-section regressions for 1950 and 1970 of the labor force participation rate of married women living with their husbands. In Table 4–3 we saw that in both years females' labor force participation is positively related to their wage

---

[15]If the minimum wage were applied to both industries (complete coverage) what is the fraction of unskilled workers made worse off?

[16]In Chapter 7 we will see that some of the economic effects of trade unions are the same as those of minimum wage legislation with incomplete coverage.

across standard metropolitan areas, but that the coefficient is much smaller in the 1970 regression. Thus, some doubt is cast on our ability to understand the dramatic increase in the labor force participation of married women. Having learned comparative statics analysis and the concept of competitive multimarket equilibrium, we are now able to speculate as to the source of the difference between the wage coefficient in the 1950 and 1970 regressions.

Figure 5–6 depicts the theoretical structure on which the "labor supply" regressions in Table 4–3 are based. The demand for labor is assumed to differ across cities (or over time), so that it crosses a fixed supply curve (holding constant y, husband's income) at successively higher wage rates, inducing more and more women to engage in market work. So, our approach in Chapter 4 is that the variation of female labor force participation is due *solely* to variation in the demand for female labor. Even if the economywide labor supply curve of married women were unchanging over time, however, only by chance would the simple regression methods described in Chapter 4 enable us to estimate this supply curve with data relating to different local labor markets (for example, cities or standard metropolitan statistical areas) for a given date.

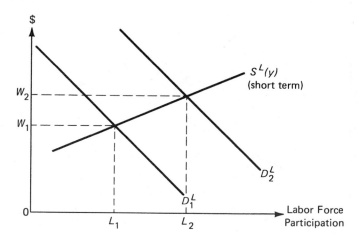

FIGURE 5–6. Short-Term Labor Supply to Cities 1 and 2

In order to see why cross-section data may not yield estimates of an economywide supply curve, suppose that points L_1, W_1 and L_2, W_2 in Figure 5–6 represent the wage rate–labor force participation relationship along the labor supply curve for married women identical in every respect except that they live in city 1 and city 2, respectively. The demand curve for labor in city 2, which for convenience we may assume is the same size as city 1, lies farther to the right than that of city 1, leading to a higher wage rate and labor force participation. In this case, the relationship between wage rate and labor force participation would represent the same thing across cities as in the entire economy; however, we would not expect this configuration of demand and supply to persist in the long term. Because families would eventually tend to relocate away from low-wage city 1 toward high-wage city 2, $S^L(y)$ in Figure 5–7 is labeled a *short-term* labor supply curve to cities 1 and 2. The long-term adjustment to multimarket equilibrium is shown in Figure 5–7 where the movement of females to city 2 causes the labor supply curve there to shift rightward so $S_2^L(y)$, while the same relocation causes the labor supply curve in city 1 to shift leftward to $S_1^L(y)$.[17] Obviously, this migration will reduce the labor force and population of city 1 while increasing that of city 2. When the wage rate equals W^* in both local labor markets, there is *long-term equilibrium* in Figure 5–7 because there is no further incentive for families (or firms) to relocate. Labor force participation has grown to L_2^* in city 2 and fallen to L_1^* in city 1.[18]

The crucial feature of long-term equilibrium, then, is that *for identical workers there will be no relationship between labor force participation and the wage rate across local labor markets*, since labor supply will adjust to differ-

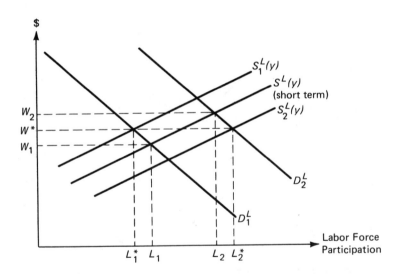

FIGURE 5–7. Long-Term Adjustment of Supply to Demand in Cities 1 & 2

---

[17] Firms would be expected to relocate in the opposite direction in search of lower costs. The effect on long-term equilibrium values of wage rates and labor force participation is the same as the relocation of the labor force, but is not depicted in Figure 5–7 in order to simplify the diagram.

[18] This does not necessarily mean, however, that the labor force participation *rate* has grown in city 2 and fallen in city 1, since *population* has moved in the same direction. Should the movers who left city 1 in response to higher wage rates in city 2 be those who are most likely to work, given wage rates and family income, then the labor force participation rate in city 2 would in the end be higher than that of city 1. See Jacob Mincer, "Labor Force Participation and Unemployment: A Review of Recent Evidence," in eds., R. A. and M. S. Gordon, *Prosperity and Unemployment* (New York: Wiley, 1966), pp. 73–112.

ences in labor demand. What is true across local labor markets within the economy is not true for the economy as a whole, an intercity migration nets out to zero when all the local labor markets are aggregated. Thus, the long-term labor supply curve of married women to the economy may well be the upward-sloping curve we have assumed, while the long-term labor supply curve across local labor markets is likely to be a different creature altogether. If the relationship between the labor force participation of married women and their wage rates across cities in the United States more closely approximates one of long-term equilibrium today than it did in 1950, this would explain the difficulty we now have in using across-cities estimates of the labor force participation–wage relationship to account for the growth in participation of married women over time.

In order to establish that the distribution of workers across local labor markets in the United States has become more responsive to interarea differences in labor demand, two steps are necessary: (1) The labor force participation relationship must be estimated using statistical techniques capable of identifying both the demand curves and the short-term supply curves (see Chapter 2). The results would show whether the short-term supply relationships estimated in 1970 are similar to those of 1950. (2) An explanation should be furnished for why the labor force participation relationship across cities in 1950 represents a greater deviation from long-term equilibrium conditions than in 1970. One possible explanation is related to the effects of World War II on population distribution. Any major war effort is likely to cause substantial economic disruptions, including the relocation of population and economic activity. To the extent that the effects of such perturbations were still felt in 1950, this could explain part of our puzzle. Evidence which supports the hypothesis that the war resulted in unusual labor market circumstances can be found in estimates of the across-cities labor force participation relationship just before the beginning of World War II. Regressions estimated by Cain and by Bowen and Finegan show that the relationship between the labor force participation of married women and their market wage rates was relatively low in 1940 compared to 1950.[19] This is what we would expect to be the case if the war generated labor market disruptions which persisted through 1950.

Frontiers of Competitive Equilibrium Analysis: The Economics of Industrial Safety

Whenever someone is injured at work, especially if a permanent physical impairment results, the costs of medical treatment, rehabilitation, and foregone earnings can be substantial. Historically, injured workers have borne

---

[19]Glen G. Cain, *Married Women in the Labor Force* (Chicago: University of Chicago Press, 1966), pp. 48 and 64; and William G. Bowen and T. Aldrich Finegan, *The Economics of Labor Force Participation* (Princeton, N.J.: Princeton University Press, 1969), p. 191.

these expenses. In 1908, however, New York passed the first workers' compensation law for the purpose of shifting at least part of the economic burden of work-related disability to the "wealthier" owners of firms; other states had enacted similar statutes by 1948.

State workers' compensation laws provide covered employees and their families with two general types of benefits: direct cash payments for death or loss of income and medical services or cash payments for such services (including rehabilitation).[20] Workers' compensation benefits stem from insurance carried by employers, and in general, direct payments are a proportion of the affected workers' earnings, up to a statutory maximum.[21] Since reductions in the frequency or severity of injuries reduces firms' insurance premiums, workers' compensation laws provide an economic incentive to improve workplace safety. Despite this, approximately 14,000 deaths and 2 million disabling injuries per year have occurred in American industry in recent years.[22] Recent research by Thaler and Rosen utilizes data from a sample of insurance company records for 1955–64 to meter the additional risk of death associated with particular occupations.[23] Specifically, the expected number of deaths was calculated for men in an occupation in an industry based on the age distribution of individuals in the sample records and standard life tables. This figure was then substracted from actual deaths in an occupation-industry category to produce the extra risk of death due to occupational hazards. Calculations for selected occupations are presented in Table 5–4. Consider, for example, the figure for boilermakers. Compared to a set of men with the same age distribution in the population at large, boilermakers endure approximately 230 additional deaths per 100,000. As a point of reference, the number of deaths (based on the 1967 life tables) for white males 35 years old was about 200 in 100,000.[24] So, if one worked as a boilermaker, the likelihood of mortality was more than two times greater than the probability of mortality in general. Remember that the figures in Table 5–4 reflect more than just fatal accidents; deaths from every aspect of an occupation, such as tension-induced heart attacks, are represented.

Political pressure to increase work safety led to the passage of the Occupational Safety and Health Act of 1970 (OSHA). Designed to "assure insofar as possible every working man and woman in the nation safe and healthful working conditions," OSHA applies to almost all employees not covered by

---

[20]For a discussion of the provisions of workers' compensation laws, see Bloom and Northrup, *Economics of Labor Relations*, pp. 550–55, and Nicholas A. Ashford, *Crisis in the Workplace* (Cambridge, Mass.: The MIT Press, 1976), pp. 386–423.

[21]Most states permit firms to self-insure.

[22]*Accident Facts* (Chicago: The National Safety Council, 1975), p. 25. As a point of reference, motor vehicle accidents killed 21,400 and injured 800,000 people in 1974.

[23]Richard Thaler and Sherwin Rosen, "The Value of Saving a Life: Evidence from the Labor Market," in Nestor E. Terleckyj, ed., *Household Production and Consumption* (New York: Columbia University Press, 1975), pp. 265–98.

[24]Ibid., p. 287.

TABLE 5-4

Additional Mortality Risk in Selected Occupations, Males, 1966

Occupation	Additional Risk*
Actors	73
Bartenders	176
Boilermakers	230
Cooks	132
Electricians	93
Elevator operators	188
Firemen	44
Fishermen	19
Guards, watchmen, and doorkeepers	267
Hucksters and peddlers	76
Longshoremen and stevedores	101
Lumbermen	256
Mine operatives	176
Power plant operatives	6
Railroad conductors	203
Sailors and deckhands	163
Taxicab drivers	182
Waiters	134

*Actuarial data were used to calculate the expected number of deaths per 100,000 male workers in each occupation based on standard life tables and the age distribution of workers in that occupation. Expected deaths per 100,000 were then subtracted from actual deaths to yield the data for additional risk. It is possible for an occupation to have a negative additional mortality risk. Why?

Source: Richard Thaler and Sherwin Rosen, "The Value of Saving a Life: Evidence from the Labor Market," in Nestor E. Terleckyj, ed., *Household Production and Consumption* (New York: Columbia University Press, the National Bureau of Economic Research, 1975), p. 288.

special statutes such as the Coal Mine Health and Safety Act. Employers are required to maintain safe and healthful places of work in general and to comply with the safety and health standards of the act in particular.[25] While workers are also expected to adhere to OSHA's rules, there are no provisions in the law for penalizing them if they do not. All responsibility for compliance is placed on employers, who are subject to fines or shutdowns for violations.[26]

It is only recently that economists have used competitive equilibrium

---

[25]Bloom and Northrup, *Labor Relations*, p. 556.

[26]For detailed descriptions of the provisions of the Occupational Safety and Health Act of 1970, see Ashford, *Crisis in the Workplace*, pp. 138–307.

analysis to examine the topic of workplace safety. We will now present some of their ideas concerning the competitive equilibrium level of job safety and utilize them to shed light on the effectiveness of workers' compensation and OSHA.[27]

THE DETERMINATION OF INDUSTRIAL INJURIES IN COMPETITION

Work-related injuries can best be thought of as undesirable by-products of the process that produces goods for consumption. In this respect, they are similar to noise, smoke, and other forms of pollution. Moreover, the limitation of injuries, like pollution abatement, is a costly activity. A formal "safety awareness" program requires instructors to lecture workers on ways to reduce accidents, time off from work for employees to attend this instruction, and plant safety inspectors. Up-to-date machinery and additional equipment such as rubber gloves and goggles will decrease accidents or their severity, but these items are not free. Lung ailments may be eliminated through the installation of a better ventilation system. More liberal sick leave benefits will reduce accidents by workers who are fatigued or not fully recovered from illness. Finally, there are implicit expenditures a firm may make to improve the health and safety of its workers, such as reducing the temperature of a chemical process below its most efficient level in order to lower the severity of burns, or slowing the pace of an assembly line. Such actions make output less than it would have been in their absence.

The curve in Figure 5–8 depicts the relationship between a representative competitive firm's expenditures on worker health and safety (E) within a given period and the fraction of its labor force that will be injured (i), holding constant total number of employees (N). Notice that many different levels of safety (injury) are possible. The firm can substantially reduce its injury rate with sufficiently large expenditures on health and safety. Alternatively, if very little is spent, relatively few employees escape harm. In the sense that the relationship depicted in Figure 5–8 represents the firm's ability to generate increased safety by devoting more resources to accident and disease prevention, it may be thought of as a **safety production function.**

What are the key properties of the (E, i) relationship as we have drawn it? The value of the slope tells us how much money the firm must spend in order to reduce i by .01 (one percentage point). The curve is convex to the origin, becoming relatively steep as it approaches the injury rate i_{min} and relatively flat as it approaches the injury rate i_{max}. This says little more than that there are minimum and maximum degrees of job safety and that decreasing the injury rate from 0.69 to 0.68, say, is much "easier" than decreasing it from

---

27The basic theoretical structure presented in this section is that of Walter Oi, "An Essay on Workmen's Compensation and Industrial Safety," in *Supplemental Studies for the National Commission on State Workmen's Compensation Laws*, vol. I, 1974, pp. 41–106.

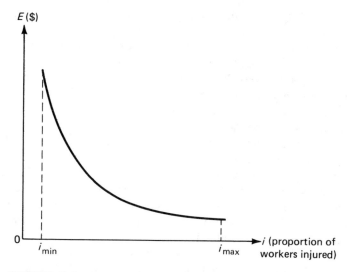

FIGURE 5–8. A Competitive Firm's Safety Production Function

0.12 to 0.11. (Can you explain why this is reasonable?) It is important to note that the position and shape of the (E, i) curve may differ across firms. What would the curve probably look like for a firm in an "innately hazardous" industry such as coal mining, as opposed to one in an "innately safe" industry such as banking?

Thus far we have noted the economic similarity between pollution and injuries—namely, that they are socially undesirable offshoots of production which are costly to eliminate. There is a crucial economic difference between the two, however. Firms usually have little or no financial incentive to reduce effluents because it is difficult to charge the parties that benefit (other firms or individuals). In contrast, there is an economic incentive for employers to improve workplace safety because their production costs decline when jobs are made less dangerous. A lower injury rate reduces labor costs in two ways. First, employee turnover is decreased as fewer new workers must be hired to replace those unable to work. Think back to our discussion in Chapter 3 (see Table 3–1) of the rather substantial expenses a firm may have whenever it hires a worker. Second, firms that offer safer working conditions can attract employees at a lower wage rate, since to most workers exposure to a hazardous situation is a "bad" for which they must be compensated financially.[28]

---

[28]For formal empirical support of this latter point, see Thaler and Rosen, "The Value of Saving a Life." As casual evidence, we offer this passage from a recent column by Jack Anderson (*The Washington Post*, March 7, 1979, p. B16), "We sent our associate Vicki Warren to work undercover at the Washington regional bulk mail center, and when she saw the appalling conditions the facility's employees must work in, she asked them why they didn't quit. The universal response was that the pay was too good to pass up. The postal workers are, in effect, being paid to risk life and limb."

Having noted that there are economic penalties and benefits to employers from improving workplace safety, we can examine the determination of the equilibrium injury rate in a competitive firm. From Chapter 3 we know that competitive firms minimize their production costs. To see that this leads to a particular injury rate, we will analyze how the various components of total production cost change when a firm adjusts job safety. Production cost is composed of three categories: purchases of labor services, purchases of capital services, and expenditures on plant safety. Consider an increase in E that results in a smaller percentage of employees suffering work-related injuries. [Remember that worker safety (s) is measured by $(1 - i)$, or the fraction of the labor force that does not sustain injuries.] The **marginal expense of safety (MES)** is defined as the increase in production costs stemming from the increase in E as a firm increases safety.[29] Depicted in Figure 5–9, the *MES* schedule is upward-sloping, indicating that when many workers are injured, it is relatively cheap to make a small improvement in safety, whereas when there is near-perfect safety, it is quite expensive to reduce injuries further. Improved plant safety also means that fewer workers must be hired to replace those injured and that a smaller wage rate premium is necessary to induce individuals to accept risk. The reduction in production

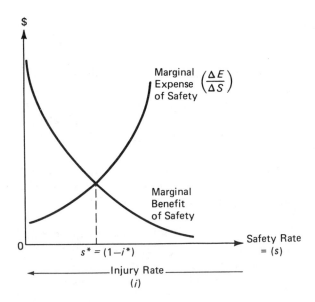

FIGURE 5–9. The Determination of the Injury Rate in a Competitive Industry

---

[29]Remember that since the safety rate is $(1 - i)$, an increase in safety is the same as a decrease in i.

cost (C) stemming from these two sources is the **marginal benefit of safety (MBS)**. Also shown in Figure 5–9, MBS is downward-sloping because the wage premium necessary to "bribe" workers into accepting a higher probability of injury is assumed to be greater when i is high than when i is low.[30]

An increase in industrial safety (a decrease in i) will lower a firm's total production cost whenever $MBS > MES$ and increase it whenever $MES > MBS$. Thus, the optimal or cost-minimizing rate of worker injuries in competition is that value of i for which the marginal expense of safety equals the marginal benefit of safety. In Figure 5–9 this occurs at injury rate i^* (safety rate s^*). At a safety rate lower than s^*, extra safety is a "good buy," while safety in excess of s^* costs more than it is worth. Notice the general result: *The firm's optimal number of work-related injuries is not zero.* While feasible, "perfect" safety is too costly.

THE EFFECT OF THE WORKERS' COMPENSATION PROGRAM ON INDUSTRIAL SAFETY

In practice, the workers' compensation program (WC) places a lower boundary on a particular aspect of the pay package, injury insurance protection. Oi points out that how this affects the level of industrial safety depends on whether in the absence of WC individuals are correctly cognizant of work hazards.[31] Suppose that in Figure 5–10 MES and MBS represent the marginal expense of safety and the marginal benefit of safety, respectively, before the imposition of the program. If individuals are initially fully informed as to the probability and severity of industrial injuries, then WC is likely to have little or no effect on work safety.[32] The reason is that the required consumption of injury insurance through the workers' compensation program is likely to be accompanied by a reduction in direct wage payments to workers, leading to a reduction by workers in expenditures for private injury insurance. Since WC does not alter work hazards directly, or (in this case) workers' willingness to accept exposure to those hazards, but rather regulates only the distribution of the pay package between direct wage payments and insurance premiums, the total hourly rate of pay in a competitive labor market should be unaffected by WC.[33] The end result is that MBS in Figure 5–10 is the marginal benefit of safety before and after WC, and the equilibrium safety rate will remain at s^*.

This scenario is not the only possibility, of course. If workers have under-

---

[30]Since we are assuming that workers are alike in their productive characteristics, the marginal benefit from replacing fewer injured workers is a constant which affects the height of MBS but not its slope. If the bribe necessary to induce workers to accept injury risk were also independent of i, what would MBS look like?

[31]Oi, "An Essay on Workmen's Compensation," pp. 69–71.

[32]Ibid.

[33]Ibid.

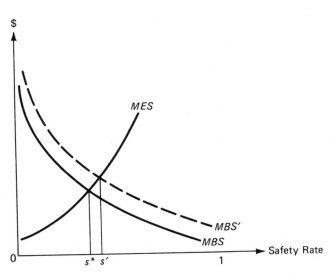

FIGURE 5–10. Possible Effects of Workers' Compensation on Industrial Safety

estimated the true risk of industrial injury, this results in a market wage rate premium which is "too low," and *MBS* lies below the marginal benefit of safety schedule associated with the "correct" premium, *MBS'*. The equilibrium safety rate, *s**, is less than that which would characterize a labor market where workers correctly gauged work injury risk, *s'*. If the forced consumption of insurance makes employees aware of the true degree of hazard associated with their jobs, then the equalizing wage rate differential will increase and the marginal benefit schedule will shift to *MBS'*, and *WC* leads to an increase in the level of industrial safety. Finally, it is also possible for *WC* to reduce *s*. Should *MBS'* represent the marginal benefit of safety before the passage of workers' compensation because workers systematically overestimate the severity of industrial injuries, then *WC* may generate a reduction in job safety if workers are led to assess injury risks more accurately. Although an interesting and important issue, the effect of *WC* on *s* has yet to be established empirically.

THE EFFECT OF OSHA ON INDUSTRIAL SAFETY

In contrast to workers' compensation, The Occupational Safety and Health Act of 1970 (OSHA) attempts to influence job safety directly by placing spending requirements, in excess of what a cost-minimizing firm would normally spend, on safety equipment and other activities designed to

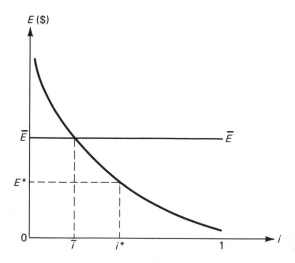

FIGURE 5–11. The Intended Effect of OSHA on Industrial Injuries

reduce work-related injuries. Figure 5–11 illustrates a representative competitive firm's equilibrium injury rate, i^*. It reproduces the firm's safety production function (introduced in Figure 5–8), which indicates the total spending on injury prevention associated with i^*. What OSHA does is to place a lower boundary on E that exceeds E^*, say $\bar{E}$. The intended effect is to reduce the rate of industrial injuries to $\bar{i} < i^*$. We know from our earlier discussions that whether i *should* be reduced from its competitive equilibrium value cannot be readily resolved with scientific economic analysis. We can, however, shed light on another key aspect of OSHA—has it succeeded in its expressed objective of reducing the incidence of work-related injuries?

In a recent monograph, Robert Stewart Smith identified some of the factors that determine OSHA's actual influence on injuries.[34] Since the act attempts to force firms to provide more safety than they have in the past found most profitable, it must impose financial punishment for noncompliance. An employer who has not satisfied OSHA's standards will compare the cost of immediate compliance [$(\bar{E} - E^*)$ in Figure 5–11] net of benefits with those of being discovered in violation of the safety standards, since once detected, violators must pay the cost of compliance plus a fine. Remember, though, that not every firm out of compliance will be caught and punished, so that a profit-maximizing firm will weight these by the likelihood of detection and punishment. In particular, let $O \equiv$ net cost of complying with

[34]*The Occupational Safety and Health Act* (Washington, D.C.: American Enterprise Institute for Public Policy Research, 1976), pp. 59–71.

OSHA's safety standards; $F \equiv$ fine if discovered out of compliance with OSHA's safety standards; and $P \equiv$ probability of being caught out of compliance and fined. Firms will choose to comply immediately with OSHA if

$$O < P(O + F) \qquad (5\text{–}1)$$

and choose noncompliance if the inequality is reversed. You should prove to yourself that if the probability of being caught and fined is, for example, 0.1 (one out of every ten violators are "nabbed"), then F must be at least nine times greater than O in order to induce firms to comply with the provisions of OSHA.

Smith reports reasonably reliable estimates from 1974 by the National Association of Manufacturers indicating that the financial outlays necessary to meet OSHA's requirements $(E^* - \bar{E})$ are substantial: \$35,000 for firms with 1 to 100 employees, \$73,500 for firms with 101 to 500 employees, and \$350,000 for firms with 501 to 1,000 employees.[35] Even if these figures greatly overstate the true cost, however, there is still little economic incentive for cost-conscious firms to comply immediately, since the probability of inspection is quite low. During fiscal 1973, only 1.3 percent of all covered plants were inspected; at this rate, the average plant is inspected once every seventy-seven years. Even workplaces receiving special attention, manufacturing plants with over 1,000 employees, have an inspection rate of only 10 percent.[36] Moreover, when violations have been uncovered, fines have tended to be rather small. The average noncomplying firm has been fined about \$170 (about \$25 per violation).[37] Incentives to comply with OSHA's standards after violations are discovered are somewhat greater, but still far from strong. Although fines for willful and repeated violations have averaged \$1,104, less than one-fourth of plants with violations received follow-up inspections.[38] Finally, even if firms comply totally with OSHA's provisions, industrial injuries will not decrease greatly if the legal safety standards do not remove the hazards that lead to accidents. Smith cites studies of accidents in Wisconsin and New York which indicate that only 25 to 33 percent of all injuries involve a permanent physical hazard capable of being eliminated by standard-setting and an inspection program.[39] Thus, it is not surprising that in a regression analysis of the safety effects of OSHA, he cannot reject the hypothesis that the trend in the injury rate for 1970–73 in heavily inspected industries was the same as it would have been in the absence of such inspections.[40]

---

[35]Ibid., p. 62.
[36]Ibid.
[37]Ibid., p. 63.
[38]Ibid., p. 64.
[39]Ibid., p. 65.
[40]Ibid., p. 69.

Conclusion

The concept of a market is central to all economic analysis. In this chapter, we examined in detail a labor market under competitive conditions and the circumstances under which a unique wage-employment transaction, satisfactory to both households and firms, occurs. Our knowledge of the underpinnings of labor supply and demand gained in Chapters 3 and 4 enabled us to predict the labor market influence of changes in the environment and to gain some insights into one economic aspect of a particular public policy, the incidence of the social security tax.

An economy is really composed of *many* labor markets. When competitive conditions apply, a wage rate for labor of a given type will persist in a labor market only if it is the same as wages elsewhere. Wage inequalities between labor markets will lead workers to leave employment in relatively low wage markets and seek employment in relatively high wage markets. This migration pattern promotes equality of wages, since only when there is equal pay in alternative markets is there no financial incentive to relocate. An important implication of this worker mobility pattern is that it leads to *economic efficiency*: the maximization of production with society's available resources. A related point is that institutions such as a minimum wage that inhibit the forces of competitive general equilibrium impose a cost on society in the form of reduced consumption of goods and services. It is impossible to conclude on scientific grounds, however, that such institutions are undesirable whenever they alter the *distribution* of income. The concept of multimarket equilibrium also proved useful in improving our understanding of the labor force participation of married women.

The area of industrial safety has recently been given special attention by labor economists. Whether the quality of industrial life is affected by workers' compensation and the Occupational Safety and Health Act of 1970, the major federal laws regulating job safety, is an interesting and important, but as yet unsettled, issue.

Exercises

*1. A market for low-wage labor has the supply and demand schedules

$$L = 2W \quad \text{(supply)}$$
$$L = 100 - 2W \quad \text{(demand)},$$

where $L \equiv$ number of workers
$W \equiv$ daily wage.

(a) Graph the supply and demand for labor. What is the equilibrium W-L combination?

The government introduces an income maintenance program that supplements the daily wage of workers by the difference between their daily wage and $40. Expressed algebraically, the program provides a daily wage supplement (S) such that

$$S = (\$40 - W) \text{ for } W \leq \$40$$
$$= 0, \text{ otherwise.}$$

Assume that individuals' willingness to supply labor at various daily wage rates is *unaffected* by this income support plan.
(b) Explain why their labor supply function to firms then becomes $L = 2W + S$. (Hint: Use a graph)
(c) What is the new market equilibrium W-L combination?
(d) Show that income support payments made by the rest of society to low-wage workers total $1,200.

2. The following are the labor supply and demand schedules for a particular labor market.

Labor Demand Schedule		Labor Supply Schedule	
Daily Wage	*Quantity of Labor Demanded*	*Daily Wage*	*Quantity of Labor Supplied*
$60	0	0	0
55	500	$ 5	500
50	1000	10	1000
45	1500	15	1500
40	2000	20	2000
35	2500	25	2500
30	3000	30	3000
25	3500	35	3500
20	4000	40	4000
15	4500	45	4500
10	5000	50	5000
5	5500	55	5500

(a) What is the equilibrium wage? Explain how you arrived at your answer.

Suppose now that Congress levies a tax on workers of $10 per unit of labor supplied. Specifically, they must "mail in checks" (have withheld from their pay) $10 for each unit of labor they sell.

(b) What is the new equilibrium wage? Explain carefully.

---

*Indicates more difficult exercises

✓ (c) Who *actually* pays the tax of $10 per unit of labor? Be as *complete* as possible in your answer.

(d) What is the *total* tax revenue collected by the government? Explain carefully.

(e) On the whole, have workers been made better off or worse off? Be as *complete* as possible in your answer.

3. Suppose that for a particular large profit maximizing firm

$C \equiv$ net cost of complying with OSHA's safety standards = $500,000,

$P \equiv$ probability of being caught out of compliance and fined = .10

$F \equiv$ fine if caught out of compliance = $200.

Demonstrate that

(a) this firm will *not* voluntarily comply with OSHA's safety standards.

(b) *Given* the above value of F ($200), how high would P have to go so as to induce the firm to voluntarily comply with OSHA?

(c) *Given* the above value of P (.10), how high would F have to go so as to induce the firm to voluntarily comply with OSHA?

(d) Suppose you are a policy-maker with the goal of getting firms to voluntarily comply with OSHA at minimum cost to society. What policy would you suggest? Justify your answer.

References

ANDERSON, JACK, "'Doors of Death' for Postal Workers," *The Washington Post*, March 7, 1979, p. B16.

ASHFORD, NICHOLAS ASKOUNES, *Crisis in the Workplace: Occupational Disease and Injury*. Cambridge, Mass.: The MIT Press, 1976.

BLOOM, GORDON F., and HERBERT R. NORTHRUP, *Economics of Labor Relations*. Homewood, Ill.: Irwin, 1977, pp. 550–57.

BOWEN, WILLIAM G. and T. ALDRICH FINEGAN, *The Economics of Labor Force Participation*. Princeton, N.J.: Princeton University Press, 1969, p. 191.

CAIN, GLEN G., *Married Women in the Labor Force*. Chicago: University of Chicago Press, 1966, pp. 48 and 64.

MILLER, ROGER LeROY, and RABURN M. WILLIAMS, *The Economics of National Issues*. San Francisco: Canfield Press, 1972, pp. 65–71.

MINCER, JACOB, "Unemployment Effects of Minimum Wages." *Journal of Political Economy*, 84, 4, part 2 (August 1976), S87–S104.

OI, WALTER, "An Essay on Workmen's Compensation and Industrial Safety." In

Supplemental Studies for the National Commission on State Workmen's Compensation Laws, vol. I, 1973, pp. 41–106.

SMITH, ROBERT STEWART, *The Occupational Safety and Health Act*. Washington, D.C.: The American Enterprise Institute for Public Policy Research, 1976.

THALER, RICHARD, and SHERWIN ROSEN, "The Value of Saving a Life: Evidence from the Labor Market." In Nestor E. Terleckyj, ed., *Household Production and Consumption*. New York: Columbia University Press, 1975.

WELCH, FINIS, "Minimum Wage Legislation in the United States." In Orley Ashenfelter and James Blum, eds., *Evaluating the Labor Market Effects of Social Programs*. Princeton, N.J.: Industrial Relations Section, Princeton University, 1976.

PART III

The Labor Market
in the Short Run
under Conditions
that Interfere
with Competition

CHAPTER 6

The Labor Market
When Buyers Are Noncompetitive

A. Educational Objectives
  1. Study of how buyers and sellers of labor interact to determine workers' economic welfare when employers are noncompetitive
  2. Comparison of how wage-employment combinations and the effect of certain public policies differ from the competitive case

B. Monopoly in the Product Market
  1. Definition of and conditions which promote monopoly
  2. The demand for labor by a monopolist with a fixed capital input
    a. Marginal revenue product of labor
    b. Role of the labor supply schedule
    c. Profit maximization and the marginal revenue product of labor as the monopolist's labor demand schedule
    d. Application: the effects of various taxes on a monopolist's demand for labor
  3. The demand for labor by a monopolist when it adjusts capital
  4. The market labor demand schedule when some or all firms are monopolists: the concept of monopolistic exploitation

C. Monopsony
  1. Definition and conditions which promote monopsony
  2. The role of the labor supply schedule: increasing marginal cost of labor services
  3. The "demand" for labor by a monopsonist when capital is fixed
    a. Application: the concept of monopsonistic exploitation
    b. Application: the effect of a minimum wage law on workers' economic welfare in the case of monopsony
  4. Evidence on the incidence of monopsony in the U.S.

Until now, our analysis of wages and employment has concentrated on the interaction between households and firms when labor and product markets are competitive. In such situations a firm maximizes profit, a household maximizes utility, and an individual buyer or seller of labor services is unable to affect wage rates or the prices of final products. In this chapter, we study markets where labor is demanded by various types of *noncompetitive* firms. Specifically, we will discuss the cases where a good or service is produced by a single firm or where labor services are purchased by only one firm. The economic theory of wages and employment is the same for competitive and noncompetitive labor markets. Equilibrium is determined by the forces of supply and demand, with marginal productivity of labor the key factor underlying the demand for labor services. So, we need only generalize some of the concepts learned in Chapter 3 to examine labor markets in which firms are noncompetitive. Our discussions will focus on two important questions: (1) How do equilibrium wage-employment combinations differ from the competitive case? (2) How do the labor market effects of certain public policies differ from the competitive case?

Product Market Monopoly

A firm is a **monopolist** when it is the sole seller of a particular good or service. The most obvious real-life examples of product market monopolists are the public utilities. Only rarely are consumers able to choose their telephone company, for example. In this case, the monopoly is usually due to average total cost reaching a minimum at a level of output large enough to supply the entire market at a price sufficient to cover full cost. Such a monopoly is typically referred to as a *natural monopoly.*[1] Monopolies may exist for other

---

*Represents more advanced material

[1] For elaboration, see Jack Hirshleifer, *Price Theory and Applications* (Englewood Cliffs, N.J.: Prentice-Hall, 1976), pp. 288–90. An interesting aspect of the natural monopolies is that they are typically subject to some form of government regulation insuring a "fair but not excessive" return to owners of capital. The result can be a markedly different utilization of labor than in the absence of such regulation. Since it is typically treated in texts on industrial organization, we choose not to discuss labor market distortion stemming from public regulation of natural monopolies. See, for example, F. M. Scherer, *Industrial Market Structure and Economic Performance* (Chicago: Rand McNally, 1970), pp. 529–37.

reasons, however. One firm may exercise complete control over an input necessary to manufacture a certain product. Alternatively, a producer may hold a government franchise giving it the exclusive rights to the production and distribution of a good or service within an area. Finally, monopoly may stem from a patent on a product or the process involved in its manufacture.

THE DEMAND FOR LABOR BY A MONOPOLIST
WHEN CAPITAL IS FIXED

In Chapter 3 we saw that when it is unable to adjust its input of capital services, the competitive firm hires that amount of labor services which equates the value of the marginal product of labor (VMP_L) with the wage rate, so that the VMP_L schedule is the competitive firm's labor demand curve. The profit-maximizing monopolist also employs labor up to the point where the last unit hired increases production cost and sales revenue by equal amounts. Once we have found something analogous to VMP_L for a monopolist, we shall have identified its demand for labor during a period of time which is too short for capital to be adjusted.

Unlike the competitive firm, which has no control over product price, the monopolist determines price by its output decision. Remember that since a monopoly firm is the sole seller of a good or service, it is also the *industry*. Therefore, the demand curve for the monopolist's output is the market demand schedule, which is downward-sloping, since as additional units are offered for sale, price declines.[2] This means that when calculating the value of an additional unit of labor services, the monopolist considers not only that it will have more output to sell at a positive price, but also that *all* its output will sell for less per unit. Economists call the monopolist's change in total revenue due to a (small) change in labor services **the marginal revenue product of labor (MRP$_L$).** A numerical example will help us understand the sense of the terminology and illustrate that MRP_L is the monopolist's labor demand curve.

In Table 6–1, column 2 lists the levels of output (Q) associated with various amounts of labor (L) for a Cobb-Douglas type production function with capital services fixed. Column 4 displays the prices (P) associated with the various outputs when the market demand schedule for final product is linear and downward-sloping. Consider what happens as L is increased from 1 to 2 units, for example. Q rises from 10 to 17, and price falls from $180 to $166. Column 6, which displays marginal revenue (MR), tells us that, on average, each of the 11th through 17th units increases total revenue by only $146. While units 11 to 17 will each sell for $166, units 1 to 10 will now sell for $14 less apiece. So, MRP_L, the extra revenue created by an additional unit of labor services, is equal to $1,022 (column 7), which is less than P times the

---

[2]We shall assume, for simplicity, that the monopolist is unable to price discriminate.

TABLE 6–1

Derivation of a Monopolist's Marginal Revenue Product of Labor Schedule

(1) ←——Production Function——→ L	(2) Q^*	(3) MPP_L	(4) $P\dagger$	(5) TR	(6) MR	(7) MRP_L
0	0	—	—	—	—	—
1	10	10	$180	$1,800	$180	$1,800
2	17	7	166	2,822	146	1,022
3	23	6	154	3,542	120	720
4	28	5	144	4,032	98	490
5	33	5	134	4,422	78	390
6	38	5	124	4,712	58	290
7	43	5	114	4,902	38	190
8	48	5	104	4,992	18	90
9	52	4	96	4,992	0	0
10	56	4	88	4,928	−16	−64

$L \equiv$ units of labor services

$Q \equiv$ units of output

$MPP_L \equiv$ marginal physical product of labor $\left(\dfrac{\Delta Q}{\Delta L}\right)$

$P \equiv$ product price

$TR \equiv$ total revenue $(P \cdot Q)$

$MR \equiv$ marginal revenue $\left(\dfrac{\Delta TR}{\Delta Q}\right)$

$MRP_L \equiv$ marginal revenue product of labor $\left(\dfrac{\Delta TR}{\Delta L}\right) \equiv (MR \cdot MPP_L)$

*Output produced according to the production function, $Q = K^\alpha L^\beta$, where $K \equiv$ capital services $= 10,000$, $\alpha = 0.25$, and $\beta = 0.75$. Output has been rounded to the nearest even unit.
†Price is obtained from the demand curve for output $Q = c - dP$, where $P =$ price, $c = 100$, and $d = 0.5$.

marginal physical product of labor (MPP_L), because the demand curve for the monopolist's output is negatively sloped. (The importance of this will soon become apparent.) Finally, notice that the figures in column 7 are the product of marginal physical product of labor and marginal revenue; hence the name, marginal revenue product of labor.[3]

Thus far we have said nothing about the availability (supply curve) of labor to the monopolist. A number of situations can exist. A monopolist may be one of only a few firms who demand workers' services in a labor market. We examine an extreme version of this, where the monopolist is the only

---

[3]For a graphic derivation of MRP_L, see C. E. Ferguson and J. P. Gould, *Microeconomic Theory*, 4th ed. (Homewood, Ill.: Irwin, 1975), pp. 400–01.

demander of labor, in the next section. Alternatively, a monopolist may compete for employees with *many* other firms, both competitive and monopolistic. In a large city, for example, the public utility monopolies compete with numerous private corporations, small businesses, and government agencies (as well as with each other) for "general" employees such as secretaries, janitors, and middle managers. We now turn our attention to a discussion of the determination of wages and employment in the situation in which a monopolist competes for labor with many other firms.

In a competitive labor market, no one firm, whether a competitor or a monopolist in its output market, is a sufficiently large purchaser of labor services to influence the equilibrium wage rate. The supply curve of labor to the monopolist in this case is the same as we are used to seeing for a competitive firm, perfectly elastic (horizontal) at the prevailing wage. Such a situation is depicted in Figure 6–1, where $\bar{W}\bar{W}$ is the supply curve of labor to individual firms. What remains to be demonstrated is that MRP_L is the monopolist's labor demand curve. All we need show is that, confronted with a particular (constant) wage rate, the monopolist maximizes profit by hiring the amount of labor services that equates the marginal revenue product of labor to that wage.

We know from our previous study of the principles of economics that any profit-maximizing firm chooses its output so that marginal revenue (MR) equals marginal cost (MC). With a little algebra it is easily shown that this decision rule is equivalent to choosing L such that $MRP_L = W$. Remember

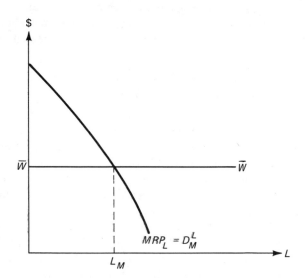

FIGURE 6–1. The Demand for Labor Schedule of a Monopolist When Capital Is Fixed and Labor Services Are Purchased in a Competitive Labor Market

that marginal cost is defined as the change in a firm's total cost (TC) due to a small change in its output (Q). Denoting the change in a variable by Δ, we have

$$MC \equiv \frac{\Delta TC}{\Delta Q} \qquad (6\text{–}1)$$

Total cost (TC) includes expenditures for the services of capital and labor,

$$TC = wL + rK \qquad (6\text{–}2)$$

where $r \equiv$ price of a unit of capital services, and $K \equiv$ quantity of capital services. Since we are considering the situation in which capital is fixed, only labor costs change when the firm adjusts its production, or[4]

$$MC \equiv \frac{\Delta TC}{\Delta Q} = w\frac{\Delta L}{\Delta Q} = W\frac{1}{MPP_L} \qquad (6\text{–}3)$$

Utilizing (6–3), when marginal cost equals marginal revenue,

$$W\frac{1}{MPP_L} = MR$$

or

$$W = (MPP_L \cdot MR) \equiv MRP_L \qquad (6\text{–}4)$$

Thus, when confronted with a given wage rate, the monopolist maximizes profit by hiring that amount of labor services which equates labor's marginal revenue product to W. In Figure 6–1 the firm will hire L_M units of labor.

APPLICATION: THE EFFECTS OF VARIOUS TAXES
ON A MONOPOLIST'S DEMAND FOR LABOR

Let us examine how the demand for labor by a monopolist is affected by three different taxes: (1) a fixed-rate profit tax, (2) a lump-sum tax, and (3) a fixed-rate revenue tax. While probably not readily apparent, the effects of all three taxes are not difficult to analyze. The profit tax means that some constant fraction of the difference between total revenue and total cost, say t, must be paid to a government revenue collection agency. The tax rate t is greater than zero and less than or equal to one. What this means is that the monopolist may keep $(1 - t) \cdot 100$ percent of each dollar of profit. If we let π stand for a monopolist's profit, which is initially assumed to be positive, this tax reduces profit to $(1 - t)\pi$. It is obvious that since t is a constant,

---

[4]What is the economic interpretation of $\frac{1}{MPP_L}$?

$(1 - t)\pi$ is maximized when π is maximized. So, the monopolist confronted with a fixed-rate tax on profit will still equate MRP_L to W, with the former serving as its labor demand schedule, since after-tax (net) profit is maximized when before-tax (gross) profit is maximized. A lump-sum tax means that the monopolist's net profit becomes $\pi - T$, where T dollars must be paid to the taxing agency whether or not production occurs. Since $\pi - T$ is maximized where gross profit (π) is maximized, the lump-sum tax does not affect the monopolist's labor demand schedule. In this case, the tax works like a fixed cost which we know affects the value of profit but not the choice of the optimal amount of labor services.

We know that in the absence of taxation, the profit-maximizing monopolist hires that amount of labor where the wage rate equals the marginal physical product of labor times marginal revenue. A fixed-rate revenue (sales) tax means that when additional dollars of sales revenue are generated, the firm may keep $(1 - m) \cdot 100$ percent of each dollar, where m is the constant tax rate on revenue. So, the monopolist's net marginal revenue when production is expanded is $(1 - m)MR$, and profit is maximized when the net marginal product of labor equals the wage rate, or when

$$(1 - m)(MR \cdot MPP_L) \equiv (1 - m)MRP_L = W \qquad (6\text{-}5)$$

Figure 6–2 illustrates the labor demand schedules of a monopolist before and after the tax in the particular situation where MRP_L is linear and $m = 0.5$. Notice that $D_M^{L'}$ is constructed by bisecting the distance between D_M^L and

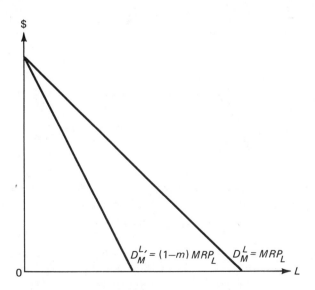

FIGURE 6–2. The Effect of a Fixed-Rate Revenue Tax on a Monopolist Demand for Labor

the horizontal axis. At any given wage, a monopolist will demand half as much labor as the result of the tax. In general, the fixed-rate revenue tax reduces the quantities of labor demanded at various wage rates to $(1 - m)$ times their pretax levels.[5]

THE DEMAND FOR LABOR BY A MONOPOLIST
WHEN IT ADJUSTS CAPITAL

In Figure 6–3, MRP_L (K_1) represents a monopolist's marginal revenue product of labor for a particular amount of capital, K_1. When confronted with labor supply curve $W_1S_1^L$, profit is maximized by employing L_1 units of labor. The question we seek to answer in this section is this: What happens to the quantity of labor employed when the wage rate changes and the monopolist is free to adjust its input of capital?

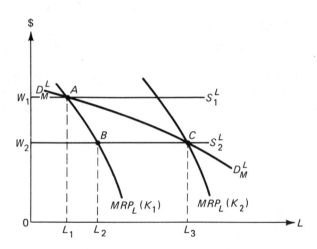

FIGURE 6–3. A Monopolist's Labor Demand Curve When It Adjusts Capital

Consider what happens if the market supply of labor schedule increases, leading to a downward shift of the labor supply schedule in Figure 6–3 to $W_2S_2^L$. If capital were fixed at K_1, the monopolist would increase its labor input to L_2 (why?). The decline in the wage rate, however, has lowered the price of labor services relative to capital services and reduced the cost of production. The first of these leads the firm to minimize the cost of any given

---

[5]As an exercise, draw your own graphs and see how D_M^L and $D_M^{L'}$ are related for various values of m and shapes of MRP_L.

output (a necessary condition for profit maximization) by using a smaller capital to labor ratio. We have called this the substitution effect of a decline in the wage. In addition, we know that the monopolist will expand production, using more of both capital and labor. This is the output effect of a decline in the wage rate. As in the competitive case, MPP_L shifts to the right with the change in K. This is depicted in Figure 6–3. The monopolist's labor demand schedule ($D_M^L D_M^L$) connects points like A and C and is flatter (more elastic) than if capital cannot be adjusted.[6] Notice that whether competitive or monopolistic in its market for output, the profit-maximizing firm's labor demand schedule is downward-sloping.

THE MARKET LABOR DEMAND SCHEDULE WHEN SOME OR ALL FIRMS ARE MONOPOLISTS

It is, of course, possible to have a competitive labor market where *all* buyers are product market monopolists. In such a situation, the derivation of market labor demand is actually less complex than when all firms are competitive in their markets for final production. Since, by definition, a monopolist is also an industry, its labor demand schedule *already* reflects the fact that product price declines with industry output. As a result, when only monopolists compete for workers' services, the demand schedule simply plots out the sum of the quantities of labor desired by each monopolist at the various wage rates. Formally stated, *the market demand curve is the horizontal sum of the monopolists' labor demand curves.* It follows directly that when both monopolistic and competitive industries purchase labor in the same market, the demand schedule is the sum of the individual component industries' demand curves.

THE CONCEPT OF MONOPOLISTIC EXPLOITATION

At this point it should be obvious that equilibrium wage and employment are determined by the interaction of supply and demand, whether buyers of labor are competitors, monopolists, or a blend of the two. We now utilize our newly acquired insight into the demand for labor by a monopolist to compare wages and employment in competitive labor markets where some buyers are product market monopolists versus competitive labor markets where only competitive industries purchase labor services.

We know that each point on a competitive industry's labor demand curve reflects the value of the marginal product of labor, which is the product of

---

[6]The interested reader is referred to C. E. Ferguson, *The Neoclassical Theory of Production and Distribution* (London and New York: Cambridge University Press, 1969), Chaps. 6 and 9, for a rigorous analytical treatment of the demand for labor by a profit-maximizing monopolist.

the price of output and the marginal physical product of labor. When an industry is a monopolist, however, it maximizes profit by hiring labor so that the wage rate equals the marginal revenue product of labor, which is the product of marginal revenue and marginal physical product of labor. Given the same production functions and demand curves for final output, a monopolist's labor demand schedule will be below that of a competitive industry, since marginal revenue is less than price.

Figure 6–4 illustrates the market labor demand schedules for two groups of n industries. The curve labeled D_c^L represents the horizontal sum of the

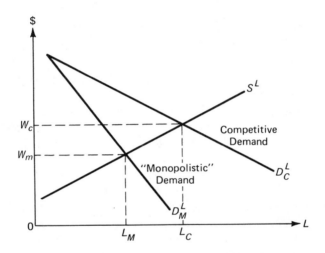

FIGURE 6–4. Competitive and Monopolistic Demands Compared

labor demand schedules of n identical competitive industries. D_M^L, the "monopolistic demand curve," is derived from the same group as D_c^L, except that one of the competitive industries has been replaced by a monopolist. Notice that in labor markets where monopolies are present, less labor will be demanded. Moreover, if the labor supply curve has any degree of inelasticity, so that it is upward-sloping, both equilibrium wage and employment will be lower than if all industries were competitive. Economists use the term **monopolistic exploitation** when referring to the wage differential $(W_c - W_M)$ caused by a product market monopoly.[7]

---

[7]Unfortunately, due to lack of data, we are unable to say anything about the incidence of monopolistic exploitation in the United States. To quote a noted authority on industrial organization, F. M. Scherer, "It is futile to attempt a quantitative summary of how much structural monopoly power exists in the whole of the American economy"; *Industrial Market Structure*, p. 59.

In our discussion thus far of the demand for labor in noncompetitive environments, we have considered only the situation in which an individual firm can affect the price of its product but not the prices of its inputs. Sometimes only a few firms purchase labor, so that one employer's actions will disturb the equilibrium wage rate. The name for this general situation is **oligopsony.** Our next two sections are devoted to formal analyses of a particular oligopsonistic labor market, **monopsony** (one buyer).

Monopsony

Although it has been declining in importance, the so-called "company town" is probably what comes to most of our minds when picturing a monopsonistic labor market. Alternatively, such a market structure may stem from an agreement by employers not to compete with each other for workers. Historically, the major professional sports in the United States have operated under a system where experienced athletes were subject to a "reserve clause" that denied them the privilege of voluntarily quitting one employer and obtaining a position with a rival team. The end of this section is devoted to an examination of the prevalence of monopsony in the United States in general, and to a discussion of one monopsony in particular—professional baseball before the recent emasculation of the reserve clause. We now turn our attention to a theoretical analysis of a labor market in which effectively only one firm purchases workers' services.

THE ROLE OF THE LABOR SUPPLY SCHEDULE

By definition, the labor supply schedule faced by a monopsonist is also that of the labor market itself. For simplicity we will consider the situation in which workers are equally capable and in which hours of work per employee do not vary so that the labor supply function relates wage rates to numbers of persons seeking employment. We know from Chapter 4 that when the quantity of labor being considered is the *number* of employees, the market supply schedule is upward-sloping. To see how this fact plays a key role in a profit-maximizing monopsonist's choice of quantity of labor, it is helpful to examine the hypothetical labor supply relation displayed in Table 6–2. Columns 1 and 2 list the numbers of individuals willing to work at various hourly wage rates. The monopsony employer's total cost per hour of different quantities of labor (TC_L) is presented in column 3, and is the product of the first two columns.[8] Finally, column 4 indicates the marginal cost of labor

---

[8] We will discuss here the case of the *nondiscriminating* monopsonist—that is, one who pays all workers an identical wage rate.

TABLE 6-2

A Monopsonist's Marginal Cost of Labor Schedule

(1) L	Labor Supply Schedule → (2) W	(3) TC_L	(4) MC_L
1	$5.00	$5.00	—
2	5.50	11.00	$6.00
3	6.00	18.00	7.00
4	6.50	26.00	8.00
5	7.00	35.00	9.00
6	7.50	45.00	10.00
7	8.00	56.00	11.00
8	8.50	68.00	12.00
9	9.00	81.00	13.00
10	9.50	95.00	14.00

$L \equiv$ units of labor services (number of employees)

$W \equiv$ hourly wage rate

$TC_L =$ total cost of labor (per hour) $\equiv (W \cdot L)$

$MC_L \equiv$ marginal cost of labor (per hour) $\equiv \left(\dfrac{\Delta TC_L}{\Delta L}\right)$

(MC_L) associated with the supply schedule in columns 1 and 2. It represents the increase in labor cost per hour associated with an additional unit of labor.

Notice that MC_L rises with L and exceeds W. Moreover, the difference between MC_L and W grows with L. When the monopsonist in Table 6–2 hires one worker, for example, it must pay an hourly wage rate of $5, which leads to a total cost of labor per hour of $5. In order to expand its labor force to two employees, however, it must increase W to $5.50. In the absence of wage discrimination, the monopsonist will pay *both* workers $5.50 per hour, and the marginal cost per hour of adding a second worker is $6. Exactly why is it that MC_L exceeds W? If the firm in Table 6–2 were a competitor, W would be fixed at $5, so that the marginal cost of expanding to a work force of two would be $5 per hour. Since the monopsonist must raise W to $5.50 to attract a second worker, its marginal cost of labor is $5.50, the second worker's hourly wage, plus $.50, the wage *increase* going to the first worker. In Table 6–2, whenever an additional worker is hired, W increases by $.50, and all existing employees, therefore, receive $.50 more per hour. So, the greater is a monopsonist's labor force, the greater is the *difference* between its current wage and its cost of adding a worker. To emphasize the relation between MC_L and the labor supply function, we have graphed in Figure 6–5 the schedules contained in Table 6–2. The important things to

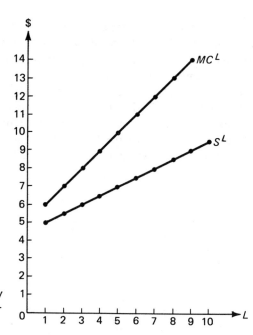

FIGURE 6–5. The Labor Supply and Marginal Cost of Labor Schedules from Table 6–2

notice are that MC^L is positively inclined, that it lies above S^L, and that (in this case) it has a slope twice that of S^L. Whenever L increases by one worker, the market wage rises by \$.50 and the marginal cost of labor by \$1.[9]

THE "DEMAND" FOR LABOR BY A MONOPSONIST WHEN CAPITAL IS FIXED

There is an old joke about a parrot who knew economics: It just kept repeating the phrase, "Marginal cost equals marginal benefit." At the risk of being put in a cage, we offer the following: as do *all* profit-maximizing firms, a profit-maximizing monopsonist hires that quantity of labor which equates the marginal cost of labor to the marginal (dollar) benefit of labor. In this section we examine the case of a monopsonist that is a product market monopolist unable to adjust its input of physical capital because it provides important background for our empirical analysis of major league baseball.

---

[9]In general, the MC_L schedule associated with an upward-sloping labor supply schedule is positively sloped and *steeper* than S_L. On this point, see Ferguson and Gould, *Microeconomic Theory*, fn. 7, pp. 408–09. In particular, when S_L is upward-sloping and linear, MC_L is positively inclined with a slope that is twice that of S_L. To see this, let S_L be described by the general linear equation, $W = a + bL$, where a and b are positive constants. From this, $TC_L \equiv WL \equiv aL + bL^2$, and $MC_L \equiv \dfrac{dTC_L}{dL} = a + 2bL$.

If a monopsonist is also a product market monopolist, profit is maximized when the quantity of labor utilized equates MC_L with the marginal revenue product of labor (MRP_L). This is illustrated in Figure 6–6, where L^* units of labor maximizes profit. Remember that since only one firm is purchasing workers' services, L^* is also total market employment. What is the equilibrium wage associated with L^* in Figure 6–6? Once a profit-maximizing monopsonist has determined its optimal amount of labor, it pays the wage rate on S^L associated with L^*. A wage lower than W^* will fail to elicit the optimal number of workers, and a wage higher than W^* is unnecessary.

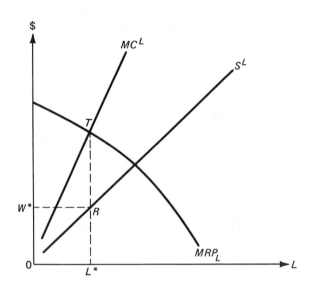

FIGURE 6–6. Equilibrium Wage and Employment for a Monopsonist That Is a Product Market Monopolist

Finally, one subtle point is worth noting: A monopsonist does not have a labor demand schedule as customarily defined. A firm that purchases workers' services in a competitive labor market faces a fixed wage rate when making its employment decision. In this situation, MC_L is constant at the particular wage rate in question, and the firm's marginal dollar benefit of labor schedule indicates its desired amount of labor services. By considering various (constant) values of W, we "trace out" VMP_L as the competitive firm's labor demand schedule and MRP_L as the monopolist's labor demand schedule. A monopsony, however, does not confront a parametric wage, but rather a *menu* of wage rates; each W is associated with a different L through S_L. Moreover, S_L implies a particular upward-sloping MC_L, which jointly determines (along with the monopsonist's marginal dollar benefit of labor curve) the equilibrium combination of wage and employment—that is, $(W^*,$ $L^*)$ in Figure 6–6. Only if the marginal cost of labor schedule shifts will the monopsony change L and therefore W. What we are saying is that there is no curve in Figure 6–6, for example, that provides the information furnished by a labor demand schedule: how much labor the firm desires at various values of W.[10]

APPLICATION: THE CONCEPT OF MONOPSONISTIC EXPLOITATION AND THE EFFECT OF MINIMUM WAGE LEGISLATION

Figure 6–7 depicts the equilibrium wage–employment combination for a monopsonistic labor market. The firm hires that amount of labor (L^*) which equates its marginal cost of labor to its marginal revenue product of labor. Having chosen its optimal level of employment, a monopsonist then offers the wage rate that elicits that employment at minimum cost. This process generates an equilibrium wage of $0C$ in Figure 6–7. Notice, however, that unlike in a competitive labor market, workers are paid less than their marginal value to the firm. This aspect of a monopsonistic labor market has been referred to as **monopsonistic exploitation,** and can be measured by the vertical

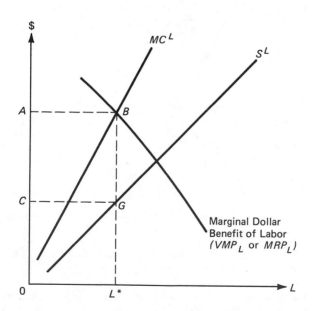

FIGURE 6–7. Monopsonistic Exploitation

---

[10]Those of you who remember your microeconomic theory of the firm will recognize that this is analogous to the absence of an output supply function for a monopoly producer.

distance AC.[11] Next we will examine a minimum wage law as a device for eliminating monopsonistic exploitation, and later some estimates of the severity of monopsonistic exploitation in professional baseball.

Consider a monopsonistic labor market where the firm is a monopolist in its output market. In such a situation, depicted in Figure 6–8, equilibrium employment is determined by the intersection of MC^L and MRP_L. This occurs at point B, which implies equilibrium employment of L^*. Workers demand, and receive, a market wage of W^* for this amount of labor. Can the resulting monopsonistic exploitation, AW^*, be reduced or eliminated by a minimum wage?

Suppose a minimum wage equal to W_{min} is imposed on the labor market depicted in Figure 6–8. It is obvious that to be effective, W_{min} must exceed W^*. In order to understand how equilibrium W and L are affected, we must first discuss how the law alters the effective market labor supply curve. To the left of point G, the market supply curve becomes a horizontal line at the

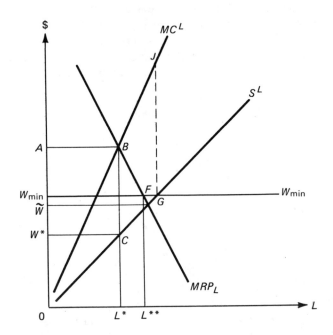

FIGURE 6–8. The Effect of a Minimum Wage Law in a Monopsonistic Labor Market

---

[11]It is important to note that AC is an *upper boundary* estimate and that alternative measures of monopsonistic exploitation have been suggested. See Ferguson and Gould, *Microeconomic Theory*, pp. 414–16. We choose to utilize the above measure because it is probably the most readily observable empirically and has been used to compute the estimates of monopsonistic exploitation in professional baseball that we discuss at the end of this chapter.

value W_{min}. As workers require a wage rate in excess of W_{min} in order to supply amounts of labor greater than that indicated by G, the market supply curve follows S^L to the right of G. So, the supply curve of labor to the monopsonist becomes the kinked line $W_{min} GS_L$. All we need to establish the new equilibrium wage-employment combination is the marginal cost of labor schedule associated with this labor supply curve. For amounts of labor less than or equal to that at G, the cost of an additional unit of labor is a constant W_{min}. When the quantity of labor exceeds that at G, the marginal cost of labor is given by MC^L. Thus, when a minimum wage of W_{min} is imposed on the monopsonist in Figure 6–8, its marginal cost of labor becomes W_{min} GJ MC^L.

Faced with this new marginal cost of labor schedule, the monopsonist again finds the amount of labor which equates its marginal revenue product of labor to its marginal cost of labor. This now occurs at point F, with the resulting equilibrium employment-wage combination, (W_{min}, L^{**}). (Can you explain why?) Notice that monopsonistic exploitation has now been eliminated. Moreover, in contrast to the effect of a minimum wage in a competitive labor market (see Chapters 3 and 5), workers have been made unambiguously better off.[12] The imposition of the minimum wage on the monopsony in Figure 6–8 has raised market wage *and* employment. You should prove to yourself that wage minimums between W^* and A will increase both W and L above their usual monoponistic values, W^* and L^*. In addition, you should be able to show that a wage minimum of $\widetilde{W}$ maximizes employment and that a wage minimum of A maximizes the wage subject to the constraint of not reducing employment below L^*. What we have shown is that in a monopsonistic labor market where the firm is a monopolist, a correctly set minimum wage, one between A and W^*, *must* improve workers' economic welfare. (What happens to workers' welfare if W_{min} exceeds A?) A number of caveats are necessary, though, concerning the *practicability* of using minimum wage legislation to eliminate monopsonistic exploitation. These have been clearly stated by George Stigler:[13]

> If an employer has a significant degree of control over the wage rate he pays for a given quality of labor, a skillfully-set minimum wage may increase his employment and wage rate and, because the wage is brought closer to the value of marginal product, at the same time increase aggregate output. . . . The minimum wage which achieves these desirable ends has several requisites:
>
> 1. It must be chosen correctly: too high a wage will decrease employment. The accounting records describe, very imperfectly, existing employment and wages; the optimum wage can be set only if the demand and supply schedules are known over a considerable range. . . .

[12]Can it be said that *society* has been made unambiguously better off?

[13]George J. Stigler, "The Economics of Minimum Wage Legislation," *American Economic Review*, 36, 3 (June 1946), 360–61.

2. The optimum wage varies with occupation (and, within an occupation, with the quality of worker).
3. The optimum wage varies among firms (and plants).
4. The optimum wage varies, often rapidly, through time.

A uniform national minimum wage, infrequently changed, is wholly unsuited to these diversities of conditions.

This completes our theoretical examination of a monopsonistic labor market.[14] We now turn our attention to evidence concerning the prevalence of monopsony in the United States in general.

Evidence: The Incidence of Monopsony in the United States

The prevalence of monopsony is an important economic issue because if labor markets are to a large extent monopsonistic, this might serve as justification for minimum wage or pro-union legislation. Alternatively, if labor markets are largely competitive, minimum wages or unions cannot be said to offer the possibility for a definite improvement in workers' economic well-being. Although not recent, a study by Bunting represents the most careful empirical examination to date of the extent of monopsony in the United States.[15] In particular, Bunting analyzed data concerning the degree of employer concentration at the *county* level during 1948. By *concentration* we mean the fraction of the total labor force employed by the largest firms. Before we summarize Bunting's results, it is important to discuss the relationship between employer concentration and monopsony power.

A monopsony is really a theoretical abstraction that is not usually formally observed. It can best be thought of as describing a situation where buyers of labor act in concert to create a wage rate lower than would have prevailed had they competed with one another for workers' services. Concentration, however, is an observable, quantifiable characteristic of a geographic area. Concentration is "high" when a few firms hire a "large" fraction of the total labor force and "low" when no one firm or small group of firms

---

[14]In the interest of brevity we do not consider a monopsony when both capital and labor services may be varied. The basic result is quite similar to the competitive and monopolistic cases discussed earlier. The profit-maximizing monopsonist also chooses K and L so that an additional dollar spent on K increases output by the same amount as an additional dollar spent on L. The difference is that the monopsonist's input prices change as it adjusts its input mix. For elaboration, see Ferguson and Gould, *Microeconomic Theory*, pp. 411–14.

[15]Robert L. Bunting, *Employer Concentration in Local Labor Markets* (Chapel Hill, N.C.: University of North Carolina Press, 1962). A summary of Bunting's findings is contained in John F. Burton, Jr., Lee K. Benham, William M. Vaughn III, and Robert J. Flanagan, eds., *Readings in Labor Market Analysis* (New York: Holt, Rinehart, and Winston, 1971), pp. 132–39.

employs a "significant" portion of the the the labor force.[16] A key assumption underlying Bunting's research is that the degree of monopsony power in a labor market is positively correlated with employer concentration. Let us elaborate somewhat on this presumed relationship.

Consider a so-called "local labor market," where employers purchase labor services of a certain type. Employers will confront a relatively elastic supply of labor if an appreciable number of jobs that are reasonable substitutes in the eyes of workers is offered by firms outside this local labor market.[17] In this situation, there will be little economic gain to local employers from collusive behavior concerning the hiring and firing of employees.[18] Monopsonistic activity, then, can be profitable only when what we have called the "local labor market" is in reality the *complete* market for the workers in question, in the sense that it encompasses all employment opportunities they perceive as reasonable.[19] Suppose, now, that we isolate a local labor market in which the elasticity of labor supply to firms is low, thus presenting the potential for monopsonistic exploitation. Since this requires collective action by employers, which should be more costly the greater the number of firms involved, a necessary (but not sufficient) condition for labor market monopsony is that such concerted activity not be prohibitively expensive to arrange and police. What Bunting does by examining employer concentration is to identify empirically the prevalence of labor markets where the potential for monopsonistic exploitation is present.

Thus far we have been quite vague concerning the measurement of employer concentration. In particular, Bunting employs three measures: CR_1, the percentage of workers in a local labor market employed by the largest firm (employer); CR_4, the percentage of workers employed by the four largest firms; and CR_{10}, the percentage of workers employed by the ten largest firms. Bunting calculated the three measures of concentration for 1,774 local labor markets in 1948, where local labor markets were defined as single counties or small clusters of counties. The 1,774 areas studied took in about 93 percent of the United States labor force. His basic findings indicated that employer concentration, and thus the potential for monopsonistic exploitation, was really quite small. Less than 10 percent of all workers were employed in labor markets where CR_{10} exceeded 50 percent, and less than 4 percent of all workers were employed in labor markets where CR_1 exceeded 50 percent.[20] Even though Bunting's data are approximately thirty years old, we feel confident that monopsony is not a widespread phenomenon today. The primary reason is that fame and financial rewards await the researcher

---

[16]Bunting, *Employer Concentration*, p. 4.

[17]Ibid.

[18]What happens to "monopsonistic exploitation" as the supply curve becomes horizontal?

[19]Bunting, *Employer Concentration*, p. 5.

[20]Burton et al., *Readings*, p. 138.

who can demonstrate empirically that a significant number of workers are victims of monopsony power of employers. As yet, no one has claimed these prizes.

Frontiers of Labor Economics: Pay and Performance in Professional Baseball

Although we have good reason to believe that labor markets are largely not monopsonistic, this is not to say that there are *no* cases in which employers have engaged in collective activities that reduce wage rates below competitive levels. An especially interesting case is that of professional baseball during the late 1960s, when the so-called reserve clause was still in effect. In particular, research by Gerald Scully attempts to measure the economic loss imposed on players (monopsonistic exploitation) as a result of the institutional structure of the professional baseball industry in the United States at that time.[21] Before we can discuss Scully's, work, however, it is necessary to understand the peculiar characteristics of the baseball players' labor market in 1968–69.

Like other workers, a baseball player was a "free agent" when initially seeking employment. This status terminated, however, once he signed a standard one-year renewable contract with a team. The **reserve clause** refers to the renewability, which was granted exclusively to the team's owner. Except for a restriction limiting the reduction in a player's salary from year to year, the standard baseball contract basically gave a team owner complete control over a player's future in the baseball industry. Scully points out that upon expiration of a player's contract, the *owner's* options were numerous; he or she could renew or terminate the contract, or sell the player to another team.[22] In this case, sale meant the transfer of exclusive control over a player's services to another team's owner(s). In contrast, a player had a much more limited set of options once an owner chose to renew his contract. He could immediately accept the owner's terms or try to negotiate an improvement by threatening to retire. Once the owner's final offer had been made, however, the player had to accept or give up playing major league baseball.[23]

It should be fairly obvious that the internal organization of the baseball industry probably had much to do with players' salaries. The reserve clause, by limiting a player to negotiation with his current team, prevented him from voluntarily moving to another team where his services were valued more highly. Such a restriction on mobility effectively granted monopsony power

---

[21]Gerald W. Scully, "Pay and Performance in Professional Baseball," *American Economic Review*, 64, 6 (December 1974), 915–30.

[22]Ibid., p. 916.

[23]Ibid.

to a team's owner, and Scully examines whether this *in fact* led to a divergence between players' salaries and their marginal revenue products.[24]

But what is a baseball player's marginal revenue product? A player's marginal physical product may best be viewed as the additional output he contributes to the team, and his marginal revenue product, the revenue created for the team by that output (performance). In particular, a player contributes to a team's win-loss record, and through this, to a team's gate (ticket) receipts and broadcast revenues. Equation (1) in Table 6–3 is Scully's production of team victories regression, from which an estimate of a player's marginal physical product may be computed. The dependent variable is a team's win-loss percentage (times 1000), and the sample employed covers two seasons, 1968 and 1969.

Of course, economic theory supplies neither the arguments nor the particular mathematical form of this equation. The linear version, which precludes diminishing marginal physical productivities of the inputs, simplifies estimation. Based on previous research into players' salaries, Scully chose to represent hitters' input by team slugging average (a measure of average total base production per time at bat) and pitchers' input by team strikeout to walk ratio.[25] Included as control variables in regression (1) are *NL*, a dummy variable designed to capture differences in the quality of play between the American and National leagues, and two other dummy variables (*CONT* and *OUT*) designed to capture differences in "team spirit." It was expected that teams in the thick of a pennant race should play better baseball, while teams out of the running should play poorer baseball. The interpretations of the regression coefficients in equation (1) are straightforward and will not be discussed, except when used in conjunction with results from the team revenue regression to calculate players' marginal revenue products by performance classes.

In equation (2) of Table 6–3, income from ticket and broadcast rights sales is expressed as a linear function of team victories (*PCTWIN*) and other variables.[26] Since a team is granted an exclusive right to play in (monopolize) an area, it is likely that the population of this geographical area is a factor in a team's ability to generate revenue. Scully chose to represent empirically this aspect of the baseball product market by the variable $SMSA_{70}$, which is the population of a team's Standard Metropolitan Statistical Area in 1970. Moreover, regression (2) yields estimates of how team racial composition and

---

[24]Remember that in monopsony, the firm and the worker *share* the worker's marginal revenue product (see Figure 6–7). Why would players' pay be their marginal revenue products and not the value of their marginal products?

[25]Scully, "Pay and Performance," p. 918.

[26]Auxiliary regressions that permitted *diminishing* marginal revenue indicated that the hypothesis of a linear relation between *PCTWIN* and *REVENUE* could not be rejected. Ibid., p. 919, fn. 6. It should also be noted that regression (2) has embedded in it the assumption that player performance does not *directly* affect a team's revenue, but rather has only an indirect effect through *PCTWIN*.

TABLE 6–3

Production, Revenue, and Salary Regressions: Professional Baseball, 1968–69*

Production of Team Victories Regression

(1) $PCTWIN = 37.24 + .92\ TSA + .90\ TSW - 38.57\ NL + 43.78\ CONT$
$\quad\quad\quad\quad\ \ (.39)\quad (4.37)\quad\ \ (5.92)\quad\quad\ (-4.03)\quad\quad (3.77)$
$\quad\quad\ - 75.68\ OUT;\ R^2 = .88;\ N = 44.$
$\quad\quad\ \ (6.17)$

Team Revenue Regression†

(2) $REVENUE = -1,735,890 + 10,330\ PCTWIN + 494,585\ SMSA_{70}$
$\quad\quad\quad\quad\quad\ \ (-1.69)\quad\quad (6.64)\quad\quad\quad\quad\ (4.61)$
$\quad\quad\ + 512\ MARGA + 580,913\ NL - 762,248\ STD$
$\quad\quad\ \ (4.28)\quad\quad\quad\ (1.84)\quad\quad\quad (2.42)$
$\quad\quad\ - 58,523\ BBPCT;\ R^2 = .75;\ N = 43.$
$\quad\quad\ \ (3.13)$

Salary Regression: Hitters

(3) $\text{Log}\ (S\ hitter) = .6699 + 1.0716\ \text{Log}\ \overline{SA} + .5220\ \text{Log}\ M + .0579\ D_{\overline{BA}}$
$\quad\quad\quad\quad\quad\ \ (.82)\quad\ (4.76)\quad\quad\quad\quad (7.53)\quad\quad\quad\ (1.61)$
$\quad\quad\ + .2746\ \text{Log}\ \overline{AB} - .0621\ \text{Log}\ SMSA_{70} + .2645\ \text{Log}\ MARGA$
$\quad\quad\quad\quad\quad\quad\quad\quad\quad\ (-.78)\quad\quad\quad\quad\ (2.81)$
$\quad\quad\ + .0194\ NL;\ R^2 = .81;\ N = 93.$
$\quad\quad\ \ (.62)$

Salary Regression: Pitchers

(4) $\text{Log}\ (S\ pitcher) = 3.3845 + .8076\ \text{Log}\ \overline{SW} + .5015\ \text{Log}\ M + .9698\ \text{Log}\ \overline{IP}$
$\quad\quad\quad\quad\quad\quad\ (4.16)\quad\ (4.00)\quad\quad\quad\quad (7.70)\quad\quad\quad (4.22)$
$\quad\quad\ - .0534\ \text{Log}\ SMSA_{70} - .0619\ \text{Log}\ MARGA$
$\quad\quad\quad\ \ (.53)\quad\quad\quad\quad\quad\ (.61)$
$\quad\quad\ - .0070\ NL;\ R^2 = .78;\ N = 55.$
$\quad\quad\ \ (.20)$

Definitions:

$PCTWIN \equiv$ [(games won/games played) · 1000].

$TSA \equiv$ team slugging average = [(total bases/official at bats) · 1000].

$TSW \equiv$ team strikeout–walk ratio = [(total opposing players struck out/total opposing players walked) · 100].

$NL \equiv$ dummy variable (= 1 if team in National League; = 0 if in American League).

$CONT \equiv$ dummy variable (= 1 if team was less than five games out of first place at the season's end; = 0 otherwise).

$OUT \equiv$ dummy variable (= 1 if team was more than 20 games out of first place at the season's end; = 0 otherwise).

TABLE 6-3 (Continued)

$REVENUE \equiv$ home game attendance revenue plus revenue from broadcasting rights.

$SMSA_{70} \equiv$ 1970 population size of team's Standard Metropolitan Statistical Area.

$MARGA \equiv$ variable designed to capture interteam differences in the "intensity of fan interest"; in particular, $MARGA$ is the coefficient of $PCTWIN$ in a regression of a team's attendance on $PCTWIN$ and other variables with data for 1957–71.

$STD \equiv$ dummy variable (= 1 for older stadium located in poor neighborhood with limited parking facilities; = 0 otherwise).

$BBPCT \equiv$ percentage of team's players who were black.

Log $X \equiv$ common logarithm of the variable X ($X \equiv SMSA_{70}$, etc.).

S hitter $\equiv$ annual salary of an individual hitter.

$\overline{SA} \equiv$ individual's lifetime slugging average [(total bases/official at bats) $\cdot$ 1000].

$M \equiv$ Number of years played in the major leagues.

$D_{\overline{BA}} \equiv$ dummy variable (= 1 if individual had a below-average lifetime $\overline{SA}$, but an above-average lifetime batting average; = 0 otherwise).

$\overline{AB} \equiv$ total lifetime at bats divided by the number of years spent in the major leagues times 5,500, which is the average season at bats for a major league team.

S pitcher $\equiv$ annual salary of an individual pitcher.

$\overline{SW} \equiv$ lifetime strikeout to walk ratio.

$\overline{IP} \equiv$ lifetime average annual percentage of innings pitched out of total possible innings (9 $\cdot$ games in a season $\cdot$ M).

*T-values are in parentheses.
†Since $MARGA$ could not be calculated for Seattle, only 43 observations were employed in the $REVENUE$ regression (2).

Source: Gerald W. Scully, "Pay and Performance in Major League Baseball," *American Economic Review*, 64, 6 (December 1974), 919, 920, 926, 927.

stadium quality affect $REVENUE$. The sign and size of the coefficient of $BBPCT$ indicate whether on the average fans "prefer" black or white players, as well as the economic magnitude of that preference.[27] Finally, Scully's variable representing intensity of fan interest ($MARGA$) requires some elaboration. It is possible that even if two teams play in similar areas, for example, revenues will differ between them because fans in the two locations differ with respect to their taste for the consumption of baseball games. To adjust for this possibility, Scully first ran a separate regression (not shown)

---

[27]What is the economic interpretation of the coefficient of STD?

for each team with time-series data for 1957–71, where attendance is the dependent variable and *PCTWIN* is one of the independent variables. The coefficient of *PCTWIN* in each of these time-series regressions became the respective teams' value of *MARGA* in regression (2). *MARGA* varied from 603 to 5,819 and represents a differential effect of winning on attendance across cities, one possible index of fan interest in baseball.[28]

For our purposes, the coefficient of *PCTWIN* in regression (2) is the one of interest. It indicates that an 0.001 increase in the fraction of games won in 1968–69 increased revenue by $10,330. This result, along with the coefficients of *TSA* and *TSW* in regression (1), may be used to calculate the dollar value of a one-point increase in a team's slugging average or strikeout to walk ratio. In particular, the value of a unit increase in *TSA* is $9,504 (0.92·$10,330), and the value of a unit increase in *TSW* is $9,297 (0.90·$10,330). Thus, we need only compute the contribution of a particular quality player to *TSW* or *TSA* in order to estimate his marginal revenue product. To facilitate calculations, Scully makes the assumption that team performance is the sum of individuals' performances. Since each team has about eight regular pitchers and twelve regular nonpitchers (hitters), the contribution of an average pitcher (strikeout-walk ratio of 2.00) to *TSW* is about 25 points (0.125·2·100), and the contribution of an average hitter (slugging average of .340) to *TSA* is about 28.3 points (0.08333·.340·1000). You should be able to show that these data imply a marginal revenue product for an average pitcher in 1968–69 of approximately $232,425 and a marginal revenue product for an average hitter of $268,963. Displayed in column 1 of Table 6–4 are various performance levels for pitchers and hitters, and contained in column 2 are marginal revenue product estimates associated with each particular performance level.

The production of victories regression employed by Scully does not hold constant nonplayer inputs, and as a result the marginal revenue product estimates in column 2 could be biased upward. (Under what conditions would this occur?) Attempts to incorporate other factors of production, such as managerial quality, into a victories regression, however, did not suggest an important role for nonplayer inputs.[29] Moreover, the data in column 1 of Table 6–4 produce the estimates presented in column 2, which are best thought of as *gross* marginal revenue products, because they are unadjusted for any player development costs or payments to nonplayer inputs. So, when compared with player salary figures, the data in column 2 suggest an upper boundary to the amount of monopsonistic exploitation in the professional baseball industry.

Such a comparison is made in column 5 of Table 6–4, which tells us the

---

[28]Scully, "Pay and Performance," p. 920, fn. 8.
[29]Scully, "Pay and Performance," p. 921.

TABLE 6–4

Marginal Revenue Products, Expected Salaries, and Rates of Monopsonistic
Exploitation: Professional Baseball, 1968–69

	(1) Perfor- mance	(2) Gross Marginal Revenue Product*	(3) Net Marginal Revenue Product†	(4) Expected Salary‡	(5) (6) Rates of Monop- sonistic Exploitation
		Hitters			E_G E_N
	270	$213,800	$ 85,500	$31,700	0.85 0.63
	230	261,400	133,100	39,300	0.85 0.70
$\overline{SA}$	390	308,900	180,600	47,000	0.85 0.74
	450	356,400	228,100	54,800	0.85 0.76
Star	510	403,900	275,600	62,700	0.84 0.77
performance	570	451,400	323,100	70,600	0.84 0.78
		Pitchers			
	1.60	$185,900	$ 57,600	$31,100	0.83 0.46
	2.00	232,400	104,100	37,200	0.84 0.64
$\overline{SW}$	2.40	278,900	150,600	43,100	0.85 0.71
	2.80	325,400	197,100	48,800	0.85 0.75
Star	3.20	371,900	243,600	54,400	0.85 0.78
performance	3.60	418,400	290,100	59,800	0.86 0.79

Definitions:

$\overline{SA}$ ≡ lifetime slugging average (total bases/official at bats times 100).

$\overline{AB}$ ≡ total lifetime at bats divided by number of years spent in the major leagues times 5,500, which is the average season at bats for a major league team.

$\overline{SW}$ ≡ lifetime strikeout to walk ratio.

E_G ≡ [(2) − (4)]/(2)

E_N ≡ [(3) − (4)]/(3)

*Calculated using the appropriate value of $\overline{SA}$ (or $\overline{SW}$) along with the regression coefficients of TSA or TSW in regression (1) of Table 6–3 and the regression coefficient of PCTWIN in regression (2) of Table 6–3. Each pitcher is assumed to comprise 12.5 percent of team pitching, and each hitter is assumed to comprise 8.33 percent of team hitting.

†Net marginal revenue product is equal to gross marginal revenue product minus estimated average player development cost of $128,300.

‡Created with the regression coefficients of equation (3) or (4) in Table 6–3. All variables except $\overline{SA}$ or $\overline{SW}$ have been set equal to their mean values.

Source: Gerald W. Scully, "Pay and Performance in Major League Baseball," *American Economic Review,* 64, 6 (December 1974), 923.

difference between a certain quality player's gross marginal product and his expected salary, expressed as a fraction of gross marginal revenue product.[30] Notice that, by definition, the rate of (gross) monopsonistic exploitation (E_G) will vary between zero and one. A value for E_G of zero means that a player is being paid his marginal revenue product. The closer is E_G to 1.0, the greater is the degree of player exploitation. The data of column 5 indicate that players' salaries average about 15 percent of their (gross) marginal revenue products. Remember, however, that E_G does not account for player development and other nonsalary expenses, and it therefore represents an upper limit to the severity of exploitation during 1968–69.

Although crude, some data are available concerning the other costs of running a major league baseball team: team costs (roster and team specific nonplayer salaries), game costs (transportation, equipment, and stadium rental), general administrative costs (salaries of front office personnel), sales costs, capital costs, and player training costs.[31] Scully used these data to create estimates of players' *net* marginal revenue products. In doing so, he chose to overstate somewhat payments to other (nonlabor) factors of production to create a lower limit on estimated marginal revenue product of labor and therefore a lower boundary on the extent of monopsonistic exploitation in professional baseball. Column 3 of Table 6–4 presents Scully's estimates of net marginal revenue products for players of various performance levels.[32] These figures have been calculated by subtracting $128,300, the mean total annual cost of fielding an average career-length ballplayer (in addition to his salary), from the figures in column 2. While this reduces substantially the estimated values of players to their teams, even the lowest-quality pitchers and hitters are paid much less than they are worth. The figures in column 6 indicate that the least productive pitcher listed in Table 6–4 received on average about 54 percent of his marginal revenue product in 1968–69 and that the least productive hitter received on the average about 37 percent of his marginal revenue product. The average gap between marginal revenue product and salary appears to be somewhat more severe for players of "star" quality.

---

[30]In order to calculate expected salaries, Scully first ran regressions with sample data for *individual* pitchers and hitters in 1968–69. The logarithm of observed salary was regressed on the logarithms of career performance, contribution to team pitching (or hitting) input, years of major league experience, and variables which capture the franchise's revenue-generating potential. These regressions appear as equations (3) and (4) in Table 6–3. Notice that they are nonlinear and that a coefficient value is interpreted as the estimated *elasticity* of salary with respect to the independent variable in question. The coefficients from these regressions were used to create the expected (predicted) salary figures in Table 6–4 by varying $\overline{SA}$ or $\overline{SW}$ and setting all other variables equal to their sample mean values.

[31]Scully, "Pay and Performance, pp. 922–23.

[32]It should be noted that the marginal revenue product of a player to his team exceeds his marginal "worth" to the baseball *industry*, since he contributes to wins for his team but to losses for other teams.

PAY IN PROFESSIONAL BASEBALL: POSTSCRIPT

Even though Scully's research suggests significant monopsonistic exploitation in professional baseball when the reserve clause was in force, players' salaries far exceeded the median earnings of even the most highly skilled occupational groupings. As a result, it has historically been difficult for major league baseball players in particular and professional athletes in general to generate legal and popular support for their fight against "low" wages. This situation is humorously captured by Jim Murray in a story in which Marvin Barnes, a professional basketball player, attempts to convince Karl Marx, Samuel Gompers, Nicolai (sic) Lenin, and John L. Lewis that he is about to be exploited. This story appears on page 212.

In the mid 1970s, however, the key source of monopsonistic exploitation in professional baseball, the reserve clause, was emasculated. The institutional structure of the baseball labor market changed to permit competition for the services of a player whose contract had expired. Such players, free agents, could sell their services to the highest bidder; this should lead to a player's receiving a salary equal to his marginal worth. An interesting research topic would be to examine data available in *The Sporting News* to see if the gap between marginal revenue product and salary in major league baseball has been reduced after sufficient time has elapsed to permit a substantial number of players to sell their services under competitive conditions.

THE EFFECT OF THE RESERVE CLAUSE
ON THE DISTRIBUTION OF PLAYERS AMONG TEAMS

It is reasonably clear that baseball players' salaries were reduced by that peculiar characteristic of the market for their services known as the reserve clause. To counter charges of monopsonistic exploitation, team owners cited the "necessity" of such an arrangement to preserve a "competitive balance" among teams. Economic analysis indicates, however, that no matter who "owned" a player's contract, the player or his team, the distribution of talent among teams should have differed little.

To see this, consider first the situation in which there is no reserve clause so that players can move between teams at will. Suppose that a player receives a wage of $50,000 from team A but is "worth" $60,000 to team B. In this case team B will offer him that amount. If this is more than his value to team A, it will permit team B to bid him away rather than offer a salary increase. If, however, the player's services are worth at least $60,000 to team A, it will make a counteroffer sufficient to induce him to stay with team A. So, in a competitive labor market for baseball players' services, a player will be a member of the team that values his services most highly.

211

Can You Help, Karl Marx?

by Jim Murray

"They couldn't get me for less than $1 million, or I'd rather work in a factory."

Thus spoke Providence College basketball star Marvin Barnes, who was drafted last week by the NBA's Philadelphia 76ers.

We take you now to a ghostly tribunal hastily convened to hear the Grievances of a basketball star about to be exploited by a soulless corporation otherwise known as the "National Basketball Assn." This celestial convocation before whom said basketball star appears consists of Karl Marx, Samuel Gompers, Nicolai Lenin and John L. Lewis. Marx is presiding.

Marx: "Comrade star, it has come to the attention of this board of inquiry that you are about to be exploited by the ruling class, that the capitalists are up to their old tricks."

Star: "I sure am, your honor."

Marx: "Now, then, try not to cry, comrade, but give us the details. Take your time. It has come to our attention that you are waging a courageous fight against the insidious forces trying to exploit the proletariat, that they are trying to trick you into low wages, long hours and poor working conditions. Can you give us the details? Is there a product connected with what you do?"

Star: "Well, not exactly, sir. You see, I make baskets for a living."

Marx: "Hah! And they bring a good price at the market! The middleman makes twice what you do on these baskets! The industrialist makes 1000 percent! The basket company stock goes up year-by-year on your sweat! A stockbroker in a plush chair on the Paris Bourse trades in it, and makes millions on your sweat while he dines at Maxim's! How well I know! And, after 50 years, they give you a gold watch and the door! How many baskets do you make a day?"

Star: "Well, I make 12-to-20 on my good days, but I don't think you understand. These aren't baskets you can put peaches in or sell or anything like that. These are just symbolic baskets, you might say."

Marx: "Wait a minute, comrade. You say these baskets have no market value?"

Star (uncomfortably): "Well, they do, sort of, your honor. Indirectly."

Marx: "Suppose we begin at the beginning here. Tell us what it is you do for the filthy plutocrats?"

Star: "Well, I bounce this ball up-and-down on a floor all night and, occasionally, I jump up and throw it through a basket."

Marx (after a silence): "Wait a minute—let me get this straight. You bounce a ball on a floor?!"

Star (excitedly): "Exactly. Some nights I do it for 48 minutes! Twice-a-week!"

Marx (pounding his ear with the flat of his hand): "Excuse me. I must have misunderstood. I thought you said '48 minutes.' And 'twice-a-week.' Surely, we are talking about hours, at least. And five times-a-week. A sweat-shop operation, right!"

Star: "Oh, I sweat all right! Sometimes it takes the trainer 10 towels to wipe me off. He has to powder me all over. You'd be surprised how hot you can get in 48 minutes. Even when they turn the air-conditioning on."

Marx: "Er, excuse me, young man. But, there is, then, danger connected with what you do? Your life is on the line! You can get killed doing it?"

Star: "Oh, there's danger all right! Some nights you can get all your shots blocked! But you can't hardly get killed, no. But I did sprain my ankle once. They called in a specialist from New York. You can see how important we are to society."

Marx: "Ah! I get it! You are a state artist! You sing! No? You paint! No? Ah, yes, you are a poet! You play the violin! Wait a minute! You compose! You are a composer! Or, do you play the cello as you do this—this, basket-throwing!?"

Star: "Oh, no. But I do have this cassette in my locker. And I sing along with it on bus trips."

Marx: "Well, then, you are a juggler! You juggle and amuse the people as you do this, this—er, what is it you call this bouncing of the ball on the floor?"

Star: "Dribbling."

Marx: "Dribbling! Indeed! Well, now, then, what pittance are the ruling classes offering you for this essential service to society, this dribbling? A few pennies-an-hour? A day? A week?"

Star: "Well, that's it! I'm demanding $1 million. At least! If I don't get it, I propose to deny the world my services. I'll go to work in a tool factory!"

Marx: "They sell tickets to watch a drill press?"

Star: "Well, no. But someone has to make a stand against these peonage conditions! Did I tell you that for their lousy $1 million I would have to play 80 games! Show up for work 80 days out of 365! I mean, what am I?! A machine?!"

Marx: "Excuse me, comrade. We'll have to continue this some other time. John L. Lewis just fainted. And I think Lenin just shot himself."

Now consider a baseball player's labor market in which a reserve clause is in effect and the same situation exists as in the previous paragraph, a player is paid $50,000 by team A but worth $60,000 to team B. In this case, team B will offer to purchase the player's contract from team A for $10,000 in cash or other player(s). Such a transaction would result in team B paying a total of $60,000 for the player's services, $50,000 to the player and $10,000 to the owner(s) of team A.[33] Should $10,000 exceed team A's "profit" on the player after it pays him his $50,000 salary, it will be in its best interest to sell his contract to team B. However, if the total worth of the player to team A exceeds $60,000, then team B's offer will be refused. So, we are led to the somewhat surprising result that even under the (monopsonistic) reserve clause, players will move from team to team in the same "way" as under competitive conditions. If a player's services are most valuable to team B, then he will move there *regardless* of whether or not there is a reserve clause in effect.[34] The primary economic difference between the baseball players' labor market in the absence versus the presence of a reserve clause is not the distribution of players among teams, but rather the way in which the value of a player's services are split between him and the team's owners.[35]

Conclusion

Workers do not always sell their services to competitive firms. In this chapter we have examined the demand for labor by firms that confront variable prices of output or labor services. Whenever possible, we attempted to compare the equilibrium wage-employment combinations in such settings to those that would exist under competitive conditions. In the process, we were able to identify certain instances in which the labor market impact of public policy differed markedly from the competitive case. No matter what type of noncompetitive labor market we examined, however, labor supply and labor productivity schedules played key roles in the determination of employment and workers' incomes.

Whereas a competitive firm has no control over the price of its product, a product market monopolist determines selling price through its output deci-

---

[33] The above example most closely describes the situation in which a player has only one year left in his career. If this is not the case, then the owner of team B(A) will offer (demand), the *present value* of the expected difference in the player's worth to the two respective teams over the remainder of his career.

[34] This result has recently been verified empirically in an article by Joseph W. Hunt, Jr., and Kenneth A. Lewis, "Dominance, Recontracting, and the Reserve Clause: Major League Baseball," *American Economic Review*, 66, 5 (December 1976), 936–43.

[35] Some of you will recognize the example in this section as an application of the famous Coase Theorem, which basically says that resource allocation will be unaffected by the assignment of property rights when those rights can be exchanged reasonably easily (costlessly). For elaboration of the Coase Theorem see Hirshleifer, *Price Theory*, pp. 450–51.

sion. As the result of a downward-sloping demand for final output, the demand curve for labor by a monopolist, while negatively inclined, is such that less labor will be purchased than by a competitive industry, all other things being equal. Thus, in labor markets in which some or all firms are monopolists in their product markets, wages will be lower than in labor markets in which all firms are competitive in their product markets. This property of wage-rate determination has been called *monopolistic exploitation*.

Monopsony is a labor market in which there is effectively one demander of labor. This also leads to exploitation in the sense that less labor is purchased and wage rates are lower than when a number of buyers compete for employees. An interesting aspect of monopsony is that there exists the possibility for a minimum wage to make workers unambiguously better off. The practicability of such a public policy is open to serious doubt, however. More important, monopsony does not appear to be a widespread phenomenon in the United States, but rather specific to a few industries. An interesting example is professional baseball before the emasculation of the reserve clause, which severely restricted the competition for a player's services. In particular, we noted that in the late 1960s major league baseball players' salaries were only about 40 to 50 percent of their marginal revenue products.

Exercises

1. Can *monopolistic* exploitation be eliminated by minimum wage legislation? Be sure to support your answer with the appropriate graph(s) and to explain carefully what is meant by monopolistic exploitation.

*2. Graphically depict a profit-maximizing monopsonist's optimal wage-employment combination in the situation where capital is fixed. (You may ignore variation in hours of work per employee and treat the labor input as simply the number of workers.) Suppose, now, that the monopsonist can "perfectly" wage-discriminate (pay *each* worker a *different* wage). What wage will it choose to pay an individual worker, and what is its new equilibrium wage-employment combination? Has the monopsonist experienced an increase in profit as the result of its ability to wage-discriminate? Support your answers with specific references to your graph.

3. The chart below provides information about the teams in the Eastern Division of the American League. Included are predictions made by Jimmy the Swede of team slugging averages (*TSA*) and team strikeout/walk (*TSW*) for the upcoming season.

---

*Indicates more difficult exercises

Team	Population in Millions (PM)	Index of Fan Interest (FI)	TSA (predicted)	TSW (predicted)
Baltimore	2.1	3	0.389	2.9
Boston	3.9	8	0.440	2.4
Cleveland	2.9	6	0.360	1.8
Detroit	4.7	5	0.300	2.1
Milwaukee	1.5	4	0.320	2.0
New York	7.2	7	0.420	2.8

Recent econometric estimates of the determination of a team's percentage of games own ($PCTWIN$) and a team's revenue ($REVENUE$) yield (1) $PCTWIN = .90\ TSA + .085\ TSW$. (2) $REVENUE = 12,500\ (PCTWIN \times 1000) + 15,500\ (PCTWIN \times PM) + 450,000\ PM + 25,000\ FI$

a. Based upon Jimmy's predictions of TSA and TSW, predict the order of finish in the Eastern Division.
b. Calculate the expected revenue for each team.
c. Consider the following predictions about individual player performances for the upcoming season.

Player	Team	Slugging Average	Fraction of Total Team at Bats
J. Rice	Boston	0.520	0.08
S. Bando	Milwaukee	0.380	0.10
G. Nettles	New York	0.400	0.07
E. Murray	Baltimore	0.390	0.11

Calculate the gross marginal revenue product for each player.

References

BUNTING, ROBERT L., *Employer Concentration in Local Labor Markets*. Chapel Hill, N.C.: University of North Carolina Press, 1962.

_____, "Employer Concentration in Local Labor Markets." In John F. Burton, Jr. et al., *Readings in Labor Market Analysis*. New York: Holt, Rinehart, and Winston, 1971, pp. 132–39.

FERGUSON, C. E., *The Neoclassical Theory of Production and Distribution*. London and New York: Cambridge University Press, 1969, Chaps. 6, 9.

_____, and J. P. GOULD, *Microeconomic Theory*, 4th ed., Homewood, Ill.: Irwin, 1975, pp. 400–01.

HIRSHLEIFER, JACK, *Price Theory and Applications*. Englewood Cliffs, N.J.: Prentice-Hall, 1976, pp. 288–90.

HUNT, JOSEPH W., JR., and KENNETH A. LEWIS, "Dominance, Recontracting, and the Reserve Clause: Major League Baseball." *American Economic Review*, 66, 5 (December 1976), 936–43.

MURRAY, JIM, "Can You Help, Karl Marx?" *The Los Angeles Times*, March 5, 1973, Sec. IV, p. 2.

SCHERER, F. M., *Industrial Market Structure and Economic Performance*. Chicago: Rand McNally, 1970, pp. 59, 529–37.

SCULLY, GERLAD W., "Pay and Performance in Professional Baseball." *American Economic Review*, 64, 6 (December 1974), 915–30.

STIGLER, GEORGE J., "The Economics of Minimum Wage Legislation." *American Economic Review*, 36, 3 (June 1946), 360–61.

CHAPTER 7

The Labor Market
When Sellers Are Noncompetitive:
The Economics of Unions

A. Educational Objectives
1. Identification of the avenues through which labor unions impact on the economy
2. Examination of how the institution of unionism alters the economic well-being of society in general and the distribution of welfare among groups within society

B. The Formation of Unions
1. A model of a union based on the theory of individual choice
   a. A worker's utility function and the objects of choice
   b. The role of the elasticity of demand for labor: Marshall's rules and union activities
2. Union membership
   a. Trade union membership in the U.S. over time
   b. Right-to-work laws and union membership among states

C. Sources and Uses of Union Power
*1. Collective bargaining backed by the threat of a strike
   a. The bargaining process with special reference to the differing preferences of the three parties involved
   b. The effect of certain economic variables on the incidence and longevity of industrial disputes
2. Methods used to reduce the supply of union labor or increase the demand for union labor
   a. Political support of "favorable" legislation
   b. "Buy union" (boycott nonunion) product campaigns

*Represents more advanced material

Throughout this book, we seek to understand how the interactions between firms and households in labor markets lead to a level of economic welfare for society and to discrepancies in welfare among groups within society. We also seek to understand the welfare effects of certain public policies. The last two chapters suggest that whether employers are competitive or noncompetitive plays a key role in determining wages and employment and in conditioning the influence of public policy. Our analysis of labor markets in the short run is incomplete, however, until we consider the situation where *sellers* are noncompetitive. In this chapter we examine the labor market when workers act in concert, forming a union to represent their mutual interests rather than vying with each other for employment opportunities.

Historically, the rights of workers to bargain collectively and to strike have been controversial issues, primarily because of their impact on the property rights of employers. Although the conflict has largely been eliminated in the United States by legislation that provides a fairly clear and stable set of guidelines protecting the rights of both parties, other frictions have arisen. The so-called right-to-work laws are still a source of controversy, and the legality of union activities by government employees is currently under debate. We will see that economic analysis has much to say about these and many other aspects of American unionism.

In this chapter we first analyze the formation of unions and their goals; this provides insight into changes in union membership over time, for example. In addition, we pay special attention to the effect of right-to-work laws on union affiliation by state. Next, we identify the sources and uses of union power, examining such topics as the bargaining process, strikes, and occupational licensing. Third, we summarize the current state of knowledge concerning the quantitative effects of unions on the American economic structure: in particular, their impact on wages in union versus nonunion sectors of the economy and gross national product. Finally, we examine the recent growth of public employees' unions.

The Formation of Unions

Unions typically have the power to raise wages, at least for a short period of time. In competitive equilibrium, firms earn just enough revenue to pay each factor of production its reservation (opportunity) price. As long as some of its plant and equipment is in fixed supply, though, a competitive firm would be willing to pay something more than the going wage rather than shut down. In response to a union's threat to withhold labor altogether, thereby forcing it to cease operating, a competitive firm would be willing to pay a higher wage rate if it could keep variable cost per unit of output below its (fixed) selling price. Although the firm would eventually not replace its plant and equipment if it could not earn a normal rate of return on them, it would minimize its short-term losses by staying in business so long as the union does not force the wage to the point that variable cost exceeds sales revenue.

To the extent that a union can control the flow of labor to a monopoly, to a competitive industry, or to a large group of firms, its power to raise wages is increased. The main reason is that in these situations the demand curve for final output is not perfectly elastic but rather downward-sloping, leading to a less elastic demand curve for labor than in the case of the single competitive firm. Another condition that would permit unions to obtain higher wages without a severe loss of employment is monopsony. (Can you explain why?) We will explore the devices unions use to raise wage rates in more detail later on. For now, it will suffice merely to point out that even under competitive conditions, firms may accede to union demands for higher wage rates.

Before we proceed with our formal discussion of the formation of unions, we must note that sometimes they bargain not only for wage rate increases, but also for preferred employment levels. We simplify our analysis by concentrating on collective bargaining agreements struck only on the wage rate, employers having the freedom to choose the amount of labor, because this is characteristic of most union contracts.

A MODEL OF UNION FORMATION BASED ON THE THEORY OF INDIVIDUAL CHOICE

It is reasonably clear that unionists seek to achieve higher wages and related benefits without "too much" employment loss. In what follows we attempt to represent these facts in a model of union formation that takes into account individuals' preferences. We begin by assuming that a union represents individuals' interests as though it were a superfamily trying to maximize group welfare.[1] In addition, we will simplify the analysis by assuming that potential unionists have identical tastes for market goods, home-produced goods, and time; and that they have equal relative productivities in the home and in the market.[2] Finally, we postulate that employment is shared equally among members of the union. These few assumptions mean that an activity which improves the welfare of any union member improves the welfare of all members.

Figure 7–1 illustrates the utility function of a representative potential unionist. Income is measured along the dashed vertical axis. We will ignore any nonlabor income, so that earnings and income coincide. The horizontal axis measures hours not worked. H_M is the total number of nonwork hours available during the period under consideration; thus, measuring from H_M to the left denotes the number of hours worked. Suppose employers purchase

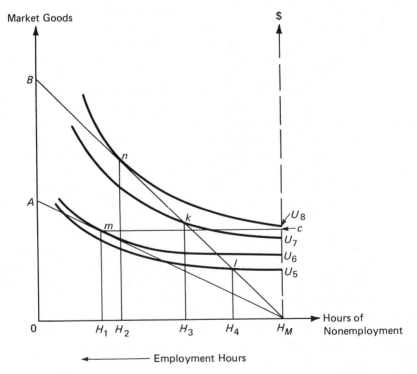

FIGURE 7–1. Utility Maximization When There Is an Employment Constraint

---

[1] For an interesting and detailed analysis of union goals when the preferences of members (and union leaders) diverge, see Wallace N. Atherton, *Theory of Union Bargaining Goals* (Princeton, N.J.: Princeton University Press, 1973), Chaps. IV, V.

[2] We will treat the wage rate as identical for all union members and as incorporating fringe benefits, paid holidays, rest periods, and "working conditions," since all these have calculable monetary equivalents as far as employers (and employees) are concerned.

$(H_M - H_1)$ hours from each worker, yielding each a total earnings of $H_M C$. Now consider the formation of a union that includes all workers and is successful in raising the wage rate to that represented by the slope of the budget line $H_M B$ in Figure 7–1. It is clear that were each member permitted to choose any point along $H_M B$, the new wage rate would definitely be preferable to the old one, and everyone could be better off than before. (Remember that union members are assumed to share equally the wage and employment impacts of their union.) However, we know that the response of firms to the wage increase is likely to be a reduction of employment from $(H_M - H_1)$ per worker to some level, say $(H_M - H_3)$ represented by point k.

It is not clear *a priori* whether union members will *want* to work more or less at the higher wage. Let us presume that the income effect of a wage increase outweighs the substitution effect so that each unionist now desires n, which is associated with increased earnings, consumption of market goods, and leisure. But, should n lie to the northwest of k, rationing of work among union members will be required.[3] In this case, the indifference curve passing through k indicates each union member's level of welfare. Since U_7 is higher than U_6, the indifference curve through m, each worker will still be better off with the higher wage rate. However, if l (any point on $H_M B$ below U_6) were the best attainable point on $H_M B$, workers would be better off with the lower wage rate. The change in the welfare of workers resulting from the wage increase depends on two factors: the elasticity of demand for labor and workers' marginal rate of substitution between leisure and market goods. The greater the elasticity of demand for labor, the greater the horizontal distance between n and k or l, and therefore, the greater the likelihood that an increase in the wage rate would reduce welfare. Remember from Chapter 4 that the marginal rate of substitution between leisure and market goods is a measure of the curvature of the indifference curves. The flatter the indifference curves, indicating that a relatively larger amount of leisure is required to compensate for the loss of a given amount of market goods, the more likely it is that workers' best attainable point will lie below U_6.[4] The key point here is that for workers to form a union requires that there be an economic (welfare) benefit to unionization, since such an activity is not free.

MORE ON THE ROLE OF THE ELASTICITY OF DEMAND FOR LABOR: MARSHALL'S RULES AND UNION ACTIVITIES

The previous section implies that unions will tend to form where the elasticity of demand for labor is relatively low. It is also true that it is in the best interests of union members to reduce the elasticity of demand for their

---

[3] If n lies to the southeast of k, the union might require overtime work or admit new members.

[4] The model just outlined concentrates on the relationship between workers' welfare and the wage level. A more complete representation of a union would incorporate a possible desire for stability of wages and employment on the part of unionists.

services thus reducing the severity of employment losses due to union induced wage gains. The economic theory of the demand for labor suggests four factors that influence the elasticity of demand for labor: (1) the ease of substituting other inputs for labor in the production process;[5] (2) the elasticity of demand for final output; (3) the importance of labor in total production cost; and (4) the elasticity of supply of other inputs. The greater is any of these factors, the greater is the elasticity of demand for labor, and thus, the more severe the adverse employment effects of a given percentage union wage gain and the smaller the benefit of continued union membership. Developed by Alfred Marshall, the relationships between the elasticity of demand for labor and these four factors are known as **Marshall's rules.**[6]

Next time the weather is bad and you are stuck inside with nothing to do, see if your friends would like to play a labor economics game, *Understanding Unions*. It is played as follows. All players first discuss the concept of labor demand elasticity and Marshall's rules. Next they take turns identifying and explaining some union activities in "the real world" that work through Marshall's rules to make the demand for union members' services less elastic. Here are some possibilities.

> *Hold the phone.* Fearing a loss of 100,000 jobs, the communications workers' union asks Congress to review the new FCC policy allowing Americans to buy telephones, instead of renting them from the phone company. The union also wants a law curbing the growing imports of foreign-made telephone equipment designed to supply the new market.[7]

> *Sizzling cinema?* A local projectionists union in Milwaukee claims new multiple-movie houses using only one operator to run several projectors risk fire from bursting bulbs, which can melt film, releasing poison gas. It may seek state laws to require theaters to hire more of its members.[8]

> *Food faddists* are costing bakery workers jobs, unions complain. The AFL-CIO food and beverage trades department blames food and diet "faddists" for encouraging less bread consumption. The group endorses legislation to promote "the use of wheat and wheat products as human foods."[9]

---

[5]A formal measure of the ability of employers to substitute capital or other inputs for labor is the *elasticity of substitution* (see p. 66).

[6]Probably the best formal treatment of Marshall's Rules is the appendix to Chapter 6 of J. R. Hicks, *Theory of Wages*, 2nd ed. (London: Macmillan, 1964), pp. 241–47. He proves that factors 1, 2, and 4 are unambiguously positively related to labor demand elasticity in the case of a competitive industry with a production function exhibiting constant returns to scale in two inputs, labor and capital. Hicks also identifies an exception to Marshall's third rule, the positive relation between the share of labor cost in total production cost and the elasticity of demand for labor. For a nice verbal explanation of the "economic logic" behind Marshall's Rules, see Albert Rees, *The Economics of Trade Unions*, rev. ed. (Chicago: The University of Chicago Press, 1977), pp. 66–69.

[7]*The Wall Street Journal*, November 29, 1977, p. 1. Reprinted by permission of *The Wall Street Journal*, © Dow Jones & Company, Inc. 1977. All rights reserved.

[8]*The Wall Street Journal*, October 28, 1975, p. 1. Reprinted by permission of *The Wall Street Journal*, © Dow Jones & Company, Inc., 1975. All rights reserved.

[9]The Wall Street Journal, February 22, 1977, p. 1. Reprinted by permission of *The Wall Street Journal*, © Dow Jones & Company, Inc., 1977. All rights reserved.

Consider "Hold the Phone." If union lobbying is successful in prohibiting Americans from installing (buying) their own telephones, this will reduce the substitutability of their labor for that of installers. Marshall's first rule tells us that this should reduce the elasticity of demand for the services of unionized telephone installers. Moreover, curbing imports of telephones should reduce the number of substitutes for domestically produced telephones available to consumers and therefore reduce the elasticity of demand for telephone equipment produced by (unionized) American workers. So, Marshall's second rule gives us even more reason to believe that the policies suggested in "Hold the Phone" are consistent with a desire to reduce the elasticity of demand for the services of union workers in the communications industry. Now try your hand at interpreting "Sizzling Cinema?" and "Food Faddists." One point is awarded for each correct example, and the player with the most points at the end of the game is declared the winner. The game ends when all players get bored. The winning player is declared an honorary labor economist, and the losers must buy him or her pizza and beer. In the case of ties, duplicate prizes are awarded.

Union Membership

In our attempt to model unions' goals based on the theory of individual choice, we have thus far assumed that the number of union members is constant. When work rationing is necessary, a reduction in union membership would increase the welfare of the remaining unionists, other things being unchanged. For example, cutting back the number of members would move point k or l closer to n in Figure 7–1, permitting those still in the union a more favorable allocation of time between labor and leisure. However, if a union allows its membership to decline, it will probably increase the elasticity of demand for its members' labor, as workers no longer in the union (or prevented from joining) offer their services to firms whose output competes with that of unionized employers. The existence of nonunion workers should reduce the effectiveness of unions in securing higher wage rates, because firms considering contract demands must now consider the competition of nonunion rivals.[10] So, unions may not be anxious to let membership dwindle, even though the short-run result could be to improve the welfare of remaining members.

A SUPPLY AND DEMAND MODEL FOR UNION SERVICES

Our discussions of Figure 7–1 point out that workers' decisions to form or join unions (the proportion of the labor force that is unionized at any moment in time) depend on the benefits from union membership. The story

---

[10]In addition, a union's prestige and political power should be increased by a large membership.

does not end here, however, as workers' tastes and attitudes toward union membership as such, the costs of organizing and maintaining worker participation in unions, and the costs of collective bargaining with employers must also be considered. This suggests that we can study the development of modern unionism in the United States within the context of the economist's favorite tool, supply and demand analysis.[11]

An individual has available a myriad of goods and services on which to spend a limited income. One consumption possibility is the services of a union. In return for negotiating wages and working conditions for its "customers," processing their grievances, and helping them search for jobs, unions are typically paid one-time initiation fees plus monthly dues. The schedule labeled D in Figure 7–2 is a demand curve for union services (U) of a given quality. It indicates the amount of U workers desire to purchase at any given price and is negatively inclined for the familiar reasons. We must remember that the price of U is not the only factor determining the quantity of union services workers desire. We know from our basic economics courses that income, tastes, and the prices of complementary and substitute services matter. Moreover, workers will consider the employment losses (opportunity cost) of union activities. So, when we draw the demand schedule in Figure

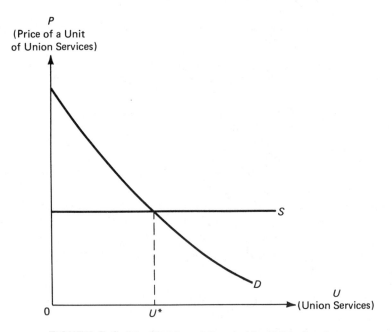

FIGURE 7–2. The Supply and Demand for Union Services

[11]Those readers interested in a detailed analysis of American trade union history should consult Foster Rhea Dulles, *Labor in America: A History*, 3rd ed. (New York: Crowell, 1966), or Joseph G. Rayback, *A History of American Labor*, 2nd ed. (New York: Free Press, 1966).

7–2, it is for a *given* set of these other factors. Should any of them change, the demand schedule would have to be redrawn. The curve labeled S is the supply of union services schedule. It reflects the cost of producing union services and is drawn for a fixed set of resource prices and a given technology for transforming those resources into U. A change in either of these factors will cause a shift in S. We assume a constant marginal cost of producing U. This simplifies our analysis, but does little violence to its basic implications. Finally, the intersection of S and D determines an equilibrium amount of union services, U^*.

It should come as no surprise that we will use the supply and demand model in Figure 7–2 to discuss how changes in the factors which underlie the supply and demand schedules affect the amount of union services consumed (purchased). But before we can perform qualitative comparative statics analyses similar to those in Chapter 5, we must first discuss how we will measure U, the quantity of union services. We will view each union member as consuming one unit of union services of a given quality. In this case, U is equal to the total number of union members, and the per capita consumption of U is simply the percentage of the labor force unionized. The latter will serve as the variable of interest in what follows. Perhaps you are troubled by our empirical representation of the theoretical variable, U. Truthfully, we know of no acceptable alternative; data on unions in the United States are just too scarce. In any event, if we understand differences in the incidence of union membership over time or among groups at a point in time, we go a long way toward understanding the institution of unionism.

Our empirical examination of union membership based on a supply and demand framework will have two parts. First, we will informally analyze the secular trends in union affiliation. We will be informal in the sense that we will merely check to see whether the interdecade movements in union membership are broadly consistent with qualitative expectations from our supply and demand model.[12] Second, we will discuss recent evidence concerning the quantitative effects of right-to-work laws on the fraction of the nonagricultural labor force that belongs to unions.

UNION MEMBERSHIP OVER TIME

Consider union membership in the United States since 1900. The year 1900 is a convenient starting point because it marks roughly the beginning of modern American unionism, which is associated with the formation of the

---

[12]Two interesting related pieces of research are John H. Pencavel, "The Demand for Union Services: An Exercise," *Industrial and Labor Relations Review*, 22, 2 (January 1971), 180–91; and Orley Ashenfelter and John H. Pencavel, "American Trade Union Growth: 1900–1960," *The Quarterly Journal of Economics*, 83, 3 (August 1969), 435–48. In both papers, supply and demand frameworks are employed to develop econometric analyses of union membership over time. Pencavel examines union membership in Great Britain from 1928 to 1966, and Ashenfelter and Pencavel consider long-run changes in United States trade union growth.

American Federation of Labor (now the AFL-CIO). Since 1900, the attitude of Americans toward unions has been characterized by a trend of increasing acceptance and tolerance—with important discontinuities and fluctuations. This, the growth of the "industrial" sectors of the economy, and the decline in the importance of foreign labor are the principal reasons for the increase in union affiliation from less than 5 percent to over 20 percent of the labor force during the twentieth century.[13] Deviations from the trend in membership also appear to be consistent with the implication of our simple model of the supply and demand for union services, and we shall discuss them in some detail.

The data in Table 7–1 indicate that union membership as a fraction of the civilian labor force grew on the average slightly less than three percentage points per decade from 1900 to 1976. Thus, the decade 1900–10 was one of average union growth, while 1910–20 was one of relatively rapid growth. The spurt in unionization during the latter period was undoubtedly aided by World War I in two ways: The demand for labor was high during the last half of the decade, and the war severely curtailed European migration to the United States. Together, these two forces should have created rather extraordinary rightward shifts in D and downward shifts in S, accelerating the long run rightward movement of the equilibrium point in Figure 7–2. The increased production due to the war increased the cost of a work stoppage to employers, thus raising the bargaining power of unions. Specifically, wage-rate increases (union services) became less costly for unions to obtain (produce). Moreover, Marshall's fourth rule tells us that the curtailment of European migration to the United States should have reduced the elasticity of demand for union labor, thus mitigating employment losses due to union activities. As a result, the opportunity cost of unionism was reduced, leading buyers to demand more U at any given (monetary) price.

Three events appear to have contributed to the decline in the 1920s in the proportion of the labor force consisting of union members. The first was the severe, albeit brief, depression of prices and economic activity in 1921–22. For obvious reasons, periods of high general unemployment can be difficult ones for unions. During such times there are unusually good substitutes for labor available to employers for workers who complain about working conditions, especially when there are few or no legal guarantees of workers' rights to organize or strike. This tended to reverse the rightward supply and demand shifts of the 1910–20 period. (Can you explain why?) Between just 1920 and 1922, for example, union membership dropped from 18.5 percent of the nonagricultural labor force to 15.6 percent.[14]

---

[13]As an exercise, see if you can explain how each of the three factors just mentioned shifts the supply or demand schedules in Figure 7–2 to produce a long-run increase in union membership.

[14]Leo Troy, *Trade Union Membership, 1897–1962*, Occasional Paper No. 92 (New York: National Bureau of Economic Research, 1965), p. 2.

TABLE 7-1

Union Membership as a Percentage of the Civilian Labor Force, 1900–1976

Year	(1) Union Membership (percent—NBER data)*	(2) Interdecade Change (percentage points)	(3) Union Membership (percent—BLS data)†	(4) Interdecade Change (percentage points)
1900	3%	—	—	—
1910	6	+3	—	—
1920	12	+6	—	—
1930	6	−6	7%	—
1933	5		5	—
1940	13	+7	16	+9
1945	22		22	—
1950	22	+9	22	+6
1953	26		26	—
1960	22		24	+2
1970	—		23	—
1976 (prelim.)	—		20	—

*The series summarized in column 1 are from Leo Troy, *Trade Union Membership, 1897–1962*, National Bureau of Economic Research, Occasional Paper 92 (New York, 1965), p. 2. These data represent individuals paying dues to a union or individuals for whom dues were paid to a federation such as the AFL, the CIO, or the AFL-CIO. In general, these data were created by dividing unions' receipts by dues per full-time worker.

†The data summarized in column 3 are from *Historical Statistics of the United States, Colonial Times to 1970*, U.S. Department of Commerce, Bureau of the Census, Series D-949 and *The Statistical Abstract of the United States, 1978*, p. 430. These data have been collected by the Bureau of Labor Statistics largely from questionnaires which requested information on unions' average annual dues-paying membership. When the BLS and NBER figures are compared, the former are nearly always larger. For more discussion of the differences between the two sets of data, see *Historical Statistics*, pp. 157–58.

A second key event was a major change in the structure of the United States economy. In particular, the 1920s marked a tremendous increase in the productivity of inputs (as conventionally measured) in agriculture. Data suggest that in 1923–29, the productivity of factors employed in agricultural production nearly doubled on the average, while at the same time output growth declined relative to the preceding twenty years.[15] What resulted was a rural-to-urban migration much greater than it otherwise would have been. For example, total migration to the states which in 1950 had the eleven largest standard metropolitan statistical areas increased by about 35 percent from 1920 to 1930 compared with 1910–20.[16] Interestingly, this net increase in population flow took place despite legal restrictions on international immigration beginning in 1924. Further evidence that economic conditions contributed to a relative "buyers' market" for labor during the 1920s is the course of real wage rates. From 1914 to 1919, the real average hourly earnings of production workers in manufacturing increased by about 4 percent per year, as opposed to approximately 2 percent per year from 1920 to 1929.[17] Thus, the change in the structure of the United States economy during the 1920s created forces that worked to intensify the adverse employment effects of union-induced wage increases leading to a reduction in the demand for union services.

A third event contributing to the decline in unionization during the 1920s was the increased tendancy of the courts to grant anti-organizational and antistrike injunctions to employers threatened by labor unions. Specifically, they tended to interpret the antitrust laws as prohibiting certain crucial forms of union activities. Moreover, the courts upheld and enforced the so-called yellow-dog contracts (agreements between employers and employees in which the latter consented not to join labor unions as a condition of employment). So, the legal environment of the 1920s reinforced the economic circumstances contributing to a relatively high cost of organizing and bargaining collectively.

The Norris-LaGuardia Act of 1932 greatly restricted employers' use of injunctions as a weapon against union organization and collective bargaining and made the yellow-dog contract legally unenforceable. The Wagner Act of 1935 ushered in the current era of union legislation, establishing the National Labor Relations Board and defining unfair labor practices. The rights of workers to organize, bargain, and strike were given clear legal sanction, and the NLRB was established as a court for the settlement of many labor-management disputes. There followed a substantial increase in union membership, despite the fact that the economy was in the midst of the Great Depression,

---

[15]Theodore W. Schultz, "Reflections on Agricultural Production, Output, and Supply," *Journal of Farm Economics*, 38, (August 1956), pp. 748–62.

[16]Everett S. Lee et al., *Population Redistribution and Economic Growth in the United States, 1870–1950* (Philadelphia: The American Philosophical Society, 1957), Vol. I, Table Pl, pp. 115–99.

[17]*Historical Statistics of the United States, Colonial Times to 1970*, pp. 170 and 211.

and economic depressions have not usually been good for union activity. This seems to be reasonably clear-cut evidence that legislation and social environment affect the success of unions, the former lowering the cost of producing union services during the late 1930s and the latter reflecting an increased desire to participate in (demand) union activities.[18]

By 1940, the proportion of the labor force consisting of union members stood at about 13 to 16 percent, or slightly more than in 1920. The tight labor market conditions of World War II, along with a social and political environment that continued to be relatively favorable toward unions, contributed to a rise in membership of 6 to 9 percentage points between 1940 and 1945. Union membership remained at approximately 22 percent of the labor force for the rest of the decade.

The 1950s saw the peak in union affiliation—26 percent in 1953. Whether the economic circumstances associated with the Korean war contributed a great deal to this is difficult to say, but historical evidence suggests that the timing of the peak is not fortuitous. Since 1953, union membership as a fraction of the labor force has fallen below its 1945 level. To what can we attribute this somewhat surprising event? We suspect that the relatively high unemployment rates during much of this time (the late 1950s, the early 1960s and the 1970s) played a role; however, legal and other economic factors were also at work. One was the changing occupational mix of the labor force. Between 1950 and 1975, for example, the blue collar workers (craft workers, operatives, and nonfarm laborers) dropped from 41 percent to about 33 percent of the labor force.[19] In contrast, between 1900 and 1910, the percentage rose from 36 percent to 41 percent.[20] To see the significance of this, consider that if 10 percent of all white collar workers are union members and about 40 percent of all blue collar workers are union members (roughly the recent averages), then the effect of an 8 percentage point decline in the proportion of blue collar workers in the labor force would be a decline of 2.4 percentage points in union affiliation. This is approximately 60 percent of the actual percentage point decline in union membership since 1945.

The relative growth of female employment from 1945 to 1975 also contributed to the decline in union membership as a fraction of the labor force. Women comprised about 40 percent of the civilian labor force in 1975, compared with about 29 percent in 1950.[21] To the extent that women are less committed to full-time labor force participation than men, they may also be less inclined to join unions (why?). However, the most important channels of influence seem to be through occupation and industry. That is, women are more likely than men to be white collar workers who, regardless of sex, are less likely to be union members.

---

[18]Remember that legislation tends to mirror the prevailing social attitudes. We shall return to this subject in our discussion of right-to-work laws.

[19]*Statistical Abstract of the United States, 1975*, p. 359.

[20]*Historical Statistics of the United States, Colonial Times to 1970*, p. 139.

[21]*Statistical Abstract*, p. 359.

In 1947, the Taft-Hartley Act, aimed at restricting some aspects of union activity, was passed. Section 14B permits states to pass "right-to-work" laws, which typically prohibit any requirement that a person become a union member or refrain from union membership in order to obtain or retain employment. If you look at the current *Statistical Abstract of the United States*, you will see that virtually all states with right-to-work laws have union membership (as a fraction of the nonagricultural labor force) below the national average. Are we justified in concluding from this observation that right-to-work laws deter union affiliation, thus contributing to the decline since World War II in union membership as a percentage of the labor force?

Where enforced, right-to-work laws raise the cost of providing union services because unions must allocate resources to persuading employees to join. In states without right-to-work laws, where union membership is a condition for continued employment, such expenses are absent. So, a right-to-work law shifts upward the supply curve in our model of union membership. There is more to the story, however. Lumsden and Petersen point out that since right-to-work laws are enacted by a vote of the populace or of a legislature which (to some extent) should reflect the popular will, it is possible that these laws merely reflect anti-union sentiment.[22] What we are saying is that people who politically support right-to-work labor are also unlikely to join unions, so that in states where right-to-work laws are in effect, the demand for union services is lower. This possibility is depicted in Figure 7–3. The key point here is that when we observe states with right-to-work laws having relatively little unionism, we cannot infer from this information alone that it is caused by extra costs of union services (the law itself).

Lumsden and Petersen attempt to separate empirically the cost effect from the taste effect. In particular, they run separate regressions for 1939, 1953, and 1968 of the form

$$U = a_0 + a_1 R + a_2 Z \qquad (7-1)$$

where $U \equiv$ percentage of a state's nonagricultural civilian labor force belonging to unions.

$R \equiv$ dummy variable capturing the (eventual or actual) presence of a right-to-work law in a state (yes = 1; no = 0).

$Z \equiv$ set of variables to control for exogenous shifts in the supply and demand for union services.[23]

---

[22]Keith Lumsden and Craig Petersen, "The Effect of Right-to-Work Laws on Unionization in the United States," *Journal of Political Economy*, 83, 6 (December 1975), 1237–48.

[23]Included are percentage (of the state's labor force that is) nonwhite, percentage female, percentage (engaged) in manufacturing and mining, percentage in construction, percentage in transportation-public utilities, and state median wage and salary income. For a discussion of the magnitude and interpretation of the coefficients of these variables, see Lumsden and Petersen, "Right-to-Work Laws," pp. 1239–48.

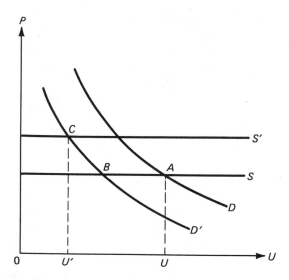

FIGURE 7–3. A Right-to-Work Law and the Supply and Demand for Union Services

In the regression for 1939, R represents whether a state would get a right-to-work law by 1968. As no right-to-work laws were actually in existence in 1939, $\hat{a}_1$, the estimated value of a_1 should reflect only relative proclivity toward union membership. In the regressions for 1953 and 1968, a_1 captures not only tastes and preferences concerning unions, but also the cost effect of right-to-work laws. If one is willing to accept that tastes concerning union affiliation changed little from 1939 to 1968, then the difference between the $\hat{a}_1$s for 1939 and 1953 and the difference between the $\hat{a}_1$s for 1939 and 1968 meter the cost effect of right-to-work laws. Put differently, the values of $\hat{a}_1$ for 1953 and 1968 are estimates of the horizontal distance AC in Figure 7–3, whereas $[\hat{a}_1 (1953) - \hat{a}_1 (1939)]$ and $[\hat{a}_1 (1968 - \hat{a}_1 (1939)]$ are estimates of the horizontal distance BC, which is the effect of the laws themselves (the cost effect). Finally, since 1953 is fairly close to when states initially adopted right-to-work laws, comparing these latter two differences in $\hat{a}_1$s tells us whether there is a time-lag effect.

Lumsden and Petersen find the estimated value of a_1 to be statistically less than zero in all three years. In the regression for 1939, $\hat{a}_1$ is -4.6. This means that in 1939, states that would have right-to-work laws by 1968 had 4.6 percentage points less union membership than states that would not adopt the laws, all other things being equal. Remember that since the laws did not actually exist in 1939, $\hat{a}_1$ (1939) can be interpreted as reflecting only interstate differences in tastes and preferences for union services. The estimated value for a_1 from the regression for 1953 is about the same, -4.5. A comparison of the coefficients for 1953 and 1939 indicates, then, no effect of the laws

231

themselves (S shifts little, implying lax enforcement). This conclusion is reinforced by a comparison of $\hat{a}_1$ for 1968 (-3.4) with $\hat{a}_1$ for 1939. Again the hypothesis that on average, right-to-work laws have no effect on union membership cannot be rejected. So, if the variables in Z adequately control for exogenous shifts in the supply and demand for union services, and tastes and preferences for union membership are not changing greatly over time, right-to-work laws are more a political than an economic issue.[24] As a result, they should have had little to do with recent downtrend in union membership in the United States.

This completes our discussion of the formation of unions and union membership. Although unions in general have grown more slowly than the total labor force during the years since the Korean war, this is not to say that *all* unions have done so. There has been a rather substantial growth of union membership among government employees, and economists have recently devoted much effort to understanding both its causes and its economic effects. We will return to the subject of government employees' unions in the last section of this chapter. Now, armed with some understanding of unions' economic goals, we examine some of the techniques they utilize to attempt to achieve those goals.

Sources and Uses of Union Power

COLLECTIVE BARGAINING AND STRIKES

Bargaining, backed by the threat of a strike, is probably the primary way unions influence their members' economic welfare. So, it seems reasonable first to attempt to understand the process through which union-management negotiations yield a wage settlement. Our analysis will touch on four aspects of the behavior of the parties involved: (1) the union's preferred outcome, (2) the dynamics of the union's wage demands during the course of negotiations, (3) the employer's preferred outcome, and (4) the dynamics of the employer's wage offers during the course of negotiations. Together, these factors determine whether or not there will be a strike, along with the duration should one occur. We begin by discussing the "ideal" wage agreement from the standpoint of the union.

The indifference curves in Figure 7–1 express a representative union member's utility in terms of his or her consumption of market goods and hours of nonemployment. It is possible to transform such a figure so that utility is expressed in terms of the wage rate and hours of employment. To do so, start at the point representing income at zero hours of work. In Figure 7–1, this is H_M, where the dashed vertical ($) axis cuts the horizontal axis

---

[24]Ibid., p. 1246.

(remember we have assumed away any nonlabor income). Now draw a straight line from H_M to one of the points on a particular indifference curve, say k on U_7. The slope of this line $(\overline{kH_3}/\overline{H_3H_M})$ is the wage rate necessary to generate utility level U_7 when the worker is employed $H_M - H_3$ hours. Now draw lines from H_M to the various points along U_7. Each line indicates a different wage-employment pairing to which the individual is indifferent. Finally, transfer this information to a two-dimensional graph where wage rate is measured along the vertical axis and hours of employment along the horizontal axis. What you have just done is to create an indifference curve indicating wage-employment combinations that yield utility level U_7.

Figure 7–4 presents three indifference curves (I_7, I_8, and I_9) derived in the manner just described. In general, such curves are U-shaped.[25] Also displayed is a market demand curve for labor in terms of hours of work per worker.[26] D^L depicts the hours per worker firms desire to purchase at various wage rates during a period of time for which a union contract is about to be negotiated. Since all union members are assumed to have identical tastes and

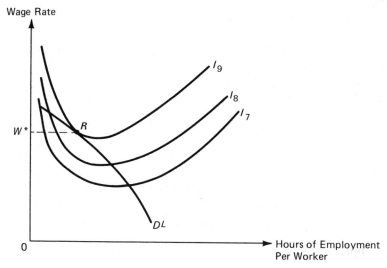

FIGURE 7–4. Wage-Employment Indifference Curves and the Union's Preferred Wage Rate

---

[25]Notice that the minimum points of the indifference curves in Figure 7–4 are arranged in a northwesterly fashion. Stated differently, let h_i^* be the hours of employment at which W is minimized along indifference curve I_i. There is an inverse relationship between h_i^* and the level of utility in Figure 7–4. See if you can show that this occurs because the income effect (of a wage increase) is assumed to outweigh the substitution effect. What would be the relationship between h^* and I_i if the substitution effect exceeded the income effect?

[26]We are assuming here that employers are concerned only with total number of work hours and that work is shared equally among union members.

preferences, the union will attempt to negotiate wage rate W^*, because this wage maximizes the economic welfare of union members, subject to the constraining force of the labor demand schedule, D^L. While W^* is the wage rate they would most like to obtain, the actual wage settlement is the result of the interaction between the parties in the bargaining process. One aspect of this interaction is the willingness of union members to settle for a lower wage in the face of stiff employer opposition to W^*.

Ashenfelter and Johnson point out that a union should not be viewed as a single entity, but rather as an organization made up of two groups with somewhat conflicting preferences, the union leadership and the rank and file.[27] The former typically places a high value on political survival within the union. Ashenfelter and Johnson feel that this objective can best be accomplished by satisfying the rank and file's expectations with respect to a wage agreement.[28] Sometimes, though, the membership's preferred wage is known by union leaders to exceed greatly what management will readily agree to. In this case, the leadership has three choices: convince workers of the desirability of a smaller wage increase than they initially hoped for, sign a wage agreement that is inferior to what workers expect, or incur a strike.[29] Should the first alternative fail, union leaders will typically prefer a strike, because an "inferior" agreement is likely to lessen their political power and appeal. In fact, a strike may even unify the rank and file behind the leadership. More important, a strike will bring members' wage demands more in line with what employers will actually agree to by making workers more aware of the "economic facts of life."[30]

Ashenfelter and Johnson believe that during the course of a strike, a union's desired wage package can be reasonably described by the pattern

$$\widetilde{W}_{t+1} = \widetilde{W}_t - \gamma(\widetilde{W}_t - \hat{W}) \tag{7-2}$$

where $\widetilde{W}_{t+1} \equiv$ wage rate package desired at time $t + 1$.

$\widetilde{W}_t \equiv$ wage rate package desired at time t (one period earlier).

$\gamma \equiv$ adjustment coefficient, which is a constant between 0 and 1.

$\hat{W} \equiv$ union's minimum acceptable wage.

What equation (7-2) says is that as a strike continues, union members adjust downward their wage demand ($\widetilde{W}_{t+1}$) by a fraction of the difference between their most recent wage demand ($\widetilde{W}_t$) and some minimum acceptable wage

---

[27]Orley Ashenfelter and George E. Johnson, "Bargaining Theory, Trade Unions, and Industrial Strike Activity," *American Economic Review*, 59, 1 (March 1969), 35–49.

[28]Remember that we are utilizing an expanded definition of the wage rate, one which incorporates the monetized values of various aspects of "working conditions."

[29]Ashenfelter and Johnson, "Bargaining Theory," p. 37.

[30]Ibid.

($\hat{W}$). That fraction, γ, reflects workers' willingness to "hold out" as well as their relative evaluation of wages received now versus in the future.

Let us now examine the pattern of union wage demands during the course of a strike implied by (7–2). First, remember that the wage demand just prior to the strike ($\widetilde{W}_0$) is equal to W^* in Figure 7–4. This information, along with equation (7–2), tells us that during the first period of the strike ($t = 1$), the union's wage demand ($\widetilde{W}_1$) is

$$\widetilde{W}_1 = (1 - \gamma)W^* + \gamma\hat{W} \qquad (7\text{–}3)$$

From (7–2) and (7–3) we can compute the wage demand during period 2 as

$$\begin{aligned} \widetilde{W}_2 &= (1 - \gamma)[(1 - \gamma)W^* + \gamma\hat{W}] + \gamma\hat{W} \\ &= (1 - \gamma)^2 W^* + [\gamma(1 - \gamma) + \gamma]\hat{W} \end{aligned} \qquad (7\text{–}4)$$

Notice, however, that (7–4) is identical to

$$\widetilde{W}_2 = (W^* - \hat{W})(1 - \gamma)^2 + \hat{W} \qquad (7\text{–}5)$$

More important, we can generalize equation (7–5) as

$$\widetilde{W}_t = (W^* - \hat{W})(1 - \gamma)^t + \hat{W} \qquad (7\text{–}6)$$

Figure 7–5 illustrates equation (7–6) for $\gamma = 1/2$. Since in general $(1 - \gamma)$ is a

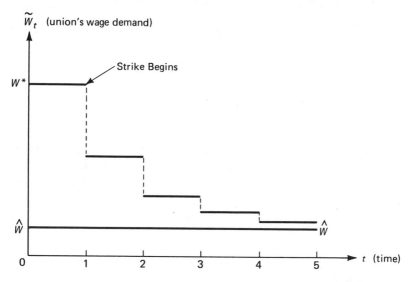

FIGURE 7–5. The Pattern of Union Wage Demands during the Course of a Strike ($\gamma = 1/2$)

fraction between 0 and 1, $(1 - \gamma)^t$ approaches 0 as time goes on, and $\widetilde{W}_t$ approaches $\hat{W}$.[31] Having identified the union's desired wage prior to a strike, as well as the pattern of its wage demands during a strike, we now turn our attention to the employer's behavior during the negotiation process.

It should come as no surprise that, other things being the same, low wage rates are preferred by employers. If you think back to our discussion of the demand for labor when capital is fixed in Chapter 3, you will realize that profit is greater the farther down its labor demand schedule a firm locates. Moreover, since a wage agreement covers a number of periods (typically three years), we must take this explicitly into account when examining the employer's decision whether to submit to a union wage demand or to refuse and incure a strike. Suppose, for the sake of argument, that a firm is negotiating a new wage agreement that is to run for some indefinite length of time. We denote the firm's sales revenue during each period by

$$R_t = p_t q_t \qquad (7\text{--}7)$$

where $R_t \equiv$ total sales revenue during period t

    $p_t \equiv$ product price during period t

    $q_t \equiv$ production during period t

To simplify matters, we will assume that capital and product price are fixed, as is output should production take place, so that either $R_t = \bar{R} = \bar{p}\bar{q}$ or $R_t = 0$. During each period, the firm's total cost is described by

$$C_t = W_t L_t + F \qquad (7\text{--}8)$$

where $C_t \equiv$ total production cost during period t

    $W_t \equiv$ wage rate during period t

    $L_t \equiv$ labor input during period t

    $F \equiv$ fixed costs (same for all t)

Since output and capital are taken as fixed, this implies a particular (constant) amount of labor during each period that production occurs, $L_t = \hat{L}$.[32] From (7–7) and (7–8) we see that the firm's profit during each period is

$$\pi_t = R_t - W_t \hat{L} - F \qquad (7\text{--}9)$$

where $\pi_t \equiv$ profit during period t

    $F \equiv$ fixed cost (assumed constant)

---

[31]For example, $(0.5)^{10}$ is less than 0.001.
[32]Can you explain why?

The firm, however, is not particularly concerned with profit during any given period, but rather with the present value of profit over the course of its existence. This means that the firm seeks to maximize[33]

$$PV(\pi) \equiv \sum_{t=0}^{T} \left[\frac{\pi_t}{(1+r)^t} \right]$$ (7–10)

where $PV(\pi) \equiv$ present value of profit stream
$\qquad r \equiv$ (constant) rate of discount
$\qquad T \equiv$ terminal period

The linkage between industrial disputes and $PV(\pi)$ can be seen more clearly if we rewrite equation (7–10), using (7–7), (7–8), and (7–9), as

$$PV(\pi) = \sum_{t=0}^{T} \frac{R_t - W_t L_t}{(1+r)^t} - \sum_{t=0}^{T} \frac{F}{(1+r)^t}$$ (7–11)

Since a fixed cost of F is incurred during every period, the only things affecting $PV(\pi)$ are the wage (W_t) and the number of periods in which production occurs.

Ashenfelter and Johnson feel that it is fruitful to treat the firm as being aware of the union's pattern of wage demands summarized by equation (7–6).[34] The decision confronting the firm at the onset of wage negotiations, then, is whether to agree immediately to a wage of W^* or, by refusing, to generate a strike. Although a strike will eventually lead to a lower wage settlement, this benefit is gained at the expense of foregone sales revenue. If the present value of the former exceeds the latter, the firm will "choose" a strike. An obvious question at this point is how long the strike will last. Since the eventual pattern of union wage demands is known by the firm at the start of negotiations, it simply decides to hold off agreeing to a wage contract until the point at which $PV(\pi)$ is the greatest. What we are saying is that during a strike, which lasts from $t = 0$ to some period $t = s$, the firm is hiring no labor and producing no output. However, union wage demands are also declining according to equation (7–6). By determining the best period in which to agree with the union, the firm implicitly chooses s (the length of the strike) so as to maximize

$$\sum_{t=s}^{T} \left[\frac{R}{(1+r)^t} \right] - \sum_{t=s}^{T} \left[\frac{\tilde{W}_t \hat{L}}{(1+r)^t} \right]$$ (7–12)

where $s \geq 0$ and R and $\hat{L} = 0$ during $0 \leq t \leq s$.[35]

---

[33] If equation (7–10) seems peculiar to you, review the concept of present value explained on pp. 271–275.

[34] Ashenfelter and Johnson, "Bargaining Theory," pp. 37–38.

[35] Why are we justified in ignoring the last term of equation (7–11)?

TABLE 7-2

The Firm's Total Revenue and Wage Bill for Strikes of Various Lengths: A Numerical Example

(1) Period (t)	(2) Total Revenue If Produce*	(3) Discount Factor†	(4) Present Value of Total Revenue If Agree on a Wage Rate at Start of Period t‡	(5) $\tilde{W}_t$**	(6) Units of Labor If Produce§	(7) Present Value of Wage Bill If Agree on a Wage Rate at Start of Period t§§
0	$1,000	1.00	$6,762	$10.00	150	$10,143
1	1,000	1.10	5,762	9.00	150	7,799
2	1,000	1.21	4,853	8.20	150	5,969
3	1,000	1.33	4,027	7.60	150	4,590
4	1,000	1.46	3,275	7.00	150	3,439
5	1,000	1.61	2,590	6.60	150	2,564
6	1,000	1.77	1,969	6.30	150	1,860
7	1,000	1.95	1,404	6.00	150	1,263
8	1,000	2.14	891	5.80	150	775
9	1,000	2.36	424	5.70	150	362

*Product price (p) and output (q) are assumed to be fixed during the periods under consideration, so that $(p \cdot q) = \$1,000$.

†Discount factor $\equiv (1.1)^t$.

‡The entry for $t = s$ ($s = 0, \ldots , 9$) is $\sum_{t=s}^{9} \frac{1000}{(1.1)^t}$ (s = date strike ends).

**Calculated from $\tilde{W}_t = 5(.8)^t + 5$ ($W^* = \$10$, $\hat{W} = \$5$, and $\gamma = 0.2$; see equation (7-6) in text).

§The fixed output of the firm is assumed to require 150 units of labor ($\hat{L}$); capital is assumed to be fixed.

§§The entry for $t = s$ ($s = 0, \ldots , 9$) is $\sum_{t=s}^{9} \frac{150\tilde{W}_t}{(1.1)^t}$.

Perhaps this all seems somewhat cryptic to you, so we have constructed a numerical example to help illuminate the nature of the decision confronting the firm. To keep things simple as possible, we assume that the hypothetical firm in Table 7-2 has a potential sales revenue of $1,000 per period that it discounts at a rate of 10 percent. When production occurs, 150 units of labor are required. At the start of negotiations ($t = 0$), the union's wage demand is $10, which it adjusts downward each period toward a minimum acceptable wage of $5. Most important, columns 4 and 7 indicate the present values of total revenue and total labor cost, respectively, for a wage agreement occurring at the start of period t, where t can range from 0 to 9. You should be able to show that the profit-maximizing firm described in Table 7-2 will hold off aggreeing to a wage contract, thus incurring a strike, until the beginning of period 7. That firms may actually "purchase" a lower wage by submitting to a strike is underscored the following statement, which appears in the *Ford Motor Company Report to Stockholders*, November 1967.[36]

> We are convinced that, in this situation, the UAW leadership concluded that no realistic settlement could be reached and ratified without a strike. . . . Given these difficult conditions, we believe the settlement we reached is a realistic one, even though it is higher than desirable. . . . A longer strike would have raised strike costs out of proportion to any resulting improvement in the outcome. In short, we believe the settlement represents the lowest possible combination of strike costs and settlement costs to the Company and the country.

It should prove useful at this point to summarize the key aspects of the above representation of the bargaining process. At the start of negotiations, the union has a desired wage which it presents to the employer. Should the firm refuse to sign a contract at that point (wage), a strike ensues. During the course of the strike, union wage demands moderate. The firm, having advance knowledge of the pattern of these wage demands, signs an agreement at the point that maximizes the present value of its profits. [37] This process determines both strike length and wage settlement. (Remember that an immediate wage settlement is equivalent to a strike length of zero.)

One subtle issue is worth noting at this point. We cannot conclude that either the union or the firm is responsible for a strike—they *both* are. The firm contributes to the strike by refusing to agree to a union's demand and

---

[36]Ashenfelter and Johnson, "Bargaining Theory," p. 38.

[37]For a simple theoretical representation of wage negotiations where each party formulates a strategy based on the anticipated response of its opponent, and where this response is not known in advance of bargaining, see Harold Bierman, Jr., et al., "Game Theory and Bargaining," in Campbell R. McConnell, ed., *Perspectives on Wage Determination* (New York: McGraw-Hill, 1970), pp. 142–49. Two excellent references on bargaining in general are John G. Cross, *The Economics of Bargaining* (New York: Basic Books, 1969), and Otomar J. Bartos, *Process and Outcome of Negotiations* (New York: Columbia University Press, 1974).

the union contributes to the strike by demanding a wage the firm finds too costly. We cannot really assign blame for a strike to one of the parties, since a strike is the result of the interaction between them. Fred Astaire said it best: It takes two to tango.

Now that we have paid the cost of learning a model of the wage negotiation process, what do we have to show for our trouble? Probably the primary benefit is that we can make qualitative predictions concerning the effects of some observable variables on strike incidence in the United States. Such an activity requires two steps. First, we must realize how changes in certain properties (parameters) of the model—γ, W^*, $\hat{W}$, or r, for example—affect strike length (s). Next, since these parameters are themselves generally not observed, we must then relate them to observed phenomena in order to generate the predictions we seek.

The following implications are somewhat obvious and will therefore be stated without formal proof.[38] A strike is more likely to occur ($s > 0$), all other things being equal, the greater the union's initially acceptable wage (W^*) or the greater the speed at which the union's wage demands are adjusted downward (γ). An agreement without a strike ($s = 0$) is more likely to occur the greater the firm's discount rate (r) or the greater the union's minimum acceptable wage increase ($\hat{W}$). In their empirical analysis of strikes in the United States during the first quarter of 1952 through the second quarter of 1967, Ashenfelter and Johnson concentrate on examining the effects of various factors influencing W^*. Among others, they view W^* as dependent on the unemployment rate and the legal structure regulating union affairs.

It seems reasonable that the union's preferred wage at the start of negotiations is negatively related to the unemployment rate (u). When u is relatively high, for example, part-time employment opportunities for strikers are relatively poor, increasing the cost of a strike. The result should be a more moderate W^* and, as a result, fewer strikes. Ashenfelter and Johnson find that, other factors held constant, a one percentage point increase (decrease) in the civilian unemployment rate is associated with a decrease (increase) of about 123 strikes per quarter.[39]

Passed in 1959, the Landrum-Griffin Act is designed to ensure democracy within unions by creating a "bill of rights" for union members and by regulating various internal union activities.[40] To the extent that it encourages the growth of dissident groups within unions and makes union leaders more responsive to their possibly less "reasonable" wage demands, we would expect the Landrum-Griffin Act to have a positive effect on W^* and therefore

---

[38]See Ashenfelter and Johnson, "Bargaining Theory," pp. 38–40, for explication. As an exercise change W^*, $\hat{W}$, r, or γ in Table 7–2 and see what happens to the firm's choice of wage settlement date.

[39]Ibid., pp. 44 and 46.

[40]For elaboration, see Martin Estey, *The Unions* (New York: Harcourt Brace Jovanovich, 1976), pp. 117–21.

strike activity. Ashenfelter and Johnson include a dummy variable in their regression equation to capture such an effect and find an increase of about 88 strikes per quarter over the pre-Landrum-Griffin period, all other things being equal.[41] Both empirical results just cited are important because they emphasize the potential for public policy to influence "industrial peace." The effect of the unemployment rate is especially important because it points out a social *cost* of reduced unemployment.[42]

ACTIVITIES THAT REDUCE THE SUPPLY OF LABOR

American unions have historically supported legislation restricting foreign immigration, since such a limitation on worker mobility decreases the supply of labor and leads to higher wages for U.S. workers, both union and nonunion. In 1866, for example, a group of union leaders held a conference in Baltimore called "the first National Labor Congress ever convened in the U.S."[43] Its purpose was to unify organized labor. One of the objectives set forth at the Baltimore conference was the restriction of immigration, particularly Chinese coolies in the West, so as to "safeguard the living standards of native workers."[44] This goal is forcefully underscored by the following stanzas from an anti-Chinese song sung by members of Denis Kearney's Working Men's party in California during the 1870s.[45]

TWELVE HUNDRED MORE

O workingmen dear, and did you hear
The news that's goin' round?
Another China steamer
Has been landed here in town.
Today I read the papers,
And it grieved my heart full sore
To see upon the title page,
O, just "Twelve Hundred More!"

O, California's coming down,
As you can plainly see.
They are hiring all the Chinamen
And discharging you and me;
But strife will be in every town
Throughout the Pacific shore,
And the cry of old and young shall be,
"O, damn, 'Twelve Hundred More'."

---

[41]Ashenfelter and Johnson, "Bargaining Theory," pp. 44 and 47.
[42]The unemployment-inflation tradeoff is discussed in Chapter 12.
[43]Dulles, *Labor in America*, p. 100.
[44]Ibid., p. 101.
[45]Philip S. Foner, *American Labor Songs of the Nineteenth Century* (Urbana, Ill.: University of Illinois Press, 1975), p. 135.

They run their steamer in at night
Upon our lovely bay;
If 'twas a free and honest trade,
They'd land it in the day.
They come here by the hundreds—
The country is overrun—
And go to work at any price—
By them the labor's done.

This state of things can never last
In, this our golden land,
For soon you'll hear the avenging cry,
"Drive out the China man!"
And then we'll have the stirring times
We had in days of yore,
And the devil take those dirty words
They call "Twelve Hundred More!"

The activities of the Working Men's party helped bring about legislation in California excluding the Chinese.[46] However, it was not until 1921 that specific numerical restrictions on immigration were established by federal legislation.[47] While the formal (legal) movement of foreign labor into the United States has been severely curtailed, (illegal) aliens are still viewed by American unions as a threat to members' economic welfare. A resolution adopted unanimously by the 12th AFL-CIO Convention in Los Angeles on December 12, 1977, urged that "Illegal immigration . . . be stopped. Employers who hire illegal aliens and those who traffic in transporting and placing illegal immigrants should be subject to stiff penalties."[48]

Political support of immigration restrictions is neither the most subtle nor necessarily the most interesting way in which organizations of workers have attempted to reduce the supply of labor to an occupation or industry. Certain occupations require a license in order for one to practice in a state. It has recently been estimated that there are over 1,500 state licensing boards. Illinois, for example, had 32 boards in 1977 which regulated entry into almost 100 professions with approximately 500,000 practitioners.[49] By raising the cost of entry, licensing serves to reduce the flow of labor into an occupation. The additional cost generally takes the form of fees, formal training in an approved institution, an apprenticeship, and a passing score on a licensing examination. Maurizi points out that a passing score may be

---

[46]Ibid.

[47]For a concise history of legal restrictions on immigration, see a recent edition of *Statistical Abstract of the United States*, "Immigration and Naturalization."

[48]*The National Economy 1977*, a pamphlet reprinted from the National Economy section of the *Report of the Executive Council of the AFL-CIO to the Twelfth Convention* (Los Angeles, Calif.: December 1977).

[49]"State Licensed Occupations Get More Criticism, But the System Is Defended as Ensuring Quality," *The Wall Street Journal*, June 14, 1977, p. 48.

difficult to obtain for a number of reasons that are not immediately obvious.[50] The exam may be held somewhat infrequently and in only one place. Applicants may be required to provide their own materials or tools; this can be quite expensive if you are a cosmetologist in need of a human model or a truck driver in need of a "rig." Finally, information concerning what types of knowledge and skills are to be examined may be withheld from examinees so that they must take the test at least once (and probably fail) in order to determine what is expected of them.

The licensing of occupations has been justified to state legislatures on the grounds that it protects the public interest. This issue is highlighted in two recent articles from *The Wall Street Journal* that deal with teachers and electrical engineers:

> *Engineers debate* a proposal to limit entry into their profession.
>
> The issue rages in the current mail election for president of the 178,000-member Institute of Electrical and Electronic Engineers. One side wants accreditation for engineering schools stiffened in order to limit the number of graduates. Others say marketplace forces alone should determine the quantity of engineers. Restricted-entry proponents really seek higher salaries, they charge.
>
> Irwin Feerst of Massapequa Park, N.Y., a maverick candidate for IEEE president, charges that engineering schools are dominated by "charlatans who never practiced," and turn out many unqualified engineers. Business likes that system because it keeps salaries low, he asserts, while academics like bulging enrollments.
>
> Mr. Feerst contends the central issue is whether the U.S. can maintain its technical superiority over competing nations such as Japan.[51]

> *Testing teachers* to assess writing and math skills nears approval in Florida.
>
> The plan, which still needs state Board of Education acceptance, would require Florida universities to give state-approved "exit exams" to prospective teachers. Those seeking teaching jobs from out-of-state or unaccredited schools would take a similar state-administered test. Passing scores would be necessary for state certification.
>
> Education officials contend the tests are needed to weed out teachers lacking basic skills. Teacher groups argue that such tests don't really assess classroom abilities, but they accept the Florida plan as long as it precludes tests for "recertifying" current teachers. Observers expect other states, encouraged by a recent Supreme Court ruling upholding teacher testing in South Carolina, to also explore such teacher-certification tests.[52]

---

[50]Alex Maurizi "Occupational Licensing and the Public Interest," *Journal of Political Economy*, 82, 2, part I (March–April 1974), 399–413. See also Milton Friedman, *Capitalism and Freedom* (Chicago: University of Chicago Press, 1962), Chap. IX.

[51]*The Wall Street Journal*, October 11, 1977, p. 1. Reprinted by permission of *The Wall Street Journal*, © Dow Jones & Company, Inc., 1977. All rights reserved.

[52]*The Wall Street Journal*, February 14, 1978, p. 1. Reprinted by permission of *The Wall Street Journal*, © Dow Jones & Company, Inc., 1978. All rights reserved.

Often, however, it is the *sellers* of a particular service, through their unions or quasi-unions such as bar or medical associations, who present the "consumer protection" argument to state legislatures. One result has been that those who have the most to gain from entry restrictions, existing practitioners, have historically been given the power to determine who may obtain a license to practice in their occupation.[53]

Although changes in fees and training requirements do occur over time to regulate the flow into a licensed occupation (compare, for example, the length of time necessary to become an M.D. today with that of a century ago), Maurizi points out that such activities happen slowly and are probably not a major instrument through which entry is "fine-tuned" from year to year.[54] For this latter purpose, he feels that licensing bodies will adjust the pass rate (the percentage of applicants who are granted licenses) on yearly examinations. The pass rate (P) is typically under the control of the licensing board. Decisions regarding P are normally made after all applications have been received, and in most cases the licensing agency is not even required to cite its reason for failing an applicant.[55]

Maurizi examines the hypothesis that when the number of applicants is relatively large, the pass rate on a licensing examination is lower, on average, than when the number of applicants is relatively small. Specifically, he runs simple linear regressions of the form

$$P = a + bA \qquad (7\text{--}13)$$

where $P \equiv$ a state's pass rate on a particular licensing examination (in a given year)

$A \equiv$ a state's ratio of the number of applicants to the number of practitioners already licensed at the time of the exam (in a given year)

$a,b \equiv$ parameters

and tests to see if b is significantly less than zero. His data cover 18 occupations[56] in each of two years, 1940 and 1950. A separate regression was run for each occupation within a given year, an individual observation being a state's pairing of P and A. The total number of observations employed in a pass rate regression are the number of states for which values of P and A are available. While most of the 18 occupations used by Maurizi were licensed in nearly all

---

[53]Recent changes in California law require its 38 boards, which are responsible for about one million licenses, to draw from one-third to a majority of their members from outside the profession they regulate. See "State Licensed Occupations Get More Criticism."

[54]"Occupational Licensing," p. 401.

[55]Ibid., pp. 404–05.

[56]Accountant, architect, attorney, barber, beautician, chiropodist, chiropractor, dentist, embalmer, professional engineer, funeral director, registered nurse, optometrist, osteopath, pharmacist, physician, real estate broker and salesman, and veterinarian.

48 states, his data typically permitted regression samples of less than 24 states.[57]

The estimated value of b is negative in 27 of his 36 regressions; it is *significantly* negative in 17 of these regressions. For simple bivariate cross-sectional regressions, Maurizi generally attains relatively high degrees of exploratory power. R^2 adjusted for degrees of freedom exceeds 0.1 in 16 of the 17 cases where b is significantly negative, exceeds 0.2 in 12 of the cases, and 0.3 in 9 cases. Finally, Maurizi uses his $\hat{b}$s, the estimated values of the bs, to calculate elasticities of the Ps with respect to the As. He finds that they generally lie in the interval -0.5 to -1.0, or that a 10 percent increase in A generates on average a 5 to 10 percent lower pass rate. Thus, Maurizi's evidence is consistent with the notion that state licensing boards use the pass rate on licensing examinations to fine-tune the flow of entrants into an occupation.

ACTIVITIES THAT INCREASE THE DEMAND FOR LABOR

Anything that increases the demand for union labor is especially good for the welfare of union workers, since it will ultimately lead to potential employment growth and upward pressure on wages. We are all familiar with attempts by unions to convince consumers to avoid nonunion products and to purchase instead union-made goods and services. Where successful, such campaigns increase the demand for union labor at the expense of nonunion labor. Perhaps somewhat less obvious, political support of high tariffs or stringent quotas on imports is another avenue through which unions frequently seek to increase the demand for union labor. Where effective, tariffs or quotas raise the relative price of foreign-produced items, leading to a substitution in consumption of American-produced goods and services and, as a result, to an implicit substitution of American for foreign workers in production. A resolution concerning international trade adopted unanimously by the 12th AFL-CIO Convention reads:

> ... We oppose the continued export of American jobs and industry, which has undermined the economy. We shall pursue ... new legislation to halt the drain on this nation's economy. ... will use all departments, legislative, education, research, public relations, publications, organization, and field services—to assure protection for American workers' jobs and living standards.[58]

In an interesting article, Silberman and Durden examine empirically the

---

[57]Maurizi's data are taken from Council of State Governments, *Occupational Licensing Legislation in the States*, Chicago, 1952.
[58]*The National Economy.*

political forces underlying minimum wage legislation.[59] Specifically, they relate statistically the socioeconomic characteristics of a congressional district in 1973 to the "vigor" with which the person representing that district supported (1973) amendments to the Fair Labor Standards Act increasing both the scope and level of the federal minimum wage.[60] The five independent variables they employ in their multivariate analysis are (1) union interests as measured by the total campaign contributions received by the district's congressional representative from organized labor in the 1972 election; (2) regional interests, as represented by a (0–1) binary variable, where 1 refers to a congressional district in a southern state; (3) small business interests as represented by campaign contributions of small business organizations; (4) low wage workers' interests, as measured by the percentage of families and unrelated individuals over 14 years of age in the district earning less than $3,999; and (5) teenage workers' interests, as metered by the proportion of the district's population that was 16 to 21 years of age.

Siberman and Durden found that union campaign contributions had a significantly positive effect on the degree of political support for minimum wage laws across congressional districts. Moreover, when the marginal impacts of the five independent variables were examined in terms of standardized units, union interest proved to have the most substantial influence. Besides a genuine desire to help the poor, is there another economic reason why unions would find it worthwhile to support federal minimum wage legislation? Fortunately, our discussions in Chapters 3 and 5 provide us with the background necessary to answer such a question.

In Figure 7–6 the markets for skilled and unskilled labor are initially in equilibrium at points a and A, respectively. For simplicity, we draw the respective supply curves as vertical and position them to reflect a relative scarcity of skilled labor. Production is assumed to take place with three factors: capital, skilled labor, and unskilled labor; capital is assumed to be fixed. To remind us that the demand for a particular class of labor depends on the capital input as well as the wage rate of the other type of labor, we write the demand schedules for unskilled and skilled labor as $D_u^L(W_s, \bar{K})$ and $D_s^L(W_u, \bar{K})$, respectively. Finally, we have drawn these schedules reflecting a

[59]Jonathan I. Silberman and Garey C. Durden, "Determining Legislative Preferences on the Minimum Wage: An Economic Approach," *The Journal of Political Economy*, 84, 2 (April 1976), 317–29.

[60]In 1973, there were two separate bills amending FLSA confronting the U.S. House of Representatives. We shall label one of them "weak" and the other "strong," based on the degree to which they increased the coverage and value of the federal minimum wage. The weak bill failed by a vote of 218 to 199. The strong bill passed, but was vetoed (successfully) by President Nixon. Arranged in ascending order of degree of support for a "tough" minimum wage law are the four voting patterns that a legislator could have exhibited: no (weak)—no (strong), yes-no, yes-yes, and no-yes. Silberman and Durden utilize trichotomous probit analysis to analyze the partial effect of an independent variable on this categorical measure of intensity of political support (the no-no class was nearly empty and therefore omitted) for the concept of a minimum wage.

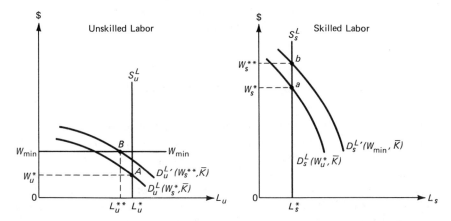

FIGURE 7–6. The Effect of a Minimum Wage on the Demand for Skilled Labor

higher marginal productivity and a smaller demand elasticity for skilled labor.

Suppose that a minimum wage of W_{min} is imposed on all workers in society. Since W_{min} is less than W_s^* but greater than W_u^*, its only direct effect will be on the market for unskilled labor. The increased relative price of unskilled labor sets about a substitution of skilled for unskilled labor in the production process. Since cost of production has also increased, there is also a negative output effect. If the substitution effect of the wage increase for unskilled labor predominates, then the demand for skilled labor shifts upward and the skilled wage rises. The increase in W_s in turn "chokes off" some of the substitution of skilled for unskilled labor, causing D_u^L to become $D_u^{L\prime}(W_s^{**}, \bar{K})$. Notice that the minimum wage has increased the wage of unskilled labor, reduced their employment, and increased the wage of skilled labor. Since unions are, in general, composed of relatively skilled workers, it is in their own best economic interests to support minimum wage legislation if the scale effect is relatively small.

Finally, the Fair Labor Standards Act is not the only federal legislation establishing a floor on wages. The Davis-Bacon Act, passed in 1931 and later amended, mandates employers engaged in federally funded construction projects valued at $2,000 or more to pay their employers the "prevailing wages."[61] Under the Davis-Bacon procedures, the secretary of labor determines the various crafts' prevailing wages, and since 1931 the secretaries have usually defined prevailing as *union*.[62] The result has been that the Davis-

---

[61] A similar wage minimum was applied to government-contract on-site services other than construction in 1965 as a result of the O'Hara-McNamara Services Act. See Gordon F. Bloom and Herbert R. Northrup, *Economics of Labor Relations* (Homewood, Ill.: Irwin, 1977), p. 498.

[62] Ibid., p. 500.

Bacon Act has worked like a tax on goods produced with nonunion labor, with effects on the welfare of union members similar to those of import tariffs discussed earlier.

Measuring the Economic Effects of Unions

We now seek to quantify some of the economic benefits of union membership in the United States. In addition, we will attempt to identify a few of the effects unions have on the economic well-being of nonunion workers in particular and society in general. Sensible decisions concerning the public regulation of union activities (for example, whether or not to pass the Labor Reform Act of 1977) require facts about the distribution of the costs and benefits of unionism among society's members.

WAGES

Our theoretical analysis of the formation of unions is built on the premise that workers join unions in order to improve their lot in life. Is it really true, however, that union workers get higher wages than they otherwise would have? This is probably the most basic economic issue concerning the institution of unionism. Unfortunately, it is also probably the one about which labor economists have the least empirical knowledge, because the presence of a significant number of union workers in the total labor force alters the structure of wages in a way that eliminates the benchmark necessary to address such an issue. That is to say, in order to conclude that unionism, or any other force, has changed the wage rate of union members, we need to know what their wages would have been were there no unions. However, since union activities also influence the wage rates of nonunion workers, the latter set of wages cannot serve as a measure of union workers wages in the absence of unions.[63]

Economists do, however, have quite extensive and reliable information on the wage rates of union workers relative to the wage rates of nonunion workers. This is an important issue for two reasons. First, differential wage rates for similar workers means that society is experiencing a welfare (GNP) loss, because too little labor is being used in the relatively high wage sectors of the economy and too much labor is being used in the relatively low wage

---

[63]It is possible to examine theoretically wages before and after unions. For an elegant, albeit complex, analytical treatment of this topic, see W. E. Diewert, "The Effects of Unionization on Wages and Employment: A General Equilibrium Analysis," *Economic Inquiry*, 12, 3 (September 1974), 319–39. As you should expect, the ultimate effect of unions on the wages of union versus nonunion workers depends on the properties of the production functions in the union and nonunion sectors and the properties of the utility functions of union and nonunion workers.

sectors. Second, it matters from the standpoint of social policy that we know whether some classes of individuals gain income relative to others due to the institution of unionism. We shall return to these topics in the course of our discussion.

Studies of relative wage effects prior to 1960 compare, across space or over time, the wage rates of groups of workers (industries or occupations) differing in extent of unionism, adjusting for the influence of factors other than unionism. Typical measures of unionism include the proportion of the group belonging to unions or the share of total group wages being paid to union members. Most of these early studies of relative wage effects have been collected, made comparable, and summarized by H. Gregg Lewis in his classic work, *Unionism and Relative Wages in the United States.*[64] It is beyond the scope of this book to examine in any detail the wealth of information presented by Lewis. (We encourage you to do that on your own.)[65] Instead, we discuss at some length one recent study of relative wage effects.

In his paper, "Union Relative Wage Effects: New Evidence and a Survey of Their Implications for Wage Inflation,"[66] Orley Ashenfelter utilizes cross-sectional data for individuals from the Survey of Economic Opportunity (SEO) and the Current Population Surveys (CPS) to examine wage differentials between union and nonunion workers during 1967, 1973, and 1975. There are a number of benefits to using these disaggregated data. Since they contain detailed, accurate measures of workers' personal attributes and job characteristics, Ashenfelter is able to purge his union relative wage effect estimates of some omitted variable biases present in studies where such information is not available. For example, labor market experience helps to determine an individual's earning capacity and is typically correlated with union/nonunion status. If, in examining statistically the difference between the wages of union and nonunion workers, a researcher ignores differences in labor market experience, part of the wage gap will be incorrectly attributed to union activity rather than to the fact that the two groups of workers differ systematically in labor market experience.[67] Moreover, the SEO and CPS contain sufficient amounts of data to permit rather precise estimates of how the union relative wage effect varies by race, sex, industry, and occupation.

Ashenfelter's empirical results come from separate linear regressions for black males, white males, black females, and white females for each of the three years mentioned above. The form of his regression equation permits the

---

[64]Chicago: University of Chicago Press, 1963.

[65]For the fainthearted, a useful summary of the Lewis volume is "Unionism and Relative Wages in the United States," in John F. Burton, Jr., et al., eds., *Readings in Labor Market Analysis* (New York: Holt, Rinehart, and Winston, 1971), pp. 438–76.

[66]In Richard Stone and William Peterson, eds., *Econometric Contributions to Public Policy* (London: Macmillan; New York: St. Martin's Press, 1978).

[67]In what direction is the estimated union relative wage effect biased if wages increase with labor market experience, all other things being equal, and the likelihood of belonging to a union also increases with experience?

estimated union relative wage effect to vary across occupation for white collar workers and to vary across both occupation and industry for blue collar workers. To get some idea of how this is done, let us suppose there were only two industries (1 and 2) and two occupations (blue collar and white collar). In addition, suppose workers were all of the same race and sex and there were only one personal trait influencing wages, X. Finally, assume that the particular mathematical equation which describes how a labor market translates an individual's amount of X, union status, industry of employment, and occupation into his or her earning capacity is

$$W_t = \tilde{\alpha}_0 e^{[\alpha_1 X_t + \alpha_2 (U_t \cdot O_{wt}) + \alpha_3 (U_t \cdot O_{Bt} \cdot I_{1t}) + \alpha_4 (U_t \cdot O_{Bt} \cdot I_{2t})]} \qquad (7\text{–}14)$$

where
$W_t \equiv$ average hourly earnings of individual t

$e \equiv$ base of natural logarithms

$X_t \equiv$ personal characteristic of individual t

$U_t \equiv$ dummy variable ($= 1$ if individual t is a union member)

$O_{wt} \equiv$ dummy variable ($= 1$ if individual t is a white collar worker)

$O_{Bt} \equiv$ dummy variable ($= 1$ if individual t is a blue collar worker)

$I_{1t} \equiv$ dummy variable ($= 1$ if individual t is employed in industry 1)

$I_{2t} \equiv$ dummy variable ($= 1$ if individual t is employed in industry 2)

$\tilde{\alpha}_0, \alpha_1, \alpha_2, \alpha_3, \alpha_4 \equiv$ constants (parameters)[68]

Fortunately, we can make equation (7–14) somewhat less formidable by taking its natural logarithm, thus yielding

$$\ln W_t = \alpha_0 + \alpha_1 X_t + \alpha_2 (U_t \cdot O_{wt}) + \alpha_3 (U_t \cdot O_{Bt} \cdot I_{1t})$$
$$+ \alpha_4 (U_t \cdot O_{Bt} \cdot I_{2t}) \qquad (7\text{–}15)$$

where $\ln W_t \equiv$ natural logarithm of average hourly earnings of individual t

$\alpha_0 \equiv \ln \tilde{\alpha}_0$

Equation (7–15) simply says that the natural logarithm of an individual's average hourly earnings is linearly related to his or her union status, personal trait (X), industry of employment, and occupation. The meaning of this expression will soon become apparent. Consider two individuals who are

---

[68] See Chapter 8 for a development of the reasoning behind this particular mathematical expression.

white collar workers and are identical except for the fact that person 1 belongs to a union and person 2 does not. If we denote the logarithm of the former's average hourly earnings by $\ln W_1$ and the logarithm of the latter's average hourly earnings by $\ln W_2$, equation (7–15) tells us that

$$\ln W_1 - \ln W_2 = \alpha_2 \qquad\qquad (7\text{–}16)$$

It is not difficult to show that when (W_2/W_1) is between about 1.0 and 1.15, $(\ln W_2 - \ln W_1)$ is *approximately* equal to $[(W_2 - W_1)/W_1]$. Thus, α_2 is approximately the proportionate difference between the wages of union and nonunion white collar workers. (For an "exact" method, see Chapter 2, pp. 42–43.) By similar reasoning, α_3 is the proportionate difference in wages for blue collar workers employed in industry 1 and α_4 for blue collar workers employed in industry 2.

The regression equation actually utilized by Ashenfelter to estimate values for the αs is much more complex than (7–15). Numerous personal characteristics such as education and marital status are included, along with six industrial classifications, five white collar occupational classifications, and three blue collar occupational classifications. The point to remember, though, is that with regression equations in the spirit of (7–15), Ashenfelter estimates union/nonunion wage gaps by occupation for those workers classified as white collar (professional, managerial, sales, clerical, service) and by occupation and industry for those workers classified as blue collar (craft, operative, laborer). Moreover, his analysis looks at the four possible race-sex pairings separately for 1967, 1973, and 1975.

Since Ashenfelter presents over 260 wage differential estimates, it would be useful if we could capture the essence of his findings in substantially less than 260 sentences. Probably the best way to do this is to examine the average wage gap for each of the four race-sex groups and for society as a whole. To see how such figures may be created, return to equation (7–15), which is a simplified version of Ashenfelter's wage-generating equation for a particular race-sex group. The weighted sum of the estimated values of α_2, α_3, and α_4 (where the weights are the fraction of white collar workers, the fraction of blue collar workers in industry 1, and the fraction of blue collar workers in industry 2, respectively) is the estimated average proportionate union/nonunion wage differential for that race-sex group. Remember that there can be a different estimated value of α_1, α_2, and α_3 for white males, black males, white females, and black females, though. The weighted sum of the estimated values of the 12 αs, where the weights are the fractions of the total labor force falling into the appropriate race-sex-occupation-industry categories, is the economywide average proportionate union/nonunion wage differential. Figures calculated in this fashion by Ashenfelter are displayed in Table 7–3. A number of interesting situations emerge. First, females seem to obtain about the same relative benefit from unionism as do white males. Second, the relative benefits of unionism appear to be quite large for black men. Third,

TABLE 7-3

Proportionate Union/Nonunion Wage Differentials
by Race and Sex, 1967, 1972, 1975*

		Males		Females	
Year	All Workers	White	Black	White	Black
1967	0.116	0.096	0.215	0.144	0.056
1973	0.148	0.155	0.225	0.127	0.132
1975	0.168	0.163	0.225	0.166	0.171

*All entries are more than twice their estimated standard errors.

Source: Orley Ashenfelter, "Union Relative Wage Effects: New Evidence and a Survey of Their Implications for Wage Inflation," in Richard Stone and William Peterson, eds., *Econometric Contributions to Public Policy* (London: Macmillan; New York: St. Martin's Press, 1978). Reprinted by permission of The International Economic Association and Macmillan, London and Basingstoke.

the relative benefits of union membership are reasonably stable in recent years for black men and white women, while they appear to be increasing somewhat for white men and substantially for black women. This leads to an upward trend in the overall average union/nonunion wage gap in recent years. It should be mentioned, however, that this last result may be due to the set of general economic conditions in the United States from 1967 to 1975. Ashenfelter notes that during this period the unemployment rate rose rather steadily from 3.8 percent to 8.5 percent. If, as we suspect, wages in the unionized sectors of the economy are less responsive to aggregate demand conditions than in the nonunion sectors, then the proportionate union/nonunion wage differential will increase or decrease as the overall unemployment rate increases or decreases.

The data of Table 7-3 identify one of the individual or private benefits of union activity, the fact that union members obtain on average higher wages than nonunion workers with similar characteristics. There is more to the story of the economic effects of unions, however, as there are a number of ways in which union activities affect society as a whole. In the remainder of this section we will examine an additional economic impact of unions, their effect on society's total output (income). To the extent that unions diminish GNP, society experiences a loss of economic welfare.[69]

---

[69]There are also social costs of inflation. (Can you name some?) If union activities contribute to inflation, this represents an additional social expense of the institution of unionism. Because of its complexity, economists have only recently begun to examine systematically the role of unions in the inflation process. See O. C. Ashenfelter, G. E. Johnson, and J. H. Pencavel, "Trade Unions and the Rate of Change of Money Wages in U.S. Manufacturing Industry," *Review of Economic Studies*, 39, 4 (January 1972), 27–54. With data for 1914–63, they present results which suggest that union membership growth and industrial strike activity have positive partial effects on the rate of inflation.

We know from our discussions in Chapter 5 that whenever identical workers receive different wage rates, society would obtain increased production (income) from its limited set of resources if more labor were to be put into the high-wage sectors of the economy and less labor into the low-wage sectors. We have just seen that unionism is one force which produces such wage differentials. There is very little evidence of the severity of the aggregate income loss in the United States due to the union/nonunion wage gap except for an analysis by Rees.[70] With data for 1957, Rees estimates that society lost at least $1.3 billion (0.3 percent) of GNP through the effects of unions on the intra-industry and interindustry wage structures. In addition, he feels that the loss due to unions' restrictive working practices (featherbedding) was at least that large, leading to a social cost of resource misallocation of about $2.6 billion, or 0.6 percent, of GNP. This, plus any welfare loss due to increased inflation, is the price society pays for permitting workers to bargain collectively with employers over wages and working conditions.[71]

Since it is somewhat difficult to interpret such a figure in isolation, consider that in 1957 the United States labor force consisted of approximately 67 million workers. This means that the social costs of unionism stemming from resource misallocation were approximately $39 per worker. Alternatively, it is generally true, but will not be proved here, that if the misallocative effects of unionism were to be eliminated, there exists a set of lump-sum taxes and transfers (subsidies) which would leave the former beneficiaries of union relative wage effects no worse off and the rest of society better off. In terms of the pie analogy of Chapter 5, we are saying that if the resource misallocation effects of unionism were eliminated, the pie representing society's total income would increase in size. More important, this increase would be sufficient to maintain the slices received by union workers in an economy where unionism leads to resource misallocation (smaller total pie) and to increase the slices of nonunion workers. Of course, political realities may be such that if union relative wage effects and restrictive working practices were eliminated, unionists would not be the ones compensated through public

---

[70]Albert Rees, "The Effects of Unions on Resource Allocation," *The Journal of Law and Economics*, 6, 2 (October 1962), 69–78.

[71]To obtain further insight into the issue, read Rees' "Resource Allocations" and make similar calculations of the economic loss due to union relative wage and work effects with current data. (All the figures you will need are contained in *The Statistical Abstract of the United States*.) It should be noted that Rees' calculations ignore any GNP loss due to union-induced unemployment. Unions (or minimum wage statutes) create wage differentials which, when imposed or adjusted, cause unemployment as workers are displaced from employment in the high-wage sectors of the economy. In addition, such wage differences will induce some workers employed in the low-wage sectors to quit their jobs and queue up for the better jobs in the unionized sectors, furthering contributing to the stock of the unemployed. The latter issue is examined in Jacob Mincer, "The Unemployment Effects of Minimum Wages," *Journal of Political Economy*, 84, 4, part 2 (August 1976), S87–S104.

policy for their earnings losses. In this case, some workers would be made worse off (union workers), others would be made better off (nonunion workers), and objective economic analysis yields no conclusion as to the social desirability of union-induced wage differentials.

To summarize, we have seen that unions increase earning capacity of members relative to nonmembers. In doing so, they affect resource allocation in a way that imposes a social cost of reduced national income. Can it be concluded from this set of facts that the U.S. would be better off without unions? No! There are a number of social benefits of unionism that, while difficult to quantify, are nonetheless important. Formal grievance processing systems appear to have relatively small effects on resource allocation but relatively positive effects on workplace equity and the meaning and status of manual work.[72] Unions also provide political representation for the working class in general. By supporting or proposing measures such as comprehensive health insurance they act as a social conscience for the U.S. economic system. This latter aspect of unionism is seen by Rees to be especially significant.[73] A stable society requires that industrial workers feel their rights are respected and that they are getting their "fair" share of the rewards. He notes that by protecting members in particular against arbitrary treatment by employers and by representing workers in general in the political process, unions contribute to this end.[74] To generalize, unionism produces a social benefit in that it helps to instill in an important group the hope of a continuing voice in the social structure and by doing so helps to insure that class differences over political or economic issues take place within a broad framework of consensus.[75] An important issue lurking under of all of this is that the "perfect" public policy toward unions is one which reduces their adverse economic effects while preserving their characteristics that work for the general good. Formulating such policy requires extreme caution and cautious evolution is what best describes the historical development of public policy toward unions in the U.S.[76] While there are costs of doing nothing about social waste, there are dangers that unwise treatment can be worse than the affliction we wish to eliminate.[77]

---

[72]Rees, *Trade Unions*, pp. 186–93. In addition, Richard B. Freeman, "Individual Mobility and Union Voice in the Labor Market," *American Economic Review*, 66, 2 (May 1976), 361–68, notes possible efficiency benefits (to employers) from unions that provide workers a way of *voicing* complaints concerning their jobs rather than articulating displeasure through an *exit* from the firm (quitting), as is typical of a competitive labor market.

[73]*Ibid.*

[74]*Ibid.*

[75]*Ibid.*

[76]*Ibid.*

[77]For an interesting, careful treatment of the issue of optimal public regulation of trade unions, see H. Gregg Lewis, "The Labor-Monopoly Problem: A Positive Program," *Journal of Political Economy*, 59, 4 (August 1951), 277–87.

Frontiers of Labor Economics:
Public Employee Unionism

In contrast to unions overall, public employee unions have grown quite rapidly in recent years. From 1956 to 1974, the number of government employees holding membership in unions or employee associations grew from 915,000 to 2,920,000.[78] The American Federation of State, County, and Municipal Employees (AFSCME) is now one of the largest unions in the AFL-CIO. One reason for this growth has been the substantial reduction in the cost of unionizing government workers.

Executive Order 10988, issued by President Kennedy in 1962, confers on all federal employees the right to hold or abstain from union membership and to bargain collectively over working conditions. Control over wages and salaries, however, was retained by Congress.[79] Federal policy was modified by President Nixon in 1969 with Executive Order 11491, which allows for exclusive union representatives based on a majority vote and defines unfair labor practices and standards of union conduct. Moreover, the order specifically makes it an unfair labor practice for a government employee labor organization to engage in a strike, work stoppage, or slowdown, to picket an agency in the course of a labor management dispute, or to support implicitly such an activity by failing to take action to stop it.[80] With very few exceptions, employees of the federal government have respected the ban on work stoppages.

In contrast to Executive Orders 10988 and 11491, the Postal Reorganization Act of 1970, establishing an independent government corporation to handle the mails, allows postal unions with exclusive bargaining rights to negotiate over wages. While postal employees are placed under the Taft-Hartley Act for purposes of regulating representation and unfair labor practices, strikes are still prohibited.[81] Finally, the Federal Pay Compensation Act of 1970 provides employee groups with additional input into the salary determination process. It gives the president, with the aid of the Office of Management and Budget and the Civil Service Commission, responsibility for establishing the salaries of classified federal employees (subject to congressional veto). In the process, they must consult with a Federal Employee Pay Council containing five representatives of employee organizations.[82]

Thus far we have said nothing about the legal structure surrounding the union activities of employees of state and local governments. Although laws differ greatly in coverage and content, by the mid-1970s, 30 states had

---

[78] Rees, *Trade Unions*, p. 182, and *Statistical Abstract of the United States: 1978*, p. 431.
[79] Rees, *Trade Unions*, p. 182.
[80] Bloom and Northrup, *Labor Relations*, p. 692.
[81] Ibid., p. 693.
[82] Ibid.

statutes giving state employees the right to bargain collectively over wages and salaries; 19 of these states extended similar privileges to local government employees.[83] Interestingly, most states also prohibit public employee strikes either by statute or interpretation of the state constitution, yet all but two of the 384 strikes involving government employees during 1974 were at the state or local levels.[84] In general, penalties imposed by states on striking unions or their leaders are either so mild as to be ineffective or so severe as to be imposed only rarely.[85] The reasons for the sharp difference in strike incidence between the federal and state and local levels of government are not obvious.

To summarize, recent legislation has legitimized (lowered the cost of) unionization of workers at all levels of government. This may not be the only factor behind the rather extraordinary growth of public employee unions, though. In addition to the fact that employment in the public sector has expanded relative to the private sector, it seems reasonable to expect public employee unions to be relatively successful in achieving wage gains, all other things being equal, especially at the state or local levels where strikes occur with some regularity. Specifically, economic analysis suggests that the demand for labor by the public sector should be relatively inelastic, so that a wage increase of a given percentage should generate a smaller (percentage) employment loss than in the private sector. It is beyond the scope of our analysis to provide formal support for this proposition.[86] As a substitute, we will simply consider a government as a firm that produces goods and services, the price of which is the tax burden taxpayers are willing to endure. This means that we can use Marshall's rules and our economic intuition to speculate as to the sources of a relatively inelastic demand for labor in the public sector.

Much of the output of government is services such as police and fire protection, education, garbage collection, and public health. Although not impossible, the substitution of capital for labor in many of these activities is relatively difficult. Except for some increased usage of visual aids and computers, the process of classroom teaching is not all that different now than what it was in the days of the one-room schoolhouse. In general, we still have a teacher lecturing and writing on a chalkboard observed by a group of note-taking students. It is difficult to believe that ignorance on the part of administrators, featherbedding by teachers, or prohibitively high prices of capital have kept the educational process so labor-intensive for so long. Instead, substitutions of other inputs for teacher services have been generally unsuccessful. So, Marshall's rules tell us that when substitution of other

---

[83]Rees, *Trade Unions*, p. 182.
[84]Ibid.
[85]Ibid.
[86]See Melvin W. Reder, "The Theory of Employment and Wages in the Public Sector," in Daniel S. Hamermesh, ed., *Labor in the Public and Nonprofit Sectors* (Princeton, N.J.: Princeton University Press, 1975), pp. 1–48.

inputs for labor is relatively difficult, the elasticity of demand for labor is relatively low. In addition, many of the things governments supply are by nature inelastically demanded relative to outputs of the private sector. Taxpayer revolts do occur, but it takes a rather drastic tax increase before the public is willing to reduce by any significant degree its consumption of, say, police protection. So, Marshall's rules give us an additional reason to expect a relatively inelastic demand for labor services by governments.

Is it true, however, that the public sector's demand for labor is less elastic than that of the private sector? Ashenfelter and Ehrenberg calculate wage elasticities for ten categories of labor services.[87] In five cases (streets and highways, public health, police protection, sanitation and sewage, and general control and financial administration) the estimated elasticity lies between 0 and −0.3. For public welfare, hospitals, and natural resources, the labor demand elasticities are between −0.3 and −0.4. The elasticities of demand for labor services in fire protection and other noneducational services are −0.53 and −0.56, respectively. By comparison, a recent survey article by Hamermesh suggests that a reasonable estimate for private sector industries is about −0.3.[88] In at least half the situations examined by Ashenfelter and Ehrenberg, then, labor demand is less elastic in the public sector than in the private sector.

We have just seen that the potential exists for public employee unions to be relatively successful in raising wages. But is the proportionate union/nonunion wage differential in fact greater in the government sector? This issue interests economists for two reasons. First, it may help to explain the rapid growth of public employee unions in recent years, the topic of this section. Second, a number of localities, New York City in particular, experienced severe financial difficulties during the 1970s. In some cases, unions were blamed for sharply rising operating costs, and proposals were made for curbing their bargaining power. So, there is an additional benefit to measuring the economic influence of public employee unions: If such unions have been relatively successful in achieving wage gains, this may imply a spread of financial difficulties among municipalities with the growth of government employee unionism.

One exceptionally elaborate empirical analysis of public sector wage determination is found in a paper by Ehrenberg and Goldstein.[89] With data for 478 cities in 1967, they examine the economic influence of municipal government employee unions. An important aspect of their research is the

[87]Orley C. Ashenfelter and Ronald G. Ehrenberg, "The Demand for Labor in the Public Sector," in Hamermesh, ed., *Labor in the Public and Nonprofit Sectors*, ed. Daniel S. Hamermesh pp. 55–78.

[88]Daniel S. Hamermesh, "Econometric Studies of Labor Demand and Their Application to Policy Analysis," *Journal of Human Resources*, 11, 4 (fall 1976), 519.

[89]Ronald G. Ehrenberg and Gerald S. Goldstein, "A Model of Public Sector Wage Determination," *Journal of Urban Economics*, 2, 3 (July 1975), 223–45.

realization that central city and suburban governments typically compete for employees from the same pool of potential applicants and must adjust their wage levels accordingly. This implies that unionization in the suburbs influences wages in the central city, and vice versa. To the extent that such geographic spillovers are significant, ignoring them may produce an underestimate of the impact of unions in the public sector.

Space does not permit us to discuss each of the regression models Ehrenberg and Goldstein employed. Many of their key results, however, emerge from estimation of wage equations of the form

$$\ln W_{jk} = a_{jo}a_{j1}g_{1k} + a_{j2}g_{2k} + a_{j3}(g_{1k} \cdot u_{jk}) + a_{j4}(g_{2k} \cdot u_{jk})$$
$$+ a_{j5}u_{jk} + a_{j6}M_k + a_{j7}X_{jk} + b_{j1}g_{1k'} + b_{j2}g_{2k'}$$
$$+ b_{j3}(g_{1k'} \cdot u_{jk'}) + b_{j4}(g_{2k'} \cdot u_{jk'}) + b_{j5}u_{jk'}$$
$$+ b_{j6}M_{k'} + b_{j7}X_{jk'} \qquad (j = 1, \ldots, 7; k \neq k') \qquad (7\text{--}17)$$

In equation (7–17), the dependent variable is the natural logarithm of the average monthly salary in 1967 of labor of type j in jurisdiction k. The data used by Ehrenberg and Goldstein permit them to examine seven disaggregated categories of noneducational municipal employees in 169 central city–suburb pairs. To test the hypothesis that the form of municipal government affects public employee wage levels, they introduce dummy variables, g_{1k} and g_{2k}, which indicate whether the jurisdiction has a city manager or an elected commissioner as its chief executive as opposed to an elected mayor. Notice that form of government also interacts with the fraction of the category's employees represented by unions or employee associations (u_{jk}) so that the effect of unionism on wage levels may depend upon the form of government. As a crude way of controlling for monopsony power of governmental units, Ehrenberg and Goldstein include as a regressor M_k, the proportion of the SMSA's population that resides in jurisdiction k. Presumably, the greater is M_k, other factors held constant, the greater is the proportion of the SMSA's public sector jobs that are located in jurisdiction k, and therefore the greater the monopsony power of jurisdiction k's government. A test of the monopsony power hypothesis is whether the estimated value of a_{j6} is statistically less than zero.[90] Since fiscal capacity, relative preferences of the community for various services, and the willingness of workers to supply labor to the different employment categories also affect wages, Ehrenberg and Goldstein include a set of variables, X_{jk}, to control for differences in these factors among jurisdictions.[91] Finally, to examine the importance of the geographical wage spillovers mentioned earlier, the same set of variables referring to the companion jurisdiction is included in (7–17). These variables, denoted by

---

[90]Ibid., p. 227.

[91]Included in X_{jk} are per capita grants from higher levels of government (excluding education) in 1967, median level of education in 1960, median value of single-family housing in 1960, average monthly earnings of manufacturing production workers in 1963, and municipal population in 1960.

the subscript k', show how factors that influence wages in one jurisdiction (k') may influence wages in another (k).[92]

Ehrenberg and Goldstein find that, depending on the type of labor under consideration, the wages of workers in central cities in which unions are present are between 0 (fire protection) and 20 (parks and recreation) percent higher than the wages of employees in central cities without unions, all other things being equal. The wage spillover from the suburb to the central city is such that the average wage in the central city is between 1 and 9 percent higher when some employees in category j in the suburbs are represented by unions than when the suburban category is totally nonunion. In the case of suburban wage levels, the direct effect of unionism varies between 5 (general control) and 15 (fire protection) percent. Although wage spillovers from central cities into suburbs are *in general* absent, central city unionization in certain cases raises suburban wage levels. In three instances (parks and recreation, streets and highways, and general control) the spillover effect exceeds the direct effect of unions on wages within the suburbs. Finally, Ehrenberg and Goldstein utilize their parameter estimates to calculate average values of the union spillover effects discussed above. They find that due to central city public employee unions, the wages of suburban employees were on average 4 percent higher in 1967 than they would have been in the absence of central city unions, whereas the wages of central city government workers were on average 4.4 percent higher due to suburban public employee unions.[93]

In 10 of 14 cases examined by Ehrenberg and Goldstein, the total effect of unionism (including spillovers) in the public sector is to place a greater proportionate wedge between the wage levels of union and nonunion workers than in the private sector.[94] Interestingly, the proportionate union/nonunion wage differentials presented by Ehrenberg and Goldstein may actually understate the true difference because their empirical analysis does not control for fringe benefit differences among workers. If the strongest unions are also the ones most successful at obtaining generous employee fringe benefit packages, and if (in equilibrium) workers who receive generous fringe benefits have lower wage rates, then ignoring fringe benefit differences biases downward estimated union/nonunion pay differentials. This can be seen more clearly with the help of a simple graph. In Figure 7–7 the line labeled U_1 indicates wage and fringe benefit payments that would "clear" a labor market in which the level of unionization is U_1. The line labeled U_0 represents a similar set of points for a labor market in which no unions are present.[95] If

---

[92]The largest central city in the SMSA is used as the *comparison city* for all other jurisdictions (central cities or suburbs) in the SMSA and the second largest city is used as the comparison city for the largest one.

[93]Ehrenberg and Goldstein, "Wage Determination," p. 243.

[94]See Table 7–3 (column 1) and Table 5 of Ehrenberg and Goldstein, "Wage Determination," p. 242.

[95]For simplicity, the lines are drawn parallel. What is the economic interpretation of this?

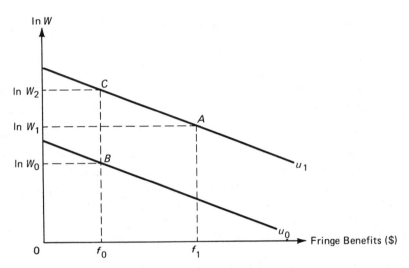

FIGURE 7–7. Fringe Benefits and the Proportionate Union/Nonunion Wage Differential

unionism also creates a more generous fringe benefit package for workers, then the equilibrium point in the unionized labor market will be something like point A as opposed to point B in the nonunion labor market. An empirical analysis of wages that standardizes for unionization but not for fringe benefits will compute a proportionate union/nonunion wage differential equal to $(\ln W_1 - \ln W_0)$ as opposed to the true differential due to unionism $(\ln W_2 - \ln W_0)$. The latter is computed by comparing union and nonunion wages with the *same* fringe benefit package.

In conclusion, we have seen that during recent years, unions of government employees have grown quite rapidly. At the same time, the costs of forming public employee unions were relatively low and the economic benefits of membership in such unions relatively high. Although we cannot "prove" that these are the chief reasons for the spread of public sector unionism, as economists we feel comfortable with how the evidence fits together.

Conclusion

In this chapter we examined the determination of wages and employment when workers have their mutual interests represented by labor unions. Our goal has been to identify the avenues through which unions impact on the economy and in the process alter the economic well-being of society and the distribution of welfare among groups within society. Figure 7–8 summarizes our general findings.

To understand the role played by unions in the economy, we considered a

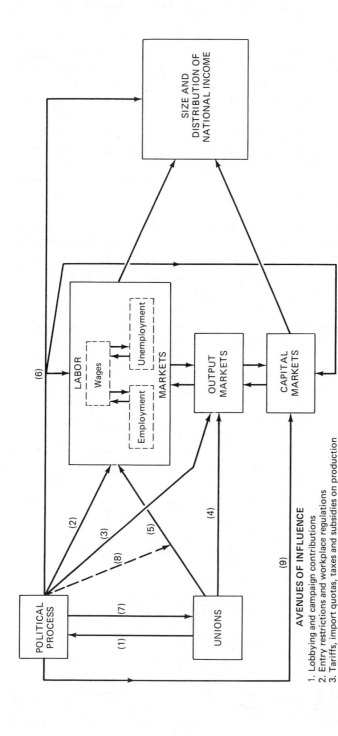

AVENUES OF INFLUENCE

1. Lobbying and campaign contributions
2. Entry restrictions and workplace regulations
3. Tariffs, import quotas, taxes and subsidies on production
4. Campaigns to buy union or boycott nonunion products
5. Collective bargaining
6. Income taxes and transfer payments
7. Laws which regulate union organizing
8. Programs which affect union bargaining power
9. Investment tax incentives

FIGURE 7–8. The Interaction between Unions and the Economy

model of the formation of unions based on the theory of individual choice. We saw that a union will be more successful in increasing the economic welfare of its members the more inelastic is the labor demand schedule. As a result, unions will tend to form where the elasticity of demand for labor is relatively low and engage in activities aimed at diminishing the elasticity of demand for union labor. More generally, the fraction of the labor force affiliated with unions will depend on the relative benefits from union activities enjoyed by workers, the relative tastes and attitudes of workers toward union membership as such, and the relative costs of union activities. These notions proved useful in interpreting the effect of right-to-work laws on union affiliation across states and the interdecade movements in overall union membership.

A variety of techniques are used by unions in their attempts to improve wages and working conditions. First and foremost is bargaining backed by the threat of a strike. Thus, we devoted considerable attention to describing the wage negotiation process, with special attention to the divergent preferences of the three parties involved—union leaders, the union rank and file, and employers. The resulting scenario aided us in understanding how certain economic variables, some of which are under the control of policymakers, affect the incidence and length of industrial disputes. Also interesting, though, are the subtle methods used by unions to reduce the supply of labor or increase the demand for workers' services, including political support of particular kinds of legislation, "buy union" (boycott nonunion) campaigns, and licensing.

The effect of unions on wage rates is one of the first topics given serious empirical attention by labor economists. Recently available data on the earnings and personal attributes of large numbers of workers have facilitated reasonably precise estimates of the earning power of union workers relative to their nonunion counterparts. Depending upon race and sex, econometric estimates place the wages of union workers 5 to 22 percent higher than those of nonunion workers. Along with these private benefits of union membership there are social costs. Crude calculations place the total (social) income loss due to union-induced resource misallocation at about 0.6 percent of gross national product.

Although overall union membership has been a relatively stable fraction of the nonagricultural labor force in the postwar period, public employee unions have grown quite rapidly, both absolutely and as a percentage of total government employment. Whether the economic factors underlying this difference can be determined is the topic of the last section of this chapter. Recent legal changes have lowered the cost of union organizing among public employees. Moreover, economic analysis suggests that the elasticity of demand for labor in the government sector should be less than in the private sector, thus presenting public employee unions with the potential for being relatively successful at increasing wages. Whether this has actually occurred is an interesting question in its own right and an important one in urban public finance. Evidence implies a somewhat greater proportionate union/ nonunion wage differential for public employees.

Exercises

1. Consider a competitive firm with
   (a) a fixed capital input, and
   (b) a collective bargaining agreement with a labor union that requires it to purchase (only) the labor services of union workers at a fixed wage of $ $\bar{W}$. (The firm may purchase as many units of labor as it wishes at that wage.)

   Explain carefully and depict graphically *two* situations in which it would be in the workers' best interests as a group to bargain for a wage cut.

2. You are confronted with the following facts:
   (a) Labor market A is competitive.
   (b) Labor market B is monopsonistic.
   (c) Both the competitive industry in market A and the monopsony in market B have identical substitutabilities of capital for labor in their production processes (σ), identical elasticities of demand for final output (η), identical shares of labor costs in their total production costs (α), and identical elasticities of supply of capital (e).
   (d) Unions are formed in both labor markets that establish *wage floors* X per cent above the normal (nonunion) equilibrium wage rates. (In other words, unions in both labor markets A and B raise wages by the same amount, X per cent.)

   Consider the following two-part statement:
   (I) Marshall's rules tell us that the demand for labor *schedules* in the competitive labor market has the same elasticity (ϵ) as the demand for labor *schedule* in the monopsonistic labor market.
   (II) Thus, the union induced wage increases will lead to *equal percentage declines* in employment in the two labor markets.

   Answer these two questions:
   (i) Is part (I) of the above statement correct? Explain carefully and support your dialogue with the appropriate graph(s).
   (ii) Does part (II) follow logically from part (I)? Specifically, will a given percentage wage increase due to a union set wage minimum above "normal" equilibrium produce the same employment loss in the two respective labor markets? Explain carefully and depict graphically. Be sure to draw a conclusion.

*3. Data for the United States indicate that states which have the *open-shop*

---

*Indicates more difficult exercises.

form of union representation (have right-to-work laws) also have on average less unionism (as measured by the fraction of nonagricultural labor force holding union membership) than states which have the *union-shop* form of representation. Using economic theory, demonstrate the accuracy of the following statement: "If the Supreme Court were suddenly to declare illegal the open shop (leaving the union shop as the only legal form of union representation), this would have no effect on unionism across states."

References

ASHENFELTER, ORLEY, and GEORGE E. JOHNSON, "Bargaining Theory, Trade Unions, and Industrial Strike Activity." *American Economic Review*, 59, 1 (March 1969), 35–42.

———, and JOHN PENCAVEL, "American Trade Union Growth: 1900–1960." *The Quarterly Journal of Economics*, 83, 3 (August 1969), 435–48.

———, G. E. JOHNSON, and J. H. PENCAVEL, "Trade Unions and the Rate of Change of Money Wages in United States Manufacturing Industry." *Review of Economic Studies*, 39, 1 (January 1972), 27–54.

———, and RONALD G. EHRENBERG, "The Demand for Labor in the Public Sector." In Daniel S. Hamermesh, ed., *Labor in the Public and Nonprofit Sectors.* Princeton, N.J.: Princeton University Press, 1975.

———, "Union Relative Wage Effects: New Evidence and a Survey of Their Implications for Wage Inflation." In Richard Stone and William Peterson, eds., *Econometric Contributions to Public Policy.* London: Macmillan; New York: St. Martin's Press, 1978.

ATHERTON, W. *Theory of Union Bargaining Goals.* Princeton, N.J.: Princeton University Press, 1973, Chaps. IV, V.

BARTOS, OTOMAR J., *Process and Outcome of Negotiations.* New York: Columbia University Press, 1974.

BIERMAN, HAROLD JR., et al., "Game Theory and Bargaining." In Campbell R. McConnell, ed., *Perspectives on Wage Determination.* New York: McGraw-Hill, 1970.

BLOOM, GORDON F., and HERBERT R. NORTHRUP, *Economics of Labor Relations,* 8th ed. Homewood, Ill.: Irwin, 1977, pp. 489, 681–703.

CROSS, JOHN G., *The Economics of Bargaining.* New York: Basic Books, 1969.

DIEWERT, W. E., "The Effect of Unionization on Wages and Employment: A General Equilibrium Analysis." *Economic Inquiry*, 12, 3 (September 1974), 319–39.

DULLES, FOSTER RHEA, *Labor in America: A History,* 3rd ed. New York: Crowell, 1966.

DUNLOP, JOHN T., *Wage Determination under Trade Unions.* New York: Macmillan, 1944, p. 44.

EHRENBERG, RONALD G., and GERALD S. GOLDSTEIN, "A Model of Public Sector Wage Determination." *Journal of Urban Economics*, 2, 3 (July 1975), 223–45.

ESTEY, MARTIN, *The Unions*, 2nd ed. New York: Harcourt Brace Jovanovich, 1976, pp. 102–3, 117–21.

FERGUSON, C. E., *The Neoclassical Theory of Production and Distribution*. London: Cambridge University Press, 1969, Chap. 11.

FONER, PHILIP S., *American Labor Songs of the Nineteenth Century*. Urbana: University of Illinois Press, 1975, p. 135.

FREEMAN, RICHARD B., "Individual Mobility and Union Voice in the Labor Market." *American Economic Review*, 66, 2 (May 1976), 361–68.

FRIEDMAN, MILTON, *Capitalism and Freedom*. Chicago: University of Chicago Press, 1962, Chap. IX.

Historical Statistics of the United States, Colonial Times to 1970. Washington, D.C.: U.S. Government Printing Office.

LEE, EVERETT S., et al., *Population Redistribution and Economic Growth in the United States, 1870–1950*. Philadelphia: The American Philosophical Society, 1957, Vol. I.

LEWIS, H. GREGG, "The Labor-Monopoly Problem: A Positive Program." *Journal of Political Economy*, 59, 4 (August 1951), 277–87.

———, *Unionism and Relative Wages in the United States*. Chicago: University of Chicago Press, 1963.

———, "Unionism and Relative Wages in the United States." In John F. Burton, Jr., et al., *Reading in Labor Market Analysis*. New York: Holt, Rinehart, and Winston, 1971.

LUMSDEN, KEITH, and CRAIG, PETERSON, "The Effect of Right-to-Work Laws on Unionization in the United States." *Journal of Political Economy*, 83, 6 (December 1975), 317–29.

MAURIZI, ALEX, "Occupational Licensing and the Public Interest," *Journal of Political Economy*, 82, 2, part I (March–April 1974), 399–413.

MINCER, JACOB, "The Unemployment Effects of Minimum Wages," *Journal of Political Economy*, 84, 4, part 2 (August 1976), S87–S104.

The National Economy 1977. Pamphlet reprinted from the National Economy section of the *Report of the Executive Council of the AFL-CIO to the Twelfth Convention*. Los Angeles, December 1977.

PENCAVEL, JOHN H., "The Demand for Union Services: An Exercise." *Industrial and Labor Relations Review*, 22, 2 (January 1971), 180–91.

RAYBACK, JOSEPH G., *A History of American Labor*, 2nd ed. New York: Free Press, 1966.

REDER, MELVIN W., "The Theory of Employment and Wages in the Public Sector." In Daniel S. Hamermesh, ed., *Labor in the Public and Nonprofit Sectors*. Princeton, N.J.: Princeton University Press, 1975.

REES, ALBERT, "The Effects of Unions on Resource Allocation," *The Journal of Law and Economics*, 6, 2 (October 1963), 69–78.

————, *The Economics of Trade Unions*, rev. ed. Chicago: The University of Chicago Press, 1977, pp. 50, 182–93.

SCHULTZ, THEODORE N., "Reflections on Agricultural Production, Output and Supply." *Journal of Farm Economics*, 38 (August 1956), 748–62.

SILBERMAN, JONATHAN I., and GAREY C. DURDEN, "Determining Legislative Preferences on the Minimum Wage: An Economic Approach." *Journal of Political Economy*, 84, 2 (April 1976), 317–29.

Statistical Abstract of the United States, "Immigration and Nationalization."

TROY, LEO, *Trade Union Membership, 1897–1962*. National Bureau of Economic Research, Occasional Paper No. 22, New York, 1965.

The Wall Street Journal, October 28, 1975, p. 1.

The Wall Street Journal, February 14, 1978, p. 1.

The Wall Street Journal, June 14, 1977, p. 1.

The Wall Street Journal, November 29, 1977, p. 1.

The Wall Street Journal, February 22, 1977, p. 1.

PART IV

The Labor Market
in the Long Run

CHAPTER 8

Long-Run Labor Supply:
Human Capital
and the Household

A. Educational Objectives
   1. Demonstrate the usefulness of an investment framework in analyzing and understanding long run labor supply decisions
   2. Develop the theory of investment in human capital and show how it serves as a framework for understanding the distribution of income and evaluating policy alternatives
   3. Apply the theory to schooling decisions and present evidence on the rate of return to schooling

B. The Household Investment Framework
   1. Present value and wealth maximization
   2. Rate of return and the investment demand curve
   3. The supply of funds for investment in human capital: the influence of family wealth
   4. Wealth-maximizing investment in human capital; human capital and earnings
   5. Evidence on the rate of return to investment in human capital in the U.S.
       a. Influences on earning power other than schooling—"ability"
       b. The rate of return approach: comparison of earnings profiles
       *c. The human capital earning power function
       d. Application: Do we have over- or underinvestment in schooling

C. Frontiers of Labor Economics: Investment in Children

---

*Represents more advanced material

269

In Chapter 4 we considered short-run labor supply decisions—whether or not to participate in the labor force, and if so, how many hours to work. In the long run, the appropriate measure of the quantity of labor supplied must reflect the quality of labor as well as hours of work. Among the factors determining the quality of the labor force are skills, health, and location in the right place (where productivity is highest). In this and the next chapter, we focus on long-run labor supply decisions. They include choices on how much schooling to obtain, whether to take a low-paying job that offers training opportunities and the promise of future wage increases, whether to change place of residence to obtain higher earning potential, and so on. Clearly, these long-run labor supply decisions are extremely important determinants of economic welfare and its distribution among individuals and families in society. Long-run labor supply decisions involve changes in all conditions affecting the quantity and quality of labor offered to the market. In order to obtain maximum economic well-being, individuals choose whether to incur opportunity costs in the form of tuition, lower current earnings, moving expenses, the cost and inconvenience of looking for a new job, and the like, in order to reap future benefits. Since long-run labor supply adjustments involve current costs and future returns, they are *investments*, and the theory of long-run labor supply is therefore the theory of decisions to invest in *human capital*.

Investments in human beings may take many forms, but it is useful to divide our discussion between the investments that take place on the job, as part of market work activity, and those acquired elsewhere. Job-associated investments in human capital consists mainly of formal and informal training programs that take place within firms. Alternatively, schooling, migration, health care, and job search primarily involve activities in the "nonmarket" sector. Of course, as with most attempts to categorize economic activities, some difficulties arise. For example, investment in health care takes place both as a household activity (having children vaccinated against diseases) and on the job (controlling exposure of workers to toxic substances). Search activities, too, are engaged in both by workers looking for good jobs and by firms looking for productive workers. This chapter deals with household investments in human capital; Chapter 9 treats investments occurring within firms.

A moment's thought should reveal that anyone who is interested in the fundamental determinants of wealth, its distribution, and government efforts to improve the lot of the poor must understand the process of investment in human capital. The answers to important economic and social questions— Why do some individuals earn more than others? Who has access to the most desirable jobs? Why do some children finish college while others drop out of high school? Why do blacks earn less than whites and women less than men?—can be better understood if one comprehends the concept of investment in human capital. Approximately 70 percent of national income in the

United States consists of wages and salaries. Thus, the distribution of economic benefits among individuals can largely be analyzed in terms of the distribution of investments in human capital and the returns obtained from them. Insofar as we may wish to alter the distribution of wealth in society, government policies toward poverty, unemployment, health, and schooling must be formulated with regard to their impact on human investments and returns to be effective and efficient. The human capital model not only helps us to understand individual long-run labor supply decisions, but can also serve as a useful guide for governmental decisions concerning society's allocation of scarce resources to develop human productive capacity.

The Household Investment Framework

As soon as we begin to deal with labor supply decisions that have consequences over several time periods, it becomes appropriate to treat them by means of a theory of human capital. At first it may seem morally wrong or factually incorrect to speak of human beings as though they were merely machines, but nothing (im)moral or (un)ethical is implied in discussing human capital. The subject matter is quite appropriate for situations in which workers have complete freedom of choice in their labor market decisions. In fact, the institutional requirement that human capital must be "owned" by the person in whom it is embodied is an important factor making the theory of human capital distinct from conventional capital theory (and more interesting). Whether the theory is "correct" can only be decided on the basis of its utility in explaining labor market phenomena.

PRESENT VALUE

The household investment, or human capital, framework describes how an individual or family chooses the "correct" amount (and type) of investment in human capital. For convenience, we will refer to this goal as *wealth maximization*. It is now necessary not only to decide how much to work in the market, but also to make choices that affect wage rates and other characteristics of the job a worker may obtain. When all other characteristics of alternative labor market choices are the same, we assume an individual achieves the most satisfaction from labor market decisions by maximizing his or her monetary earning power. A note of caution is called for here: The nonmonetary characteristics of alternative labor market choices are not always the same. Some regions are more desirable to live in than others; some jobs less injurious to the health than others, and so on. Utility-maximizing individuals should be expected to consider these characteristics in their long-run labor market decisions. Thus, utility maximization does not necessarily imply opting for the labor market choice yielding the greatest monetary income opportunities. "Compensating differentials" among wages in different occupations, industries, and geographic locations complicate the study of long-run labor supply decisions.

✓ What does it mean to maximize one's potential money return in the labor market over the long run? Often, discussions of the total amount of earnings in alternative occupations take the form of urging young people to continue their education because high school degrees may add, say, $100,000 to total lifetime earnings. Yet maximization of total lifetime earnings may not lead to utility or wealth maximization, even when we ignore all nonpecuniary aspects of labor market decisions. Obviously, the $100,000 is not gained without cost. One reason why a young person may hesitate to acquire additional schooling is that even if the tuition is "free," the *opportunity cost* of more education is by no means zero. Market earnings must be sacrificed while attending school, and unless a sizable scholarship is available, these foregone earnings must be subtracted from future income gains. But even if the net gain is positive, this would not necessarily mean that acquiring more schooling would increase wealth, because a dollar received in the future does not have the same weight in calculating the net returns to a long-run labor market choice as a dollar's cost paid in the present. One of the essential features of the theory of investment and capital (human or nonhuman) is the role of time—the comparison of future and present dollars.

Suppose you are interested in maximizing your monetary wealth and you face two alternatives: (1) to repay a $10,000 debt immediately; or (2) to repay the same debt one year from now. Which alternative do you prefer? If you think about it carefully, you will probably choose the second. If you already have the $10,000, you can place it in a savings account or invest it for a year and earn interest—say 5 percent. Thus, one year from now you can pay the $10,000 debt and have $500 left over. Alternatively, you could put a little over $9,500 in the bank now and spend the remainder; a year from now you would have $10,000 in your account that could be used to satisfy your creditors. The same analysis applies even if you have to borrow money to repay the debt. For if you were to borrow $10,000 now, but place it in your savings account for the year instead of repaying your debt, you would be better off at the year's end by the annual interest payment on your savings.

As long as there is an interest rate, decisions among economic alternatives must consider the timing of costs and returns. A dollar today is not the equivalent of a dollar tomorrow—it is worth more than that. There is a simple technique for evaluating costs and returns that occur through time, and that is to express the value of a future expenditure or receipt in terms of an amount paid out or received today. The value today of a future receipt or expenditure is called its **present value**. By expressing monetary amounts that occur at different points in the future in terms of their present values, we have a valid means of comparing costs and returns that occur over a period of years. In terms of the example given above, if the rate of interest were 5 percent, it would be necessary to put only $9523.81 in a savings account today in order to have enough to make a $10,000 payment one year hence. In other words, if interest is paid annually, the *present value* of $10,000 to be paid (or reveived) one year from today is $9523.81 or $10,000/(1 + i)$, where i, the rate of interest, is 0.05.

Consider the alternative of repaying the $10,000 debt two years from now. What is the present value of $10,000 two years hence? We follow the same procedure as above. If you have $10,000 now, you can save it, earning $500 the first year, if the interest rate is 5 percent. The second year, if you let the interest accumulate, you will earn $500 plus 5 percent on the first year's interest, or $25. Thus, you could repay the debt at the end of two years and have $1,025 left. The longer you can delay repaying the debt, the better off you are; the present value of the $10,000 debt is smaller, the further away the date of repayment. This is because the longer you can wait before paying out the $10,000, the smaller the sum of money you have to set aside today in order to have $10,000 when the debt is due. In our example, in order to have $10,000 two years from now, you only have to set aside $10,000/(1 + i)^2$ today, or $9070.29. The present value of $10,000 two years from now is $10,000/(1 + i)^2$. The present value of a debt of $10,000 one year from now plus a debt of $10,000 two years from now is $10,000[(1 + i)^{-1} + (1 + i)^{-2}]$. Similarly, if someone *owed* you $10,000, the present value of the payment to you would be smaller the further in the future you received it. This is because you must forego receiving the interest on the payment for every year it is not paid to you. Thus, the formula for the present value of a future payment to you is identical to that for a future payment by you to someone else.

The present value concept is easily applied to long-run labor market choices. Consider an individual faced with deciding between two occupations, one of which (Y) requires two additional years of schooling but promises a greater future income than the other occupation (X). (The individual is *already* capable of doing X without further education or training.) The occupations are equally "pleasant." The problem, then, is to decide which occupation will yield the greatest present value in monetary terms. Suppose the additional schooling required to gain access to occupation Y is "free," so that the only cost of entering occupation Y is the earnings not received in X while going to school. Assume that if occupation Y is chosen, part-time work is available yielding a small income during the two years of schooling and that the individual views the net income in each year for the two occupations to be as shown in Table 8–1. (Our example is limited to six years for illustrative purposes.)

The present value of future earnings in occupation X (PV_x) is the sum of the present values of each year's anticipated income. Denoting each year's expected earnings as X_j where the subscript j represents the year (starting

TABLE 8-1

Income Received and Present Values in Occupations X and Y at Various Interest Rates

| | Net Income | | Present Value | | | | | | | |
| | | | $(1+i)^{-j}X_j$ | | | | $(1+i)^{-j}Y_j$ | | | |
Year (j)	X	Y	$i = 0$	$i = 0.05$	$i = 0.20$	$i = 0.25$	$i = 0$	$i = 0.05$	$i = 0.20$	$i = 0.25$
0	$10,000	$ 1,000	$10,000	$10,000	$10,000	$10,000	$ 1,000	$ 1,000	$ 1,000	$ 1,000
1	10,000	1,000	10,000	9,524	8,333	8,000	1,000	952	833	800
2	10,000	18,000	10,000	9,070	6,944	6,400	18,000	16,327	12,499	11,520
3	10,000	18,000	10,000	8,638	5,787	5,120	18,000	15,549	10,417	9,216
4	10,000	18,000	10,000	8,227	4,822	4,096	18,000	14,809	8,680	7,373
5	10,000	18,000	10,000	7,835	4,018	3,277	18,000	14,103	7,232	5,899
Sum	$60,000	$74,000	$60,000	$53,294	$39,904	$36,893	$74,000	$62,740	$40,661	$35,809

from the present, $j = 0$) during which income is received, we know from the formula for present value given above that[1]

$$PV_x = \sum_{j=0}^{5} X_j(1 + i)^{-j} \qquad (8\text{--}1)$$

Similarly, the present value of future earnings in occupation Y is

$$PV_y = \sum_{j=0}^{5} Y_j(1 + i)^{-j} \qquad (8\text{--}2)$$

As Table 8–1 shows, whether X or Y is the most advantageous occupation (whether X or Y offers the earnings stream with the greatest present value) depends not only on the net earnings in each year, but also on the rate of interest relevant to this particular individual. The wealth-maximizing decision is to choose occupation Y at relatively low rates of interest. But when the rate of interest equals 25 percent, the present value of future earnings in occupation Y falls below that of occupation X, and the net economic advantage goes to occupation X.

In this example, the only cost of choosing occupation Y is the earnings foregone by not choosing X. Foregone earnings constitute an *indirect cost* of choosing occupation Y. *Direct costs* include outlays for tuition, books, and the like, which we assumed were nonexistent in order to keep the example simple. Direct costs are extremely easy to treat, however. They are simply subtracted from any earnings received in the year during which the costs are incurred. If, say, there were tuition payments of $500 to attend school during years 0 and 1, then Y_0 and Y_1 would each equal $500 ($1,000 less tuition), and PV_x would be correspondingly smaller.

Whether PV_y exceeds PV_x depends on the rate of interest, the direct and indirect costs of investing in occupation Y, the excess of earnings in Y over those in X after the schooling (or other investment) necessary to enter occupation Y, and the number of years during which the returns from investing in Y are received. By carefully studying the present value formulas, you should be able to see that $PV_y - PV_x$ is more likely to be positive the smaller the costs of choosing Y, the greater the returns, the greater the number of time periods during which net positive returns to Y are received, and the lower the rate of interest.

RATE OF RETURN

In exploring human capital decisions, it is often convenient to deal with the rate of interest at which the present value of investing in human capital exactly equals the cost of doing so. In the preceding example, the cost of

---

[1]To be precise, we must specify whether income is received at the beginning or end of each year. We assume that income is received at the beginning of each year.

choosing Y is the earnings foregone by not choosing X. From the figures in Table 8–1, we can see that the critical rate of interest, at which $PV_y - PV_x = 0$, is between 20 and 25 percent, since when $i = 0.20$, PV_y is greater than PV_x, while when $i = 0.25$, PV_x is greater than PV_y. In Table 8–2, it can be seen that the critical rate of interest is approximately equal to 22 percent.

TABLE 8–2

Calculation of Rate of Return to Investing in Occupation Y

	Net Income			
Year (j)	Occupation X	Occupation Y	$Y_j - X_j$	$(Y_j - X_j)(1 + r)^{-j}$
0	$10,000	$ 1,000	$-9,000	$-9,000
1	10,000	1,000	−9,000	−7,377
2	10,000	18,000	8,000	5,375
3	10,000	18,000	8,000	4,406
4	10,000	18,000	8,000	3,611
5	10,000	18,000	8,000	2,960
Sum	$60,000	$74,000	$14,000	$ −25
				$(r = 0.22)$

We use the symbol r to denote the **rate of return**, which is the rate of interest at which $PV_y - PV_x = 0$. From equations (8–1) and (8–2) and the above definition, you should see that the rate of return, r, is defined implicitly as

$$\sum_{j=0}^{5} X_j(1 + r)^{-j} = \sum_{j=0}^{5} Y_j(1 + r)^{-j} \tag{8–3}$$

The factors affecting the rate of return are the same as those determining whether PV_y exceeds PV_x. The rate of return is higher the smaller the direct and indirect costs of choosing occupation Y, the greater the excess of net earnings in Y over those in X, and the greater the length of time during which net positive returns to Y are received.

THE DEMAND CURVE FOR INVESTMENT IN HUMAN CAPITAL

The concept of the rate of return, which is equal to the rate of interest at which it makes no difference to an individual's wealth whether a particular investment is undertaken or not, is extremely useful because it permits us to construct a demand curve for investment in human capital. To see this, assume that investments in human capital need not be made in discrete jumps of, say, an entire additional year of schooling, but rather may be carried out in very small increments which can be measured in monetary units. For example, suppose that it is possible to acquire one dollar's worth of additional training, schooling, or investment in health, where the dollar may measure both direct costs (tuition, fees, books, doctor bills) and indirect costs (foregone earning opportunities due to time spent in schooling, engaging in healthful recreation activities). The demand curve for investment in human capital describes of the relationship between the rate of interest at which an individual or family can borrow (or lend)[2] money and the amount of desired investment in human capital. From the preceding discussion you should see that all investments will be undertaken for which the rate of return exceeds the rate of interest, because so long as the rate of return exceeds the rate of interest, the present value of an investment exceeds its cost. *Therefore, the demand curve for investment in human capital is the relationship between the rate of return on an additional investment (the marginal rate of return) and the amount of investment already undertaken.* In order to draw the demand curve for investment in human capital, we need to discover how the marginal rate of return varies as investment increases.[3]

We assume that there are no institutional barriers preventing individuals or families from undertaking all wealth-maximizing human capital investment activities—namely, all those for which the rate of return exceeds the rate of interest. We also assume that at any moment of time those investment "projects" are undertaken which yield the highest return. (This does not mean that those projects which are rejected at one point in an individual's life cycle may not be especially worthwhile later on. For example, the rate of return to investing in apprenticeship training for a ten-year-old boy or girl may be lower than investing the same resources in an additional year of schooling, while the opposite may be true for an eighteen-year-old.) What happens to the rate of return on additional investment as more and more resources are devoted to human capital depends on a number of factors, but two are probably especially important. One, which is similar to forces affecting the firm's demand for factors of production, is the law of diminishing returns or the law of variable proportions. When a firm uses more and more labor with a fixed amount of other productive factors, labor's marginal product declines. Similarly, we may expect that as increasing amounts of human capital are invested in a single individual, the rate of return to further

---

[2]We must emphasize that this analysis applies equally when it is not necessary to borrow money to invest in human capital. The opportunity cost of investment in this case is the foregone interest on funds that could have been used elsewhere. For example, if you don't go to college, you could invest your earnings in a savings account.

[3]The discussion of the demand and supply curves for investment in human capital draws heavily on Gary S. Becker, *Human Capital*, 2nd ed. (New York: National Bureau of Economic Research, 1975) pp. 94ff.

investment will diminish. In general, we may think of human capital as produced using a fixed human input, market goods, and previously acquired human capital. One of these inputs, the individual human being, cannot be varied. Thus the ratio of previously produced human capital to the fixed capacity of an individual human being (to absorb more training, schooling, health, or whatever) grows over time, and the efficiency of additional resources devoted to producing human capital diminishes.

The second factor affecting the marginal rate of return as the amount of human capital invested in an individual increases results from the effect of previously produced human capital on the cost of investing in more human capital. Individual earning power grows as human capital increases. Since one's own time is required to produce human capital, and since the cost of time rises as the wage rate rises, as human capital accumulates the amount of additional capital that can be produced for a given monetary expenditure declines. This rising indirect cost of investing in human capital also induces a negative relationship between the total amount invested and the marginal rate of return.

Both diminishing returns and rising opportunity cost lead to a negative relationship between the rate of return to additional investment and the amount of human capital already acquired. Since wealth maximization requires investing in human capital up to the point where the rate of interest (i) equals the rate of return (r) to additional investment, the marginal rate of return schedule shown in Figure 8–1 is also the demand for investment in human capital of a wealth-maximizing individual or family.

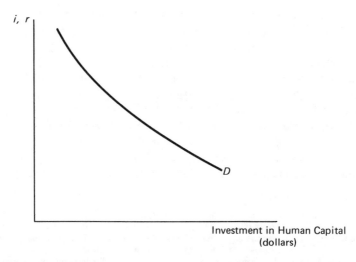

FIGURE 8–1. Marginal Rate of Return Schedule and Individual Demand for Human Capital

THE SUPPLY OF FUNDS FOR INVESTMENT
IN HUMAN CAPITAL

If human beings could be used as collateral against loans made to finance human capital (if indentured servitude or slavery were currently legal), then the supply curve of funds for investment would be like that for investment in physical capital. If you want to buy an apartment house for investment purposes, or if an established business firm wishes to purchase new equipment, there is a well-defined market for loanable funds in which it is possible to borrow at a market-determined rate of interest. The apartment house or equipment can be repossessed if there is a default in loan repayment. This is not to say that lenders are indifferent to the risk associated with lending very large amounts to a single investor. Rather, the collateral provided by the physical asset(s) financed with borrowed funds reduces risk sufficiently to make the supply of funds relatively elastic, in contrast to the supply of funds to finance human capital.

In Figure 8-2, S_h and S_p represent supply curves of funds for investment in human and physical capital, respectively. They depict the relationship between the marginal rate of interest and the amount of funds borrowed (or not lent) to finance investment opportunities. The cost of certain human capital investments, from the investor's (although not society's) point of view, may be nearly zero. Since child labor and compulsory school attendance laws greatly reduce foregone labor market earnings of children while they

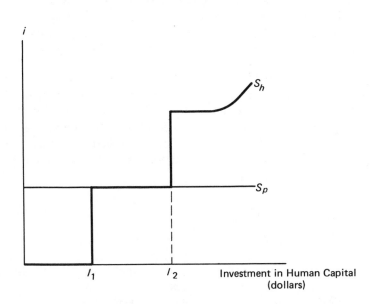

FIGURE 8–2. Supply Curves of Funds for Investment Purposes

are enrolled in the earlier years of (subsidized public) schooling, the private cost of investing in some schooling for the children in most families is extremely low. The low opportunity cost of financing modest amounts of investment in human capital is represented by the initial portion of S_h which lies along the horizontal axis of Figure 8–2 up to I_1.

Some families can finance further investments in human capital (say up to I_2) by selling stocks or bonds, or using them as collateral for borrowed funds to finance college tuition. For such families, the supply of loanable funds for additional investment in human capital will coincide with S_p, the cost of funds for investment in physical capital. Eventually (very soon for less wealthy families), as more human capital investment is undertaken, financing becomes increasingly difficult as assets that may be sold or used to provide collateral for borrowed funds are exhausted. It becomes necessary to rely on increasingly costly sources of funds. For example, a young family may desire to invest in human capital by accepting low-paying jobs that promise increased earnings in later years. The family may be able to maintain current consumption of goods and services by borrowing. It may purchase a home, making a smaller down payment than if members were not foregoing some current income in the expectation of better jobs later on. Essentially, they are financing part of their investment in human capital by using their home as collateral for the funds they want to borrow. Additional sources of funds will be more costly. New furniture may be purchased, despite low current income, by resorting to the market for instalment loans. The interest rate on instalment loans is higher than on home mortgage loans. The interest rate on unsecured loans is higher than the rate on loans secured by, say, furniture or an automobile. As more investment is undertaken, funds may be available, but only at higher rates of interest, as shown by the upward-sloping portion of S_h beyond I_2. Eventually, borrowing difficulties may become so great that the only source of investible funds is reduced current leisure (a part-time job while attending college, for example) and reduced current consumption. We have drawn the supply curve of funds for investment in human capital as an upward-sloping step function to reflect the difficulties created by the unavailability of human capital as collateral. For convenience, however, we will usually draw S_h as a conventionally smooth, upward-sloping curve, as in Figure 8–3.

EQUILIBRIUM INVESTMENT IN HUMAN CAPITAL AND EARNINGS

Figure 8–3 depicts the interaction of the supply and demand curves for investment in human capital from the point of view of an individual investor. Since wealth maximization requires investing in all "projects" for which the rate of return exceeds the rate of interest, it is easy to see that H_0 represents the amount invested, while i_0 and r_0 represent the equilibrium interest rate

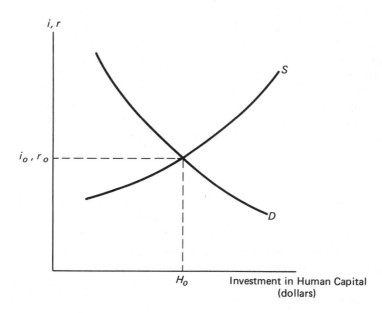

FIGURE 8–3. Supply and Demand for Investment in Human Capital

and marginal rate of return, respectively. Factors making it easier to finance human capital investments, such as greater family wealth, will shift the supply curve to the right, increasing the amount invested and lowering the equilibrium rate of return to human capital. Similarly, equilibrium investment and rate of return are influenced by the position of the demand curve.

One important condition underlying the demand curve is the "ability," or capacity, of the individual. For example, some individuals benefit more from schooling than others (in the sense that they are able to obtain higher-paying jobs). To the extent that such differences are systematically related to identifiable characteristics such as "ability" or "intelligence" as measured by IQ tests, we may think of the position of the demand curve as lying farther to the right for relatively "able" persons. These individuals will invest in more human capital and have a higher equilibrium rate of return than others, all other things being equal. (One of the most important areas of current research is the relationship between individual demand curves for human capital and prior investments. This research is an attempt to answer the old nature vs. nurture question regarding human abilities.)

HUMAN CAPITAL AND EARNING POWER

The simple model of human capital developed here is also a theory of market earning power, since market wages are assumed to constitute a major return to investing in human capital. (Investing in human capital may well raise efficiency in household production as well. For example, relatively well-educated parents presumably are better able to rear children.) In order to relate investment in human capital to observed earnings of individuals, a bit of further analysis is required.

If human capital never depreciated in value (which would require among other things an infinite life span), and if the returns to an investment in human capital were constant over time, then the dollar value of the annual return to an investment in human capital would simply be

$$R = rH \qquad (8\text{--}4)$$

where R is the annual return to an investment in human capital (in dollars), r is the rate of return, and H is the dollar value of the investment. Compare equation (8–4) with the more complicated equation (8–3). Equation (8–3) also relates returns to investment in human capital. In order to understand the relationship between equations (8–3) and (8–4), we rewrite (8–3) in terms of the numerical example in Table 8–2, distinguishing between the periods when investment occurs (periods 0 and 1) and the periods when the returns are reaped (periods 2 through 5).

$$\sum_{j=0}^{1} (X_j - Y_j)(1 + r)^{-j+2} = \sum_{j=2}^{5} (Y_j - X_j)(1 + r)^{-j+2} \qquad (8\text{--}5)$$

Rewriting equation (8–3) this way focuses separately on the *investment* in human capital [the left-hand side of equation (8–5)] and the *returns* [the right-hand side) of (8–5)].

Notice that 2 has been added to the exponent on both sides of equation (8–5). This is because we are now looking at the investment in Y from the point of view of the beginning of period 2 rather than the beginning of period 0. From the point of view of the beginning of period 2, the investment required to enter occupation Y is $\$13,396 + \$10,980 = \$24,376$. $\$24,376$ corresponds to $\sum_{j=0}^{1} (X_j - Y_j)(1 + r)^{-j+2}$ in equation (8–5) and to H in equation (8–4). Why is the cost of investing in Y $\$24,376$, not $\$18,000$ (the simple sum of $X_0 - Y_0$ and $X_1 - Y_1$)? Because from the point of view of the beginning of period 2, the opportunity costs, $\$9,000$, foregone in periods 0 and 1 could have been invested elsewhere, yielding a return. If we assume that choosing occupation Y over occupation X is a marginal decision (that is, barely worthwhile) for the investor in human capital, then the additional $\$9,000$ earned at the beginning of period 0 if occupation X had been chosen could have been invested elsewhere to yield a compounded annual return of 22 percent for two years, while the $\$9,000$ that would have been received in period one could have been invested at 22 percent for one year. Thus, by the beginning of period 2, period 0's foregone earnings of $\$9,000$ have resulted in an opportunity cost of $9,000 \times (1.22)^2 = $13,396, while the earnings foregone in period 1 now "costs" $10,980. These figures yield the total investment in Y of $24,376.

We have already seen that the rate of return in the numerical example of Table 8–2 is 0.22. If we were to substitute 0.22 for r and $24,376 for H in equation (8–4), we would obtain a value for R equal to $5,363. This is considerably smaller than the $8,000 difference between Y_j and X_j for the periods $j = 2, \ldots, 5$ in Table 8–2. When the payout period is short, the annual returns must be larger to make an investment worthwhile. For equation (8–4) to "work," the returns to investing in human capital must occur over more than four periods, since equation (8–4) holds strictly only when the returns continue forever. Fortunately, equation (8–4) is a fairly good approximation to the relationship between investment costs and returns in studying many aspects of human capital investment, even though no human capital investments yield returns indefinitely. Equation (8–4) is a useful approximation because the discounting process reduces the present value of future returns to nearly zero in a period of time shorter than the average work life expectancy after most human capital investments occur. Equation (8–4) "works" because the present value of a future sum approaches zero as the period in which it occurs becomes further away in time

$$\lim_{j \to \infty} (1 + i)^{-j} = 0 \qquad (8–6)$$

For interest rates on the order of magnitude of 10 percent, the present value of a $1 of return occurring, say, twenty-five years in the future, while not zero, is small. More precisely, $\dfrac{\$1}{(1.1)^{25}} = \$.092$.

Let us compare the approximation in equation (8–4) to the numerical example of Table 8–2 once again. Suppose the cost of investing in occupation Y were $24,376 and the rate of return were 0.22, just as in the example, but that the returns continued for twenty-five years rather than only four years. Applying equation (8–4) we obtain $rH = 0.22 \times $24,376 = $5,363. Now this would be strictly correct only if the annual returns $5,363 continued forever. How large is the error involved using the approximation given by equation (8–4)? The *present value* of $5,363 received for twenty-five years, evaluated at an interest rate of 22 percent, equals $24,209, only $167 less than the amount invested. In other words, the equation (8–4) approximation is about 99 percent accurate when the rate of return or interest is 22 percent. For lower rates, the degree of error is somewhat larger, but still acceptable. For example, using equation (8–4) and assuming a 10 percent rate of return, the addition to earning power resulting from a $100,000 investment lasting forever would be $10,000. However, the required annual increase in earning power for an investment yielding a 10 percent return over a period of only twenty-five years would be $11,017. Thus the error from using the equation

(8–4) approximation when the rate of interest or rate of return is near 0.10 is about 10 percent.

Equation 8–4 can be used to relate individual investment in human capital to market earning power as follows: We assume that one's market earning power results from some initial amount of human capital endowed at birth (this is presumably minimal), plus the returns to all investments in human capital made throughout each individual's lifetime. In Figure 8–3, the total of these investments is the wealth-maximizing amount, H_o. The rate of return to each successive dollar of investment is measured by the height of the demand curve for investment in human capital. The annual market earning power (R) resulting from each dollar invested in human capital, using equation (8–4), is r, where r is its rate of return. Therefore, the total effect of human capital on earning power is represented by sum of the rates of return times each dollar invested; this is the area under the demand curve to the left of H_m. This area is shaded in Figure 8–4. If we make these additional assumptions—(1) that human capital affects market earning power, but not efficiency in home production; (2) that hours of work are not affected by increased earning power resulting from investment in human capital; and (3) that there is currently no investment in human capital taking place—then the return to each dollar invested is fully reflected in increased labor market income. In this case the area under the demand curve to the left of H_m is

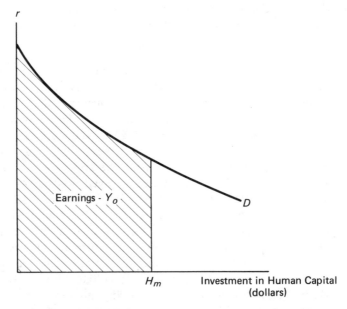

FIGURE 8–4. Relationship between Human Capital and Market Earnings

measured by observed market earnings, except for the basic earnings obtainable with no investment in human capital, if any. In terms of equation (8–4), observed market earnings (Y_0 plus the shaded area in Figure 8–4) can be approximated by

$$Y = Y_0 + \sum_{h=1}^{m} r_h H_h \qquad (8\text{--}7)$$

where Y is observed market earnings, Y_0 represents earnings with zero human capital, and r_h is the rate of return to investing the H_hth dollar in human capital.

Evidence on the Rate of Return to Investment in Schooling

One of the most important applications of human capital theory is in helping us to understand the distribution, or dispersion, of income among individuals in our society. Indeed, this is such an important topic that we have reserved part of Chapter 10 to discuss it. At this point we want to take a few steps further in understanding the basic application of human capital theory to long-run labor supply decisions by summarizing a few empirical studies. As we have pointed out, human capital theory is applicable to a broad spectrum of human activities—schooling, formal and informal job training programs, job search, health, and child-rearing, for example. In fact, economists have applied the analysis of investment in human beings to all these topics. However, by far the greatest amount of applied human capital research has dealt with investment in schooling because of its importance as measured by the quantity of indirect and direct costs devoted to it, its presumed importance as a determinant of incomes, and the relatively high quality of available data. We will review some studies of schooling as a form of human capital here.

ANALYZING INVESTMENT IN SCHOOLING: RESEARCH OBSTACLES

Two related but distinct procedures have been used to analyze investment in schooling. One we may call the internal rate of return method, corresponding to Table 8–2 and equation (8–3); it involves the direct comparison of income streams of persons or groups of persons who differ in their levels of acquired schooling. The other method is called the earnings function approach, corresponding to equation (8–7); this method relates wage rates or earnings directly to schooling by means of regression analysis of a simple mathematical transformation of equation (8–7). The principal goals common to most studies using these procedures have been to estimate the rate of return to schooling, to relate the rate of return schedule to the demand for schooling, and to draw inferences for educational policy. For example, has there been underinvestment or overinvestment in education? What would happen to the earning power of a typical individual if he or she received more schooling?

The two approaches have been used to achieve similar research goals, and those who wish to apply them must surmount common obstacles to successful empirical research. The most obvious of these obstacles—one that perhaps subsumes all others—is the well-known potential bias due to omitted variables. Just think of it. If we simplistically apply the approach of Table 8–2 or equation (8–3) to estimate the rate of return to schooling, we are implicitly assuming that schooling is the only systematic force affecting the incomes of, say, college graduates by comparison with others who have received less schooling—high school graduates, for instance. This is a very strong assumption, and students of the effect of schooling on market earning power are not in general agreement as to the degree, or even the direction, to which it results in biased estimates of the return to investment in schooling. It does not take great insight to suspect that college graduates come from wealthier families (thereby making it easier for them to finance higher education), may have greater ability ("intelligence") to benefit from college, and also are likely to invest in forms of human capital other than college which also affect market earning power. To what extent does the omission of these conditions, which may be correlated with both schooling and subsequent market earning power, bias estimates of the return to schooling?

Let us examine the possible sources of bias listed above one at a time.[4] (1) The influence of family wealth on returns to investment in human capital can be analyzed in terms of the supply and demand framework outlined above. Insofar as the only influence of family wealth is to lower the effective rate of interest in financing human capital investment, we have a situation like that depicted in Figure 8–5. If everyone benefited equally from a given amount of schooling, observed schooling levels would be S_1, S_2, S_3, and S_4, and the rates of return inferred from the corresponding earnings streams would be r_1, r_2, r_3, and r_4, respectively.[5] With only one demand curve and many supply curves, variation in family wealth *by itself* does not bias estimates of the rate of return. Quite the contrary, it is the source of variation in supply conditions, given the demand curve, that is necessary to identify the relationship between the rate of return and the amount invested.

Individual differences in "intelligence" or "ability" as measured, say, by IQ tests, may affect the benefits derived from schooling—the demand curve for investment in human capital—and the supply curve as well. The direction

---

[4] Once again our discussion draws heavily on Becker's *Human Capital*, pp. 94ff.

[5] Note that the horizontal axes of Figures 8–4—8–7 measure human capital in *dollars* corresponding to each year of schooling. The dollar amount corresponding to each year of schooling is the sum of foregone earnings plus direct costs incurred during that year.

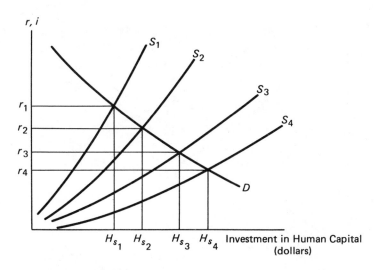

FIGURE 8–5. Possible Influence of Family Wealth on Investment in Human Capital

of the effect of ability on the demand for investment in human capital is uncertain.[6] More able persons may have access to higher paying jobs, independent of the amount of schooling acquired, thus raising indirect schooling costs and lowering demand. Alternatively, ability may increase the benefits derived from schooling, partly by enabling students to succeed in school with relatively little effort. Whether through reducing indirect schooling costs or by interacting with schooling to increase wage rates more than ability could do by itself, a positive effect of ability on schooling benefits would result in raising the demand for investment by relatively able persons. In Figure 8–6 we describe the case in which ability increases the demand for schooling but has no effect on supply. The observed relationship between schooling and incomes would then describe the supply curve of funds for investment in human capital, not the demand curve, as might be supposed. A strong possibility is that ability will influence not only the demand for human capital (in an unknown direction), but also the supply. Insofar as selective admission policies (to favored high schools and colleges) and scholarship and fellowship aid make it easier for able persons to attend school, the supply of investable funds for such persons is increased. If the effect of ability is also to increase demand, as in Figure 8–6, then a positive correlation between demand and supply results, as depicted in Figure 8–7. The observed relationship between income and schooling yields no direct information about demand or supply. If one were mistakenly to think that a demand curve had been observed, one

---

[6]See, for example, Zvi Griliches, "Estimating the Returns to Schooling: Some Econometric Problems," *Econometrica*, 45, 1 (January 1977), 1–22.

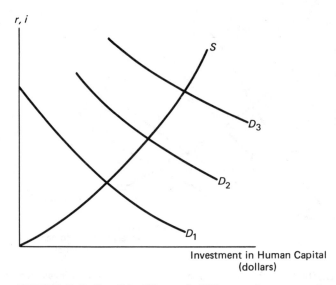

FIGURE 8–6. Possible Effect of Ability on Investment in Human Capital

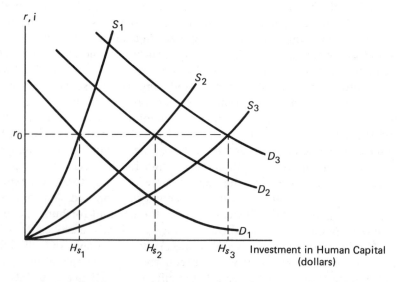

FIGURE 8–7. Effects of Ability on Supply and Demand of Investment in Human Capital

might infer that the rate of return declines very little, if at all, as an individual acquires more schooling. In fact, if a typical individual who attends school S_1 years (because he or she has demand and supply curves D_1 and S_1, respectively) were to increase schooling beyond S_1, the rate of return (for him or her) would fall below r_0; it would not remain at r_0, as the observed pattern of income and schooling might suggest.

Still another problem in attributing observed differences in earnings or earning power only to differences in schooling is that persons who acquire additional schooling are not unlikely to acquire other forms of human capital as well. So it would be wrong to attribute the entire additional income of such persons to schooling alone. This is an important problem when we wish to assign observed income differences among persons to their correct causes. Surprisingly, however, investment in different kinds of human capital may not be a very serious problem if an estimate of only the rate of return to schooling is desired. Ignorance of other investments in human capital made by individuals who acquire different amounts of schooling will not result in a biased estimate of the rate of return to schooling if two conditions hold: (1) All the costs of the other investments are indirect—foregone earnings—rather than direct expenditures; and (2) the rate of return to the other investments is not different from the rate of return to schooling.

These conditions are not as restrictive as they may at first appear to be. It is widely believed that on-the-job training is the most important from of investment in human capital other than schooling made by those who acquire relatively large amounts of schooling and that the principal cost of on-the-job training from the individual worker's point of view is foregone earnings. (A detailed analysis of on-the-job training is presented in Chapter 9.) Furthermore, as we pointed out above, wealth maximization implies that the individual will undertake only those human capital investments whose rate of return is expected to be the highest among the alternatives available. Therefore, on-the-job training would not be undertaken if still more schooling promised a higher rate of return.

To see why (given the two conditions enumerated in the preceding paragraph) ignoring the possibility of on-the-job training or other investments in human capital whose costs are principally indirect need not bias an estimate of the rate of return to schooling, look at Table 8–2 once again. Table 8–2 purports to show the effect of a two-year schooling program on earning power by providing access to occupation Y. Suppose now that the schooling required to enter occupation Y lasted only one year (year 0), but that during the first year of employment in Y (year 1), the worker receives only $1,000 in earnings. The $9,000 gap between year 1 earnings in occupations X and Y represents a cost of entering occupation Y, regardless of whether it arises from a combination of tuition payments and foregone earnings due to attending school or to the fact that the worker is not worth much to an employer during the first year of employment in Y because further training is required. If only one year of schooling (and one year of training) were required to enter occupation Y, and if the rate of return to the training were the same as that to schooling, then using equation (8–3) to calculate the rate of return would still be correct. The rate of return would be equal to the rate of interest at which the present value of the earnings stream in occupation X equals that in occupation Y.

ESTIMATING RATES OF RETURN: COMPARISON OF EARNINGS STREAMS

Using equation (8–3) to estimate rates of return to schooling involves the direct comparison of market earning power—usually measured by earnings—among individuals who have received different amounts of schooling. Since no existing set of data contains information over the actual lifetimes of individuals, it is necessary to develop artificial cohorts using observations on a cross section of persons at a given date—usually a decennial census year. An *artificial cohort* essentially involves assuming that the earnings next year of an individual who has acquired say, twelve years of schooling, will be equal to the earnings this year of someone else who also acquired twelve years of schooling but who is one year older. Similarly, earnings two years hence are estimated with data for someone who is two years older, and so on.

In practice, for large data sets, the artificial cohort may itself be constructed by means of regression analysis. One pioneering and well-known study is that of Giora Hanoch,[7] who used disaggregate data from the 0.001 sample of the 1960 U.S. Census of Population for 34,180 men. Employing information on their 1959 earnings, Hanoch used regression analysis to relate the earnings of these men to a large number of variables including years of schooling and age. Hanoch's regression equations are of the general form

$$Y = a_0 + a_1 S + a_2 A + \sum_{a_{i=3}}^{n} a_i Z_i \qquad (8\text{–}8)$$

where Y is 1959 earnings, S is years of schooling, and A is age, and Z_i represents a number of additional variables such as urban or rural residence, marital status, and so on. The coefficients a_1 and a_2 represent the net effect of schooling and age, respectively, on earnings. Hanoch used these coefficients to estimate earnings, by age, for men who had completed different amounts of schooling.[8] Regressions were estimated separately for whites and blacks living in the North and South so that separate earnings profiles could be constructed for whites living in the north, blacks living in the north, whites living in the south, and blacks living in the south, respectively. These artificial cohort earnings profiles are an attempt to answer this question: What would

---

[7]Giora Hanoch, "Personal Earnings and Investment in Schooling" (unpublished Ph.D. dissertation, University of Chicago, 1965); "An Economic Analysis of Earnings and Schooling," *Journal of Human Resources*, 2, 3 (summer 1967), 310–29.

[8]Schooling and age are actually represented in Hanoch's regressions by sets of dummy variables ($S_1 = 1$ if schooling $= 0$–4 years; $S_2 = 1$ if schooling $= 5$–7 years). This enabled Hanoch to capture any nonlinear relationship between earnings and these variables.

happen to the lifetime earnings of an individual if he were to receive more schooling, but remain the same in all other respects? (The variables that schooling changes, thus altering income, such as occupation, are not held constant.) Some of the resulting earnings figures are shown in Table 8–3. Figure 8–8 is a graphic representation of the age-earnings profiles of various schooling levels for white men living in the north.[9]

Two features of the earnings profiles described in Table 8–3 and Figure 8–8 merit attention. One is the lack of earnings figures for certain age groups (for example, persons 18 years old and less who received twelve years of

TABLE 8–3

Selected Estimated Expected Earnings (dollars per year)
by Age and Schooling, Persons Out of School, 1959,
by Race and Region

	Years of School Completed		
Age	8	12	16
Whites/North			
20	1,737	2,233	—
42	4,934	6,222	9,561
62	3,667	5,239	8,298
Whites/South			
20	1,337	1,883	—
42	4,004	5,792	8,821
62	3,127	4,798	7,557
Nonwhites/North			
20	1,038	1,519	—
42	3,543	4,291	5,395
62	3,046	2,414	1,481
Nonwhites/South			
20	832	1,134	—
42	2,158	2,750	4,040
62	1,649	1,305	1,054

Source: Giora Hanoch, "Personal Earnings and Investment in Schooling" (unpublished Ph.D. dissertation, University of Chicago, 1965), pp. 55–56.

---

[9]The earnings profiles shown in Table 8–3 and Figure 8–8 are not taken directly from the relevant regression coefficients. They are first "smoothed," using an averaging procedure to eliminate bumps due to random effects.

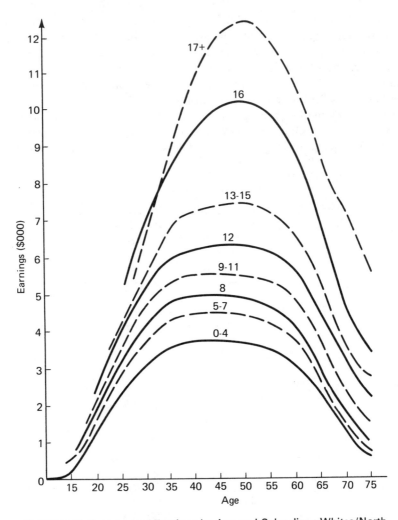

FIGURE 8–8. Estimated Earnings by Age and Schooling : Whites/North

Source: Giora Hanoch, "Personal Earnings and Investment in schooling" (unpublished Ph.D. dissertation, University of Chicago, 1965), pp. 55–56.

schooling; persons 24 years old and less with sixteen years of schooling). Since good data on actual private direct costs of schooling are not available, Hanoch assumed that the earnings received by persons who were attending school were exactly offset by tuition and other direct schooling costs; thus zero net earnings is shown for persons still attending school. This means that the full private cost of completing college is measured by the earnings estimated for high school graduates during the first four years after leaving school. The second important feature of the earnings profiles is their steep decline after reaching their peak. It is highly unlikely that the earnings received by typical individuals actually decline so steeply as they become older—at least before retirement. The steep declines observed in the artificial cohorts described in Figure 8–8 and Table 8–3 do not reflect the effect that economic growth—economywide increases in the general level of the real wage rate—is likely to have on a typical person's earnings over a lifetime. Moreover, in an artificially constructed earnings profile, the later years of the life cycle are represented by earnings of men who received their schooling in earlier years than men who make up the younger years of the life cycle. Insofar as the content of what is taught in school, particularly at professional levels, changes over the years, a schooling quality element depresses observed earnings in the later years of an artificial cohort in a manner that does not affect actual earnings over a typical individual's lifetime. These two causes of exaggerated decline in artificial cohort earnings during the years of middle age and beyond probably do not have a serious effect on estimated rates of return, since all the earnings streams are depressed and since the earlier years' figures enter much more importantly into the rate of return and present value computations than do those of the later years.

The four estimated earnings profiles were used to calculate rates of return to different levels of schooling.[10] As mentioned above, since direct schooling costs were assumed to exactly offset earnings received while in school, the private cost of attending school is the full amount of earnings received by persons who received the next smallest amount of schooling. Some of these rates of return are shown in Table 8–4. They range between 5 and 23 percent. Table 8–4 is read as follows: the number 0.161 appearing in the 8-year column and 12-year row for whites/north indicates that if a white man living in the north who had completed eight years of school were to complete high school, the rate of return he would receive for doing so would equal 16.1 percent. (As we show later on, this means that by completing high school, his earnings would be about 16.1 percent higher. See pp. 295–299, especially footnote 13.) The figure 0.115 immediately below is the rate of return he would receive for completing *both* high school and college. The number 0.096 in the 12-year column and 16-year row for whites/north is an estimate of the rate of return to completing college for someone who has completed the twelfth year of schooling.

Bearing in mind all the possible biases described above, Table 8–4 can be used to construct a demand curve for investment in schooling. Instead of dollars, we can (for convenience) plot schooling on the horizontal axis and the rate of return on the vertical axis. This is done in Figure 8–9. The numbers

---

[10]More detailed numbers than those of Table 8–3 are used to construct the earnings profiles. A computer program designed to set the present value of the differences between alternative earnings stream equal to zero is used to solve for the rate of return by means of numerical methods. That is, successive rates of return are tried until the earnings profile differences finally equal zero.

TABLE 8–4

Estimates of Private Internal Rates of Return between Schooling Levels, by Race and Region

Higher Level of Schooling (Years)	Lower Level of Schooling (Years)	
	8	12
Whites/North		
12	0.161	
16	0.115	0.096
Whites/South		
12	0.186	
16	0.128	0.101
Nonwhites/North		
12	0.23	
16	0.07	no data
Nonwhites/South		
12	0.11	
16	0.08	0.06

Source: Giora Hanoch, "Personal Earnings and Investment in Schooling" (unpublished Ph.D. dissertation, University of Chicago, 1965), p. 71.

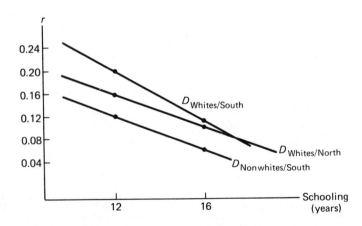

FIGURE 8–9. Rates of Return to Schooling Estimated from 1960 Earnings

along the diagonals of Table 8–4 represent marginal rates of return and are used to construct the demand curves shown in Figure 8–9. They show the rates of return for obtaining 12 years of schooling rather than 8 years and 16 years rather than 12 years.[11] It is simple to convert the horizontal axis to dollars. It is necessary only to find the earnings of each level of schooling below the level measured—up to 11 years when measuring the rate of return to obtaining the twelfth year of schooling, for instance—calculate the present value as of the beginning of the school year measured, and add up the present values cumulatively along the horizontal axis. The present value of the cumulative foregone earnings will be *greater* than the simple sum because the interest on these earnings is part of the opportunity cost of schooling. (See the discussion relating to this problem on pages 282–83.)

ESTIMATING RATES OF RETURN: THE HUMAN CAPITAL EARNING POWER FUNCTION

A simple transformation turns equation (8–7) into a "human capital earning power function" that can be used, and has frequently been so employed, to estimate the rate of return to schooling directly by means of regression analysis. Recall equation (8–7): $Y = Y_0 + \sum_{h=1}^{m} r_h H_h$. To see how it is transformed into an earning power function relating observed market earnings to schooling, we once again make use of the assumption that *direct schooling costs are equal to earnings while in school.* Thus H_h in equation (8–7) is equal to the earnings that would have been received had no schooling been undertaken during the period. Therefore, earning power in the year following the last year of schooling *and for all subsequent years* can be expressed in terms of earning power if no schooling were undertaken plus the return on all foregone earnings during schooling years, as shown in Table 8–5.[12] In other words, when all schooling costs can be expressed in terms of foregone earnings (because direct schooling costs cancel earnings received while attending school), equation (8–7) becomes

$$Y_S = Y_0 \prod_{j=1}^{S} (1 + r_j) \qquad (8\text{–}8)$$

where S is the number of years of school acquired.

For simplicity, assume that r_j is a constant. This means that the rate of return does not rise or decline with schooling, but we will relax this assump-

---

[11]Many more than just the two points shown for each demand curve were calculated by Hanoch. Only two are shown in Table 8–4 and Figure 8–9 for reasons of simple exposition.

[12]If you really understand this example, you should be able to apply it to the numerical example of pages 275–76 based on Table 8–2. *Hint:* Investment costs in each year equal foregone earnings less $1,000.

TABLE 8-5

The Human Capital Earning Power Equation

Schooling (j)	Earning Power If Schooling Equals Only j Years	Cost of jth Year of Schooling
0	Y_0	0
1	$Y_1 = Y_0 + r_1 Y_0 = Y_0(1 + r_1)$	Y_0
2	$Y_2 = Y_1 + r_2 Y_1 = Y_0(1 + r_1)(1 + r_2)$	Y_1
3	$Y_3 = Y_2 + r_3 Y_2 = Y_0(1 + r_1)(1 + r_2)(1 + r_3)$	Y_2
.		.
.		.
.		.
S	$Y_S = Y_{S-1} + r_S Y_{S-1} = Y_0(1 + r_1)(1 + r_2) \cdots (1 + r_S)$	Y_{S-1}

tion shortly in order to permit estimation of a downward-sloping rate of return schedule. Equation (8–8) then becomes

$$Y_S = Y_0(1 + r)^S \tag{8–9}$$

Taking the natural logarithm of (8–9), we obtain

$$\ln Y_S = \ln Y_0 + S \ln (1 + r) \tag{8–10}$$

We now make use of an approximation. For the value of r lying between zero and 0.3 or so, $\ln (1 + r)$ is approximately equal to r. Therefore, we may write the human capital earning power function as

$$\ln Y_S = \ln Y_0 + rS \tag{8–11}$$

For "reasonable" values of r, the rate of return is the partial derivative of the natural log of earning power with respect to schooling![13] Of course, other

---

[13]If you know differential calculus, then another interpretation should be clear. Since $\dfrac{d \ln Y}{dx} = \dfrac{dY}{dx} \dfrac{1}{Y}$, the rate of return is measured by the proportionate change in earning power due to an additional year of schooling.

Equations (8–9) and (8–10) implicitly assume that "interest" on prior investments is paid and compounded annually. If we assume that interest is paid and compounded every instant, then equation (8–11) holds exactly. The proof is as follows. If we were to divide each year into n equal periods, with interest paid and compounded each period, (8–9) would become

$$Y_S = Y_0\left(1 + \frac{r}{n}\right)^{nS} \tag{8–9'}$$

Instantaneous payments and compounding of interest requires n to become infinitely large. From a well-known algebraic formula,

$$\lim_{n \to \infty} Y_0\left(1 + \frac{r}{n}\right)^{nS} = Y_0 e^{rS} \tag{8–9''}$$

where e is the base of natural logarithms. Therefore, taking the natural log of (8–9'')

$$\ln Y_S = \ln Y_0 + rS \quad \text{(Q.E.D.)}$$

variables may be, and often are, included in regression analysis based on equations like (8–11). The additional variables included depend on what it is considered necessary to hold constant in order to answer this question: How would one more year of schooling affect the earning power of a typical individual? The problems with this interpretation of the human capital earning power function are the same as those involved when interpreting rates of return based on direct comparisons of earnings streams discussed above. The advantage of the human capital earning power equation is its simplicity, in that the two-step procedure of relating earning power to schooling and subsequently computing rates of return as in the earnings profiles comparison procedure is reduced to one operation.

Two difficulties in the empirical application of equation (8–11) are that it implies constant earning power after leaving school and that it must be estimated using data for synthetic cohorts of individuals who differ in their schooling and, consequently, their earning power. The straightforward application of equation (8–11) assumes that the age–earning power profiles of persons who differ in years of schooling look like Figure 8–10. In Figure 8–10, age 0 represents the age of leaving school for an individual who has acquired S_1 years of schooling and who has earning power equal to Y_1 dollars per year. By comparison, a typical individual who acquires S_2 years of schooling does not leave school until age $= S_2 - S_1$ years; while in school, net earnings are zero, but they rise to $Y_2 > Y_1$ at age $S_2 - S_1$ years and remain constant throughout the individual's lifetime. If actual earning power profiles looked like Figure 8–10, then equation (8–11) could be estimated using earning power information for any year after leaving school. The earning power profiles in Figure 8–10 do not possess the inverted U-shape of "actual"

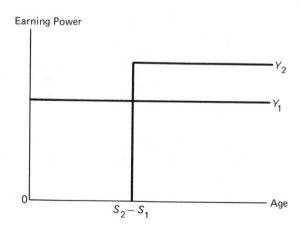

FIGURE 8–10. Graphical Representation of Equation (8–10) for Two Individuals Who Differ Only in Level of Schooling

profiles as depicted in Figure 8–8, however. The most important reason for this is the neglect of the investment in human capital through on-the-job training and experience, which imparts an upward tilt to earning power after leaving school. In Chapter 9 we will explore this aspect of human capital investment at length. For now, however, you should see that on-the-job training is omitted from equation (8–11), and unless proper precautions are taken, biased estimates of the return to schooling may result.

In order to obtain unbiased estimates of the rate of return to schooling using equation (8–11), investment in on-the-job training must be held constant either by explicitly including it as a variable when applying regression analysis or by constructing a sample in which all the individuals have invested approximately the same amount in this form of human capital. Jacob Mincer[14] has shown that the return to schooling alone can be estimated to a reasonable approximation, without explicitly including a variable representing on-the-job training, by constructing a sample of individuals who have acquired about eight years of postschooling labor market experience. Thus, he has estimated equation (8–11) using a sample of 2,124 white nonfarm men with 7 to 9 years of experience drawn from the same data set Hanoch used.[15] Mincer finds an average rate of return to schooling for all levels of schooling of 16.5 percent. Equation (8–11) can be modified to allow for the likelihood that the rate of return declines as additional years of schooling are acquired. This is done by adding the term S^2, obtaining

$$\ln Y = \ln Y_0 + r_1 S + r_2 S^2 \tag{8–12}$$

Those of you who have learned calculus will see that the rate of return to an additional year of schooling is no longer simply the coefficient of S, r_1, but is now a function of the *level* of schooling, namely, $r_1 + 2r_2 S$. If the estimated value of r_1 is positive, while that of r_2 is negative, the rate of return to incremental years of schooling declines, as depicted in Figure 8–9. Mincer estimated $r_1 = 0.42$ and $r_2 = -0.010$, suggesting a negative relationship between schooling and the rate of return. These estimates imply that the rate of return to the twelfth year of schooling is 0.18, while for the sixteenth, it is 0.10. These values are not far from those calculated by Hanoch and shown in Table 8–4. In Table 8–4, the rate of return to completing four years of high school for northen whites (given the completion of high school) is 0.16, while that to obtaining four more years of schooling is 0.096.

The Mincer and Hanoch studies differ not only in the technique used to estimate rates of return, but also in the degree to which variables other than schooling (and training) are held constant. Hanoch's study is quite elaborate in this respect, whereas Mincer's boils down to a relatively simple comparison

---

[14]Jacob Mincer, *Schooling, Experience, and Earnings* (New York: National Bureau of Economic Research, 1974), Chap. 1.

[15]Ibid., Chap. 3, Table 3–3.

of incomes among persons who differ in level of schooling acquired. Thus, it is somewhat surprising that the two studies arrive at such similar results. Hanoch tested the sensitivity of his estimates to his method of estimating age-earnings profiles for different schooling levels. He found that results did not change appreciably when a simple comparison of earnings profiles, not derived from his rather elaborate regression analysis, was used.

DO WE HAVE OVER- OR UNDERINVESTMENT IN SCHOOLING?

Entire books can (and have) been devoted to answering this question, and we will provide only the sketch of an answer here, concentrating on the investment decision from the private individual's point of view. We have assumed that the individual investor is interested in maximizing wealth. If schooling's only effect were to increase market earning power, then wealth maximization would require that schooling be undertaken up to the point where the rate of return to the last dollar spent on schooling equaled that obtainable to other forms of investment, physical capital included. To the extent that schooling is an enjoyable experience yielding consumption value in addition to increased future earnings, and to the extent efficiency in home production is increased, the rates of return as usually estimated are too small. On the other hand, most studies ignore the effect of progressive income taxation on private rates of return, and thereby may present estimates that are too large.[16] Note that the bias from ignoring income taxes when estimating the rate of return may not be as large as it at first seems, since income taxation reduces the *cost* as well as *returns* to schooling. Why?

Many studies of schooling and the educational system focus on the *social* return to schooling as opposed to the private return we have discussed thus far.[17] The social rate of return to schooling is less than the private rate of return to the extent that public contributions supplement private expenditures on the direct cost of schooling. The social rate of return is greater than the private rate of return to the extent that individuals with more schooling (say, a college degree) increase not only their own earning power, but that of others. For example, workers whose supervisors are well educated may be more productive than other workers and thereby earn more. Income taxes, which probably should be subtracted from calculations of private rates of return (because taxpayers may not value government expenditures as highly as an equal amount they would spend themselves), should not be subtracted from calculations of social rates of return.

What then do estimated private rates of return suggest about wealth-maximizing behavior? Both Hanoch and Mincer estimated a private marginal

---

[16]If taxes are viewed as payment for "value received," then it would not be appropriate to reduce private rate of return calculations to correct for income taxes paid.

[17]For a more detailed discussion, see Becker, *Human Capital*, Chap. V.

rate of return for white male college graduates of about 10 percent, based on 1959 data. It would not be correct to compare this figure with the return obtainable on a highly liquid, low-risk investment such as a government bond, because investments in human capital have a relatively uncertain outcome and are relatively illiquid (human beings cannot legally be sold for cash). The cost of investment in human capital, then, includes not only the interest that must be given up by not placing funds in a safe, liquid investment, but also a premium that most investors require if they are to invest in less secure projects, such as common stocks or business firms.

A widely used benchmark against which to measure the rate of return to investment in schooling has been the rate of return to corporate manufacturing investments. Stigler[18] has estimated this to be approximately 7 percent, which is lower than the rate of return to acquiring a college education estimated by Mincer or Hanoch (and many others) using 1960 census data. Taken at face value, a comparison of the rate of return to college education with that on physical capital in manufacturing suggests that wealth could have been increased if additional white males had invested in college education—even acquiring some graduate school experience. In drawing this conclusion, however, it is essential to bear in mind all the possible biases inherent in estimating the rate of return to investment in human capital. Economists are not in agreement as to whether the rate of return to schooling has been correctly estimated or, if so, whether the rate of return to acquiring a college degree for a typical college graduate is that which would accrue to a typical high school graduate were a college degree to be obtained.[19]

The rate of return estimates calculated by Hanoch and Mincer are derived from 1959 data. Does more recent information yield comparable estimates? Richard Freeman[20] has calculated rates of return for various years from 1959 through 1974 using decennial census and Current Population Survey data. He finds that the rate of return to a college degree was about the same in 1969 as in 1959. However, it declined in the early 1970s, and Freeman's estimate of the private rate of return in 1974 is only 8.5 percent, compared to 11.5 percent in 1969. A possible explanation of this decline is discussed in

[18]George J. Stigler, *Capital and Rates of Return in Manufacturing Industries* (Princeton University Press for the National Bureau of Economic Research, 1963).

[19]Another interpretation of the excess of the rate of return to schooling over that to physical capital is possible. Acquiring schooling may be distasteful (a "bad" instead of a "good") to the average individual. If so, then pecuniary wealth maximization and utility maximization do not amount to the same thing, because the displeasure of attending school must be taken into account. In a recently published study, Edward Lazear reaches the conclusion that schooling affects utility negatively and that is why rates of return to schooling exceed those to physical capital. ["Education: Consumption or Production," *Journal of Political Economy*, 85, 3 (June 1977)].

[20]Richard Freemand, "Overinvestment in College Training," *Journal of Human Resources*, 10, 3 (summer 1975); "The Decline in the Economic Rewards to College Education," *Review of Economics and Statistics*, 59, 1 (February 1977).

Chapter 10, pp. 355–358. Whether the decline in the economic rewards to a college degree that Freeman observes are the result of temporary or permanent forces remains to be seen. It is worth noting, however, that even the lower rates of return estimated by Freeman appear not to have fallen below the earlier estimates of the return to investment in physical capital.

From the point of view of the private individual, investment in schooling does not appear to have exceeded the amount implied by the assumption of wealth maximization. Even with the possible decline in the rate of return to a college degree in recent years, it is still likely that the rate of return to investment in human capital for most persons has not fallen below that to physical capital. The rate of return to graduation from high school is likely to be considerably higher.[21]

Frontiers of Labor Economics: Investment in Children

In Chapter 4, we integrated the presence of children who require care into the short-run theory of labor supply. Greater insight into the economics of family size and human development can be obtained within the human capital framework. The time and other scarce resources parents devote to child care may be viewed as investments in human capital, the returns to which include the satisfaction parents derive from rearing children who have characteristics pleasing to them, such as good health, good manners, respect for the mores of society, the ability and desire to do well in school, and the capacity to do well in the labor market. These various characteristics are often studied as *child quality*.

Child quality, like health, is a form of human capital produced in the household with parental time and purchased inputs. (Schooling, which also requires the child's time, requires market inputs purchased through direct tuition payments or indirectly through taxation and public expenditure.) The time allocated to the household production of child quality cannot be

---

[21]Because of its complexity, we do not discuss the problem of the socially optimum amount of schooling and that of justifying publicly subsidized education. These issues involve questions of both economic efficiency (Do individual borrowing difficulties make private opportunity costs of schooling greater than the social opportunity cost? Do external benefits of education warrant the encouragement of more schooling than individuals would normally choose for themselves?) and equity (Should government support education through grants to individuals or through loans? Should the rich receive these forms of aid as well as the poor?). The interested reader may wish to consult one or more of several books and monographs on these topics. Some suggested sources are: Gary S. Becker, *Human Capital*, 2nd ed. (New York: Columbia University Press, 1975), Chapter 5; *Journal of Political Economy*, 80, 3 (May–June 1978, Part II), particularly the paper by T. W. Schultz; Byron W. Brown and Daniel H. Saks, "The Production and Distribution of Cognitive Skills within Schools," *Journal of Political Economy*, 83, 3 (June 1975), 571–94.

supplied to the labor market. Therefore, family decisions on the number and quality of children must ultimately be viewed as determined simultaneously with labor supply decisions. Given the household child quality production function and input costs, the greater the quality desired for each child, the greater the time and purchased inputs required and, hence the greater the cost of rearing a child. Given the quality desired, the cost of rearing a child will depend on input costs and the parents' efficiency in producing child quality. Thus, an important determinant of variation in the cost of children among families will be the market wage rate of parents. Although the traditional child-rearing pattern in which the major time input is that of the mother is gradually changing, it is still probably a useful assumption to use the mother's market earning power as an index of the family's time cost of child rearing. Since the prices of market goods vary less among families than the mother's market earning power, the latter variable is usually viewed by economists as an extremely important determinant of variation in child costs.

Efficiency in the production of child quality is also likely to vary considerably among families. In other words, the parents' own accumulated human capital should enhance their ability to produce human capital in their children. For example, a relatively well-educated mother through the stories she reads to her preschool children, through the activities in which she encourages them to participate, through the supervision of homework, and so on, is more likely to produce well-educated children than is a mother with a less advantageous background. Numerous studies have shown that parental background characteristics are positively associated with corresponding characteristics (schooling, economic success, for example) in their children.[22] Of course, merely to establish a correlation between, say, parents' schooling or wealth and that of their offspring tells us nothing about the causal mechanism involved. The correlation by itself is as consistent with a model of intergenerational wealth transfer based on a social caste system[23] as with the human capital–household production approach. In addition to the empirical correlation between parental and child characteristics, knowledge of the mechanism through which desired child characteristics are developed and a measure of the relationship between returns and cost is needed in order to gain support for the hypothesis that parents produce desired qualities in their children by means of costly inputs that bear a rate of return.

Many studies are aimed at discovering the linkages between parental background and child characteristics. Several of these focus on the role of mother's time in child rearing and the effect of her education on the charac-

---

[22]One well-known study is that of Otis Dudley Duncan, David L. Featherman, and Beverly Duncan: *Socioeconomic Background and Achievement* (New York: Seminar Press, 1972).

[23]For example, Samuel Bowles, "Schooling and Inequality from Generation to Generation," *Journal of Political Economy*, 80, 3, part II (May–June 1972).

teristics of her children. In one such study, Fleisher[24] has examined the effect of mother's time spent out of the labor force, and presumably in the home, on the production of child quality, where child quality is measured by intelligence (IQ), level of schooling attained, and market earning power. The study attempts to discover whether well-educated mothers have a greater impact on the quality of their children than do other mothers.

Fleisher's method involved estimating human capital equations similar to equation (8–1), modified to take into account the effects of family background variables on IQ, schooling, and market earning power. The data consisted of a 1971 national sample of several hundred young men (age 19 to 29). Little effect of mother's time spent out of the labor force (during the child's first fourteen years) was found on IQ or level of schooling obtained. However, a significant effect of mother's time on the earning power of children was observed. Fleisher found that the average impact of eleven years of mother's home time on a son's market wage (in 1971) ranged from $0.57 per hour for mothers with ten years of schooling, to $1.17 per hour for mothers who were college graduates. In other words, not only do mothers appear to be able to affect the development of child quality (as measured by market earning power) by devoting time to child rearing, but well-educated mothers are more efficient than others.

Moreover, the relative advantage of well-enducated mothers in child-rearing efficiency appears to be greater than their advantage in market earning power. The results reported above suggest that college-educated mothers are 105 percent more effective than those with only ten years of schooling in producing market earning power in their children; the market wages of college graduate mothers are higher than those of high school dropouts by only 74 percent, however. The differential productivity effect suggests that well-educated mothers find it less expensive to develop market earning power in their children than do mothers with less schooling. This may explain why relatively well-educated mothers tend to reduce their labor force participation when young children are in the household more than do mothers with less schooling.[25]

However, Fleisher also estimated that the present value (at a 10 percent rate of interest) of increased sons' lifetime earnings was less than the cost, in

---

[24]Belton M. Fleisher, "Mother's Home Time and the Production of Child Quality," *Demography*, 14, 2 (May 1977). This paper also contains references to other studies of mother's time in the development of child quality. A number of other studies provide estimates of parental time and material resources devoted to child rearing. Among these are Thomas J. Espenshade, "The Price of Children and Socio-Economic Theories of Fertility," *Population Studies*, 26 (July 1972); and C. Russell Hill and Frank P. Stafford, "Allocation of Time to Preschool Children and Educational Opportunity," *Journal of Human Resources*, 9 (summer 1974).

[25]See, for example, Arleen Leibowitz, "Women's Allocation of Time to Market and Nonmarket Activities: Differences by Education" (unpublished Ph.D. dissertation, New York, Columbia University, 1972). Other references are cited in Fleisher, "Mother's Home Time."

terms of foregone earnings, of mother's home time. It would be difficult to support an argument that simple maximization of the family's wealth in monetary terms is the sole force governing family decisions to allocate the mother's time from market work to child rearing. Since parents doubtless value many child characteristics besides future earning power and may derive pleasure from child care itself, it should not be surprising that a naive human capital approach does not capture the full set of forces underlying parental decisions in allocating time between child-rearing activities and market work.[26]

Conclusion

In this chapter, we introduced the analysis of long-run labor supply decisions by focusing on human capital from the household point of view. Investment in human capital involves long-run labor supply decisions in that the forces affecting the allocation of time between market and nonmarket activities which were assumed to be outside the control of the household in Chapter 4 are now seen to be the subject of economic decision-making. Although short-run labor supply decisions and long-run decisions involving investments in schooling, health, job search, movement from one labor market to another, and the like (for oneself and for one's children) affect the constraints under which time allocation decisions are made, it is also true that work-leisure choices feed back to human capital investment decisions as well. For example, the rate of return to investment in schooling will be greater, the larger the amount of time one expects to supply to the labor market and thereby reap the benefits of higher wage rates. These interdependencies between short-run and long-run labor supply decisions constitute the framework within which some of the most recent and advanced studies of labor supply and human capital behavior have been conducted.[27]

Coupled with the household production framework, the human capital approach is an extremely poweiful and flexible tool of economic analysis that has yielded insights into a broad spectrum of social behavior and institutions which had not previously been viewed as within the province of economic analysis. Thus, health, child-rearing activities, and family size, as well as occupational choice and schooling, are all seen to require the investment of scarce resources that yield both pecuniary and nonpecuniary future returns. Future economic research will hopefully shed more light on how differences

---

[26]These calculations assume that when children are present and a mother leaves the labor force, all her time is devoted to child care. Insofar as she performs other activities in the home as well, the costs of child rearing (in terms of mother's time) have thereby been over-estimated relative to the benefits.

[27]See, for example, James J. Heckman, "A Life-Cycle Model of Earnings, Learning, and Consumption," and Sherwin Rosen, "A Theory of Life Earnings," *Journal of Political Economy*, 84, 4, part 2 (August 1976); also Alan Blinder and Yoram Weiss, "Human Capital and Labor Supply: A Synthesis," *Journal of Political Economy*, 84, 3 (June 1976).

in family capacities to produce these investments determine their allocation within the population.

Exercises

1. Betty Basher has just graduated from high school. A staunch feminist, Betty desires to maximize her human wealth (present value of her income stream), having forsaken marriage and children. Unfortunately, she is also terminally ill and has only two years left to live. As the result of recent equal opportunity laws, Betty may borrow or lend as much money as she desires at a constant market interest rate of 10 percent. Finally, she has available (only) the following three occupational possibilities:

Occupation	Pays Income This Year of	Pays Income Next Year of
Professional Football Player	$ 21,000	0 (body wears out)
Secretary	$ 9,000	$13,000
Tennis instructor	$ −10,000 (training costs)	$33,000

a. Which occupation will Betty choose? (You may assume that income is received or costs paid at the *beginning* of a year.) Justify your answer mathematically.

b. If the government were to abolish formal participation in contact sports so that there is no longer a market for her services as a football player would her choice be different?

2. At a recent meeting of the Rocky Mountain Economic Association, Professor Berry Bush, chairman of the department of economics, Aspen State Teacher's College, was heard to remark: "Human capital theory implies that individuals with the same amounts of investment in human capital will have equal labor market incomes." Is he right? Explain your answer carefully and support it graphically.

3. Suppose a government program is implemented that enables everyone to invest as much as they wish in human capital at no cost to themselves whatsoever. (Demonstrate your answers with the graphical model of investment in human capital.)

a. How much will a wealth-maximizing individual invest?

b. Will such a government program produce earning power equality across individuals?

References

BECKER, GARY S., *Human Capital*, 2nd ed. New York: National Bureau of Economic Research, 1975, pp. 94–144, 191–200.

BLINDER, ALAN, and YORAM WEISS, "Human Capital and Labor Supply: A Synthesis." *Journal of Political Economy*, 84, 3 (June 1976), 449–72.

BOWLES, SAMUEL, "Schooling and Inequality from Generation to Generation." *Journal of Political Economy*, 80, 3, part II (May–June 1972), 219–51.

BYRON W. BROWN and DANIEL H. SAKS, "The Production and Distribution of Cognitive Skills within Schools." *Journal of Political Economy*, 83, 3 (June 1975), 571–94.

CARNOY, MARTIN, and DIETER MARENBACH, "The Return to Schooling in the United States, 1939–69." *Journal of Human Resources*, 10, 3 (summer 1975), 312–31.

DUNCAN, OTIS DUDLEY, DAVID L. FEATHERMAN, and BEVERLY DUNCAN, *Socioeconomic Background and Achievement*. New York: Seminar Press, 1972.

FLEISHER, BELTON M., "Mother's Home Time and the Production of Child Quality." *Demography*, 14, 2 (May 1977), 197–212.

FREEMAN, RICHARD, "Overinvestment in College Training?" *Journal of Human Resources*, 10, 3 (summer 1975), 287–311.

FREEMAN, RICHARD B., "The Decline in the Economic Rewards to College Education." *Review of Economics and Statistics*, 59, 1 (February 1977), 18–29.

GRILICHES, ZVI, "Estimating the Returns to Schooling: Some Econometric Problems." *Econometrica*, 45, 1 (January 1977), 1–22.

GROSSMAN, MICHAEL, *The Demand for Health: A Theoretical and Empirical Investigation*, National Bureau of Economic Research Occasional Paper 119. New York: Columbia University Press, 1972.

HANOCH, GIORA, "Personal Earnings and Investment in Schooling." Unpublished Ph.D. dissertation, University of Chicago, 1965.

———, "An Economic Analysis of Earnings and Schooling." *Journal of Human Resources*, 2, 3 (summer 1967), 310–29.

HECKMAN, JAMES J., "A Life-Cycle Model of Earnings, Learning, and Consumption." *Journal of Political Economy*, 84, 4, part II (August 1976), S11–S44.

LAZEAR, EDWARD, "Education: Consumption or Production?" *Journal of Political Economy*, 85, 3 (June 1977), 569–98.

LEIBOWITZ, ARLEEN S., "Women's Allocation of Time to Market and Nonmarket Activities: Differences by Education." Unpublished Ph.D. dissertation, Columbia University, 1972.

MINCER, JACOB, *Schooling, Experience, and Earnings*. New York: National Bureau of Economic Research, 1974, pp. 7–23.

ROSEN, SHERWIN, "A Theory of Life Earnings." *Journal of Political Economy*, 84, 4, part II (August 1976), S45–S68.

STIGLER, GEORGE, *Capital and Rates of Return in Manufacturing Industries*. New York: National Bureau of Economic Research, 1963.

CHAPTER 9

Investment in Human Capital: Firms

*Represents more advanced material

In Chapter 8 we focused on human capital investment that takes place for the most part outside of firms. The most important form of human capital examined was investment in schooling. Ignoring nonpecuniary considerations (for example, there may be positive or negative consumption value to schooling), rational investment policy implies investing in each form of human capital up to the point that the rate of return to the last dollar spent on each type is the same. Numerous activities enhance human capital. Within the relatively narrow definition of human capital that encompasses only those investments that increase market earning power, an important investment activity we mentioned only in passing in Chapter 8 is human capital generated by job-training activities outside formal schooling. Schooling increases labor market productivity in a multitude of ways—communications skills, mathematical and logical facility, occupation-specific instruction in business administration, data processing, medicine, and so on, but few individuals enter the labor market with sufficient knowledge to perform a job as efficiently as an experienced worker. It is necessary to gain occupation-specific knowledge not conveyed in school through actual practice—how to sell a pair of shoes, take a blood sample, write a will, prepare an income tax statement. Moreover, each business firm has its own special way of doing things that requires *firm-specific* knowledge to perform properly.

Workers' value to employers increases with the accumulation of such productivity-enhancing *training*. Training is an intrinsic component of most jobs, leading to improved performance on given tasks and, in many cases, to advancement toward supervisory roles in the firm. Economic incentives emerge from the labor market to acquire training, just as with other forms of human capital. *Job training* is a much broader concept than formal training programs. It is probably safe to assume that the great bulk of investment in job training is informal—learning by doing—rather than well-defined formal programs. The relatively small amount of data on firms' training activities supports this assumption. For example, Mincer[1] reported results of a survey of New Jersey industries made by the New Jersey Bureau of Apprenticeship and Training which indicated that about 5 percent of workers were participating in formal training programs. Only 16.2 percent of New Jersey firms had formal training programs. Such programs—especially apprenticeship training—seem to have declined historically, having been supplanted to some extent by increased schooling.[2] Thus, in order to capture the full dimension and impact of on-the-job training (OJT), indirect measures that focus mainly on informal training must be used.

---

[1] Jacob Mincer, "On-the-Job Training: Costs, Returns, and Some Implications," *Journal of Political Economy*, 70, 5, part 2 (October 1962).

[2] Paul G. Keat, "Long-Run Changes in Occupational Wage Structure 1900–56," *Journal of Political Economy*, 68, 6 (December 1960).

An Overview of Measurement Problems

Such measurements of OJT are needed because firms do not typically keep track of training costs as they do, say, raw material costs. This is not to say that firms are unaware of the informal training process. Profit-maximizing firms could hardly remain unaware of the growth in worker productivity that goes with experience and the costs to the firms of losing experienced workers and hiring replacements. Mincer[3] quotes the following passage from a New York Merchants and Manufacturers Association study:

> [On-the-job training costs include] the expense brought about by substandard production of new employees while learning their job assignments and becoming adjusted to their work environment; the dollar value of time spent by supervisors and other employees who assist in breaking in new employees on their job assignment, and costs of organized training programs.[4]

These costs, incurred during the early years of experience, yield returns throughout the term of employment and hence represent an investment in human capital. To them should be added the costs of a personnel department whose function is to search for, recruit, and process new employees. (These costs of recruiting new employees were treated briefly in the Frontiers section of Chapter 3.)

It is quite difficult for a firm to assess accurately OJT costs (although some firms attempt to do so). The effort involved in accurately apportioning supervisory time between overseeing new and experienced employees, in evaluating the expense brought about by substandard production, and so on, will in many cases be so great compared to the benefits to the firm that relatively casual information is used to guide the firm's employment policies. Even if such cost data were readily available, it would not tell us who—the firm or the employee—actually bears the costs and reaps the returns of investment in OJT human capital. It is the answer to this question, as well as knowledge of the magnitude of OJT capital, that is of interest in helping us to understand the way in which OJT affects earnings and other important aspects of labor market behavior.

Whether the firm or the employee actually bears the cost (and reaps the return) of OJT has no relationship to who makes the nominal payment ("writes the check"). Just as with a tax or subsidy on the sale of a good or service, who bears the cost depends on the interaction of market supply and demand forces and not upon whom the tax is levied or to whom the subsidy is paid by law. (Recall the example of the social security tax in Chapter 5.)

---

[3] Mincer, "On-the-Job Training," p. 62.
[4] See Table 3–1 for some relatively recent data.

Some firms may have the reputation of providing excellent training programs on which they spend substantial sums. They may be very selective in their hiring policies and offer employees fine opportunities for advancement as their tenure with the firm grows. On the other hand, employees may actually be paying for these OJT investments by accepting relatively low rates of pay during the early years of employment. Other firms, who pay higher starting salaries, may not increase wage rates as rapidly as job tenure grows. In the former case, the worker, through accepting a relatively low rate of pay to begin with, is actually bearing a substantial portion of the cost of investing in OJT. The return to this human capital investment occurs in later years in the form of a higher rate of pay. In the latter case, assuming the growth in workers' productivity is the same, the firm is actually bearing OJT costs by paying workers more than their value when they are first hired, and it is the firm which reaps the returns as worker productivity grows along with job tenure, while wage rates rise less rapidly.

Investment in OJT is extensive and an important component of total human capital in the United States. Mincer,[5] in a pathbreaking empirical study of OJT, estimated annual aggregate investment in OJT actually paid for by workers in 1958 as $13.5 billion, and investment in schooling as $21.6 billion. Since 1958 was the midst of the postwar "baby boom," the proportion of school-age persons in the population was relatively large, and the proportion of investment via schooling was larger than usual. Mincer estimated that in 1949, the amount of annual human capital investment via OJT was approximately equal to that taking place via schooling. As we develop the theoretical analysis of OJT in the next section, it will become clearer to you how Mincer arrived at his estimates. To anticipate, however, Mincer's (and practically all others') analysis of OJT builds on the study of investment in schooling through examination of age-earning power profiles presented in Chapter 8. The estimates of the amount of investment and rate of return to OJT apply only to investment by workers, not to those actually paid for by firms. In order to obtain information on the amount of OJT investment actually paid for by firms, data on the value of workers' marginal product comparable in detail to wage or earnings data would be needed. Since such information is not generally available, studies of the cost and returns to OJT have usually been limited to the worker's point of view.

Theoretical Analysis

The theoretical analysis of OJT is an extension of the framework developed to study investment in schooling. Complications arise, however, because, as suggested above, OJT investment may be undertaken either by firms or

---

[5]Mincer, "On-the-Job-Training," p. 62.

workers. In order to understand this problem, recall that if schooling were the only form of investment in human capital, typical worker value to an employer—the value of the worker's marginal product—would depend only on schooling (ignoring interpersonal differences in "luck" and ability). Therefore, ignoring depreciation of human capital attributable to aging, obsolescence of knowledge, and so on, the relationship between a worker's age and marginal product would look something like the profile shown in Figure 9–1. Along the horizontal axis, age is measured in years. The origin

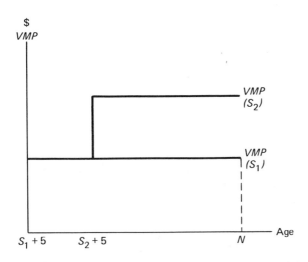

FIGURE 9–1. Age–VMP Relationship with No OJT

represents the age at leaving school when S_1 years of school are obtained (say, $S_1 + 5$ years if children typically enter school when they are 5 years old). The vertical axis measures *VMP* in dollars. A worker who acquires S_1 years of schooling would have a constant *VMP* equal to $VMP(S_1)$ dollars until the age of retirement, which we assume to be age N years. Another worker, like the worker with S_1 years of schooling in all respects except that S_2 years of schooling have been acquired, would have a *VMP* equal to $VMP(S_2)$ starting at age $S_2 + 5$ and continuing until retirement. Under competitive labor market conditions, market wage rates would equal *VMP* for each worker, and a worker's return to acquiring $S_2 - S_1$ additional years of schooling would be $VMP(S_2) - VMP(S_1)$ dollars per year.

When OJT occurs, age-*VMP* profiles no longer look like those of Figure 9–1. Rather, as training occurs, a worker's *VMP* grows as a result. Thus the relationship between *VMP* and age has an upward tilt, leveling off as training ceases. If once again we assume no depreciation of skills with age,

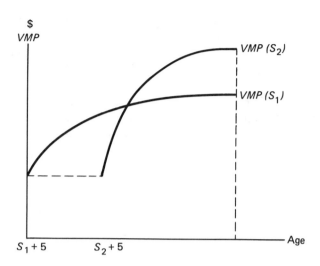

FIGURE 9–2. Age–VMP Relationship with OJT

VMP then remains constant until the age of retirement, as shown in Figure 9–2. When schooling ceases, *VMP* does not necessarily jump up to a new, higher level, but grows over time as training occurs, eventually attaining a level higher than that attainable with a smaller amount of schooling. The analysis of OJT introduces an important new problem in labor market analysis. Whereas, under competitive conditions, we have so far seen that wage rates must always equal *VMP*, with the possibility of OJT this equality need no longer hold at each moment in time. To explore this relationship further, we take a closer look at a *VMP* curve like those of Figure 9–2 by redrawing it in Figure 9–3, along with two possible wage rate-age relationships for a typical worker.

VMP depends on schooling and the amount of training. Any direct costs (salaries of instructors, materials used, and so on) or other expenses associated with hiring a worker (aptitude tests, filling out forms, and so on) are subtracted from the value of any output produced to find *VMP*. It is quite possible, therefore, that *VMP* is zero or even negative during the early part of a worker's tenure with a firm. One possible pattern of payment to the worker would be to set the wage rate (W) equal to *VMP* at all times. This wage profile (W_1) would coincide exactly with *VMP* and satisfy the competitive condition established in Chapter 4 that $W = VMP$ at all times. With $W = VMP$, the firm would have no incentive to hire additional workers, and the workers would be unable to earn a higher wage anywhere else, because no other employer would be willing to pay a higher wage rate (why?). Suppose, now, that the employer knows a typical employee will stay on the job for *N-S-5* years. (This knowledge need not be held with certainty for

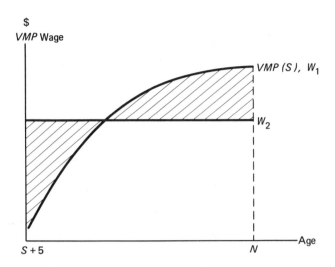

FIGURE 9–3. Wage Rates and VMP over the Working Life with OJT

each employee, but may be an expectation based on experience with a large number of employees or on evidence gathered by observing the experience of other firms.) Under these circumstances, the employer would be willing to pay workers an amount greater than *VMP* during the early years of tenure with the firm, provided that this "loan" could be recouped with interest later on. Workers might prefer this, because it would be one way of maintaining spending capacity without borrowing money formally while *VMP* is relatively low. Each year (t) that *VMP* fell short of W, the employer would be "lending" an amount $W_t - VMP_t$ to the employee. Eventually, *VMP* rises above W_t and the employer's "loan" is repaid. (The subscript t equals the employee's age.)

Suppose that during the first year an employee works for a firm (which happens to be the first year after the employee leaves school), *VMP* falls short of the wage paid by x dollars. The firm is said to invest x dollars in the OJT of this worker. If this were the only year during which training took place and subsequently *VMP* grew sufficiently to exceed the wage rate, the rate of return on the employers' investment would be r, such that

$$x = W_{S+5} - VMP_{S+5} = \sum_{t=S+6}^{N} (VMP_t - W_t)(1 + r)^{-(t-S-5)} \qquad (9\text{–}1)$$

where once again the subscript t represents the employee's age. Under the extreme circumstances represented by wage pattern W_2 in Figure 9–3, W_t is a constant throughout the worker's tenure with the firm, while *VMP* rises over time. Equation (9–1) is easily adapted to situations in which the number of years during which the firm pays for OJT is greater than one, or even unknown a priori. Subtracting $W_{S+5} - VMP_{S+5}$ from both sides of (9–1), we obtain

$$0 = \sum_{t=S+5}^{N} (VMP_t - W_t)(1 + r)^{-(t-S-5)} \qquad (9-2)$$

which holds for any number of years during which W exceeds VMP, so long as VMP exceeds W during at least one year. In the case of wage profile W_1, it should be clear that since $VMP - W$ is always 0, there is no investment by the firm in OJT, and equation (9–2) holds trivially as $0 = 0$, with r undefined.

The "loans" in the form of $W_t - VMP_t$ represent *investment* by the firm in the OJT human capital of its employees. Under the assumption that firms want to maximize profits, we have the same rule for investing in human capital as we derived for the household in Chapter 8: The firm will maximize its profit, or wealth, by undertaking all investments for which the rate of return (r) exceeds the market rate of interest (i). In equilibrium, therefore, the rate of return on the firm's last investment will equal the market rate of interest. If r exceeded i, it would pay the firm to take advantage of this opportunity to earn more profits by hiring additional workers and investing in their training, or additional firms would enter the industry, increasing the demand for workers. Given increasing costs for each firm and a downward-sloping demand curve for the industry's output (and possibly an upward-sloping supply curve of labor), VMP must eventually fall (and wage rates rise) so that equality of r and i on investments in human capital is achieved (why?).

An important implication of the preceding paragraphs is that once the possibility of the firm's investing in OJT is considered, wage profile W_1 (Figure 9–3) need not hold: VMP need not equal W at every moment in time, even under conditions of competitive equilibrium. All that need hold is that the *present value* of a typical worker's VMP over the period of expected job tenure with the firm equal the *present value* of the wages paid. This can be seen in equation (9–2), if we make use of the profit- or wealth-maximization condition $r = i$. When the firm maximizes its profit, (9–2) becomes

$$\sum_{t=S+5}^{N} W_t(1 + i)^{-(t-S-5)} = \sum_{t=S+5}^{N} VMP_t(1 + i)^{-(t-S-5)} \qquad (9-3)$$

which says that the present value of wage rates paid equals the present value of marginal products. Once again (9–3) holds trivially under conditions of wage profile W_1, since W and VMP are always equal. The insight that, under competitive conditions, wage–marginal product equality need hold only in the present value sense is one of the most profound in labor market analysis and bears implications for numerous forms of economic behavior including migration, quits, layoffs, and unemployment rates. The economists who pioneered in developing the theory and implications of investments in OJT human capital are Walter Oi, Gary Becker, and Jacob Mincer.[6]

GENERAL AND SPECIFIC TRAINING

Under what circumstances will the rate of return be sufficiently high to induce an employer's investing in OJT? The answer is very complex and depends in part on the effect of OJT on the length of time a typical employee is expected to remain with the firm. In this section we develop the answer to a first approximation. The employer's decision whether to invest in OJT depends crucially on expected returns. Obviously, if an employee is likely to quit as soon as training is completed and take a job elsewhere, it will not pay an employer to invest in training. Other things being equal, an employee will quit to take a new job if it pays more than the current job. Suppose a worker receives OJT that raises his or her *VMP* in other jobs by the same amount as in the firm providing the training. In this case, if the firm adopts wage profile W_2 (Figure 9–3), thus paying for the full amount of OJT investment, a typical worker will soon be able to earn more than W_2 in alternative jobs. The employee would quit, and the employer's investment in OJT would be lost. When OJT increases *VMP* in a large number of jobs by the same amount, we say that the worker receives *general training*. Clearly, a profit-maximizing firm will not invest in general OJT. Employers will not adopt wage profile W_2 when training is general; rather, they will adopt wage profile W_1, which implies that the employees, not employers, must bear the cost (and reap the returns) of general OJT.

General OJT is formally similar to schooling. Schooling presumably increases an individual's earning power equally in a large number of alternative jobs, and it is normally paid for by the individual or the family, possibly with public aid. Thus, the analysis of investment in schooling readily meshes with that of investment in OJT paid for by the individual. Postschooling OJT investment paid for by the individual is simply reflected in wage or earnings amounts that remain below the figures which would be observed if no such training occurred and the returns to schooling were immediately reflected in money wages. There are numerous examples of general OJT. Perhaps the most apparent is apprenticeship training in various crafts, where apprentices receive considerably lower rates of pay than journeymen or master craftsmen. Young lawyers typically work for experienced practitioners at relatively low rates of pay before going out on their own. Physicians seeking to become specialists earn much less as residents in hospitals than they could receive

---

[6]Walter Y. Oi, "Labor As a Quasi-Fixed Factor," *Journal of Political Economy*, 70 (December 1962); Gary S. Becker, *Human Capital* (New York: National Bureau of Economic Research, 1975); Mincer, "On-the-Job Training."

in private practice without specializing. An "exception that proves the rule" regarding the employer's willingness to pay for general training is found in the armed services. One of the enticements used to induce voluntary enlistment by the military is the provision of vocational training. A major cost of military personnel is the loss of trained enlisted men who seek civilian employment at the end of their first or second terms in order to receive higher rates of pay than can be obtained in the military. The armed services may attract enlistments by paying for general training, but unless the enlistment terms are sufficiently long, these investments will not yield returns to military employers because enlisted men tend to quit after their VMP rises above their military rates of pay.

Not all OJT is general training. Work experience with a firm may also raise an employee's VMP to the current employer, but not to others. For example, work practices differ among firms, and employees become more valuable to their employees as they adjust to the firm's characteristic ways of doing things, to the personalities of supervisors and co-workers, and perhaps learn trade secrets. Such increases in VMP are firm-specific, because if an employee were to quit and take a job with another firm (even if the job were similar), all of these OJT investments would be lost; hence they are called *specific OJT*. Human capital investments in specific OJT raise workers' VMP where they are currently employed, but not elsewhere; consequently, specific OJT does not increase the wage rates workers can obtain in alternative employment. This means it is possible for an employer to reap returns from investing in specific OJT. If a typical worker accumulates specific OJT human capital as job tenure lengthens, so that VMP rises over time as in Figure 9–3, the employer will not automatically lose by adopting wage profile W_2, thus investing in all of the worker's specific OJT and reaping all of the returns. Other employers will not be willing to pay more than W_2, so the worker will have no incentive to leave, thus destroying the employer's investment in OJT.

Any condition that reduces the probability of a worker's quitting and thus reducing an employer's returns to OJT investment will increase the willingness of an employer to pay for OJT. Thus, when there are significant money and psychic costs to a worker of leaving one job to take another (moving expenses, leaving friendly neighbors and co-workers), it would not necessarily be inconsistent with the theory of OJT to observe employers investing in the general training of workers. Such a situation might come about due to the geographic isolation of the place of employment. A likely example due to legal barriers to interfirm movement until a few years ago was in professional baseball (recall our discussion in Chapter 6), where the reserve clause may have protected the employer's interest in the general training of young players. Employers claimed the reserve clause was necessary because of the expense of running farm teams in which young players could be brought up to major league quality. From the players' point of view, however, the reserve clause was simply a tool with which management was able to retain players at lower salaries than would otherwise have been possible, since a disgruntled athlete's only option was to quit baseball or move to a different country to play.

Specific OJT raises the *VMP* of workers in the firm in which they are employed, but not elsewhere. Consequently, employers may invest in specific OJT. They may also invest in general OJT if conditions inhibit worker mobility to other jobs. It would be easy to assume that whenever opportunities to invest in specific OJT arise such that *r* exceeds *i*, the firm will always undertake the investment. However, the problem is not so simple. If the rate of return to specific OJT exceeds the rate of interest, it pays the wealth-maximizing worker as well as the employer to undertake the investment. Who, then, pays for and receives the returns to firm-specific OJT? A little reflection on this problem suggests that employees and employers will share specific OJT investments, whereas employees are most likely to pay for investments in general training. The reason is that the expected rate of return to OJT investments is greater if both employer and employee share costs and returns. Suppose, to the contrary, that an employee paid for all training investments and received all returns. The employee's wage rate would then always equal *VMP*. Under these circumstances, any unforeseen decline in the worker's value to the employer due, say, to adverse business conditions, would cause *VMP* to fall below *W*. The profit-maximizing employer would then lay off the worker, and the worker would lose all or part of his OJT investment, depending on the probability of being recalled, the length of time it takes to find a new job, and the proportion of specific and general training acquired.

On the other hand, if the firm pays for all specific OJT investments, the worker's wage will never exceed the amount warranted by general training, and *VMP* will exceed *W* after the firm begins to reap the returns to its investment. Under these circumstances, the worker is much less likely to be laid off if *VMP* declines unexpectedly, because a "cushion" exists representing the employer's investment returns—the excess of *VMP* over *W*. In fact, the employer may not lay off the worker even if *VMP* falls below *W*, because to do so increases the probability that the employee may not be available when recalled, and the employer will then have to go to the expense of hiring and training new workers when business conditions improve. (What determines the employer's decision to lay off a worker when *VMP* falls below the wage rate?) Unfortunately for the employer, however, if the worker's wage rate is based only on general training, an unanticipated increase in *VMP* in other firms will cause the worker's opportunities to improve, and he or she may therefore quit to take another job. The employer's OJT investment would thus be lost.

Suppose for simplicity that all OJT is firm-specific and that firm and worker share specific OJT costs and returns. This situation is described in

Figure 9–4. The horizontal line g in Figure 9–4 represents the marginal productivity of the worker with S years of schooling and no OJT. Assuming that the skills acquired through schooling do not depreciate, VMP due to schooling is constant over the working life. The worker's VMP may be less than g, however, during the initial time on the job if OJT occurs, because of direct expenditures on supervisory and training personnel, materials, and so on. Thus, Figure 9–4a shows VMP to lie below g at first, rising above it later on. If the employer paid for all firm-specific OJT, W would always coincide with g, while if the worker paid, W and VMP would always be equal. In Figure 9–4, firm and worker share the firm-specific OJT costs and returns as indicated by the fact that W lies between the g and VMP curves. During the early years of tenure with the firm, the worker receives more than VMP, but less than what could be earned if no firm-specific OJT were undertaken. During later years, the worker earns more than could be earned elsewhere, since W exceeds g; nevertheless, the firm is also profiting from its earlier willingness to pay a wage higher than VMP, since VMP now exceeds W. The sharing of the costs and returns to firm-specific OJT is reflected in the shaded areas of Figure 9–4. The shaded area reflects the worker's investment in OJT to the left of the intersection of the W and g curves, while the area to the right reflects the worker's returns. (These areas do not show costs and returns precisely, as the next section shows.) Similarly, the shaded area to the left of the intersection of the W and VMP lines represent the firm's investment, while the area to the right indicates returns.

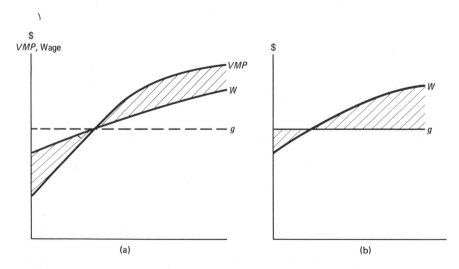

(a)   (b)

FIGURE 9–4. Firm and Worker Share OJT Costs. (a) Shaded area shows employer's investment and returns to OJT; (b) shaded area shows worker's investment and returns to OJT

Before going on to discuss applications and empirical studies of OJT, we need to deal with a common objection to the approach developed above. It has been argued that earning power in some jobs just "grows with experience," without any training taking place at all. This objection, while possibly accurate, does not invalidate the human capital approach. In a competitive economy, if the wages obtainable in a given job were represented by a curve like W in Figure 9–4, and W were always higher than the wages of an alternative job, like g (that is, if W and g did not cross), workers would leave the low-paying occupation and seek jobs in the high-paying occupation. This would cause the W curve to fall and the g curve to rise until they crossed, as in Figure 9–4. In other words, competition for jobs would force workers who desire to obtain the excess of W over g in later years to pay for it by investing in the job which pays W, less than g, during the early years on the job. This payment is a human capital investment, and the analysis of OJT helps us to understand the relationship between investment cost and later returns.

Measuring OJT Costs and Returns

In Chapter 8 two statistical methods of analyzing investments in schooling were presented. One method involved the direct comparison of earnings streams of persons or groups of persons who differ in levels of schooling. This method is readily adaptable to dealing with OJT provided all OJT investment costs are indirect (that is, consist of foregone earnings). Even if there are direct OJT costs, they are likely to be reflected in foregone earnings from the worker's point of view. That is, the firm may "pay" for direct costs, but to the extent that workers actually bear OJT investment costs, it is through accepting a wage lower than they could earn in an alternative job rather than laying out cash in the form of direct payments. It is a relatively simple matter to compare earnings streams of workers in order to measure human capital costs and returns, because the required data are readily obtainable. Therefore, much work has been done involving worker investments in schooling and OJT. Unfortunately, in order to measure firm investments and returns directly, we require information on the VMP of typical workers in each year of job tenure, and such data are not readily available. Therefore, very little is known about the magnitude of firm OJT investments. In other words, available information on earnings or wage rates by age of worker provide the needed data to measure the W and g curves of Figure 9–4, but since it is extremely difficult to find information on VMP, we cannot discuss the costs and returns to firm investments in OJT.

The second method of analyzing investments in schooling involved development of a *human capital earning power function*. It was shown that a simple form of this function is

$$\ln Y = \ln Y_0 + rS \tag{9-4}$$

where Y is a measure of earning power, Y_0 represents what earning power would be in the absence of any schooling, r is the rate of return, and S is years of schooling completed. Equation (9–4) was equation (8–11) in Chapter 8. One difficulty in implementing equation (9–4) empirically is that Y is affected by other nonschooling investments in human capital, particularly OJT. While it is possible to estimate (9–4) as it stands (as we showed in Chapter 8), it is easier to adapt the equation to accommodate information on training as well. Indeed, a principal advantage of the human capital earning power equation approach over the earnings stream comparison approach is its flexibility. It can, and often is, modified to estimate rates of return to OJT and other forms of human capital investments as well as to study the effects of other variables such as "ability" and family background on earning power and the rate of return to schooling and OJT investments.

Equation (9–4) was derived by assuming that all schooling costs could be treated as foregone earnings and that the amount of earnings foregone in acquiring an additional year of schooling is the full amount which would have been received working with the lower level of schooling and acquiring no OJT. It is the assumption that net earnings received while attending school are zero which allows the use of the simple number of years of schooling in equation (9–4). However, net earnings are not typically zero while the worker invests in OJT. Assuming that all worker-financed OJT investments are indirect—paid for by accepting a wage (W) below that which would otherwise be received based on the worker's prior human capital investments—we may define the ratio $k = (W/f)$, where f represents the "full" wage based on prior investments. k may also be thought of as the proportion of the employee's time on the job devoted to OJT. Then, the human capital earning power function can be modified to become

$$\ln Y = \ln Y_0 + r_1 S + r_2 kX \qquad 0 < k < 1 \tag{9-5}$$

where r_1 and r_2 represent the rates of return to schooling and OJT, respectively, and X represents years of job experience.[7] Bear in mind that k and r_2 relate to *all* worker-financed OJT investments, whether they involve general or specific training. Just as in Chapter 8, equation (9–4) can be modified to accommodate the possibility that the rate of return to schooling is not constant. Equation (9–5) can be modified to reflect the possibility of declining r_2 or k by adding X^2.

---

[7]A more detailed development of equation (9–5) is found in Jacob Mincer, *Schooling, Experience, and Earnings* (New York: National Bureau of Economic Research, 1974), Chap. 1.

Our examples of empirical investigations of OJT are both taken from the work of Jacob Mincer, who has pioneered in applying both the earnings stream comparison and human capital earning power equation approaches.

THE EARNINGS STREAM COMPARISON METHOD

Mincer employed the earnings stream comparison approach in his 1962 paper, "On-the-Job Training: Costs, Returns, and Some Implications."[8] Table 9–1 shows some of Mincer's earnings stream calculations, taken from the March 1959 Current Population Survey and other data. (Note Mincer did not assume that direct schooling costs exactly equal earnings while in school. In fact, he estimated that direct costs exceeded the earnings of those attending college; hence the negative figures for 18- to 21-year-old persons who were attending college.) The figures in Table 9–1 are age-earnings profiles based on artificial cohorts (described in Chapter 8). Recall that in Chapter 8 we showed how, using artificial cohorts, the rate of return to additional schooling could be calculated as long as we were prepared to assume the rate of return to schooling equaled that to OJT. Making this assumption, Mincer computed the "interest rate" that makes the present value of the sum of the earnings differentials in column 3 of Table 9–1 equal to zero. He thus estimated the rate of return to college education and to OJT for college-

TABLE 9–1

Net Earnings Streams for U.S. Male High School
and College Graduates, 1958

Age	(1)	(2)	(3) Differential in Earnings (1) − (2)
	Years of Schooling		
	16+	12	
18–21	$ −682	$2,800	$−3,482
22–24	3,663	3,537	126
25–29	5,723	4,381	1,342
30–34	7,889	5,182	2,707
35–44	10,106	6,007	4,099
45–54	11,214	6,295	4,919
55–64	10,966	6,110	4,856

Source: Jacob Mincer, "On-the-Job Training: Costs, Returns, and Some Implications," *Journal of Political Economy*, 70, 5, part 2 (October 1962), Table A3. Reprinted by permission of The University of Chicago Press.

[8] *Journal of Political Economy*, 70, 5, part 2 (October 1962).

educated males (compared to acquiring a high school education and concomitant OJT) to be 11.5 percent in 1958. Having computed this rate of return, Mincer was then able to go back to the earnings streams and calculate the magnitude of the additional OJT investments of college graduates year by year. In showing how this was done, we can also demonstrate why the point at which the earnings streams "cross" (that is, where the earnings differentials of Table 9–1, column 3, equal zero) does not show where OJT ceases to occur.

The procedure for using comparative earnings streams to calculate a rate of return and OJT for college graduates (compared to high school graduates) is demonstrated in Table 9–2. Column 1 shows the earnings differentials

TABLE 9–2

OJT Calculations Based on Data Supporting Table 9–1

Age	*(1)* *Earnings Differential*	*(2)* *Return on Last Year's Cost*	*(3)* *Return on All Previous Cost*	*(4)* *Cost at Age Shown* $[-(1) + (3)]$
18	$-3,246	$ —	$ —	$3,246
19	-3,403	373	373	3,776
20	-3,561	434	807	4,368
21	-3,719	502	1,308	5,027
22	- 203	578	1,887	2,090
23	126	240	2,127	2,001
24	455	230	2,357	1,902
25	685	219	2,576	1,891
26	913	217	2,793	1,880
27	1,349	216	3,009	1,660
28	1,672	191	3,200	1,528
29	2,009	176	3,376	6,367
30	2,336	157	3,533	1,197
31	2,522	138	3,671	1,149
32	2,707	132	3,803	1,096
33	2,892	126	3,929	1,037
34	3,077	119	4,048	971
35	3,260	112	4,160	898
36	3,448	103	4,263	815
37	3,638	94	4,357	719
38	3,824	83	4,440	616
39	4,010	71	4,511	501
40	4,145	58	4,568	423
41	4,278	49	4,617	339
42	4,411	39	4,656	245
43	4,540	28	4,684	144
44	4,674	17	4,701	27

between college and high school graduates for single years for ages 18 to 44. Direct schooling costs are subtracted to obtain net earnings of college students. The earnings of high school graduates are affected by the opportunity cost of the OJT they are undertaking. Therefore, the earnings differential (Table 9–2, column 1) for age 18 represents the indirect plus direct costs (times -1) of attending the first year of college, over and above the OJT cost born by a typical high school graduate during the first year after graduation. This differential, $3,246, is entered in the age 18 row of column 4. Following this logic, it would be easy to assume that the additional cost of attending the second year of college is therefore $3,403, the negative of the earnings differential at age 19. This would be incorrect, however, because the earnings differential at age 19 is an understatement of the cost of attending the second year of college! Since $r = 11.5$ percent, the student who attends the second year of college is not only giving up the earning power of a high school graduate and direct costs, but also the return on the first year of college attendance, which is $3,246 \times 0.115 = $373 (column 3). Assuming, as we have, that human capital does not depreciate, this return of $373 remains part of the student's earning power until the age of retirement. Thus, the cost of attending the second year of college is shown in column 4 to be $3,776. Similarly, the additional cost of attending the third year of college is the sum of foregone earnings at age 20 ($3,561) plus $0.115 \times $3,776 = 434, the return on the second year's cost, plus $373, the return on the first year's cost. $434 + $373 = $807, shown in column 3, and the total additional cost of the third year of college is consequently $4,368. The same calculations, adding $0.115 \times $4,368 = 502, the return to the third year of college, yields $5,027, the additional cost of the last year of college.

Age 22 is assumed to be the first year on the job. By now you should see that the earnings differential of $203 between college students who are performing their first postschool year of market work is a gross understatement of the cost of whatever OJT they undertake during that year. According to our human capital model, if the typical college graduate undertook no OJT during the first or any subsequent year of postschool employment, his or her market earnings would be equal to full earning power, or the earning power of a high school graduate plus the returns to all previous training. In other words, the earnings of the college graduate would exceed those of a high school graduate by $1,887, not fall short by $203. The sum of $1,887 and $203, $2,090, is therefore an estimate of the dollar amount of OJT incurred by a typical college graduate during the first year of employment in excess of that incurred by a high school graduate during the fifth year of employment. Now you should be able to see why the point at which the earnings differential becomes zero (between ages 22 and 23) does not reveal the age at which OJT ceases. Investment in OJT vanishes when no additional investment cost is implicit in the earnings stream differential—that is, when the excess of the earning power of a typical college graduate over that of a typical

high school graduate is sufficient to cover the returns on all prior investments. This does not occur in the 1958 data used to develop Table 9–2 until
age 44.

The procedure described above compares the earnings of college graduates
with those of high school graduates. Since high school graduates also invest
in OJT, which affects their earning power and observed earnings, the investment costs from age 22 on tell us only the OJT investments made by college
graduates in addition to those made by high school graduates of the same
age. Mincer also developed OJT estimates for high school graduates and
elementary school graduates. By assuming that persons with only one to
four years of schooling received no OJT,[9] he was able to cumulate the OJT
investment calculations across schooling groups to obtain the total OJT
investment costs for college graduates. To illustrate, while the additional
OJT investment at age 30 is shown in column 4 of Table 9–2 to be $1,197,
total investment at that age was estimated by Mincer to be $1,547. The addi-
tional investment by a typical college graduate is considerably greater than
that of a typical high school or elementary school graduate ($1,197, $350,
and $161, respectively). In general, the amount invested in OJT is consider-
ably greater, the higher the level of formal schooling. Evidently schooling
and OJT are complementary factors of production. Mincer calculated the
total lifetime OJT investment of a typical college graduate to be $30,700,
based on 1958 data, while he estimated total schooling costs to be $26,000.
In order to put these dollar amounts in perspective, remember that they are
based on earnings data for twenty years ago. Considering the inflation and
economic growth that has occurred over the years since, the investments
measured in terms of today's wage levels would be much higher.

Although the OJT investments of persons with less schooling were calculated to be considerably smaller, the age at which investment ceased was
always around 40, with the annual amount declining with age. It makes sense
that human capital investments tend to occur relatively early in life, since
their rate of return declines as one grows older (why?).

THE HUMAN CAPITAL EARNING POWER FUNCTION

Mincer followed up his earlier work with a more elaborate study published
in 1974.[10] In this study he made extensive use of human capital earning power
functions. One difficulty in using the simple form of the earning power function shown in equation (9–2) is that it assumes k, the proportion of work time

---

[9]This assumption is undoubtedly false and Mincer relaxed it, obtaining new estimates
of the amount of OJT in his later work, *Schooling, Experience, and Earnings*. The OJT
estimates for college graduates were not changed much, however.

[10]Mincer, *Schooling, Experience, and Earnings*.

devoted to OJT, is constant with work experience. We saw in the preceding section that OJT very likely declines with age, ceasing around age 40 for the average worker. Therefore, the human capital earning power function should be capable of capturing this behavior. One form of the function which does this adds the term X^2 to equation (9–2). Mincer estimated this form of the human capital earning power function to data for approximately 31,000 white, nonfarm, nonstudent men up to age 65 from the 0.001 sample of the 1960 U.S. census of population. He obtained the following result:[11]

$$\ln Y = 6.20 + .107S + .081X - .0012X^2 \quad \bar{R}^2 = 0.29$$
$$\quad\quad\quad (72.3) \quad (75.5) \quad (-55.8)$$

The figures in parentheses are t values. Y is 1959 earnings, S is years of schooling, and X is experience measured as age minus S minus 5. The results show that a substantial proportion of annual earnings can be "explained" by two variables—schooling and experience.

As mentioned previously, one major advantage of the human capital earning power equation is its flexibility and the richness of the information it can yield. For example, it is not necessary, as in the earnings streams comparison approach, to assume that the rate of return to schooling, r_1, equals the rate of return to OJT, r_2. Through a chain of mathematical manipulation which we will not repeat here, Mincer shows that if an assumption is made regarding the period over which some OJT occurs (T), then r_2 and k can be identified. For $T = 20$, $r_2 = 6.3$ percent, and k during the first year of OJT (k_0) is 0.58 (that is, over half of a typical worker's time is devoted to OJT); for $T = 30$, $r_2 = 11.9$ percent, and $k_0 = 0.42$. Since the earnings comparison approach suggested that for high school and college graduates T is closer to 20 than to 30 years, it may be inferred from these results that the rate of return to OJT is somewhat lower than that to schooling. If that were true, individuals would be investing too little in schooling relative to OJT if they desire to maximize their wealth. Too little is known about the correct form of the human capital earning power function, however, to be sure that this comparison between r_1 and r_2 is correct.

Frontiers of OJT Analysis

There are numerous applications of OJT theory to economic behavior, and we will treat only two of them briefly here. We will discuss the implications of OJT for employment turnover (quits and layoffs) and geographical mobility.

---

[11]Ibid., Table 5–1, equation p(1).

The two most important implications of OJT theory are: (1) market earning power will tend to rise after the typical worker leaves school; and (2) for the worker who has received some OJT, the wage rate in his or her current job will exceed the wage that would be received in the next best alternative job while falling short of the worker's VMP (see Figure 9–4). The second implication departs from the strict $W = VMP$ equality of marginal productivity theory when human capital considerations are ignored. Consequently, it affects our view of the firm's policy toward hiring and laying off workers, as well as our view of a worker's willingness to quit a job or seek alternative employment in another firm.

If $W = VMP$ always held, then a competitive, profit-maximizing firm would lay off workers or attempt to lower wages whenever some change, even a temporary decline in demand for the firm's product, caused VMP to decline. However, we observe firms retaining many more workers in the presence of adverse product market conditions than might seem warranted by simple marginal productivity theory, and when workers are laid off, certain groups (mainly those in less-skilled occupations) are laid off with greater frequency than others. On the supply side of the market, workers do not always respond to interfirm and interregional wage differentials by quitting their present jobs and moving to seemingly higher-paying alternatives. Moreover, when laid off, many employees do not immediately begin to seek new jobs.

Much of layoff and quit behavior can be understood by reference to OJT theory. Since for experienced workers, VMP typically exceeds W because of the firm's investment in specific OJT, it pays the firm to retain employees when VMP falls relative to W so long as some excess of VMP over W remains. The reason is found in recognizing that the firm's previous investments in employees are akin to *fixed costs*. So long as the firm receives some return on these investments, it is preferable to retain workers rather than to discharge them, reducing the firm's return on previous investments to zero. Although it may at first seem strange, it may pay the firm not to lay off workers even when VMP falls below W. The reason is that if the decline in VMP is thought to be temporary, the profit-maximizing firm will weigh the cost of retaining workers when VMP falls below W against the risk of incurring future costs to hire and train new workers to replace those who were laid off and found jobs in other firms.

From the worker's point of view, to quit a job and take one elsewhere means foregoing future returns on worker-financed investment in OJT specific to the old firm. In other words, the relevant wage alternative is not that which is received by a worker with comparable experience in another firm, but the wage paid to workers with equivalent general training only.

This could well involve a cut in pay even if workers with comparable experience in the alternative firm are earning more. Look again at Figure 9–4: just as the probability of an experienced worker's being laid off is smaller, the larger the excess of VMP over W, so is the probability of the worker's quitting smaller, the greater the excess of W over g. In other words, layoffs and quits are expected to be negatively related to firm and worker investments in (and returns from) OJT, respectively.

Simple as the preceding propositions sound, they are not easy to test, because, as mentioned earlier, we have no direct information on VMP by year of experience. Nor is it possible to obtain accurate information on g by year of experience. Thus, an indirect method of estimating firm and worker investments in specific human capital is required. Early studies relied on an assumed positive correlation between wage rates and firm-financed specific investment to explain worker turnover.[12] There are some difficulties with this procedure, since the wage rate is correlated with numerous other variables that could also explain quits and layoffs.[13]

In a 1972 paper, Donald O. Parsons[14] used an indirect procedure to capture separate effects of employer-financed firm-specific investment in human capital (S_F) and of specific investments financed by workers (S_w). He achieved a good degree of success in explaining variation in quit and layoff rates (the number of quits or layoffs expressed as a proportion of the number of employees) across 47 narrowly defined manufacturing industries for the years 1959 and 1963. Parsons' method is based on three basic relationships we have already discussed:

$$S_F \equiv S - S_w \qquad (9\text{–}6)$$

$$S \equiv T - G \qquad (9\text{–}7)$$

$$W = a_1 G + a_2 S_w \qquad (9\text{–}8)$$

Identity (9–6) states that, for trained workers, S_F is the difference between total firm-specific investment (S) and worker-financed firm-specific investment, while (9–7) states that specific investment equals the difference between total human capital (T) and the capitalized value of general training (G). (G is the present value of g in Figure 9–4 less any transfer costs involved in changing jobs.) Equation (9–8) is a wage equation which holds strictly only if the returns to human capital were constant over time and if working life were infinite. Then a_1 would represent the return to a unit of general training and a_2 the return to a unit of worker-owned specific training.

---

[12]Oi, "Labor as a Quasi-Fixed Factor"; Sherwin Rosen, "Short-Run Employment Variation on Class I Railroads in the U.S. 1947–63," *Econometrica*, 36, 3-4 (July 1968), 511–29.

[13]Mincer, "On-the-Job Training."

[14]"Specific Human Capital: An Application to Quit Rates and Layoff Rates," *Journal of Political Economy*, 80, 6 (November–December 1972), 1120–43.

Assuming that the worker's returns to human capital investments, a_1 and a_2, are equal to each other, equation (9–8) can be solved for worker-owned specific capital, yielding

$$S_w = \frac{W}{a_2} - G \qquad (9\text{–}9)$$

The next step in Parsons' approach is to define two lists of variables for which data are available and which are assumed to be associated with T and S, respectively. These lists will not be reproduced here, but one feature of them is that each must contain some variables not included in the other.[15] The assumed functions for T and S are then substituted into equation (9–8) (since $G \equiv T - S$), permitting S_w to be expressed as a function of observed W and the variables assumed to be associated with T and S. Finally, since quit rates are hypothesized to be negatively correlated with S_w, this hypothesis can be tested by estimating the regression relationship between industry quit rates on the one hand and the wage rate and the variables substituted for G in equation (9–9), on the other. Since layoffs are hypothesized to be negatively correlated with S_F, a similar procedure allows layoffs to be used as a dependent variable in a regression equation in which the right-hand variables are based on substituting for T and making use of identities (9–6) and (9–7).

Parsons was able to hypothesize the signs of four variables in the quit regression described above and of twelve variables in the layoff regression. (The difference between the regressions in the number of variables whose signs are predictable arises because it is necessary to substitute for both T and S in the quit regression but only for T in the layoff regression.) In the quit-rate regressions, all four coefficient signs were the same as predicted under the specific human capital hypotheses in both 1959 and 1963 data sets. In the layoff regression, eleven of the twelve "predictable" regression coefficients are as hypothesized. Parsons' results offer substantial support for the ability of human capital theory to explain firms' hiring and layoff policies and worker mobility. These are topics economists had little success in understanding before the concept of human capital, in particular that of OJT, was brought to bear on labor market behavior.

GEOGRAPHICAL MOBILITY AND THE FAMILY

Wealth maximization requires that individuals accept jobs in those geographic areas (labor markets) where the present value of their real earnings will be highest, all other things being equal. Since moving from one place to another is costly, the gain in earning power obtained by leaving one labor

---

[15] The interested reader should consult Parsons' article to gain further insight into the intricacies of his approach.

market and moving to another must exceed the cost of doing so. Formally, individual wealth is increased through geographic mobility between markets i and j so long as

$$\sum_{t=1}^{n} (Y_{it} - Y_{jt})(1 + i)^{-t} > C_{ij} \qquad (9\text{--}10)$$

where Y represents real earnings, t represents time, n is the expected period of residence in either location, and C is the cost of moving from i to j. Inequality (9–10), taken simply, implies that workers will quickly move from one labor market to another whenever persistent wage differentials exist that are sufficiently large to cover the costs of moving. Nevertheless, although considerable migration does occur in the United States, many individuals who apparently could gain from moving do not do so. Research by economists into the reasons for individual differences in the propensity to move from one labor market to another has dealt with improving the accuracy with which the returns and costs of moving are measured. Understanding labor mobility is desirable not only because of the insights gained into individual human capital investment decisions, but also because the outcome of mobility decisions has important implications for the efficiency of labor markets. As we saw in Chapter 5, movement of workers to jobs where their marginal productivity is highest generally promotes the efficient allocation of labor in the economy. Geographic mobility is a crucial component of this allocative process.

Observed Wage Differentials Are Not What They Seem. Job tenure and age have long been recognized as deterrents to all kinds of labor market mobility—between employers within a labor market as well as between employers in geographically separate locations. Is this negative correlation between the probability of job change and tenure, given observed wage differentials due to "noneconomic" behavior, inconsistent with equation (9–10)? An understanding of human capital theory and OJT suggests it is not. The difference between the average level of wage rates in two labor markets reflects not only returns to the general human capital investments of workers in those markets, but also returns to job-specific investments. Worker investments in job-specific OJT will eventually result in the worker earning a wage higher than he or she could obtain elsewhere. Therefore, observed wage differentials among labor markets tend to overstate the gain that would be obtained by a typical worker who moved from the low-wage market to the high-wage market. This overstatement is greater the longer a given worker has remained on his or her current job.[16]

[16]A recent study of this aspect of labor mobility is Boyan Jovanovic and Jacob Mincer, "Mobility and Wages: On the Job and Over the Life-Cycle" (Conference on Low Income Labor Markets Sponsored by the Universities–National Bureau Committee for Economic Research, June 9–10, 1978).

Individual and Family Gains Are Not Necessarily the Same.   Even after observed wage differentials have been corrected for specific OJT investments, an individual worker may not respond to a potential wage gain because of family considerations. Following Jacob Mincer,[17] we can reformulate the condition for geographic mobility, equation (9–10), as

$$G_f \equiv R_f - C_f > 0 \qquad (9–11)$$

where G_f is the net real income gain from migration *to the family*, R_f the returns (in present value), and C_f the costs.

$$G_f \equiv \sum_i G_i \qquad (9–12)$$

where i denotes the individual family members. Clearly, if we denote the principal earner of the family (usually the husband) as 1, it is possible that $G_1 > 0$ while $G_f < 0$. Some obvious reasons for such an intrafamily conflict of interest include these: (1) the pressure of school-age children, and (2) the labor force participation of the wife. It is costly to search for satisfactory new school arrangements for children; although the husband may be able to improve *his* labor market position by moving, the wife may be forced to relinquish a job in which she has acquired a specific OJT investment without an equally satisfactory job prospect in the new destination. These sources of conflict do not eliminate geographic mobility, but they will tend to reduce it. If the gains from the marriage itself are great enough, the wife will be willing to sacrifice her job prospects to facilitate the husband's labor market advancement. (A similar argument applies to the husband, of course. But since the husband's labor market attachment is generally stronger than the wife's, the "sacrifice" is usually that of the wife.)

Table 9–3 shows the negative influence of husband's age (a proxy for job tenure) and of wife's employment status on family migration. The proportion of married men who moved from one state to another between 1965 and 1970 declines steadily with age and is smaller for husbands with working wives. The right-hand column of Table 9–3 suggests the negative impact on the wife's labor market opportunities of the husband's mobility. Of the employed wives of movers, 40 percent or more were not working in 1970. Some of these women would have left the labor force in any event, but much of the reduction in labor force participation can be attributed to the loss of specific human capital resulting from migration.[18] Table 9–4 shows that not only does wife's employment inhibit family migration, but the family is less likely to move the

[17]"Family Migration Decisions," *Journal of Political Economy*, 86, 5 (October 1978), 749–74.

[18]Data from National Longitudinal Surveys shows that between 1966 and 1969, only 24 percent of wives (husband's age 45–59) who worked at least one week in 1966 did not work in 1969.

TABLE 9-3

Percentage of Married Men 30 to 59 in 1965 with Nonfarm Occupations
in 1970 Who Moved between States between 1965 and 1970,
by Age and Wife's Employment Status in 1965

Husband's Age in 1965 and Wife's Employment Status in 1965		Percentage of Wives Employed in 1970
30–39		
Wife employed	7.7%	54.7%
Wife not employed	9.0	23.9
40–49		
Wife employed	4.1	61.7
Wife not employed	5.4	22.8
50–59		
Wife employed	2.5	57.4
Wife not employed	3.1	16.8

Source: Jacob Mincer, "Family Migration Decisions," *Journal of Political Economy*, 86, 5 (October 1978), Table 6. Reprinted by permission of The University of Chicago Press.

TABLE 9-4

Probability of Family Migration, 1967–1972

Wife's Job Tenure	Children 6–18	
	None	Some
0	0.132	0.107
5	0.079	0.063
10	0.055	0.044

Source: S. H. Sandell, "The Economics of Family Migration," *NLS Report on Dual Careers*, vol. 4, (December 1975) Columbus: Center for Human Resource Research, Ohio State University. Reported by Jacob Mincer in "Family Migration Decisions."

longer the wife has been employed at her current job. This is what the theory of human capital would lead us to expect. Table 9–4 also shows the negative association between the presence of school-age children and migration.

Since the labor force participation of both wife and husband creates a potential strain on family ties when one family member expects to gain from geographic mobility while the other does not, it is tempting to attribute the upward trend in divorce rates over the past thirty years to the rising labor force participation of married women. Of course, causation may also run in the opposite direction. Women may expect their marriages to be less stable than they did before World War II and thus engage in labor force activity as a hedge against future disruption. In an exploratory study of this fascinating question, Robert Michael concludes: ". . . the labor force participation rate of married women (with spouse and young children present) is causally prior to the divorce rate and fertility."[19] The application of the theory of human capital to socioeconomic behavior promises to be a rewarding area of future research.

Conclusion

In this chapter we extended the theory of human capital developed in Chapter 8 to cover investment in the context of the firm through on-the-job training. The analysis of general and specific human capital investments provides important insights into the determination of wage rates after the period of formal schooling and explains why age–earning power profiles are rising, rather than flat, over much of the working life for those individuals with continuous labor force experience. One of the most important insights provided by OJT theory is that the value of a worker's marginal product need not equal his or her wage rate at any moment in time under competitive conditions. The $W = VMP$ equality derived in Chapter 3 is replaced by a comparable equality between the *present value* of wage costs and returns from the employer's point of view, and important implications are derived for the behavior of labor turnover.

Many of the topics treated in this chapter are the subject of on-going research on the frontiers of labor economics, and unsettled issues remain. One interesting avenue of research brings the theory of human capital full circle by applying the analysis of firm-oriented investments to the behavior of the family as an entity. In the study of the "economics of divorce," years of marriage, the growth of common interests, and the accumulation of property and children are treated as investments in specific human capital that reduce the probability of "quits" in the form of divorce or separation. This is not just topical; it bears potentially important implications for understanding other aspects of the labor market—the supply of labor, for example, which we have analyzed in previous chapters as resulting from intrafamily decisions on the allocation of time between home and market. Time allocated to home activities is often devoted to child care—investment in children. It should now be apparent that the theory of human capital is a powerful economic tool, one which provides insights into a broader spectrum of social behavior than almost any other body of economic analysis.

---

[19] "Causation among Socioeconomic Time Series," Working Paper No. 246 (Stanford, Calif.: National Bureau of Economic Research, 1978).

Exercises

1. Consider a competitive labor market in which only *general* on-the-job training is available, mobility of workers between firms is costless, and where training occurs only during the first period of a worker's job tenure (period 0). Let

$$W_t \equiv \text{wage rate in period } t \ (t = 0, i, ., T)$$
$$VMP_t \equiv \text{value of marginal product in period } t \ (t = 0, 1, .., T)$$
$$C_t \equiv \text{cost of training in period } t \ (t = 0)$$

   (Assume that W_t, VMP_t, and C_t occur at the *beginning* of a period.)
   (a) What wage rate will a trained worker receive in a period after training is completed? [Present an algebraic expression for W_t ($t = 1, 2, .., T$).] Be sure to justify your answer.
   (b) What wage rate will a worker receive *during* training? (Develop an algebraic expression for W_0.) Support your answer with reference to your solution to part A.

*2. Consider a competitive labor market in which only *specific* training is available, and where training occurs only during the first period of a worker's job tenure (period 0). Let

$$W_t \equiv \text{wage rate in period } t \ (t = 0, 1, .., T)$$
$$VMP_t \equiv \text{value of marginal product in period } t \ (t = 0, 1, .., T)$$
$$C_t \equiv \text{cost of training in period } t \ (t = 0)$$

   (Assume that W_t, VMP_t, and C_t occur at the *beginning* of a period.)
   In the Beltom Corporation (BC), a profit-maximizing organization, the VMP of an untrained worker is (a constant) $200 per period, and C_0 is equal to $130. Moreover, after training VMP rises to a constant $400 per period.
   (a) Beltom needs a new worker. Mr. Y walks into the personnel office and makes Beltom the following offer: He will work for a wage of $200 during his initial employment period (period 0), BC will absorb the cost of specific training, and after he is trained, he will work for two periods (periods 1 and 2) at a wage of $325 in each period. What is Beltom's rate of return on this investment in specific training?
   (b) While they are thinking about Mr. Y's offer, an equally productive potential employee, Ms. X, walks into the personnel office and makes Beltom the following offer: She will work for $200 during her first period of employment (period 0), BC will pay for her specific training, and after completing training, she will work for one period (period

---

*Indicates more difficult exercises

1) for a wage of $244. What is the rate of return to investment in the specific training of Ms. X?

(c) If Beltom can hire only one of the two, which will it hire? Why?

(d) Suppose that society has an "equal opportunity" law that says that Ms. X must be paid the same in each period as Mr. Y since they are equally productive workers; in particular, after training Ms. X must receive a wage of $325 for the one period she desires to work. If Beltom can hire only one of the two individuals, which one will it hire? Support your answer. If the equal opportunity law was designed to "protect" Ms. X, has it in fact made her better off?

*3. Consider Parsons' model of investment in specific human capital, quits, and layoffs described by equations (9-6) to (9-9) and discussed on pages 327–28. Equation (9-9) states that

$$Sw = \frac{W}{a_2} - G,$$

where

$Sw \equiv$ worker financed investment in firm specific human capital, and
$G \equiv$ present value of investments in general human capital.

(a) What is the economic interpretation of $\frac{W}{a_2}$?

(b) Show that if T (total human capital) and S (total firm specific investment in human capital) are described by the linear relations,

$$T = b_0 + b_1 X_1 + b_2 X_2$$
$$S = c_0 + c_1 X_1 + c_3 X_3,$$

where c_i, b_i $(i = 0, \ldots, 3)$ are constants and X_i $(i = 1, \ldots, 3)$ are variables, equation (9-9) may be rewritten as

$$Sw = (c_0 - b_0) + \frac{1}{a_2} W + (c_1 - b_1) X_1 + c_3 X_3 - b_2 X_2.$$

(c) What are the economic interpretations of $(c_1 - b_1)$, c_3, and b_2?

(d) What are the expected qualitative effects of increases in X_1, X_2, and X_3, respectively, on worker quits?

(e) What special information is imparted by empirical knowledge of the effect an increase in X_1 on worker quits?

References

BECKER, GARY S., *Human Capital*. New York: National Bureau of Economic Research, 1975, pp. 16–36.

MINCER, JACOB, "On-the-Job Training: Costs, Returns, and Some Implications." *Journal of Political Economy*, 70, 5, Part 2 (October 1962), pp. 50–79.

————, *Schooling, Experience, and Earnings*. New York: National Bureau of Economic Research, 1974, pp. 7–23; 83–96.

————, "Family Migration Decisions." *Journal of Political Economy*, 86, 5 (October 1978), 749–74.

OI, WALTER Y., "Labor as a Quasi-Fixed Factor." *Journal of Political Economy*, 70, 6 (December 1962), 538–55.

PARSONS, DONALD O., "Specific Human Capital: An Application to Quit Rates and Layoff Rates." *Journal of Political Economy*, 80, 6 (November–December 1972), 1120–43.

ROSEN, SHERWIN, "Short-Run Employment Variation on Class I Railroads in the U.S." *Econometrica*, 36, 3–4 (July 1968), 511–29.

PART V

Some Labor
Market Aspects
of Economic Welfare

CHAPTER 10

Wages
and Wage Structure

A. Educational Objectives
   1. Utilize the theoretical structure developed in previous chapters to help identify the factor(s) underlying the general growth of real wages in the U.S. over time and the distribution of returns to labor in recent years
   2. Examine alternative theoretical interpretations of the observed positive relation between investments in human capital and individuals' earning capacities

B. The Historical Behavior of Real Wage Rates in the United States
   1. Wage growth since 1800
   2. Reasons for the wage growth
      a. Growth of physical capital per worker
      b. Growth of human capital per worker

C. The Distribution of Earning Capacity among Individuals
   1. Overview: Why of interest to economists
   2. Some theoretical considerations
   3. Some statistical considerations
   4. Empirical analysis
      a. The roles of schooling and labor market experience in the distribution of earning capacity in general
      b. Male-female differences: the role of intermittant labor force participation
      c. Occupational and industrial differences: how much insight is provided by the simple human capital framework
      d. Changes over time in wage differences among skill levels

D. Frontiers of Labor Economics: Does Investment in Human Capital Really Increase Labor Market Productivity
   1. Overview: orthodox versus segmented labor market theory
   2. Noncompeting groups: the core of segmented labor market theory

3. Empirical Issues
    a. Estimating the "true" relationship between earning capacity and schooling
    b. Estimating the role of screening in the determination of earning capacity

In this chapter we extend our discussions of the economic rewards to labor to encompass the historical trends in real wages[1] and the structure of earnings in recent years. Knowledge of the determinants of the general structure of payments to labor provides insight into a variety of important issues, including poverty. Among other things, by the time we are finished we hope to have a better idea of why the earning power of a typical individual or family unit may lie below some "poverty level" as established by common agreement, custom, or legislation.

Although we will apply the tools of supply, demand, and investment in human capital developed in previous chapters, understanding real wages and the wage structure is an extremely difficult task. Moreover, this is an area of considerable disagreement among economists. We will often have to admit that the behavior of wages, while consistent with the competitive framework, is also consistent with other interpretations. It is reasonable to say that comprehending wage structures and trends currently constitutes *the* major challenge to researchers in labor economics.

The Historical Behavior of Real Wage Rates
in the United States

Economic theory implies that, in a competitive economy, wage rates tend to equal labor's value of marginal product (VMP). When investment in on-the-job training is considered, the equality between wage rates and VMP still holds, but in a lifetime context—that is, the *present value* of workers' mar-

---

[1]Real wage rates are measured in terms of the goods and services they can buy. Theoretically, the real wage is the slope of the budget constraint describing the individual's tradeoff between hours of leisure and market goods (see pp. 100–101). In practice, real wage rates are usually estimated by dividing a measure of nominal (paycheck) wage rate by an index of the cost of living (for example, the consumer price index). Thus, real wage rates are usually measured in terms of dollars, with reference to a base period when the "purchasing power" of a dollar is taken to be unity. A simple numerical example is useful. Consider a man who earns $5 per hour in 1975 and $5 per hour in 1978, while the consumer price index rises from 1 to 1.10. (The consumer price index is typically multiplied by 100 and recorded in standard sources as having risen from 100 to 110.) He will have experienced a decline in his real wage rate of [$5 − ($5/1.10)] = $0.45. That is, his real wage rate in 1978, in terms of a price index equal to 1.00 in 1975, would be approximately $4.55, while his nominal or money wage rate would still be $5.

ginal contribution to output will tend to equal the *present value* of their lifetime earnings. Even in an economy permeated with monopolies and monopsonies, though, wage rates should rise with productivity (see Chapter 6). Thus, in order to understand the general growth of real wages in the United States, we must identify the factors that have influenced the productivity of labor. In particular, we will take note of increases in nonhuman capital per worker and human capital per worker.

DATA ON REAL WAGES SINCE 1800

Data on real wage rates prior to 1890 are difficult to find. Prior to 1860, they are difficult to find and unreliable. What information there is suggests a moderate and unsteady secular (long-term) increase prior to 1860 and a rather steady increase from around 1880 to 1920. Except for the period of approximately 1930 to 1938, the secular increase in wage rates has continued over the past five and a half decades.[2]

Table 10–1 shows some indicators of real wage rates before 1890. Until 1860 relatively many workers (slaves and the self-employed) were not represented in these average wages. Furthermore, a large portion of wages was paid in kind. Therefore, these data must be interpreted with appropriate caution. Having been warned of their defects, real wage rate data prior to 1860 suggest an average annual rate of growth in the neighborhood of 1 percent. While real wage growth appears to have halted between 1860 and 1880, it seems to have resumed at an annual rate of about 1 percent during the 1880s.[3]

Wage rate data in manufacturing for the period since 1890 are presented in Table 10–2. These data are considerably more reliable than those of Table 10–1, and show that the growth of real wage rates continued at about 1 percent per year through 1915. Since 1915, real wage rates have been increasing by more than 1.5 percent annually.[4] If we consider the period 1890–1975, over which the best data are available, we see that real wage rates in manufacturing were almost four times higher in 1975 than in 1890, and that the average annual rate of growth was about 1.7 percent.

---

[2]Stanley Lebergott, *Manpower in Economic Growth* (New York: McGraw-Hill, 1964), pp. 137–64.

[3]Clarence Long's figures in *Wages and Earnings in the United States, 1860–90* (Princeton, N.J.: Princeton University Press, 1960), Tables A-11 and A-12, suggest that real wage rates rose between 1870 and 1880 as well as from 1880 to 1890. Thus, we are unsure of the behavior of real wage rates, by decade, between 1860 and 1890.

[4]Long reports average real wage increases of about 1.5 percent annually from 1860 to 1890 and about 2.8 percent from 1914 to 1953. While these figures are higher than those derived from Tables 10–1 and 10–2, the change around 1915 is similar. See Ibid., p. 109.

TABLE 10-1

Some Indicators of Real Wage Rates in the United States: 1832–1890

Year	(1)	(2) a	b	(3)	(4)	(5)	(6) a	b
1830				100				
1832	$313	$0.62				$313	$0.62	
1840				91				
1849	292					400		
1850		0.61	$0.87	73			.84	$1.19
1859	346					444		
1860			1.06	78	78			1.35
1869	524		1.55			430		1.27
1870					122			
1879	394					410		
1880			1.23		96			1.28
1889	522				95*	549		
1890			1.46		95*			1.54

Definitions:
  (1) Full-time and full-time equivalent average annual earnings in iron and steel manu-
      facturing.
 (2a) Average daily earnings of common labor, with board.
 (2b) Average daily earnings of common labor, without board.
  (3) Weighted index of retail prices of textiles, shoes, rum and whiskey, coffee, and tea
      (1830 = 100).
  (4) Consumer price index (1830 = 100); *1889 and 1890 figures are the author's estimates.
  (5) (1) ÷ (3) and (4)(× 100).
 (6a) (2a) ÷ (3) and (4)(× 100).
 (6b) (2b) ÷ (3) and (4)(× 100).

Source: Stanley Lebergott, *Manpower in Economic Growth* (New York: McGraw-Hill, 1964),
pp. 541, 545, 548–49.

REASONS FOR THE WAGE GROWTH: RELATIVE INCREASES IN PHYSICAL AND HUMAN CAPITAL

Is the historical growth of real wages consistent with the theory of supply, demand, and investment in human capital under competitive conditions? In particular, can this theory provide insight into the rather sharp increase in wage growth after 1915? If so, then we should be able to find evidence of concomitant growth in the value of the marginal product of labor. We will focus on two sources of growth in labor's *VMP*: (1) an increase in the ratio of physical to human capital in the economy; and (2) an increase in the amount of human capital embodied in each worker. The first source of *VMP* growth is an implication of the *principle of variable proportions*: the marginal productivity of labor rises with the (physical) capital to labor ratio (see Chapter 3). Concerning the second source of growth, *VMP* refers to the extra value of output generated by a small increment in labor of a given

TABLE 10–2

Real Wage Rates in Manufacturing in the United States: 1890–1965

Year	(1)	(2)	(3)	(4)	(5)
1890	$.199		91	.219	
1895	.200		84	.238	
1900	.216		84	.257	
1905	.239		89	.269	
1910	.260		95	.274	
1915	.287		101	.284	
1920	.663	.55	200	.331	.28
1925	.645	.54	175	.368	.31
1930		.55	166		.33
1935		.54	137		.40
1940		.66	140		.47
1945		1.02	179		.57
1950		1.44	240		.61
1955		1.86	267		.70
1960		2.26	294		.77
1965		2.61	314		.83
1970		3.36	386		.87
1975		4.81	536		.90

Definitions:
(1) Average hourly earnings in manufacturing.
(2) Average hourly earnings of production workers in manufacturing.
(3) Consumer price index (1914 = 100).
(4) (1) ÷ (3)(× 100).
(5) (2) ÷ (3)(× 100).

Sources: (1): *Historical Statistics of the United States, Colonial Times to 1970*, Series D766. (2): Ibid., Series D802, *Statistical Abstract of the United States, 1976*, p. 378. (3): *Historical Statistics of the United States*, Rees index through 1914, Series E186; consumer price index, all items 1915–1975, Series E135 (1975 from *Statistical Abstract, 1976*, p. 439). The indexes were adjusted to 1914 = 100.

quality. A greater amount of human capital per worker is equivalent to an increase in labor quality that raises the marginal physical productivity of labor and therefore *VMP*. Not only, then, is a marginal unit of labor more productive when used with a greater amount of capital, but it is also more productive when it is of higher quality (has more human capital embodied in it).[5]

---

[5]To see how these factors positively influence *VMP*, consider a basic neoclassical production function, such as the Cobb-Douglas $Q = \gamma K^\alpha (aL)^{1-\alpha}$, where Q is total output, K is the input of physical capital, a is human capital per unit of labor, L is the quantity of labor, and γ and α are parameters. Thus, we are expressing output as a positive function of the services of physical capital and human capital (aL). To see (1) and (2) in the text, remember that the marginal physical product of labor (*MPP*) is the effect of a change in L on Q, other things remaining the same. For this production function $MPP = \gamma K^\alpha (aL)^{-\alpha} a$. This can also be expressed as $MPP = \gamma \left(\dfrac{K}{L}\right)^\alpha a^{(1-\alpha)}$, which is a positive function of $\left(\dfrac{K}{L}\right)$ and a.

Data on the value of the stock of nonfarm nonresidential structures and equipment (in constant prices) provide an indicator of the amount of physical capital in the United States for the period 1850–1958.[6] This stock increased at an average annual rate of slightly less than 5 percent from 1850 to 1912. From 1912 to 1958, the average annual rate of growth was only 1.6 percent. During similar periods, the labor force grew at rates of 2.5 percent (1850–1910) and 1.2 percent (1920–60), respectively.[7] Clearly, the capital-labor ratio was increasing at the same time wages were rising. However, we are concerned with whether the growth of the capital to labor ratio *accelerated* around 1915, the year in which the growth in wages increased from about 1 percent to 2 percent per year. If in year t the capital to labor ratio is $\frac{K_t}{L_t}$, and if the numerator and denominator grow at the annual rates of r and i, respectively, then in year $t + 1$, the ratio is $\frac{K_t(1 + r)}{L_t(1 + i)}$. From this we see that the annual rate of growth of K/L is $\left[\left(\frac{K_t(1 + r)}{L_t(1 + i)} - \frac{K_t}{L_t}\right)\Big/\frac{K_t}{L_t}\right] = \left[\left(\frac{K_t(1 + r)}{L_t(1 + i)} \div \frac{K_t}{L_t}\right) - 1\right] = \left[\frac{(1 + r)}{(1 + i)} - 1\right]$. Before 1915, the rate of growth of capital to labor was approximately $[(1.05/1.025 - 1] = 0.024$, while after this date it slowed to about $[(1.016/1.012) - 1] = 0.004$. Thus, acceleration in the rate of wage growth is not readily attributable to the behavior over time in the ratio of capital to labor. What, then, is a likely cause of the remarkable increase in the rate of growth of real wages around 1915?

There is evidence that a significant increase in labor force quality (human capital per worker) coincided with the wage trends we seek to understand. Between 1870 and 1910, the proportion of the 17-year-old population graduating from high school rose from 2 percent to 8.8 percent, or by about 2.2 percentage points per decade, while from 1910 to 1930, the proportion rose to 50.8 percent, or by slightly more than 10 percentage points per decade. Further evidence that the United States was increasing its rate of investment in human capital per person is that the fraction of gross national product going into direct educational expenditures rose sharply during the last four decades of the nineteenth century, as shown in Table 10–3. At the same time, the population of school-age children was growing more slowly. The rate of growth of the 5- to 19-year-old population fell fairly sharply after 1890. The growth of this age group had been about 25 percent per decade following the Civil War, but declined to about 16 percent from 1890 to 1900 and fell to less than 13 percent by 1910–20.[8]

Judging from data on direct educational expenditures in the twentieth century, the rising trend of the share of such expenditures in GNP continued

---

[6] *Historical Statistics of the United States*, p. 255.
[7] Ibid., pp. 127, 139.
[8] Ibid., Series A121–123.

TABLE 10-3

Fraction of Direct Educational
Expenditures in Gross National
Product—United States,
1840–1900*

Year	Fraction
1840	.006
1850	.007
1860	.008
1870	.013
1880	.011
1890	.015
1900	.017

*Includes public school expenditures at all levels.

Source: Albert Fishlow, "American Investment in Education," *Journal of Economic History*, 26, 4 (December 1966), 430.

through at least 1930.[9] These trends in the school-age population and educational expenditures combined to increase the per capita quantity of resources devoted to schooling. In addition, declining immigration probably contributed to rising labor force quality, since immigrants tended to have less schooling than the native-born population. For example, the illiteracy rate among native-born whites in 1900 (age 10 and over) was 4.6 percent, while among foreign-born whites it was 12.9 percent.[10]

So, while data on the trends in human capital per worker "match up" better with data on real wages in the United States over time than do the data on the growth of physical capital per worker, the accuracy of these data plus an inability to control for possible intervening factors prohibit us from creating what could be called a thorough explanation of the historical trend of real wage growth over the past century. We hope these defects are remedied in our ensuing analyses of earnings in recent years in the sense that by formulating more precise hypotheses from the theory of supply, demand, and investment in human capital, along with more and better data on earning capacity, our understanding of the levels and distribution of economic welfare exceeds our understanding of the historical trends of wages in general.

Before turning our attention to the distribution of earned income during the last few decades, however, we must at least speculate about the roles of

[9]T. W. Schultz, "Capital Formation by Education," *Journal of Political Economy*, 68, 6 (December 1960), 578.

[10]*Historical Statistics of the United States*, Series H666, 667.

two institutional factors, unionism and minimum wage legislation, in the historical trends of real wages. Although they may have played a part in the upward trend of real wages in recent years (this is somewhat unlikely, however, due to their potentially unfavorable effects on the wages of "uncovered" workers—see pp. 163–66), it certainly would be difficult to attribute the wage growth before 1915, as well the increased wage growth around 1915, to unions or minimum wage legislation. The proportion of the labor force consisting of union members was too small and unstable to have been an important influence on wages, and nationwide minimum wage legislation was not enacted until much later.

The Distribution of Earning Capacity among Individuals

In this section we examine the structure of individuals' earning capacities. The topic has occupied a great deal of the attention of economists for two reasons. One is a concern with the determinants of income inequality; the other is a concern about how well labor markets function to allocate labor among alternative employments and, concomitantly, to determine wages. These two concerns are certainly not unrelated. If we wish to alter income distribution, a knowledge of how it is generated is essential. Moreover, our evaulation of the desirability of an existing wage structure may depend in part on the degree to which workers seem to be paid according to their productivities. If the former concern is not obvious, suppose that society decides the earnings of executives are too high relative to the earnings of production workers and imposes a progressive income tax as a "remedy." If the earnings of executives are relatively high because they are remunerated for specialized skills acquired through education and training and for a willingness to assume risk and responsibility, a tax may eventually reduce the willingness of individuals to supply these qualities. In this case, the pretax remuneration of executives will increase and, after an adjustment period, the pretax income distribution may become *more* unequal than before the income tax. However, if the relatively high remuneration of executives occurs because they possess special talents which are inborn traits whose only use is in executive activities, an income tax would reduce the "rents" (payments in excess of value in their most attractive employment alternatives) received for these talents, but probably not reduce the amount of executive talent supplied to the economy in the long run.

SOME THEORETICAL CONSIDERATIONS

There are many ways to define wage structure, the appropriate definition depending on what is of interest from the point of view of economic analysis or public policy. The basis for understanding the wage structure, however, is the theory of supply, demand, and human capital developed in previous chapters and used to help interpret the historical course of real wage rates in the last section. This analytical framework was summarized in Chapter 8 in terms of the individual's supply and demand for human capital. It is repeated in Figure 10–1. Individual investment in human capital is determined by the relevant human capital supply and demand curves. A particular individual could be characterized, for example, by demand curve D_a or D_b and supply curve S_1 or S_2. Factors such as individual differences in aptitude, ability, or family wealth determine the relative positions of the demand and supply curves. Since wealth maximization requires investing up to the point where the relevant supply and demand curves intersect (so long as the rate of return to human capital surpasses that to nonhuman capital), the correlation between demand and supply is an important influence on the distribution of wage rates and earnings.

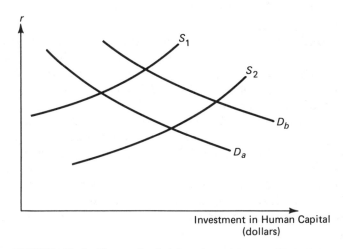

FIGURE 10–1. Human Capital Supply and Demand Schedules

For example, if persons who are able to enjoy relatively large benefits from investment in human capital also have relatively easy access to investable funds (perhaps due to scholarships given out on the basis of ability), S_2 goes with D_b and S_1 with D_a. Since earning power is determined by the area under the demand curve up to the amount invested, the difference between the earning power of individuals "a" and "b" will be greater if their supply curves are 1 and 2, respectively, than if the relationship were reversed. That is, a positive correlation between the demand and supply of human capital investment will work toward increasing the dispersion of labor market earning power among individuals.

If everyone had the same demand curve but differed in the availability of funds for investment in human capital, the only reason for differences in human capital investment would be variation in supply curves, and the intersections of supply and demand would constitute a locus of points describing the demand curve for human capital. Earnings would increase, and the rate of return decline, with rising investment per person in schooling, training, and other forms of human capital. On the other hand, if everyone had the same supply curve but different demand curves, the rate of return (and earning power) would rise with human capital investment. Finally, if everyone had the same demand and supply curve, there would be equality in the amount of human capital investment (for example, there would be no individual differences in schooling) and real earning power would be equal. The only reason for wage rate inequality would be nonpecuniary differences in job characteristics. Persons who worked at relatively unpleasant or hazardous jobs would receive compensatory wage premiums (see the discussion in Chapter 5 on job hazards).

SOME STATISTICAL CONSIDERATIONS

Before proceeding, let us reflect a bit on the nature of the statistical tools we will employ in the investigation of wage structure, most of which are covered in Chapter 2. In the remainder of this chapter we will apply the methodology discussed there to observed behavior, guided by the competitive theory of wage determination.

In utilizing competitive theory to help understand the observed wage structure, we are forced, because of limited information, to test very simple hypotheses; specifically, we must assume that many variables omitted from our regressions are uncorrelated with the independent variables under consideration. Another reason we must test simple hypotheses from competitive theory is the "low" level at which we have contrasted the behavioral implications of the theory of competition with those of theories with noncompetitive postulates (that is, monopoly or monopsony). Realistically, we are not in a position to confirm or refute competitive theory with a high degree of certainty. Nevertheless, testing simple hypotheses derived from competitive theory does provide insights into the determinants of wage behavior.

INCOME INEQUALITY AMONG INDIVIDUALS IN GENERAL: EMPIRICAL ANALYSIS

Underlying any of the measures of wage structure we could study is the distribution of labor market earning power among individuals in general. To gain insight into this distribution, we rely on the model of human capital investment depicted in Figure 10–1 and summarized in the human capital earning power function developed in Chapters 8 and 9, the simplest form of which is

$$\ln Y = \ln Y_0 + r_1 S + r_2 k X \qquad (10\text{–}1)$$

where r_1 and r_2 represent the rates of return to schooling and OJT, respectively; k represents the proportion of the worker's time devoted to OJT investment; and X, years of labor market experience. Inequality of market earning among individuals is captured by variation in the left-hand side of equation (10-1). In the human capital framework, this inequality is explainable in terms of variables on the right-hand side that represent human capital investments. Schooling and OJT need not be the only forms of human capital investment used to explain income inequality, but the practical matter of the availability of quality data limits the extent to which other variables are incorporated in empirical work.

The human capital approach emphasizes the importance of life-cycle considerations in determining the distribution of wages in the economy and points out the importance of a theoretical framework when interpreting economic data. The natural measure of economic welfare emerging from human capital analysis is the present value of lifetime earnings, rather than wages received in any particular year. Equation (10-1) makes it clear why this is so; market earning power is not given once schooling is complete, but rises over the years as experience is acquired. This is illustrated in Chapter 9, where the annual earnings of someone who completes five years of schooling initially falls short of the earnings received by a worker who receives slightly less schooling, later overtakes, and finally surpasses them. Moreover, in a population with persons of the same age but different amounts of schooling, we would obtain quite different pictures of the degree of income inequality depending upon which year we measured annual income, *even if the lifetime present value of persons with five years of schooling were equal to that of persons who acquired one to five years* (why?).

Unfortunately, data on individuals' lifetime earnings streams are not generally available, so it is virtually impossible to study the personal distribution of present values of lifetime earnings. Moreover, interpersonal differences in current earning power often represent a concomitant disparity of lifetime earnings prospects. Therefore, there seems to be some merit, as well as necessity, to analyzing earning-power dispersion with data on current wage rates, or earnings.[11]

When the human capital earning power equation is used to estimate the returns to schooling and experience with data for individuals, it also provides some evidence concerning the importance of investment in human capital in understanding the personal distribution of income. Recall the following esti-

---

[11] In what follows we approach the issue of the dispersion of labor market success among workers somewhat casually. Specifically, we do not go beyond the level of theoretical and statistical analysis of earning capacity determination developed thus far and introduce any of the formal measures of wage dispersion such as the variance of the natural logarithm of earnings $[\sigma^2(\ln y)]$ or the Gini coefficient. For a simple explanation of and recent data for the latter, see Lloyd G. Reynolds, *Labor Economics and Labor Relations*, 7th ed. (Englewood Cliffs, N.J.: Prentice-Hall, 1978), pp. 273–77. For a formal statistical analysis of $\sigma^2(\ln y)$, see Jacob Mincer, *Schooling, Experience and Earnings* (New York: Columbia University Press, for The National Bureau of Economic Research, 1974), Chap. 2.

mate reported in Chapter 9, based on work of Mincer with 1960 census data for out-of-school nonfarm white men aged 64 and less

$$\ln Y = 6.20 + .107S + .081X - .0012X^2, \; R^2 = 0.29 \qquad (10\text{--}2)$$

where Y is annual earnings in 1959, S is schooling, and X is a measure of experience. In studying the personal distribution of earning power, we focus on the R^2 statistic to a greater extent than when our major interest was just the returns to schooling and experience. The coefficient of determination (R^2) equals 0.29, which tells us that the variables representing investment in human capital are capable of accounting for between one-fourth and one-third of the variation in the earnings of a large group of the United States population. When you think of the host of additional factors that must also influence earnings, such as individual differences in ability, health, luck, the pleasantness or unpleasantness of particular jobs, and unemployment experience, the statistical performance of schooling and experience is quite impressive.

A word of caution is called for, however. Some of the variables omitted from Mincer's estimate of the human capital earning power function reported above may be correlated with schooling and experience (can you cite some examples?), and their influence on income may therefore be represented indirectly. Ability and time unemployed are likely possibilities. Of course, to the extent that schooling and other investments in human capital increase economic welfare by reducing the risk of unemployment,[12] it may not be "unfair" to omit unemployment experience from the human capital earning power function when attempting to explain the personal income distribution. Another problem with Mincer's approach also arises from the use of labor market earnings rather than the rate of pay for a fixed time period as the dependent variable. By using a measure of earnings rather than earning power more strictly defined, individual work-leisure decisions may confound estimates of the human capital earnings function, since hours and weeks of work will be influenced by earning power and hence affect earnings (see Chapter 4).

Evidence that these omitted variables and specification problems are not responsible for the explanatory power of schooling and experience is found in another study. Using data for a national sample of out-of-school men aged 27 years old or less in 1969, Griliches[13] found that years of schooling and age alone account for 29 percent in the variation of hourly wage rates on current or last job. Given his dependent variable, omission of unemployment experience as an independent variable in equation (10–2) is probably not a serious problem.

---

[12]Recall from Chapter 9 that firm-specific OJT reduces the probability that the firm will lay off a worker when there is a decline in demand for the firm's output.

[13]Zvi Griliches, "Estimating the Returns to Schooling: Some Econometric Problems," *Econometrica*, 45, 1 (January 1977), 1–22.

In summary, interpersonal differences in human capital investments appear to be capable of accounting for a significant amount of income inequality. Later on in this chapter, we ask the important policy question of whether this explanatory power tells us that, by promoting equality in human capital investments through access to schooling and experience opportunities, we can enhance the economic opportunities of the poor.

MALE-FEMALE EARNINGS DIFFERENTIALS:
EMPIRICAL ANALYSIS

Worker investments in OJT cause wage rates to increase with work experience. For individuals with a strong labor force attachment—reflected in more or less continuous labor force participation—wage rates tend to rise more or less continuously with age over their working lives. However, those who devote much time to activities in the household will not obtain as much OJT, and their market wage rates will accordingly show a relatively small increase (if any) over their working lives. Not only will there be less investment in human capital simply because there is less work experience, but there will also be less incentive to invest in OJT while working, since the expected returns to such investment are positively related to expected future labor force participation. Depreciation of skills when an individual is out of the labor force may also occur. Thus, the theory of investment in human capital may help us to understand some of the causes of differences in the market earning power of men and women—particularly married women who devote a substantial proportion of their lives to the care of children.[14] This is not to say that there has not been discrimination against women in the labor market that has resulted in lower wage rates for women than for men of equal training and ability. However, in order to gain any idea of the likely magnitude of the effect of discrimination on the wage rates of women, or any other group, it is absolutely essential to know what wage rates would be in the absence of discrimination. Thus, applying the theory of human capital is a necessary step toward ultimately understanding why some parts of the population receive lower wage rates than others.

Applying human capital theory to explain male-female wage differentials involves, first of all, a simple modification of the human capital earning power function, equation (10–2). The empirical results are then used to "explain" the difference in earning power between men and women. Modifica-

---

[14]The material in this section draws heavily on two papers: Jacob Mincer and Solomon W. Polachek, "Family Investments in Human Capital: Earnings of Women," *Journal of Political Economy*, 82, 2, part II (March–April 1974), S76–S108; and Steven H. Sandell and David Shapiro, "The Theory of Human Capital and the Earnings of Women: A Reexamination of the Evidence," *Journal of Human Resources*, 13, 1 (winter 1978), 103–17. See also Jacob Mincer and Solomon W. Polachek, "Women's Earnings Reexamined," *Journal of Human Resources*, 13, 1 (winter 1978), 118–34.

tion of equation (10–2) is necessary to explain the wage rates of women because women who leave the labor force to care for children do not have continuous labor force experience. Specifically, the single variable X in equation (10–2) is replaced with a set of variables designed to reflect discontinuous, or segmented, labor market experience. One such modification results in the earning power function

$$\ln Y = \ln Y_0 + r_1 S + r_2 X_1 + r_2 X_2 + r_3 h \tag{10–3}$$

where X_1 is total number of years of labor market experience since leaving school, X_2 is the number of years worked on current or last job, and h is years in which at least six months were spent out of the labor force. A difference between r_1 and r_2 would reflect a difference in the amounts of time devoted to OJT or in the rates of return between the most recent job and earlier jobs, (those before the birth of children). The coefficient r_3 is expected to be zero or negative, reflecting the possibility that human capital depreciates during periods of absence from the labor force.

Sandell and Shapiro[15] estimated equation (10–3) by means of two-stage least squares regression analysis, using a sample of 1,028 white married women age 30 to 44 who were working and living with their husbands in 1966. The data are from the National Longitudinal Surveys. Two-stage least squares is called for because of a likely simultaneous equations problem, as discussed in Chapter 2. The simultaneity would arise because, given the variables included in equation (10–3), some women will have better labor market opportunities than others, and this may influence their lifetime participation decisions. Consequently, causation could run from the wage rate to the experience variables as well as in the hypothesized direction from experience to market earning power. Two-stage least squares is designed to permit the estimation of the effect of experience on earning power, unbiased by the possibility of "reverse causation."[16]

Sandell and Shapiro obtained the following regression coefficients when they estimated equation (10–3) by means of two-stage least squares regression analysis:

Variable	Estimated Coefficient	t Value
S	0.058	10.5
X_1	0.008	2.5
X_2	0.016	6.7
h	−0.006	1.8

---

[15]"Earnings of Women." The original formulation of equation (10–3) is from Mincer and Polachek, "Family Investments."

[16]For more details, including the list of "exogenous" variables used in the two-stage estimation procedure, consult the original article, cited above.

One of the most striking aspects of these regression results is that a considerably smaller coefficient of the effect of experience on market earning power was estimated for women than for men.[17] Evidently women obtain a smaller rate of return to OJT than do men, or devote a smaller proportion of their market working time to human capital investment. The reason why married women may invest less than men was discussed above. From the marginally significant coefficient of h we may infer that some depreciation of labor-market-oriented human capital may occur during years spent outside the labor force, but the magnitude is not extremely large. Time spent on the most recent job results in twice as rapid an increase in the current wage rate as experience on other jobs. This is presumably due to job-specific aspects of current OJT which would have been lost when previous jobs were given up.

The regression coefficients shown above can be used to help explain the difference in wage rates between white married men and women age 30 to 44. (In 1966 this wage gap was a little more than $1 per hour, or about 50 percent of the average wage rate for married women.) The procedure is to answer the question, "How much would the sex differential in wage rates narrow if the work experience of women were the same as that of men, but the female coefficients remained as they are?" That is, the differences between men and women in the variables X_1, X_2, and h are multiplied by the female regression coefficients. The sum of these products is then added to the mean wage rate of women to see how close the wage of women would be to that of men if they were like men in work experience.[18] Approximately one-quarter of the male-female wage gap is eliminated with this procedure, leaving three-quarters unexplained by the difference in labor market experience (average schooling is about the same for men and women). The unexplained male-female wage gap may be taken as the upper boundary of the effect of discrimination, although caution is called for in drawing this inference.[19]

OCCUPATIONAL AND INDUSTRIAL EARNINGS DIFFERENCES: HOW MUCH INSIGHT IS PROVIDED BY THE SIMPLE HUMAN CAPITAL FRAMEWORK?

Finally, the human capital approach to the study of wage rates should also lead to an understanding of wage differences among occupations and industries. Almost by definition, we should observe wage differences among workers in the various occupations. Since occupations are defined, by and large, according to the nature of the tasks or skills performed, it is through a focus on schooling and training as avenues through which individuals

---

[17]Comparable estimates for men are not shown. Data for married men aged 30–44 in 1966 were taken from the *Survey of Economic Opportunity*.

[18]For more detailed analysis of such a statistical technique, see the three articles cited in footnote 16.

[19]Solomon W. Polachek, "Potential Biases in Measuring Male-Female Discrimination," *Journal of Human Resources*, 10, 2 (spring 1975), 205–29.

develop job skills that human capital theory lends insight into the occupational wage structure. So, in examining evidence on human capital investments in Chapters 8, 9, and in the preceding section of this chapter we have indirectly acquired some insights into the determinants of the occupational wage structure. The understanding of interoccupational wage differences and its behavior over time rests on our ability to organize available information on occupations through the systematic approach of human capital theory.

A competitive economy in equilibrium should exhibit interindustry wage-rate differences that reflect only interindustry differences in worker skill mixes and employment conditions such as region, pleasantness of work, risk to health, and cyclical variability of employment, to name a few. There should be no *persistent* interindustry wage differentials due to conditions such as difference in capital-to-labor ratios because workers will seek employment where wage rates are highest and because employers will seek to pay workers of given quality the lowest possible wage rates; both of these activities produce forces that tend to equalize wage rates. Nor should there be an association (*cet. par.*) between wage rates and the *amounts* of labor and capital employed. Judging when other things are in fact equal or have remained unchanged, however, so that economic theory in its simplest (usually competitive) form can be applied and tested, is one of the most difficult aspects of applied work in economics.

The hypotheses about the occupational and industrial wage structures presented pertain mainly to conditions of long-run labor market equilibrium. Occupations and industries also differ among themselves with respect to recent changes in the demand for workers. When there is a change in demand for workers, we cannot expect the supply response to be highly elastic over *short* periods of time. Human capital theory emphasizes that it takes time and money to acquire information about changing labor market conditions and to engage in any formal and informal training that may be required to change jobs. When workers have acquired knowledge about their jobs and firm specific human capital, they will certainly be reluctant to quit and accept new jobs (which may require a costly geographical relocation) for only a slight and perhaps uncertain improvement of pay. Expanding industries and occupations may therefore exhibit extraordinarily high wage rates, and contracting industries or occupations the opposite. Moreover, trade unions may act to limit the number of workers in particular industries and occupations. Unionism and recent changes in labor demand, then, will contribute to the variation of wage rates among occupations and industries.

To what extent can occupational and industrial wage data be interpreted in terms of a long run equilibrium labor market in which there exist interindustry and interoccupation differences in worker productivities? Specifically, once schooling and age (experience) and other worker characteristics are taken into consideration, is there any systematic variation remaining among occupational and industrial categories? If so, such differences may be attributable in part to short-term demand or supply forces, unionism, pleasantries of work, or risk to health and life, and so on.

One study that can be used to explore the answer to the questions posed in the last paragraph is that of Hanoch, based on 1960 U.S. Census data for 34,180 men (see Chapter 8). Table 10–4 exhibits partial results of Hanoch's research, which consists of a regression analysis of annual earnings expressed as a function of the variables indicated, plus others (not shown) representing place of residence, birth, family characteristics, residential characteristics, and weeks worked.[20] Note that almost all the occupation and industry groups have large and significant differences in annual earnings, despite the fact that education, age, race, sex, and other relevant worker characteristics are held constant.[21]

When occupational and industry variables and weeks worked are removed from the regression reported in Table 10–4, the R^2 statistic falls by 8 percentage points to .265. This figure is quite close to the degree of explanatory power exhibited by schooling and age (experience) *alone* in the human capital earning power functions estimated by Mincer with similar data (p. 350). Thus, interindustry and interoccupational factors other than the personal characteristics reflected in Table 10–4 reduce the variation in wages unexplained by schooling and experience by only about 20 percent. Although industry, occupation, race, and region variables no doubt capture the influence of noncompetitive elements in the economy, such as discrimination, unions, monopsony, and product market monopoly, these variables also reflect short-term deviations from equilibrium, nonpecuniary differences in employment conditions, and variation in the cost-of-living among regions of the United States. Similarly, the variation in wages, *unexplained* by the variables included in the regression reported in Table 10–4 is also attributable to the above noncompetitive forces, as well as to our failure to capture fully the effects of "luck," ability, and other personal characteristics.

CHANGES OVER TIME IN WAGE DIFFERENTIALS AMONG SKILL LEVELS

One reason an understanding of changes in the wage structure over time is of interest is because it identifies many of the forces affecting the personal distribution of earning power. We believe that the preponderance of evidence available suggests that rates of return to schooling decline with the amount of

---

[20]Since the dependent variable is annual earnings in 1959 and weeks worked was included as a right-hand variable in the regression (although it is not shown in Table 10–4) the regression coefficients approximate those which would have been obtained had the dependent variable been the weekly rate of pay.

[21]All the variables shown in Table 10–4 are dummy variables. The use of dummy variables is discussed in Chapter 2.

TABLE 10-4

Estimates of the Wage Function: Males of Age 25–64 with Earnings in 1959

Variable	Coefficient (in dollars)	St. Error	Variable	Coefficient (in dollars)	St. Error
Constant Term	−1,750	282	Occupation		
			Professional	414	93
Schooling (years)			Farmers & Farm Mgrs.	−1,966	270
0–4	−1,073	106	Managers, Officials, Prop.	1,821	83
5–7	−938	76	Clerical & Kindred plus Sales	−38	77
8	−755	69	Craftsmen, Foremen	0	
9–11	−446	61	Operatives	−402	65
12	0		Service & Private Household	−677	101
13–15	650	78	Farm Laborers	−383	285
16	1886	98	Not Reported	760	118
17+	3,191	115			
			Industry		
Age			Agriculture	−747	238
25–34	0		Contract Construction	−20	75
35–44	789	55	Manufacturing	0	
45–54	941	61	Transportation	−81	76
55–64	782	74	Trade	−816	66
			Services & Industry	−936	74
Race Region			Not Reported		
Southern Whites	−410	52	Public Administration	−848	88
Northern Whites	0				
Southern Nonwhites	−1,069	105	$R^2 = .345$		
Northern Nonwhites	−725	106			

Notes: The sample, from the 1:1,000 sample of the 1960 U.S. *Census of Population*, consists of 34,180 males with mean earnings of $5,530.60 in 1959. The unit of measurement of the coefficients is dollars. Variables included in the regression whose coefficients are not reported here, but whose influence is, however, not reflected in the coefficients reported, include residence (rural, urban, etc.), family characteristics, weeks worked, and marital status. Coefficients measure deviations of income from the category whose coefficient is zero. *E.g.*, men with 0–4 years of schooling earned $1073 less per year than high school graduates, *cet. par.*

Source: Giora Hanoch, "Personal Earnings and Investment in Schooling" (Ph.D. dissertation, University of Chicago, 1965), pp. 24–25.

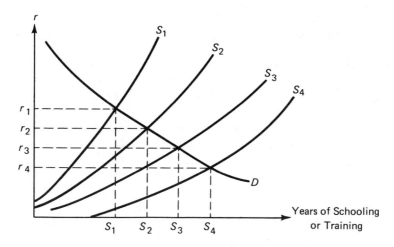

FIGURE 10–2. The Effect of Increases in Nonhuman Wealth on the Level of and Rate of Return to Schooling or Training

investment. Moreover, both theory[22] and evidence[23] suggest that the rate of return to years of schooling does not increase markedly with ability. These considerations suggest that we can adopt Figure 10–2 as a reasonable framework for analyzing wage differentials over time. (Note that the horizontal axis of Figure 10–2 measures years of schooling or training rather than the dollar amount of investment in human capital.)

What does the model of human capital characterized by Figure 10–2 imply for the behavior of the economy-wide wage structure over time? The difference between individuals who face supply curves like S_1 and those who face S_2, S_3, or S_4 is presumably access to family nonhuman wealth that can be used to finance human capital investment. If r_4 (the rate of return to completing four years of college and concomitant OJT) is about equal to the rate of return to investment in nonhuman capital in the economy, then increases in nonhuman wealth for this group of individuals would not lead to further investment in human capital. On the other hand, for less wealthy families, increases in wealth, shifting S_1, S_2, and S_3 to the right, would tend to increase human capital investment per person. Thus, increasing real income levels over time should lead to *rising levels of schooling* and other forms of human capital investment.

As the proportion of the population completing high school and college increased, it would not be surprising to observe the rate of return to these

[22]Zvi Griliches, "Estimating the Returns to Schooling"; Thomas J. Kniesner and Solomon W. Polachek, "Ability, Schooling, and the Rate of Return to Education: Toward a More Complete Representation," Department of Economics, University of North Carolina, Working Paper 77–78, September 1978.
[23]Ibid.

levels of investment declining because of a clockwise rotation and leftward shift of the *demand* curve in Figure 10–2. To see this more clearly, recall that the rate of return is approximated by the *proportionate increase* in earning power attributable to a unit increase in human capital investment (Chapter 8, equation 8–10). For example, what happens to the rate of return depends in part on the economy-wide demand for college graduates relative to high school dropouts, as rising levels of income facilitate the completion of four years of college. There is no reason to believe, however, that there will also be a concomitant growth in the *relative demand* for college graduates. In the face of an increasing labor force ratio of college grads to high school dropouts, the relative reward to completing college should decline (reflected in a leftward shift and clockwise rotation of D in Fig. 10–2) unless there is an offsetting increase in relative demand for college graduates.

Evidence suggests that there has been both a long-term narrowing of wage differentials by degree of skill and of the rate of return to completing college (and high school) in the United States.[24] On the basis of admittedly skimpy evidence, Becker concludes that " . . . rates of return on both high school and college education declined rather significantly during the first forty years of the (twentieth) century, and then stopped declining and even rose during the next twenty years."[25] Until 1940 the decline would have coincided with the unprecedented increase in schooling levels that in the first part of this chapter we asserted was a basic cause of real wage growth and is consistent with the hypothesis on wage differentials presented in the preceding paragraphs. Freeman[26] provides evidence that the rate of return to a college degree dropped from the late 1960s through the early 1970s. Although he notes that this decline in the reward of a college education coincides with the coming of age of the "baby boom" cohorts of the 1950s and a possible temporary decline in the economy's relative demand for college-trained workers, what Freeman has observed may also be a resumption of the earlier downward trend in the rate of return to schooling.

Frontiers of Labor Economics: Does Investment in Human Capital Really Affect Labor Market Productivity?

We have focused on the role played by human capital investment, particularly schooling, in influencing the level and structure of real wage rates. The associations observed between schooling and earning power have been

---

[24]See, for example, Paul G. Keat, "Long Run Changes in Occupational Wage Structure 1900–56," *Journal of Political Economy*, 68, 6 (December 1960), 584–600; and Becker, *Human Capital*, Chapter VI.

[25]*Human Capital*, p. 212.

[26]Richard B. Freeman, "Overinvestment in College Training?" *Journal of Human Resources*, 10, 3 (summer 1975), 287–311; "The Decline in the Economic Rewards to College Education," *The Review of Economics and Statistics*, 59, 1 (February 1977), 18–29.

assumed to reflect a causal relationship in which schooling (and other human capital investments) result in higher wage rates because they increase labor market productivity. This subject has important implications for social policy. If our interpretation is true, then low incomes are correctable by appropriate "doses" of schooling, training, and other forms of human capital. In particular, should interpersonal differences in human capital investments be due primarily to differences among families in the availability of funds to finance these investments, as depicted in Figure 10–2, then the provision of subsidies to schooling and training for "disadvantaged" persons ought to improve their market earning power. A belief in the efficacy of schooling in raising market productivity is one of the traditional reasons for support of government subsidies to education. If, on the other hand, the observed association between schooling and wage rates does not represent a causal relationship, the outlook for improving the lot of the poor through schooling, training, and other "manpower" approaches is dim. Those social scientists who adopt the latter view generally favor either more direct interference in labor markets (government creation of new jobs, for example) or income transfers as means of alleviating poverty.[27]

The orthodox approach to the subject of human capital investments, labor market productivity, and earning capaicty has its roots in the eighteenth-century writings of Adam Smith,[28] and criticism of it goes back at least as far as the works of Karl Marx and J. S. Mill.[29] Despite the diversity of approaches and the 125 years over which these critical studies have appeared, there is a common thread running through them that may be called the concept of **noncompeting groups**, or **segmented labor markets**.[30] In this section we will highlight some of the basic features of these criticisms of the orthodox, or neoclassical, approaches to wage differentials. In doing this we will try to shed light on whether the SLM theories are truly distinct from neoclassical analysis or whether they merely emphasize certain features of labor markets already recognized but given relatively little attention by orthodox economists. Finally, we will examine briefly some empirical implications of the segmentation theories, contrast them with those of neoclassical theory where possible, and suggest how these contrasting hypotheses fare when confronted with available data. This subject matter is controversial, and the conclusions we reach do not represent general agreement among economists.

---

[27]Of course, not all low-income persons could be helped by schooling and training even under the most favorable circumstances. Mental and physical handicaps and old age can create conditions, which cannot be corrected by after-the-fact human capital investments.

[28]*The Wealth of Nations* (New York: Modern Library, 1968). See Book I, Chap. 10.

[29]A summary of the history of economic thought in this area and a critique of alternative approaches is found in Glen G. Cain, "The Challenge of Segmented Labor Market Theories to Orthodox Theory: A Survey," *Journal of Economic Literature*, 14, 4 (December 1976), 1215–57.

[30]Ibid.

The concept of noncompeting groups or segmented labor markets can be understood in terms of the human capital demand and supply curves depicted in Chapter 8 and the age-earning power profiles of Chapters 8 and 9. In terms of age-earning power profiles, the neoclassical view is depicted in Figure 10–3. A typical individual is assumed to have sufficient prior knowledge and ability to choose between job x with age–earning power profile x and job y with its age–earning power profile y, where earning power is defined to be net of any direct costs of human capital investments. Profile y cannot lie completely above x. If it did, workers would leave job x for job y, raising wage rates in x and lowering them in y until the lifetime present values of earning capacity in the two respective employment alternatives were equal. This requires that the two curves cross, as is shown in Figure 10–3.

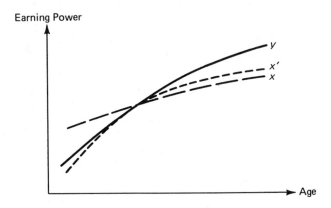

FIGURE 10–3. Neoclassical and SLM Views of Alternative Age-Earning Power Profiles

In the SLM approach, y and x are not viewed as feasible alternatives for the same individual. If someone who were a typical x worker were to become a y by, say, acquiring a college education, he or she would not earn y, but a lower amount—say x'. This might be due to race or sex discrimination—for example, where employers refuse to hire the worker with a college degree to fill a job which provides the OJT necessary to generate age–earning power profile y. A second reason why the amount of schooling normally associated with y might not result in the typical x worker obtaining job y is that he or she lacks other forms of human capital or "ability," which enhance the effectiveness of schooling in creating labor market productivity. For example, if one comes from a "disadvantaged" background in which good work habits, knowledge of how to get the most out of school, and so on, are not acquired, this can lower the effectiveness of schooling in providing access to job y.[31]

Orthodox economists who view human capital theory as a valuable tool of labor market analysis certainly recognize the possibility that discrimination against workers on the basis of race, sex, or other personal characteristics influences wage rates and the allocation of labor. Moreover, human capital theory has not been limited to the analysis of investments in schooling and OJT. Theoretical and empirical analyses have dealt with parents' allocation of time to child rearing, the effectiveness of this time as conditioned by parents' schooling and other characteristics in altering an offspring's "ability," schooling, and labor market earning power, and the direct association between parental characteristics and an offspring's labor market achievements. So, there is little doubt that more than just schooling and OJT is involved in the determination of ones labor market "success." From the point of view of policy, the crucial issues separating orthodox economists and those who seriously question the usefulness of human capital analysis are, then: (1) the degree to which "family background" variables interact with (dominate?) schooling and OJT in determining labor market success, and (2) the most effective and proper means of offsetting adverse background influences.[32]

In terms of the simple human capital supply and demand curves developed earlier, it is probably fair to characterize the SLM approach as emphasizing the importance of individual differences in demand for human capital investment, relative to differences in supply, in determining labor market outcomes. In the SLM view, as depicted in Figure 10-4, family background, (correctly) pessimistic expectations about the future, and discrimination may all interact to cause the demand for human capital investment of x workers to lie far to the left of that for y workers. Since families of x workers also have relatively low incomes, their supply curves of investible funds also lie far to the left, resulting in less human capital investment and lower earnings. Bear in mind that when we say x workers' demand curves lie to the left of those for y workers, we are not saying that the former individuals necessarily desire less income than the latter, or that they have less "ambition," but rather that their view of the productivity of investing in human capital leads

---

[31]Insofar as family background influences manner of speech, social behavior, and the like, and these individual characteristics alter the effectiveness of schooling and training in generating labor market success, the difference between the effect of family background on forms of human capital other than schooling and discrimination against certain groups of workers becomes rather hazy.

[32]The word "proper" is used advisedly. Suppose we were certain that parental behavior in the home was diminishing a child's future earning prospects. When is it ethically permissible to deprive the parents of their freedom of choice in rearing their children? In the United States, supporters of neither orthodox nor SLM views typically advocate interfering directly with parental prerogatives in child rearing beyond compulsory school attendance and making available programs such as Head Start.

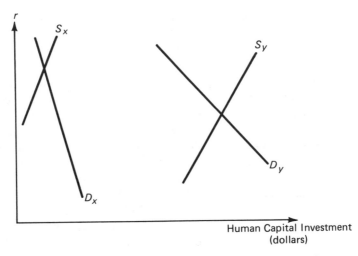

FIGURE 10–4. Human Capital Supply and Demand Curves: Noncompeting Groups

them (rationally) to demand less of it than *y* workers. Moreover, social policy that makes it easier for *x* workers to invest by providing free tuition, low-cost loans, subsidized training, and so on, will not increase the incomes of *x* workers as much as might be expected on the basis of *y* workers' experience, because the human capital demand curves reflect the efficacy of these forms of investments in generating labor market productivity. Thus, without more drastic forms of action, the SLM approach views *x* workers as doomed to holding "bad" jobs with little opportunity for advancement, while *y* workers get "good" jobs with higher incomes and plentiful opportunities for OJT. Low-income workers not only acquire relatively little schooling, but also have little incentive to do so. Efforts to increase their schooling would not provide them with the more favorable labor market opportunities of *y* workers.

Underlying the SLM approach is the concept of a "dual" labor market, consisting of "internal" and "external" components.[33] In the external market, " . . . pricing, allocating, and training decisions are controlled directly by economic variables. These two markets are interconnected, . . . and movements between them occurs at certain job classifications which constitute *ports of entry and exit.* . . . The remainder of the jobs within the internal market are filled by promotion or transfer of workers who have already gained entry. Consequently, these jobs are shielded from the *direct* influences

---

[33]This concept has been popularized, although by no means originated, by Peter B. Doeringer and Michael Piore in their *Internal Labor Markets and Manpower Analysis* (Lexington, Mass.: Heath, 1971).

of competitive forces in the external market."[34] If Doeringer and Piore's description of the dual labor market does not seem altogether strange to you, it is because you should recognize that it is also consistent with a labor market characterized by the importance of firm-specific OJT in many jobs, as implied by neoclassical human capital theory! In neoclassical terms, the external market is populated by workers whose human capital is not firm-specific, while the internal labor market is governed to a greater extent by the implications of firm-specific investment in workers.[35] So, it is consistent with *both* orthodox and SLM theories that workers in the "external" market also have acquired less total human capital and have lower earning power than workers in the "internal" labor market.

The ability of the dual labor market approach to rationalize observations that are also consistent with orthodox labor market and human capital theory reemphasizes the difficulty in empirically differentiating between the SLM and neoclassical labor market theories. So far, no one has integrated the various strands of segmented labor market theories into a cohesive, internally consistent whole, distinguishing SLM hypotheses from those of neoclassical labor market theory in a manner generally accepted by both sides. In the next section we present our view of a few of the important empirical issues that have been treated by economists on both sides of the fence.

EMPIRICAL ISSUES

The policy significance of the SLM approach is that schooling and OJT—particularly the former—will generally be unsuccessful in bettering the economic welfare of the poor. Observed positive relationships between schooling and earning power are thought to be spurious, interpreted as the result of forces that have nothing to do with a causal relationship between schooling and labor market productivity. Two explanations of the alleged spurious relationship are these: (1) Those who achieve higher schooling levels are more able than others, and the more able also happen to obtain more schooling, and (2) schooling acts as a "screen" or "filter," distinguishing productive workers from others but not creating productivity as such. We will not delve into issue 1 except to note that some kinds of "ability" which also enhance the effectiveness of schooling can be produced by human

---

[34]Ibid., p. 2.

[35]A cogent analysis of the operation of a "dual" labor market and its implications for wage structure, written from a neoclassical point of view, but not explicitly using a formal human capital framework, can be found in several papers by M. W. Reder, particularly "The Theory of Occupational Wage Differentials," *American Economic Review*, 45, 5 (December 1955), 833–52; "Wage Differentials: Theory and Measurement," in *Aspects of Labor Economics* (Princeton, N.J.: Princeton University Press, 1962); and "Wage Structure and Structural Unemployment," *Review of Economic Studies*, 21, 3 (October 1964), 309–21.

capital investments in the home. Insofar as poor families are less capable of producing "able" children, schooling alone may yield a lower return than in more favorable situations, but the effect of ability on the return to schooling can go in either direction.

The "True" Relationship between Schooling and Earning Capacity.   Before dealing with issue 2, let us first address a question underlying the entire issue of the connections between schooling, labor market productivity, and poverty. Does schooling have a smaller effect on the earning power of low-income workers than others? If we return to Chapter 8, we see that evidence suggests a greater effect of schooling on earning power at lower levels of schooling than at higher levels. On the other hand, Cain cites at least a half-dozen studies by advocates of the SLM view that find a small or negligible effect of schooling on the earning power of workers who typically work at "external" type jobs—that is, jobs with relatively insecure status and little opportunity for advancement. These studies are based on a faulty method-ology, however. What they have done is essentially to ignore the fact that, even if there is a causal relationship running from schooling through labor market productivity to earning power, it is not deterministic, but rather stochastic. Some individuals with a given level of schooling will achieve greater than average earning power, others less. This is shown in Figure 10–5.

Suppose that instead of estimating the "true" relationship, a sample is constructed consisting only of "disadvantaged" individuals. Such a sample might be created by simply excluding everyone with a wage in excess of W_0— truncating the sample at W_0 as shown in Figure 10–5. Alternatively, a similar effect would be achieved by focusing on low-wage occupations or including

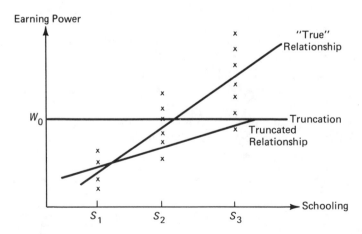

FIGURE 10–5. The Effect of Sample Truncation on the Estimated Relationship between Schooling and Earning Power

in the sample only those persons living in low-income areas. Any of these selection methods will result in a sample that is truncated with respect to the dependent variable. In the simple case demonstrated in Figure 10–5, truncation means that as schooling increases, an individual included in the sample is more likely to have achieved less than average market earning power as compared with the other persons who have acquired the *same* level of schooling. If the hypothesis that schooling enhances labor market productivity is indeed true, so that schooling leads to good jobs and higher earnings, then a truncated sample such as that depicted in Figure 10–5 will not yield a true picture of this relationship. A downward bias will be imparted to the estimated effect of schooling on earning power, lending support to the SLM view when it is unwarranted.[36]

Screening. The role of schooling as a "filter" or "screen" versus its role in creating labor market productivity has been the subject of a number of recent studies.[37] In the screening hypothesis, schooling and worker productivity are positively correlated, but schooling does not produce or create increases in worker efficiency on the job. A simple way of viewing this complex problem is that individuals differ in their value to employers who cannot differentiate among the workers prior to hiring because of imperfect knowledge. Completion of a certain level of schooling is a signal to employers that a worker has certain desirable characteristics for which they are willing to pay a particular wage. Thus, there is some incentive for workers to acquire schooling even though providing additional schooling for disadvantaged workers would not bring their market earning power up to the level of those who have obtained good jobs. Paradoxically, not only would increasing the schooling of low-income workers such as teenage dropouts through public policy schooling be a waste of resources if schooling provided no more than a screening function, but a further waste of resources would also be created if individuals who had previously been able to obtain good jobs by acquiring a given level of schooling now had to acquire further schooling to create an effective signal to potential employers.

We will not dwell here on the complex issue dealing with whether there would be too little or too much schooling from the point of view of social

---

[36]When there is more than one independent variable, a downward bias in the estimated effect of schooling is not assured. (Arthur S. Goldberger, "Linear Regression in Truncated Samples," Social Science Research Institute, University of Wisconsin, 1975.) Empirically, however, the bias is generally negative. (David L. Crawford, "Estimating Earnings Functions from Truncated Samples," Discussion Paper 287-75, Institute for Research on Poverty, University of Wisconsin, 1975.)

[37]Three well-known ones are Michael Spence, "Job Market Signaling," *Quarterly Journal of Economics*, 87, 3 (August 1973), 355–379; Kenneth Arrow, "Higher Education as a Filter," *Journal of Public Economics*, 2, 3 (July 1973), 193–216; and Joseph Stiglitz, "The Theory of 'Screening,' Education, and the Distribution of Income," *American Economic Review*, 45, 3 (June 1975), 283–300. A more recent analysis is Kenneth I. Wolpin, "Education and Screening," *American Economic Review*, 67, 5 (December 1977), 949–58.

welfare if its only purpose were to differentiate workers on the basis of characteristics schooling itself did nothing to create. Suffice it to say that schooling could well be socially useful under such circumstances,[38] even if it were not effective in raising the market earning power of low-income workers by raising their labor market productivity. The question that concerns us here is whether there is evidence that the main function of schooling has been to serve as a screening device rather than as a means of generating human capital in the traditional sense. Unfortunately, we will have to rely on rather indirect evidence. In order to discern whether schooling increases labor market skills, we would need knowledge of worker productivity before and after obtaining schooling. However, if such direct information on worker skills (as opposed to observing the wage rates of workers with different amounts of schooling) were available to social scientists, it would presumably also be available to employers, and the problem of schooling as a screen would not arise. It is primarily because there is no general agreement on just how skills are enhanced by education that the screening question is a live issue.[39]

Orthodox economists do not deny the potential importance of screening in labor markets, although they tend to be skeptical of the view that screening is a significant function of schooling. The reason for this skepticism is simply that schooling is so expensive. Entrepreneurs have an incentive to develop lower-cost methods of obtaining information about workers and implicitly sell such credentials for a profit. It is difficult to believe that schooling is the least-cost method of discriminating among workers according to their "innate" talents.

It might be argued that a firm will have little incentive to develop low-cost techniques for screening employees. Once such information is produced, it cannot be kept secret and all other employers will be able to take advantage of the information without paying for it. This is the same argument that applies to the firm's unwillingness to "pay" for investment in general OJT for its workers. As you might have already guessed, the problem has the same solution. The cost-minimizing firm need only specify the use of the least-cost screening technique; it need not pay for it. The firm concerned about losing its general investment in screening workers would require that they obtain screening before they are hired from a firm specializing in producing ability "credentials" or offer screening in return for workers' accepting lower initial rates of pay. Workers would thus invest in their own screening. Those whom the screen identified as particularly desirable would reap a return on their investment in the form of particularly good job opportunities. Individuals who are "filtered out" as less valuable might actually do worse than if there were no screening. But workers could avoid the screen only by

---

[38]Stiglitz, " 'Screening' "; Wolpin, "Education."
[39]It should be obvious that the main concern here is with "general" education as opposed to "professional" education, where the labor market skills imparted are more apparent.

seeking employment in a firm that did not care to distinguish between "skilled" and "unskilled" workers. Individuals who were uncertain about their ability to pass the screen would choose between these alternatives on the basis of expected earnings in a firm that screens versus a firm that does not screen and their willingness to bear the risk of being classified as less desirable employees.

Wolpin[40] has proposed a test of the importance of the screening function of schooling. In his test, the individual supposedly knows his or her skill potential in alternative employments much better than does a prospective employer. Therefore, schooling as a screen is assumed to be much less important among self-employed persons than among salaried workers. There are problems with this test of the screening hypothesis, particularly that those who ultimately become self-employed may not have decided to do so before completing their schooling. Moreover, customers may demand the screening function in the case of the self-employed.[41] In order to minimize the former problem, Wolpin examined only workers who were either self-employed or salaried throughout their observable working lives (which cover a twenty-year period in the data he uses). He also limited his sample to nonprofessional workers, since the contribution of professional education to productivity is not as much in doubt as the contribution of general education. He found that the average level of schooling for self-employed workers in his sample was 13.95 years, while that of salaried employees was 14.55 years.[42] While the direction of the difference in average years of schooling between these two groups is that implied by the screening hypothesis, it is small, and is not statistically significant by conventional standards.[43] On the basis of this rather crude test, it would appear that schooling has only a minor screening function, if any.

Conclusion

In this chapter we looked at the behavior of market earning power from many perspectives. However, we have consistently tied our discussion to the central question of what forces affect differences in earning power among

---

[40]"Education and Screening."

[41]Consider the concerned patient who will only permit himself to be treated by a board-certified, Harvard-educated surgeon.

[42]Wolpin's data are taken from the "National Bureau of Economic Research-Thorndike" sample consisting of approximately 5,000 men who were Air Force pilot, navigator, and bombardier candidates in 1943. Practically all of these men were at least high school graduates. For a more detailed description, see P. J. Taubman and T. J. Wales, "Higher Education, Mental Ability, and Screening," *Journal of Political Economy*, 81, 1 (January–February, 1973), 28–55.

[43]The standard deviations of the two mean schooling figures are 1.92 years and 1.81 years.

individuals. Thus, the study of the level and distribution of wages becomes a testing ground for the validity of neoclassical labor market theory based on the concepts of labor supply, demand, and human capital.

We contrasted the neoclassical or orthodox view of labor markets with what has been called the segmented labor market (SLM) concept. In doing this, we compared some of the theoretical implications of these competing views and assessed them against available evidence. We are persuaded that the orthodox approach offers much help in understanding the behavior of wage rates and their distribution among individuals. There is considerable evidence that schooling is causally related to labor market productivity and that rising levels of economic well-being are attributable to rising levels of physical and human capital.

It cannot be denied, however, that despite increases in schooling and other forms of investment over time, there remain many families and individuals whose labor market productivity and market earning power are insufficient to support a minimum socially acceptable standard of living. Numerous individuals do not enjoy labor market success commensurate with what might be expected on the basis of their schooling (as others enjoy above-average earning power). The questions of what kinds of investment in human capital, at what stage of the life cycle they would be most effective, and the point at which more direct approaches through income maintenance and employment policy become more efficient means of aiding society's poor remain an important challenge to advocates of the neoclassical view of wage determination.

Exercises

1. According to the human capital model, why might earnings differ between persons of equal ability in a world where there is no labor market discrimination? Would an *exogeneously* imposed minimum schooling law increase or decrease the differences in earnings among individuals? Explain carefully and depict graphically.

2. Suppose you know that female earning power is generated according to the following function:

$$\ln Y = 1.15 + .06S + .008X_1 + .016X_2 - .006h$$

where: $\ln Y$ = natural logarithm of hourly wage rate

S = years of schooling

X_1 = years of labor market experience since leaving school

X_2 = years worked on last or current job

h = number of years since leaving school in which at least six months were spent out of the labor force.

(a) Calculate the hourly wage rate of a woman who is a high school graduate, has worked a total of 10 years (five of which are on her current job), and has spent 5 years out of the labor force. Show your work.

(b) Consider two women, Ms. A and Ms. B, who have the same amounts of schooling. Ms. A leaves the labor force for 10 years to bear and raise children while Ms. B works continuously at the same job during this period. Use the above earning power generating function to calculate the percentage difference in their wage rates at the end of the 10 year period. Show your work.

3. Suppose that in estimating the rate of return to schooling a researcher decides to construct a sample consisting only of "disadvantaged" individuals by excluding everyone with a schooling level in excess of $\bar{S}$ (some arbitrary level, i.e., 12 years). Will this procedure yield a false (biased) empirical picture of the earning-schooling relation? (In formulating your answer you may ignore the existence of any other factors determining earning power.)

References

ARROW, KENNETH, "Higher Education as a Filter." *Journal of Public Economics*, 2, 3 (July 1973), 193–216.

CAIN, GLEN G., "The Challenge of Segmented Labor Market Theories to Orthodox Theory: A Survey." *Journal of Economic Literature*, 14, 4 (December 1976), 1215–57.

CRAWFORD, DAVID L., "Estimating Earnings Functions from Truncated Samples," Discussion Paper 287-75, Institute for Research on Poverty, University of Wisconsin, 1975.

DOERINGER, PETER B., and MICHAEL PIORE, *Internal Labor Markets and Manpower Analysis*. Lexington, Mass.: Heath, 1971.

FREEMAN, RICHARD B., "Overinvestment in College Training?" *Journal of Human Resources*, 10, 3 (Summer 1975), 287–311.

———, "The Decline in the Economic Rewards to College Education." *The Review of Economics and Statistics*, 59, 1 (February 1977), 18–29.

GOLDBERGER, ARTHUR S., "Linear Regression in Truncated Samples." Social Science Research Institute, University of Wisconsin, 1975.

GRILICHES, ZVI, "Estimating the Returns to Schooling: Some Econometric Problems." *Econometrica*, 45, 1 (January 1977), 1–22.

HANOCH, GIORA, "Personal Earnings and Investment in Schooling," Ph.D. Dissertation, University of Chicago, 1965, pp. 24–27.

Historical Statistics of the United States, Colonial Times to 1970. Series D766, D802, E186, E135, F450, D167, D11, C-89, A120-123, H666, D196, D781, D782, D787, F187.

KEAT, PAUL G., "Long Run Changes in Occupational Wage Structure 1900–56." *Journal of Political Economy*, 68, 6 (December 1960) 584–600.

KNIESNER, THOMAS J. and SOLOMON W. POLACHEK, "Ability, Schooling, and the Rate of Return to Education: Toward a More Complete Representation." Department of Economics, University of North Carolina, Working Paper 77–8, September 1977.

LEBERGOTT, STANLEY, *Manpower in Economic Growth.* New York: McGraw-Hill Book Company, 1964, pp. 137–64.

LONG, CLARENCE, *Wages and Earnings in the United States 1860–1890.* Princeton, N.J.: Princeton University Press, 1960, pp. 153–154; 109.

MINCER, JACOB, and SOLOMON W. POLACHEK, "Family Investments in Human Capital: Earnings of Women." *Journal of Political Economy*, 82, 2, pt. II (March/April 1974), S76-S108.

———, "Women's Earnings Reexamined." *Journal of Human Resources*, 13, 1 (winter 1978), 118–34.

POLACHEK, SOLOMON W., "Potential Biases in Measuring Male-Female Discrimination." *Journal of Human Resources*, 10, 2 (spring 1975), 205–29.

REDER, MELVIN W., "Theory of Occupational Wage Differentials." *American Economic Review*, 45, 5 (December 1955) 833–52.

———, "Wage Differentials: Theory and Measurement." *Aspects of Labor Economics*, Princeton, N.J.: Princeton University Press, 1962.

———, "Wage Structure and Structural Unemployment." *Review of Economic Studies*, 21, 3 (October 1964), 309–21.

SANDELL, STEVEN H., and DAVID SHAPIRO, "The Theory of Human Capital and the Earnings of Women: A Reexamination of the Evidence." *Journal of Human Resources*, 13, 1 (winter 1978), 103–17.

SCHULTZ, T. W., "Capital Formation by Education." *Journal of Political Economy*, 68, 6 (December 1960), 571–83.

SMITH, ADAM, *The Wealth of Nations*, Book I. New York: Modern Library, 1968, Chapter 10.

SPENCE, MICHAEL, "Job Market Signaling." *Quarterly Journal of Economics*, 87, 3 (August 1973), 355–79.

Statistical Abstract of the United States, 1976, pp. 378, 439, 368.

STIGLITZ, JOSEPH, "The Theory of 'Screening,' Education, and the Distribution of Income." *American Economic Review*, 65, 3 (June 1975), 283–300.

TAUBMAN, PAUL J., and TERENCE J. WALES, "Higher Education, Mental Ability, and Screening." *Journal of Political Economy*, 81, 1 (January/February 1973), 28–55.

U.S. Census of Population 1970, DC(2)-7A, "Occupational Characteristics," Tables I and II.

WOLPIN, KENNETH I., "Education and Screening." *American Economic Review*, 67, 5 (December 1977), 949–58.

CHAPTER 11

Unemployment

A. Educational Objectives
  1. Define unemployment in labor markets
  2. Elaborate the diverse causes of unemployment and its effects on economic welfare
  3. Provide a framework for understanding fluctuations in unemployment over time and differences in unemployment among demographic groups and geographic areas

B. Unemployment in Labor Markets
  1. What is unemployment
     a. It is incorrect to view unemployment simply as excess labor supply caused by "sticky" wage rates
     b. The theory of choice among alternatives can be used to analyze and understand unemployment behavior
     c. Just as there are always unemployed workers, there are also always unfilled job vacancies
  2. How people become unemployed
  3. Unemployment and social welfare

C. The Varieties of Unemployment and Their Causes
  1. Unemployment as a form of search
     a. Searching is a form of investment in human capital
     b. The sequential search model
  2. "Frictional" unemployment
     a. Frictional unemployment arises from search behavior and can be explained by the search model
     b. Measuring frictional unemployment
  3. Structural unemployment is associated with industrial, occupational, or demographic shifts

4. Cyclic unemployment
   a. Cyclic unemployment is associated with aggregate economic fluctuations
   b. Layoffs are important in cyclic unemployment
   c. The theory of OJT and the concept of income insurance help explain fluctuations in layoffs and the relative stability of wage rates during economic downturns
D. Frontiers of Labor Economics
   1. What is the "full employment" level of unemployment
      a. Changes in the demographic structure have probably raised the normal level of unemployment
      *b. Regression analysis of the effect of demographic changes
   2. The effect of unemployment insurance (UI) and eligibility on unemployment
      a. UI lowers search costs
      b. UI subsidizes layoffs
      *c. Empirical studies of UI and unemployment

Unemployment, along with wage rates, is one of the most important determinants of economic welfare. However, the association between unemployment and economic well-being is not clearly negative. Whereas it is difficult to conceive of a situation where an increase in the real rate of pay would not make a worker better off, all other things being equal, it is not at all clear that a reduction in unemployment is always a good thing. In this chapter we explore why this seemingly paradoxical statement is true by investigating in some detail the behavior of unemployment in the United States and its incidence across geographic areas and groups of workers.

Unemployment in Labor Markets

WHAT IS UNEMPLOYMENT?

As we saw in Chapter 2, the concept of unemployment is precisely defined in labor market data. A worker is considered unemployed if he or she has not worked during the preceding week, wants to work, is able to work, and has actively sought work in the recent past. A helpful way to envision how the population breaks down into the various categories of labor force attachment and unemployment is shown in Figure 11–1. The official definition of

---

*Represents more advanced material

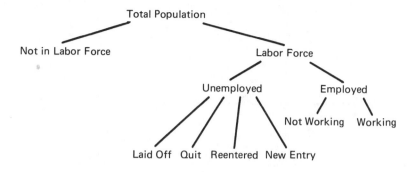

FIGURE 11–1. Labor Force Attachment

unemployment makes no reference at all to the wage rate at which an unempolyed worker would accept a job offer. While an ideal unemployment definition might well incorporate such an acceptance wage concept, our discussion takes the official definition as given.[1]

Unemployment is probably the most misunderstood economic concept among nonspecialists. The average person as well as many public officials view unemployment in the manner portrayed in Figure 11–2. Labor is supplied elastically at some constant wage rate W_0 up to some "full employment" level L_F, beyond which the labor supply curve becomes completely inelastic. The labor demand curve has the typical negative slope with respect to the wage rate, but often or typically intersects the supply curve to the left of L_F. Thus the level of employment L_F is "determined" by demand, as is the level of unemployment $L_F - L_E$. In this naive view, unemployment is simply excess labor supply, and any reduction in the gap between L_F and L_E would appear to be "good," in that more individuals who wish jobs at wage W_0 are able to obtain them. Incomes, and hence economic welfare, are increased. One of the problems with this naive view of unemployment is that it begs the question of why the wage remains at W_0 when $L_F - L_E$ is greater than zero. The theory of labor supply developed in Chapters 5, 8, and 9 is based on the assumption that time has economically valuable uses in activities other than working. Individuals who cannot find work at a given wage will either use their time to search for work, adjust downward the wage they are willing to accept, or devote their time to nonlabor market activities. Modern analysis of unemployment recognizes that if the market wage rate does not fall to W^*, the reason must be found in forces impinging on labor supply (and demand), and that unemployment in general cannot be interpreted as a simple form of excess labor supply.

[1] Melvin Reder has suggested an intriguing way of incorporating an acceptance wage concept in his article "The Coming Demise of Unemployment," *Proceedings of the American Statistical Society*, 122, 3 (June 1978), 139–44.

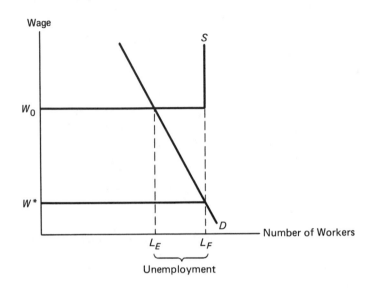

FIGURE 11–2. A Naive View of Unemployment

Economists have begun to view unemployment as a form of labor market behavior that can be analyzed with the general theory of choice. Unemployed workers who are not temporarily laid off and waiting to be called back to their jobs are viewed as choosing to look for work (search) rather than to accept the best job offered at the moment or to quit active search and, by definition, withdraw from the labor force. *Job search* is viewed as a means of improving one's labor market circumstances (finding a better job) and hence is a form of investment in human capital. In this view, unemployment is no more a "bad" than is schooling, since it may result in a worker's obtaining a better job. Clearly, the job search approach to unemployment does not imply that all workers would be better off if they were unemployed; nor does it imply that individual labor force members feel happy about being unemployed. To say that a worker "chooses" to be unemployed means only that he or she is attempting to do as well as possible *given a set of constraints*; the constraints may be very unfavorable by comparison to previous expectations or with respect to the constraints faced by other workers.

Remember, though, that the job search approach to unemployment tells us no more about worker happiness than does, say, the theory of labor supply. In labor supply theory, a worker chooses to work a certain number of hours, given the market wage rate obtainable and nonemployment income. This is not to say that the worker would not be better off if the wage or nonemployment income were higher and it were possible to obtain the same income with less work. Similarly, a worker would prefer to find a given job with less unemployment. A positive theory of unemployment analyzes how individuals determine their optimal job search strategies (that is, the amount of unemployment) subject to the constraints imposed on them by the operation of labor markets.

From the preceding remarks, you should see that even if it were possible to reduce measured unemployment to zero, it would be undesirable to do so. Severe restriction workers' free choice among alternative job opportunities would almost certainly be required, as in the China or the Soviet Union. Positive unemployment will always be observed in a free labor market where information is a scarce commodity. When is the labor market in *equilibrium*, then? Is there a level of unemployment consistent with equality between supply and demand in labor markets? We will deal with the difficult problem of the "full employment" level of unemployment later in this chapter. For now, we want to emphasize that simply to compare the number of persons looking for work with the number of job vacancies is not adequate. For example, there could be precise equality between the number of unemployed workers and the number of job vacancies, with the unemployed either not desiring to accept available jobs or employers not wishing to hire workers from among the unemployed. Employers might perceive a shortage of workers, while the unemployed perceived a shortage of jobs. A more sophisticated measure of equilibrium is required than a mere matching of numbers of workers and jobs in labor markets.

HOW PEOPLE BECOME UNEMPLOYED

To understand the causes of unemployment and its implications for economic welfare, it will help to know something about how people become unemployed, and how the unemployment rate is measured. Before proceeding, a word of caution is called for, however. In examining *how* workers become unemployed, we do not learn automatically *why* they become unemployed. This is not merely an effort on our part to play with semantics; rather, the distinction between the *how* and *why* of unemployment is a fundamental problem in the analysis of social behavior. As you know, unemployment is measured by means of tabulating answers to questions on individual labor force behavior during a "survey week." We can more or less objectively observe through this technique whether an individual worked, whether he or she was on layoff or actively sought work, and the kind of activity pursued before entering the unemployed state. What we cannot observe nearly as easily are the reasons why individuals seek work in a particular occupation, industry, or labor market; the reasons individuals quit a job before a new job is found, or the reasons they (explicitly or implicitly) reject job opportunities even though they are unemployed. If we knew the answers to these questions, we could understand the *why* as well as the *how* of unemployment behavior. Even if we were to design an elaborate and costly questionnaire to elicit this crucial information, however, most economists would probably be skeptical of our ability to use the resulting data to understand the *causes* of unemployment. Indirect methods of inferring causal relationships explaining unemployment behavior are called for, as in most other branches of economics.

With the preceding caveats in mind, we can again some insight into the nature of unemployment by examining Table 11–1. These data show why we have emphasized the complexity of unemployment and the difficulty in drawing welfare implications from the mere observation that an individual experiences unemployment. 1975 was a year of relatively high overall unemployment in the United States. In particular, one heard a great deal about the difficulties facing youth in the labor market. Table 11–1 shows that the unemployment rate among 16- to 19-year-old persons was nearly three times higher than that for adult men. However, when we examine the distribution of unemployed persons by prior activity, we see that two-thirds of the unemployed youth were experiencing unemployment in connection with labor force entry or reentry. The unemployment rate among young men who had lost their previous jobs was no higher than that for adult men. A similar, but less extreme, pattern exists for adult women. Much unemployment among youth and women is associated with job search almost necessarily accompanying mobility from outside the market labor force to jobs in the market sector. Of course, the individuals seeking work would be better off if they could find jobs with given characteristics with less search and unemployment experience. The point is that a substantial share of unemployment is attributable to the process of learning about the job market and what it has to offer to those who have relatively little labor market knowledge and experience—an inherently costly process.

As one might expect, among adult males, the principal "reason" for being unemployed was the loss of the previous job (75 percent). Loss of previous job through layoff or firing is the explanation the ordinary person most frequently associates with unemployment. Even though the transition from employment to unemployment can mean economic misfortune, in many jobs periodic layoffs are a way of life and largely are offset by other conditions of employment (higher hourly wage rates, "guaranteed annual wage"). The auto and construction industries and stevedoring are examples of areas in which such compensation for frequent unemployment is important.

UNEMPLOYMENT AND SOCIAL WELFARE

In few markets are buyers and sellers matched to each other without expenditure of time and material resources. Why then is unemployment in labor markets singled out for so much attention? The answer lies in the fact that human capital accounts for the lion's share of wealth of most families and individuals. Therefore, failure to find a match between buyer and seller can result in considerable hardship, even though an important function of unemployment is to facilitate selection of a suitable job and hence to improve

TABLE 11-1

Distribution of Unemployed by Prior Labor Status and Reason for Leaving Last Job, 1975

	Percent Distribution of Unemployed			Proportion of Total Civilian Labor Force for Group Shown		
	Both Sexes 16–19 Years Old	Male 20 Years +	Female 20 Years +	Both Sexes 16–19 Years Old	Male 20 Years +	Female 20 Years +
Total	100.0%	100.0%	100.0%	19.9%	6.7%	8.0%
Working	34.3	83.5	63.9	6.7	5.7	5.1
Lost last job	25.6	75.0	50.0	5.0	5.1	4.0
Left last job	8.7	8.5	13.9	1.7	0.6	1.1
Out of labor force	65.7	16.6	36.1	13.1	1.1	2.9
Reentered labor force	29.9	14.5	31.9	6.0	1.0	2.6
Never worked before	35.8	2.1	4.2	7.1	0.1	0.3

Source: Employment and Training Report of the President 1977, Table A–25.

the worker's economic situation. If unemployment were mainly an activity of the wealthy, it would probably not be of much social concern.

Unfortunately, unemployment is more common among low-wage workers than high-wage workers. In 1975, for the experienced civilian labor force, 4.7 percent of white collar workers were unemployed, compared to 11.7 percent of blue collar workers; within the latter group, 15.6 percent of laborers (the lowest-paid) experienced some unemployment.[2] While nonfarm laborers accounted for only 4.9 percent of the labor force in 1975, they accounted for over 10 percent of workers who were unemployed 27 weeks and over.[3] Unemployment is an important contributing factor determining whether family incomes fall below the poverty line. For example, in 1975, one-fourth of male heads of families below the poverty level (who were not ill or disabled) did not have year-round full-time jobs. Although unemployment is a phenomenon that disproportionately affects the poor, this need not be so. Why unemployment and low income happen to be related is a question to which we will return. Now let us look more closely at the varieties of unemployment and what we know about their causes.

The Varieties of Unemployment and Their Causes

As we saw in Table 11-1, people enter the unemployed state from various previous states. In order to understand how the flow of individuals into and out of unemployment affects economic welfare and the relationship between unemployment and labor market equilibrium, it is useful to develop an unemployment taxonomy. That is, we want to categorize different types of unemployment experience according to their underlying economic causes. What proportion of unemployment is due to depressed demand for aggregate output? How much to shifts in the structure of demand and supply of output for particular industries? How important are labor market "frictions"? Our attempts to answer these questions should help us understand the determinants of unemployment and provide insights into the development of policies appropriate to "cure" unemployment when desired and to reduce its harmful effects on social welfare. But first let us explore the concept of job search in greater detail.

UNEMPLOYMENT AS A FORM OF SEARCH

We will derive much more insight into the nature of unemployment if we first elaborate on the concept of unemployment as a form of the search behavior proposed earlier in this chapter, even though not all job search is carried

---

[2] *Employment and Training Report of the President 1976*, Table A-21.
[3] Ibid., Tables A-15 and A-29.

on while a worker is unemployed and not all unemployed individuals are looking for new jobs. The basic premise of the search approach to unemployment is that the unemployed individual actively seeks work while refraining from working at a job. The decision to remain unemployed is based on the benefits and costs of continued search. The cost of unemployed search is clearly the greater of foregone earnings on the best immediately available job or the value of commodities (including various forms of investment in human capital as well as "leisure") that could be produced if the worker devoted all search time to such pursuits. The benefit to search is the expected improvement in job offers over immediately available alternatives. The benefit of remaining unemployed derives from the expectation that a higher market wage will be obtained through further search. Insofar as an unemployed individual typically expects to hold a future job for several years, the present value of increased future earnings is the appropriate measure of the gain to remaining unemployed. Job search activity, not surprisingly, is a form of investment in human capital.[4]

Information about labor market alternatives (or any other alternatives) is a valuable asset that can be *produced* with inputs of one's own time and market goods (for example, advertisements, transportation). Time costs will vary among individuals in accordance with their labor market and household opportunities. What determines variation in benefits? Clearly, given the increase in the wage rates one can obtain by searching, the expected gain will be greater, the greater the proportion of time devoted to market work and the length of the period one expects to remain on the new job. The other important source of gain is the expected wage increase resulting from further search, and this depends on the degree of information imperfection in the labor market. If perfect information were freely available about all alternative jobs, no search would be necessary. A person could immediately decide whether, and where, to work. In the world as we know it, however, different employers pay different wage rates to similar workers doing similar work. The spread among these wage rates is limited, of course, by workers' search behavior, as well as being a partial determinant of the search behavior, and of unemployment itself.

In order to see how costly information and imperfect knowledge about alternative jobs interact to determine unemployment, we will develop a simple model of search behavior by means of a numerical example. We will show that wealth-maximizing search behavior involves the individual's choosing a wage rate, called the **acceptance wage**, such that if a job offering the acceptance wage or more is received, it will be accepted; otherwise the job will be rejected and the search continued. This search procedure is called **sequential search**, because it involves rejecting each job offered until the first

---

[4]For a seminal treatment of search as investment, see George J. Stigler, "Information in the Labor Market," *Journal of Political Economy*, 70, 5, part 2 (October 1962). For a more recent summary, see Steven A. Lippman and John J. McCall, "The Economics of Job Search: A Survey," *Economic Inquiry*, 14, 2 (June 1976).

offer equal to or exceeding the acceptance wage is received. In order to develop our example, let us assume that a job, if accepted, is expected to last for two years, that it would involve 2,000 hours work per year, and that the interest rate for calculating the present value of prospective wage offers is zero. The jobs offered to the individual differ only in their rate of pay, all other working conditions being the same. In Figure 11–3 we depict a situation in which 20 percent of the job offers an unemployed worker might receive would have a present value of $20,000 ($5 per hour × 2,000 hours per year × 2 years), 30 percent a present value of $24,000, 30 percent $28,000, 15 percent $32,000, and 5 percent $36,000. Although search is required to find out just which employers offer the highest wage, the searcher does have knowledge of the information contained in Figure 11–3. That is, he or she does know that the probability of receiving a job offer with a present value less than $20,000 is zero, the probability of being offered a job worth as much as $36,000 is only 5 percent, and so on. On the basis of these assumptions, we can begin to analyze how the wealth-maximizing job searcher arrives at an acceptance wage (W^*).

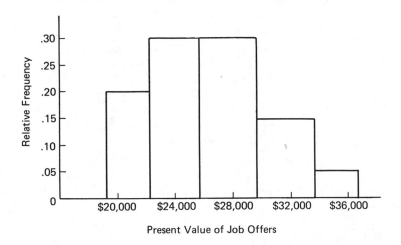

FIGURE 11–3. Frequency Distribution of Present Value of Job Offers

At first glance it may seem that W^* will be $9 per hour, since if the searcher has sufficient patience, he or she will eventually receive a job offer with a present value of $36,000. Why settle for less? The answer, you will immediately see, is that it would be all right to wait for the best possible job to come along if there were no opportunity cost of doing so. Unfortunately, search uses scarce time and other resources, so the searcher must weigh the expected gains from further search, should the $36,000 job not be immediately offered, against the cost of search. The solution to the search problem, like so many others in economics, involves comparing marginal benefit with marginal cost! Wealth-maximizing search involves formulating a search strategy such that the marginal benefit of further search is equal to the marginal cost. Therefore, in order to complete our example, we must make an additional assumption about the search costs. We will assume that each job offer received requires two months of searching, that time is valued at $600 per month,[5] and that other costs such as transportation and telephone calls amount to $100 per month. Thus, the cost of generating one job offer (C) is $1,400.

The information contained in Table 11–2 allows us to calculate the expected returns to search, and we know the cost per search period. How does a wealth-maximizing individual use this information to formulate an optimal search strategy? The optimal strategy involves establishing an acceptance wage (W^*) that maximizes the difference between the expected present value of the search process and the expected cost.

TABLE 11–2

Corresponding Values of W*, PVW*, and PV*

W*	PVW*	Probability of Receiving an Offer of at Least W*	PV*
$5	$20,000	1.0	$26,200
6	24,000	0.8	27,750
7	28,000	0.5	30,000
8	32,000	0.2	33,000
9	36,000	0.05	36,000

Source: Figure 11–3.

The Expected Present Value of the Search. By establishing the value W^* at which a job offer will be accepted, the searcher establishes the expected present value of search. The expected present value of the job accepted, PV^*, is greater than the present value of the job offering the acceptance wage, PVW^*. By setting an acceptance wage W^*, the searcher is assured that the job ultimately accepted will pay at least W^*. For example, if W^* is set at $6, PVW^* is $24,000, as shown in Figure 11–3 and Table 11–2. However, to calculate PV^*, we must take into consideration that there is a chance the offer extended to the searcher (and accepted) will exceed $6. Since W^* equals $6, the probability that from among the set of acceptable offers

---

[5] The $600 represents the greater of either the value the individual places on a month's "leisure" or the amount that could be earned in a known job opportunity.

($6, $7, $8, and $9) the offer will actually equal $6 is calculated as follows: On the basis of the information contained in Figure 11–3, we know that the probability a job offer will equal or exceed $6 is the sum of the probabilities attached to each offer of $6 or more—namely, $0.3 + 0.3 + 0.15 + 0.05 = 0.8$. If we divide 0.3, the *unconditional* probability that a job offer will equal $6, by the sum 0.8, we obtain 0.375, the probability of *accepting* an offer of $6, *conditional* on $W^* = \$6$. Similarly, we divide 0.3 by 0.8 to obtain .375, the conditional probability of accepting an offer of $7; .15 divided by .8 equals .1875, the conditional probability of accepting an offer of $8; and .05 divided by .8 equals .0625, the conditional probability that a job offering $9 per hour will be accepted. Note that the sum of these conditional probabilities, $.375 + .375 + .1875 + .0625$, equals 1, the probability that the job *accepted* will offer a wage equal to or exceeding $6, conditional on $W^* = \$6$.

To calculate PV^*, we simply multiply each value of PVW^* corresponding to a wage offer of $6 or more by its respective conditional probability and take the sum of the products. Thus, PV^* for $W^* = \$6$ is calculated as $24,000 $\times$ $.375 + \$28,000 \times .375 + \$32,000 \times .1875 + \$36,000 \times .0625 = \$27,750$, which is shown in the fourth column of Table 11 -2. By a similar procedure, you should be able to calculate that the PV^* corresponding to $W^* = \$7$ is $30,000, and so on. (*Hint*: Begin by recognizing that the unconditional probability of receiving an offer equal to or exceeding $7 is .5. Thus, the conditional probabilities of accepting a job worth $7, $8, or $9 per hour if W^* is set at $7 are .6, .3, and .1, respectively.)

The Expected Cost of Search.   Just as the present value of search increases with W^*, so does the cost. Since the probability of receiving an offer equal to or exceeding W^* falls as W^* rises (Table 11–2), the *expected number of periods of search*, N^e rises with W^*. As shown in Table 11–3, N^e equals the *reciprocal* of the probability (p) that an offer equal to or exceeding the acceptance wage will be received. Calculating N^e is analogous to calculating the expected

TABLE 11–3

Calculating Expected Search Costs

W^*	Probability of Receiving an Offer of at Least W^* (from Table 11–2) (p)	$N^e = \dfrac{1}{p}$	Expected Cost $(N^e C)$
$5	1	1	$1,400
6	.8	1.25	1,750
7	.5	2	2,800
8	.2	5	7,000
9	.05	20	28,000

number of times a six-sided die must be thrown before coming up with a number equal to, say, 4 or more. Since there are six possibilities (1, 2, 3, 4, 5, or 6), the probability of any throw yielding a 4 or more is $3/6 = 1/2$; thus the expected number of throws is $1/(1/2) = 2$.[6]

If we assume it is possible to search for a fraction of a period (for example, an offer might be received closer to the beginning of the period than to the end), then N^e can be multiplied by the cost per period of search, C, to derive the *expected cost* associated with each value of W^*. This calculation is carried out in the fourth column of Table 11–3. The expected cost of search, N^eC, rises with the acceptance wage because of the rise in the expected waiting time before accepting a job.

Maximizing the Net Gain from Search.   The net gain from search is maximized by setting W^* so that the difference between PV^* and N^eC is largest. As shown in Table 11–4, this occurs with a reservation wage of $7 per hour. Note that for W^* less than $7, the marginal benefit of raising W^* and increasing the expected duration of unemployment (N^e) exceeds the marginal cost of doing so. Tor W^* greater than $7, marginal cost exceeds marginal benefit. (The marginal benefit and cost columns are simply the changes in PV^* and N^eC, respectively, as W^* increases.)

TABLE 11–4

Net Gains from Search

W^*	PV^*	Marginal Gain	N^eC	Marginal Cost	Net Gain ($PV^* - N^eC$)
$5	$26,200	$26,200	$ 1,400	$ 1,400	$24,800
6	27,750	1,550	1,750	350	26,000
7	30,000	2,250	2,800	1,050	27,200
8	33,000	3,000	7,000	4,200	26,000
9	36,000	3,000	28,000	21,000	8,000

[6]Mathematically, to derive N^e, we need to calculate the probability that the first offer equal to or greater than W^* will occur during the kth search period. That is, we wish to calculate the probability (P) that the number of periods (N) before an acceptable offer is received equals $K - 1$. This probability [$P(N = K)$] is equal to the *joint probability* of two events: (1) during the first $K - 1$ searches, no offer equal or exceeding W^* is received; and (2) such an offer is received during the kth search period. Thus $P(N = K) = p(1 - p)^{K-1}$ where p is the probability of receiving an offer equal to or exceeding W^* during any search period. (Values of p for our numerical example are given in Table 11–3.) N^e is the *expected value* of N. It is the mean of $P(N = K)$ over all values of K—that is, $\sum_{K=1}^{\infty} Kp(1 - p)^{K-1}$. Since $p(1 - p)^{K-1}$ is a convergent geometric series, it is easy to show that $N^e = \sum_{K=1}^{\infty} Kp(1 - p)^{K-1} = (1/p)$.

It is important to recognize that, even assuming the individual searcher has perfect knowledge of the *probability distribution* of wage offers, the outcome of the job search process is uncertain. A large number of individuals with search costs and a probability distribution of wage offers equal to those in our example would receive an *average net gain* from search of $27,200 by setting $W^* = 7$. They would experience an *average duration of unemployment* of two search periods. Some would be lucky and receive an offer exceeding $7 the first search period, while others might be so unfortunate as to remain unemployed a large number of periods, receiving no offers greater than $6. Nevertheless, regardless of what an individual searcher's experience may be under the sequential search strategy, the beginning of each period is a "new ball game." Past bad luck does not alter the fact that the expected net gain from setting $W^* = 7 is still the maximum expected net gain. Past search costs are "sunk" and do not affect present wealth-maximizing search strategy. A more complex search strategy than that in our example would postulate uncertain knowledge of the probability distribution of wage offers. Then the searcher would adjust W^* with information gathered through the search process. (We will not complicate our discussion with this problem yet.)

Assuming the net benefits to searching at least one period are positive, the wealth-maximizing search requires that the acceptance wage be set as shown in Figure 11-4. In Figure 11-4, we assume that the acceptance wage can be "fine-tuned" by very small amounts, so that wealth maximization occurs at the point where the marginal cost of increasing W^* by one more cent just equals the marginal gain. The marginal gain curve rises as W^* rises, since clearly the expected present value of the job accepted rises as the minimum acceptable wage rises. The marginal cost curve (and the expected duration of unemployment) rises even faster, however, so that in general it pays to stop short of the maximum conceivable wage offer. "Going for broke" would in fact seriously reduce the expected net gain from search.

A change in the cost of search will cause the acceptance wage to change in the opposite direction. For example, a decline in the cost of search to $750 per period would raise W^* in our example from $7 to $8, and the expected length of unemployment would rise to 10 months. In general, the marginal cost curve in Figure 11-4 shifts downward when the cost of search falls, causing the intersection with the marginal benefit curve to shift to the right.

A change in the gains from search will cause the acceptance wage to change in the same direction. One of the important factors determining the gain to search is the degree of wage dispersion for labor of a given quality. This amounts to saying that the greater the disparity of wages, the greater the payoff to investing in labor market information. We can show this by slightly modifying the numerical example of Figure 11-3 and Tables 11-2 through 11-4. Suppose that the *average* present value of wage offers stays the same (at $26,200), but the *dispersion* of wage offers increases as shown in Figure

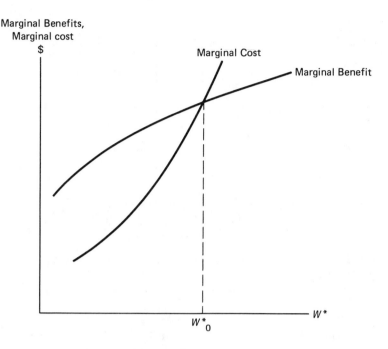

FIGURE 11–4. Marginal Gain and Expected Marginal Cost of Search Related to the Acceptance Wage

11–5. In Figure 11–5, the dispersion is greater because the highest and lowest possible wage offers are farther apart. The economics of the situation is that a worker who is lucky can do better under the conditions of Figure 11-5 than under the conditions shown in Figure 11-3.[7] To see this, look at Table 11-5. PV^*, the expected gain from search, is greater for every value of W^* than in the first example with a smaller wage dispersion. The net gain from search, $PV^* - N^eC$, also rises so that it now pays the searcher to set $W^* = \$8$ as the acceptance wage, rather than \$7. The expected duration of unemployment rises from two to five search periods. This example illustrates that the greater the degree of information imperfection in the labor market, the more it pays to invest in unemployment, all other things being equal.

Before going on, we should note briefly that job search need not involve unemployment. A worker may search for a better job while on his or her old job. Whether he or she quits before or after finding a better alternative depends upon the gains and costs of doing so. Searching while unemployed may be more productive, but the gain over a slower, less efficient search

[7]The *ceteris paribus* assumption is very important here. Increased dispersion of wage offers may result from a relatively high cost of search (see below). In this case, a higher acceptance wage may not result.

FIGURE 11–5. Frequency Distribution of Present Value of Wage Offers with Increased Dispersion

TABLE 11-5

Gains and Costs of Search with Increased Wage Dispersion

W^*	PVW^*	PV^*	p	$N^e = \dfrac{1}{p}$	N^eC	$PV^* - N^eC$
$ 4	$16,000	$26,200	1.0	1	$ 1,400	$24,800
5	20,000	26,736	.95	1.05	1,470	25,266
6	24,000	28,000	.8	1.25	1,750	26,250
7	28,000	30,400	.5	2	2,800	27,600
8	32,000	36,000	.2	5	7,000	29,000
9	36,000	38,000	.1	10	14,000	24,000
10	40,000	40,000	.05	20	28,000	12,000

while working at a job may or may not exceed the cost of giving up one's labor market income for a while. Thus, although we deal here with unemployment in terms of job search, not all search involves being unemployed. All the forces we analyze affect both the decision to choose more or less unemployment as well as the decision whether or not to search while holding a job or while unemployed.

The search view of unemployment implies that the acquisition of information by workers and employers should narrow the dispersion of rates of pay for workers of given quality. One implication of this is that as means of communication have improved, reducing search costs, the variation of wage among regions of the United States should have declined over time.

We should also expect to observe that the variation of wage rates is greater among older workers who, because of the limited length of expected working life, have a shorter period of time in which to collect the benefits of search. Stigler found that between 1904–1909 and 1947–1954 the average coefficient of variation[8] of average earnings in selected manufacturing industries among a set of identical states declined by about one-third; data on monthly earnings of engineers by age in 1929 show that the coefficients of variation increase with age. Stigler also found evidence of a higher coefficient of variation of wage rates among women (who typically are in the labor market a shorter time, and therefore to whom the rate of return to a given expenditure on search is probably lower) than among men in the same occupation.[9] Stigler's findings are consistent with the importance of information search theory for understanding market prices.

FRICTIONAL UNEMPLOYMENT

"The cause of a man's being unemployed is not that which led him to lose his last job but that which prevents him from getting another job now." Loss of a job for any cause results in frictional unemployment if there are other jobs available reasonably well suited to the worker's abilities.[10]

We might add that not only must jobs be available, but workers must be able to find them with a reasonable expenditure of time and other search costs and without adjusting their customary work or their acceptance wage rate.

Even if there were no business cycles or unanticipated reduction in industrial production, there would still be unemployment. New workers will always be entering the labor market, and they must seek information about the best alternatives. Moreover, experienced workers who feel that their present or previous jobs do not represent the best they can obtain in the job market will be searching for better opportunities. Scarcity of information

---

[8] The coefficient of variation is the standard deviation divided by the mean. The standard deviation of a set of numbers is a measure of dispersion. Let X_i, $i = 1 \cdots n$, represent one of a set of n numbers. The standard deviation is defined to be

$$\sigma = \left[\frac{\sum_{i=1}^{n} (X - \bar{X})^2}{n} \right]^{1/2}$$

where $\bar{X}$ is the arithmetic mean of the set of numbers. The coefficient of variation is $\frac{\sigma}{\bar{X}}$.

Thus the standard deviation of the set of numbers 1, 2, 3, 4, 5 is $\left(\frac{4+1+1+4}{5} \right)^{1/2}$,

which equals $(2.00)^{1/2}$. The coefficient of variation would thus be $\frac{(2.00)^{1/2}}{3}$.

[9] Stigler, "Information in the Labor Market," pp. 99–100.

[10] Albert Rees, quoting William H. Beveridge, in "The Meaning and Measurement of Full Employment," *The Measurement and Behavior of Unemployment* (Princeton, N.J.: Princeton University Press, 1957), p. 27.

about alternatives ensures that many of these labor force participants will actively seek (better) jobs while unemployed. Similarly, there are employers who believe they can improve the quality of their work forces by laying off some workers and searching for others. In other words, labor market "frictions" due to lack of perfect foresight and all-encompassing knowledge are constantly replenishing the pool of unemployed workers.

In terms of the search theory developed in the preceding section, frictional unemployment exists because there is a dispersion of wage rates (and other job characteristics) anticipated by a given worker. Thus, even in periods of high overall labor demand, it will pay workers to engage in some search. In general, experienced or "mature" workers have formed a pretty firm picture of their labor market opportunities as depicted in curve E of Figure 11–6.

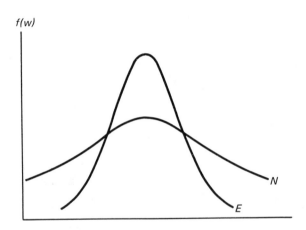

FIGURE 11–6. Relative Frequency Distribution of Wage Offers for (E) Experienced Workers and (N) New Labor Force Entrants

Nonetheless, it will still pay some of them to engage in some search (1) before accepting a new job if they have been laid off or (2) to quit their jobs and to seek new ones if they are presently employed. New workers, of course, have less experience upon which to draw to assess their alternative job prospects and will generally view their alternatives as depicted by curve N in Figure 11–6. In addition, young workers expect to benefit from their search for a longer period of time and have lower search costs per period of time than do older workers. (An offsetting factor, however, may be that young workers are less efficient searchers, requiring a longer time to generate a job offer than experienced, older workers.) These considerations suggest that the marginal benefit of unemployment for new workers (R_N in Figure 11–7) will be greater relative to opportunity cost, than for experienced workers.

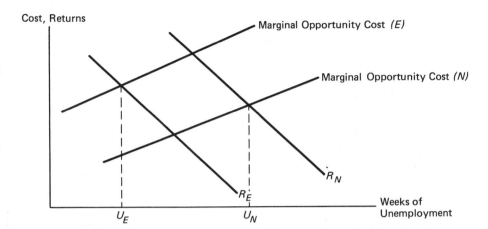

FIGURE 11–7. Cost and Returns to Unemployment for Experienced Workers (*E*) and New Workers (*N*)

Thus, new workers would be expected to choose more unemployment than experienced workers, as shown in Figure 11–7.

Frictional unemployment such as U_E for experienced workers or U_N for new workers would be stable magnitudes if there were no changes in (1) aggregate demand for goods and services in the economy, (2) the demand or supply of output of particular industries or geographic regions, or (3) opportunity costs of search (why?). When these conditions change, workers' views of their labor market alternatives will be modified. The result is a different mixture of frictional and other types of unemployment in the economy. R_E, R_N, and the opportunity cost curves in Figure 11–7 will be modified.

Measuring Frictional Unemployment. There is no obvious way to discern from the answers provided to current labor force surveys whether unemployed workers owe their circumstances to frictional or other causes. Not only would the information required be difficult to obtain, but also the degree to which labor market "frictions" and structural changes affect unemployment depend on each other as well as on the state of the whole economy. For example, a young person entering the labor market will face different job prospects and search costs in a labor market characterized by depressed demand than in boom times. A downturn in economic activity will affect the cost and returns to search for experienced workers differently than for inexperienced members of the labor force. During especially prosperous times (a "tight" labor market), an experienced worker may decide that the probability of regaining his old job is fairly high even if a period of job search proves unrewarding. The *frictional* unemployment of mature workers might therefore rise when labor market conditions are improving. On the other hand, a new labor force entrant might find the job offers available without search so attractive that frictional unemployment among younger workers could decline.

It should be apparent, then, that it is probably impossible to separate unemployment due to labor market frictions from other (cyclical and structural) forces in such a way that they add up to total unemployment. Too many important interrelationships are involved. The search view of unemployment does, however, give us valuable insights that help us understand the causes of the wide dispersion of unemployment experience of different labor force groups. As suggested above, one of the most widely noted differences in unemployment experience is that between young persons and experienced labor force participants. Lack of experience means that knowledge of labor market alternatives is quite limited, leading to a wide dispersion of anticipated wage offers as well as possibly low search costs. These forces imply a high level of search-related unemployment. On the employer's side as well, youthful workers have relatively unknown characteristics, increasing the likelihood of a poor match of worker to job and hence a higher likelihood of layoff. Similar differences, although perhaps not quite as pronounced, may be expected to affect the unemployment experience of men versus women.

Table 11–6 shows monthly average unemployment rates by age, sex, and race over the six-year period 1967–73, along with corresponding data on labor force participation rates. Vast differences in average unemployment experience among these population groups are apparent and are clearly negatively associated with labor force participation. Of course, participants and nonparticipants might never wish to change their labor force status, so there need not be any association between participation and exposure to the possibility of unemployment. Although search theory does not unequivocally imply that frictional unemployment will be negatively correlated with labor force participation, the negative association is suggestive of an underlying relationship between mobility from one labor force state to another (for example, between out of the labor force and unemployed search for a job) and overall unemployment experience.

In order to assess the validity of viewing these intergroup differences in unemployment as essentially frictional in nature, we have related them to differences in flows into and out of the labor force and employment.[11] In Figure 11–8 we have plotted the simple relationship between the group unemployment rates and (1) the average proportion of the group not in the

---

[11]These flows have been analyzed in a lucid and instructive paper, albeit with more complicated techniques, by Stephen T. Marston in "Employment Instability and High Unemployment Rates," in Arthur M. Okun and George L. Perry, eds., *Brookings Papers on Economic Activity*, 1, 1976. The gross flows between labor force states are measured from unpublished data of the monthly *Current Population Surveys*.

TABLE 11-6

Unemployment and Labor Force Participation Rates
by Age, Sex, and Race, Monthly Averages, 1967–1973

Age, Sex, and Race	Unemployment Rate (%)	Labor Force Participation Rate (%)
White males		
16–19	12.4%	58.4%
20–24	6.7	83.7
25–59	2.3	95.3
White females		
16–19	13.0	46.1
20–24	6.9	57.5
25–59	3.8	48.6
Nonwhite males		
16–19	25.5	47.9
20–24	11.8	83.3
25–59	4.2	90.6
Nonwhite females		
16–19	32.5	33.9
20–24	15.0	57.4
25–59	6.1	58.6

Source: Stephen T. Marston, "Employment Instability and High Unemployment Rates," in Arthur M. Okun and George L. Perry, eds., *Brookings Papers on Economic Activity*, 1, 1976. © 1976 by the Brookings Institution.

force which enters the labor force each month, and (2) the average proportion of the employed segment of the group who are either laid off or quit each month. Since these averages are computed over a six-year time period, it is probably safe to view them as representing rather stable differences among age-sex-race groups. The data plotted in parts (a) and (b) of Figure 11–8 show a strong positive relationship between movement into and out of the labor force (and employment), and unemployment. Marston has confirmed these relationships in a multiple regression framework as well.[12]

Close examination of the observations plotted in Figure 11–8 indicates that young black (nonwhite) persons appear to experience more unemployment than do whites or older blacks, given their tendency to move into and out of the labor force. These black-white differences in unemployment rates for younger workers, given their mobility into and out of the labor force and employment, appear to be due to a tendency for blacks to remain unem-

[12]Ibid.

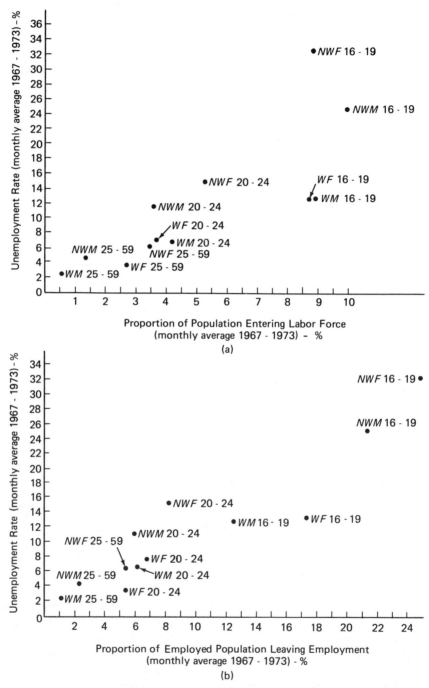

FIGURE 11–8. Labor Force Flows and Unemployment by Age, Sex, and Race

Source: Stephen T. Marston, "Employment Instability and High Umemployment Rates," in Arthur M. Okun and George L. Perry, eds., *Brookings Papers on Economic Activity,* 1, 1976. © 1976 by the Brookings Institution.

ployed longer than whites once they have entered the unemployed state. In Figure 11–9, the group unemployment rates are plotted against the monthly average proportion of unemployed persons who become employed within a month. As can be seen, young blacks exhibit a much slower tendency to move out of unemployment than do other groups, and this is strongly and negatively correlated with their average unemployment rates.

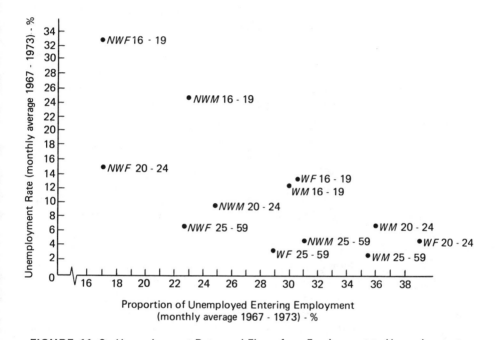

FIGURE 11–9. Unemployment Rates and Flows from Employment to Unemployment

Source: Stephen T. Marston, "Employment Instability and High Umemployment Rates," in Arthur M. Okun and George L. Perry, eds., *Brookings Papers on Economic Activity*, 1, 1976. © 1976 by the Brookings Institution.

The preceding discussion treats frictional unemployment as arising from the ever-present need to match workers and jobs in an environment that is always changing—if for no other reason than because of the entrance of new workers into the labor force, and the aging and retirement of existing workers. The fact that we have shown a pronounced correlation between group unemployment rates and measures of employment instability does not, however, establish that the economy tends to generate the "correct" amount of frictional unemployment, that economic policies cannot or should not be undertaken to reduce the typical period of job search, or that discrimination is not a factor influencing the relatively large unemployment rates of young blacks and mature women.

STRUCTURAL UNEMPLOYMENT

The line between frictional and structural unemployment is by no means clear and distinct. A rough and ready distinction, however, can be drawn along the lines of whether difficulties in matching workers to jobs arise because information depreciates on both sides of the market due to the constant entry and exit of individual employers and workers, or because of sharp changes in the industrial structure of labor markets or the demographic composition of the labor force. When, for example, there is an important and perhaps unanticipated change in the demand for workers by a firm or industry whose production activities constitute an important component of employment in a labor market (or among a particular skill group of workers), previous information reflected in workers' anticipated job offers or the number and quality of workers firms can expect to attract by offering given job characteristics may need to be revised. The crucial issue, though, is the speed with which these revisions occur. When a substantial number of the workers in a market are slow in perceiving that the wage offers they can anticipate receiving have deteriorated and when firms do not quickly realize they can attract workers of a given quality with conditions more favorable to themselves than previously, the speed with which unemployed workers move to an employed state or decide to leave the labor force will be reduced. Structural unemployment is the result of such slow adjustment to major changes in labor market circumstances.

Structural unemployment derives its name from the idea that it is caused by changes in the industrial, occupational, and demographic structure of the economy. The key question is, given changes in the industrial and occupational structures of the economy, why doesn't the economic system always adjust quickly enough to eliminate structural unemployment? It would be wrong to think that structural unemployment always results when changes occur in the demand and supply of different kinds of labor; it does not. Most economists agree that the economy adjusts reasonably well even to rather major changes in conditions; sluggish responses are the exception rather than the rule. Nevertheless, such situations warrant careful attention. Let us explore why the adjustment of labor markets to changing conditions may occur too slowly to keep structural unemployment from reaching undesirably high levels. First of all, adjustments to a changing economic structure are costly, often requiring relocation or reeducation of workers, installation or alteration of plant and equipment, production slowdowns until new methods are effectively incorporated into the production process, and so on. Thus, neither firms nor workers will take steps to adjust to changing conditions unless the changes are thought to be permanent enough to justify the necessary expenses. In the presence of imperfect information, it takes time to decide whether the investment in information and adjustment will pay. In addition to the adjustment and information costs, which are more or less

directly measurable in terms of money, the psychological costs of adjustment, especially when the migration of workers is involved, may also be
a serious deterrent to adaptation. Still another cause of structural unemployment is the interdependence of the supply of and demand for labor. That is,
adjustment of the labor force to changing demand conditions—for instance,
moving out of a declining community—often further reduces the demand
for labor. Finally, wage rigidity due to firms' fear of social disapproval,
unions, or minimum wage rates may hinder or prevent adjustment of the
wage structure that would otherwise quickly bring about a balance between
the amounts of labor supplied and demanded.

Let us consider a hypothetical example to help clarify the possible causes
of structural unemployment. Suppose that, in a small agricultural and mining
community in the Appalachian region, technological changes make the
introduction of labor-saving mining machinery economical at existing wage
rates. If miners were willing to quickly accept substantial reductions in wages,
the decline in the quantity of labor demanded would be offset. However,
wages are not immediately reduced, and people are thrown out of work.
The ensuing reduction in the price of coal does not bring about a sufficient
increase in the amount of coal demanded to restore mining employment to
its old level. There will, of course, be some smaller mines in which the
introduction of the new machinery is not feasible, and any decline in wage
rates that does occur may make previously marginal mines economical to
operate. However, we may imagine that substantial unemployment remains.
Some of the unemployed may find work in agriculture, but the elasticity of
demand for labor in local agriculture is so small that it cannot absorb large
numbers of such workers.

As some of the unemployed emigrate from the area, repercussions are felt
in industries that have supplied local needs (services, construction, and so on)
as the demand for their output falls. Thus, a decline in demand for labor
in mines has the effect of reducing the demand for labor in other industries
in the area. Workers who are in the prime working-age group, who have few
or no children, and who have favorable attitudes toward moving will leave
the area and find jobs in more prosperous locations. Thus, the remaining
population tends to be made up disproportionately of those who, for reasons
having to do with their age, the likelihood of their finding work elsewhere,
the size of their families, or their attitudes toward moving per se, have
remained in the declining area despite the increasing difficulty of earning a
living.

Now, if this area happened to be marginally attractive to some industry
(for example, textiles or apparel) that had not yet located there, the declining
wage rates and the increasing availability of workers might be sufficient to
induce a change in the local industrial structure and restore the demand for
labor to a level high enough to keep unemployment reasonably low. This is
more likely to happen if the unemployed workers are of a relatively high

skill level or are readily adaptable to new kinds of jobs. Workers are more likely to have such characteristics if they are relatively well educated and have been employed in jobs where the work contributes to adaptability. Alternatively, high unemployment may persist, with no new industries being attracted; able workers will continue to leave until the community is indeed depressed, with few readily employable workers among the unemployed. Gradually, discouraged workers leave the labor force, lowering both the labor force participation and the unemployment rates of the community.

CYCLICAL UNEMPLOYMENT

Modern concern with unemployment dates from the prolonged period of deficient aggregate demand which we call The Great Depression of the 1930s. Most economists and policy-makers still associate the principal problem of unemployment with the economy's periodic reductions in the rate of growth of aggregate demand for output and the derived demand for labor. These business fluctuations result in parallel movements in the overall unemployment rate. The relationship between fluctuations in national income and unemployment is shown in Table 11–7 and Figures 11–10 and 11–11. Figure 11–10 shows gross national product in 1958 prices for the period 1946–75. A trend line has been fitted to this GNP series by means of a regression equation. The formula for this trend equation is $Y_t = (307.0)e^{.0359t}$, where Y is GNP from Table 11–7, and t takes on the value of 0 in 1946, 1 in 1947, and so on through 30 in 1975.[13] The deviations of Y_t from the trend have been plotted against the unemployment rate in both Figures 11–10 and 11–11. The pronounced negative relationship between these two variables suggests that when aggregate demand for goods and services is higher than normal, the demand for labor is also high, resulting in lower than average unemployment. Similarly, higher than normal unemployment is attributable to relatively low aggregate demand.

The Nature of Cyclical Unemployment. We have described frictional unemployment as resulting from the constant search by employers for workers to match their job requirements and by workers for suitable jobs. Cyclical unemployment cannot be fully understood within the search framework used to analyze frictional and structural unemployment, however.

---

[13] The trend equation represents the value per capita GNP would have equaled in each year if it had grown at a constant proportional rate. To see that this is true, note that the proportionate rate of growth over time is $\frac{dY}{dt}\frac{1}{Y}$. This expression for the proportionate growth rate is the coefficient of t in the trend equation. This can be seen by taking the natural log of both sides of the equation, and differentiating, obtaining

$$\frac{d\ln Y}{dt} = \frac{dY}{dt}\frac{1}{Y} = .0359, \text{ since } \ln e = 1.$$

TABLE 11-7

GNP, Deviations from Trend, and Unemployment Rate,
United States, 1946–1975

Year	(1)	(2)	(3)	(4)
1946	$312.6	307.0		
1947	309.9	318.3	−8.4	.039
1948	323.7	330.0	6.3	.038
1949	324.1	341.7	−17.6	.059
1950	355.3	354.2	1.1	.053
1951	383.4	367.2	16.2	.033
1952	395.1	380.3	14.8	.030
1953	412.8	394.3	18.5	.029
1954	407.0	408.7	−1.7	.055
1955	438.0	423.3	14.7	.044
1956	446.1	438.8	7.3	.041
1957	452.5	454.9	−2.4	.043
1958	447.3	471.1	−23.8	.068
1959	475.9	488.3	−12.4	.055
1960	487.7	506.2	−18.5	.055
1961	497.2	524.8	−27.6	.067
1962	529.8	543.5	−13.7	.055
1963	551.0	563.4	−12.4	.057
1964	581.1	584.1	−3.0	.052
1965	617.8	604.9	12.9	.045
1966	658.1	627.0	31.1	.038
1967	675.2	650.0	25.2	.038
1968	706.6	673.2	33.4	.036
1969	725.6	697.8	27.8	.035
1970	722.5	723.4	−0.9	.049
1971	744.1	749.2	−5.1	.059
1972	786.9	776.7	10.2	.056
1973	829.8	805.1	24.7	.049
1974	815.7	833.8	−18.1	.056
1975	800.7	864.4	−63.7	.085

(1) Gross national product, 1958 prices (billions of dollars).
(2) "Predicted" values of (1) based on estimated trend $Y = (307.0)e^{.0359t}$ ($t = 0$ in 1946).
(3) (1) − (2).
(4) Civilian unemployment rate.

Source: (1) 1946–1970, U.S. Census Bureau, *Historical Statistics of the United States, Colonial Times to 1970* (Part 1), Series Fl-5, 1970–1975; U.S. Department of Commerce, *Statistical Abstract of the United States, 1976*; (4) U.S. Department of Labor, *Manpower Report of the President, 1976*.

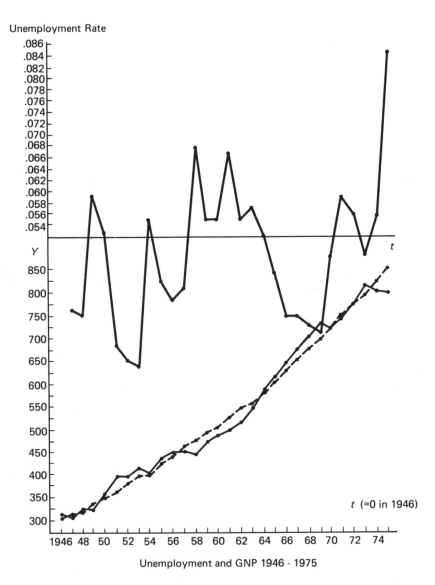

Unemployment Rate

Y

t

t (=0 in 1946)

Unemployment and GNP 1946 - 1975

FIGURE 11–10. Gross National Product, 1946–1974 (1958 dollars) and Unemployment

To be sure, more workers are laid off and the opportunity cost of search time falls in recessions, since known alternative jobs are few and their character- istics relatively undesirable. This reduced cost by itself would tend to lengthen the optimal unemployment period; on the other hand, the cost of generating a job offer of given quality is increased as the numbers of expected job offers

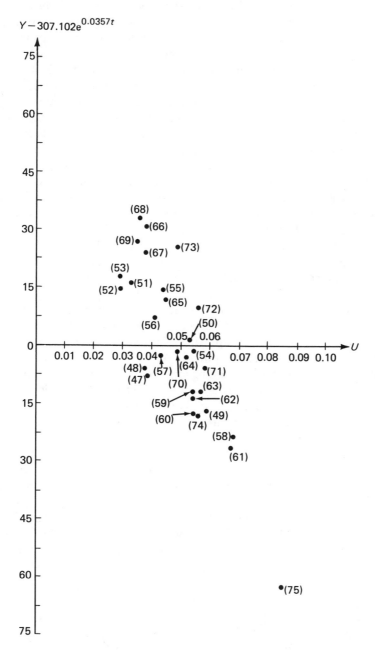

FIGURE 11–11. Unemployment and Deviations of Trend from GNP: 1946–1975

diminishes (possibly to zero). The diminished net gain to search during recessions reduces quits and makes it less attractive for some workers to enter the labor force. To the extent that workers lag in their realization that labor market opportunities have deteriorated, they may also overestimate the net gain to search and remain unemployed longer than usual.[14] The single most important source of unemployment during recessions is the increased number of workers who have been laid off from their jobs. Many of these laid-off workers do not appear to seek work actively, because they expect eventually to be recalled to their old jobs or because they believe that equally attractive opportunities are not worth searching for.[15] It is to this process that we must turn to understand why unemployment rises during recessions.[16]

The question that arises concerns why employers choose to lay off workers when aggregate demand declines rather than temporarily lower wage rates. One possible answer is that collective bargaining agreements preclude such wage reductions and thus force layoffs as the only alternative. This cannot be the entire story, however, or even most of it. Layoffs, rather than downward-flexible wage rates, occur in firms, industries, and occupations that are not covered by collective bargaining agreements as well as those in which unions are present. Moreover, the negative relationship between unemployment and aggregate economic activity is not peculiar to the past thirty years, during which unions have claimed as members 25 to 30 percent of the labor force. Layoffs and resulting unemployment have long been associated with—even the measure of—depressed economic activity. Even today, most workers are not covered by collective bargaining agreements. Although unionism plays a role, forces more fundamental to labor markets must be called upon to explain the basic nature and behavior of cyclical unemployment.

If firms could predict the course of fluctuations in economic activity, and if goods could be stored for future sale without cost, a temporary downturn in aggregate demand would not necessarily result in a concomitant decline in labor demand. Firms would find it profitable to maintain production and employment, and store output for future sale. Because these conditions do not hold in general (firms do not know how long a given recession will last; how long it will affect their particular product line; production cannot be stored without cost; fashions will change in unknown ways), the demand for labor shifts in the same direction as the demand for output. Thus, during recessions, profit-maximizing firms will want to reduce wage rates or the number of employees.

---

[14]The influence of lags in the perception of one's "true" labor market alternatives on unemployment will be dealt with in Chapter 12, where inflation is also analyzed.

[15]See, for example, *Employment and Training Report of the President 1977*, Table A-25, "Percent Distribution of Unemployed Persons 16 Years and Over and Unemployment Rates, by Reason for Unemployment: Annual Averages, 1968–76."

[16]See, for example, Martin Feldstein, "Temporary Layoffs in the Theory of Unemployment," *Journal of Political Economy*, 84 (September–October, 1976).

To help understand the interrelationship between the firm's demand for output, the derived demand for labor, wage rates, and layoff behavior, it will be helpful to recall the theory of human capital and OJT developed in Chapter 9. Figure 11–12 is a recapitulation of Figure 9–4 and shows that investment in firm-specific OJT creates a wedge between VMP and W so that even when there is a downturn in economic activity, the value to the firm of a worker with, say, t_0 years of experience, will not necessarily fall below W.

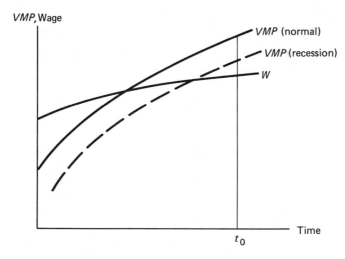

FIGURE 11–12. Relationship between VMP and W When There Is Firm-Specific OJT

Thus the firm may receive a positive return from employing a worker even though VMP is less than normal. Even if VMP should fall below W, the profit-maximizing firm will not lay off the worker unless it believes that the risk of the worker's finding another job and thus not being available for recall when VMP once again exceeds W is sufficiently high. Studies by Oi, Rosen, and Parsons[17] have shown the importance of the OJT concept in explaining patterns of layoffs in the presence of depressed labor demand. However, these studies do not explain why, when VMP falls far enough below W to make layoffs profitable, the firm does not reduce wage rates rather than discharge workers. Moreover, when aggregate demand is temporarily low, making it difficult or impossible to switch jobs, why do employers not take advantage of the situation by lowering W regardless of the level of VMP?

---

[17]W. Y. Oi, "Labor as a Quasi-Fixed Factor"; Sherwin Rosen, "Short-Run Employment Variation on Class I Railroads in the U.S."; Donald O. Parsons, "Specific Human Capital: An Application to Quit Rates and Layoff Rates." (For full citations, see References.)

Two reasons are generally given for the apparent unwillingness of employees to lower W. These reasons are also consistent with the downward inflexibility of wage rates associated with collective bargaining agreements— which are, after all, not imposed upon employers unilaterally, but involve agreement by both sides. The first reason bears on the credibility of the employer and his or her long-term ability to attract new employees. The theory of OJT implies an unwritten contract between employer and employee regarding the terms of employment over time. Lowering wage rates to take advantage of depressed labor market conditions might be profitable in the short run, but would feed back negatively on long-run profits as workers discovered that an employer could not be trusted to keep his or her side of the human capital contract. The second reason for stable wage rates is related to employees' assumed preferences to avoid the risk of fluctuating incomes and employers' interest in long-term cost minimization and profit maximization. The firm is seen as providing not only the opportunity for OJT to its employees, but insurance against fluctuating income as well.[18] Thus, employees agree to accept a stream of wage payments lower than it might otherwise be (in present value terms) in return for freedom from the risk of a reduced wage rate when the demand for their services declines. The terms on which employees can "purchase" income insurance are governed by the expected course of future fluctuations in VMP. Since income insurance is not free, employees do not typically demand complete freedom from the risk of fluctuating incomes. Thus, during periods of particularly low output demand, the implicit contract for "income insurance" permits the firm to lay off workers. Why do implicit income insurance contracts not provide for wage reductions rather than layoffs when VMP falls below a critical level? One appealing explanation is that if the wage rate were cut sufficiently severely to make the firm willing to maintain employment, workers would find it preferable to use their time in nonmarket activities—that is, the home wage rate would exceed the market wage rate and it would be optimal to withdraw from the labor force temporarily. Thus, the firm lays off workers because it knows that if it did offer the lower wage rates it would be willing to pay, workers would choose to quit until wages rose again.[19] The "preference" by workers to be laid off rather than to accept wage cuts is augmented by

---

[18]Recent studies along these lines are those of C. Azariadis, "Implicit Contracts and Underemployment Equilibria," *Journal of Political Economy*, 83 (December 1975); M. N. Baily, "Wages and Employment under Uncertain Demand," *Review of Economic Studies*, 41 (January 1974); and D. F. Gordon, "A Neoclassical Theory of Keynesian Unemployment," *Economic Inquiry*, 12 (December 1974).

[19]An interesting development that suggests the relevance of thinking of layoffs as a kind of vacation has been the adoption of "inverse seniority" in a few industries. Senior workers have a kind of first option on being laid off when the firm wishes to reduce employment temporarily. See Sheldon Friedman, Dennis C. Bernstead, and Robert T. Lund, "Inverse Seniority as an Aid to Disadvantaged Groups," *Monthly Labor Review*, 99 (April 1976), 36–37.

the availability of nonwage income in the form of unemployment compensation.[20]

Distinguishing among Frictional, Structural, and Cyclical Unemployment

The theory and taxonomy of unemployment presented above should make it clear that it is impossible in practice to develop a neat separation of unemployed persons into categories of frictional, structural, and cyclical unemployment. Frictional unemployment grows during cyclical downturns in the economy partly because acceptance wage rates do not adjust downward sufficiently rapidly to offset the decline in labor demand. Structural unemployment and frictional unemployment are difficult to distinguish as the definition of the market grows in size. Nevertheless, it is important from the point of view of policy-makers to know, to the extent possible, whether a change in unemployment experienced by the economy's labor force is attributable to cyclical forces or, say, to changes in labor market "frictions," because the appropriate policy actions are different. Cyclical unemployment may be offset by monetary and fiscal policies, while changing structural and frictional unemployment may be offset by altering the flow of information, workers, and firms within and among labor markets.

An illustration of how easy it is to confuse one kind of unemployment with another is found in the behavior of the United States economy from 1958 to 1967. During these ten years, it would have been easy to conclude that a major structural change had taken place in the demand for goods and services, resulting in substantial structural unemployment. In retrospect, it is evident that the unusually high unemployment rates experienced between 1957 and the "heating up" of the war in Southeast Asia were due to aggregate demand forces. The immediate cause of concern can be seen in Table 11-8. The unemployment rate rose to a postwar high of 6.8 percent in 1958 and did not fall below 5 percent for seven years. During this period, a number of economists argued that a long-term decline in the relative output and employment of goods-producing industries (manufacturing, construction, mining, and related transportation and utilities), coupled with an increase in the relative importance of service industries, was resulting in structural unemployment. It was also argued that capital-labor substitution in these industries ("automation") was exacerbating the unemployment problem.

As Tables 11-8 and 11-9 show, employment actually declined in many of the goods-producing industries between 1957 and 1962. Unemployment in these industries was concomitantly high. From the point of view of that

---

[20]See Feldstein, "Temporary Layoffs in the Theory of Unemployment."

TABLE 11-8

Average Annual Changes in Employment: Goods Producing
and Related Industries, 1948–1966 (thousands)

Industry	(1) 1948–53	(2) 1953–57	(3) 1957–62	(4) 1965–66
Manufacturing	339	−94	−85	1,052
Mining	−26	−10	−36	−4
Contract construction	91	75	−45	100
Transportation and public utilities	20	−12	−63	103

Sources: (1)–(3), Walter W. Heller, "The Administration's Fiscal Policy," in Arthur Ross, ed., *Unemployment and the American Economy* (New York: Wiley, 1964), p. 98. Reprinted by permission of John Wiley & Sons, Inc., (4), U.S. Department of Labor, *Manpower Report of the President, 1967*, p. 20.

TABLE 11-9

Unemployment Rates in Goods-Producing Industries
and Manual Occupations, 1953–1975

Industry or Occupation (Experienced Workers)		1953	1957	1961	1962	1966	1975
Craftsmen, foremen and kindred workers		.026	.038	.063	.051	.028	.083
Operatives and kindred workers		.032	.063	.096	.075	.043	.132
Laborers, except farm and mine		.061	.094	.145	.124	.073	.156
Manufacturing		.025	.050	.077	.058	.032	.109
Mining, forestry, fishery	wage and	.049	.063	.116	.086	.038	—
Transportation and public utilities	salary workers	.018	.031	.051	.039	.020	.056
Total unemployment		.025	.043	.067	.056	.039	.085

Source: U.S. Department of Labor, *Manpower Report of the President, 1967*, pp. 217–18; *Employment and Training Report of the President, 1976*, pp. 171–72.

time, it was easy to conclude that the high unemployment rates in goods-producing industries and manual occupations had indeed resulted from a major structural shift. From our vantage point, we can more easily see that the high unemployment rates in these industries and occupations were not unusual, given the overall depressed state of the economy that prevailed. The causation was running from a slow rate of growth in overall aggregate demand to particularly high unemployment in goods-producing industries and manual occupations rather than from structural shifts to an unusually high rate of joblessness. We have since observed that unemployment rates generally rise more in the goods-producing industries and in manual occupations than elsewhere during recessions. This is probably due to the concentration of manual occupations in goods-producing industries and to the volatile nature of demand for production. Relatively large fluctuations in output demand make layoffs more likely to occur despite the demand of workers for a certain amount of income insurance. Less-skilled manual workers are likely to have less firm-specific OJT. Therefore, the cushioning gap between VMP and W is likely to be smaller for the average worker in, say, manufacturing, than elsewhere in the economy.

Evidence that no major structural change had occurred can be seen by examining relative unemployment rates both before and after the nine-year period of prolonged high overall unemployment. In 1957, a year of more or less normal business activity, the total unemployment rate was 0.43, the unemployment rate experienced laborers (manual workers) was 0.094, and that of workers in manufacturing was 0.050. The differences in the unemployment rates between laborers, workers in manufacturing, and the general average were, respectively, 0.051 and 0.007. However, during 1961, the worst year of the depressed period, these differences had risen to 0.078 and 0.010. If a permanent change in the structure of demand for labor in goods-producing industries and in manual occupations had been the principal causes of high unemployment rates, then we might have expected 1961 unemployment rate differences to persist. But they did not: By 1966, the difference between the unemployment rate of laborers and the general average had fallen to 0.034, and the difference between the unemployment rate in manufacturing and the average unemployment rate was once again 0.007. A similar conclusion was reached by some economists during the early 1960s, even before data for the entire period were available. For example, Walter W. Heller showed that as of 1962, there had been no change in interindustry or interoccupational differences in unemployment rates that was not observed in previous periods of depressed aggregate demand.[21] A decade later, our economy once again experienced a prolonged recession. In 1975, the total unemployment rate rose to 8.5 percent of the labor force. As Table 11–10 shows, laborers and employers in manufacturing had the highest proportion of unemployed workers, the excess of their unemployment rates over the economy average being 0.071 and 0.024, respectively. It is gratifying to observe that there was virtually no attempt to blame the economy's woes on structural shifts in 1975. The uneven impact of cyclic changes on industries and occupations is now generally recognized.

---

[21]"The Administration's Fiscal Policy," in Arthur M. Ross, ed., *Unemployment and the American Economy* (New York: Wiley, 1964), pp. 93–115.

Frontiers of Labor Economics

WHAT IS THE "FULL EMPLOYMENT" LEVEL
OF UNEMPLOYMENT?

This question naturally arises as soon as we recognize that much unemployment represents job search activity necessarily arising in a labor force with a changing demographic, industrial, and occupational structure. It certainly is important to policy-makers, who are constantly searching for a value of the unemployment rate to serve as a trigger for initiating antirecessionary monetary, fiscal, and labor market policies. It is tempting to define the "full employment" unemployment rate as that which would coincide with a zero rate of inflation in the economy. We shall see in the next chapter, however, that unemployment will tend toward a "normal" level regardless of the long-run rate of inflation. While there is probably no single indisputable value that can be calculated to measure the full employment unemployment rate, something can be learned from an application of the theory of search and frictional unemployment.

Because unemployment arising from labor force entry and normal job search varies among groups, changes in the relative size of these groups in the population will influence the overall unemployment rate observed in the economy. Michael Wachter[22] has found that not only is the unemployment rate of young persons normally higher than that for other groups, but also that this disparity widens when there is an increase in the proportion of these groups in the population. The reason for this widening is presumably that young persons are complementary to older workers in firms' production functions. Thus, when there is an increase in the proportion of young persons their productivity declines, and this is reflected in job offers. While this change in the nature of job offers (and perhaps the cost of search) does not necessarily raise the optimal period of search, it may do so.

Wachter estimated regressions of the following form for fourteen age-sex labor force groups

$$\ln (U_i) = a_0 + a_1 \ln (U_{pm}) + a_2 \ln (RP_y) \qquad (11\text{--}1)$$

where U_{pm} is the unemployment rate among prime-age males, 25 to 54 years of age; U_i is the age-sex specific unemployment rate, and RP_y is the population of individuals 16 to 24, relative to the total population 16 to 64. As an example of his results, for males 16 to 19, Wachter estimated $a_0 = 5.05$, $a_1 = 0.60$ and $a_2 = 1.37$, with t values of 17.4, 16.5 and 10.4, respectively. In other words, the 16- to 19-year-old unemployment rate tends to be higher

---

[22]"The Changing Cyclical Responsiveness of Wage Inflation," *Brookings Papers on Economic Activity*, 1, 1976.

than that of "prime-age" males, even in the best of times, and when the unemployment rate of prime-age males rises by 1 percent (a rough measure of cyclical effects), that of males 16 to 24 rises by 0.6 percent. However, an increase of 1 percent in the relative size of the 16- to 24-year-old population raises the unemployment rate of 16- to 19-year-old male youth by 1.37 percent. raises the unemployment rate of 16- to 19-year-old male youth by 1.37 percent.

Since the unemployment rate of young persons is normally higher than that of others, an increase in the proportion of young persons in the population will tend to raise the rate of unemployment for the entire labor force. This tendency is reinforced by a positive value of a_2, the effect of the proportion of young persons on their own unemployment rate (but offset by a tendency for the unemployment rate of male workers 35 and over and female workers 55 to 64 to fall when RP_y rises). Wachter used the results of his age-sex specific regressions to calculate a weighted average normal unemployment rate for the entire economy. To do this, he needed to insert a value for U_{pm} that prevails in "normal" times—that is, when the economy is at "full employment." With this value of U_{pm}, U_{pm_N}, it is possible to use the fourteen regressions to calculate a normal unemployment rate for each age-sex group and then, using the proportion of each group in the population as a weight, to construct a weighted sum, or average unemployment rate for the entire economy. Of course, the validity of interpreting this average, U_N, as the full employment rate of unemployment depends on the validity of the value selected for U_{pm_N}. Nevertheless, *changes* in the calculated value of U_N will provide a good indication of how the full employment rate of unemployment has changed over time purely as a function of demographic factors, even if the level of U_N is not known with certainty.

Wachter chose a value for U_{pm_N} of 2.9 percent, a figure he justified on grounds that this is the average value of U_{pm} during periods which can reasonably be considered as neither recessions nor booms in our economy. Using this value, he calculated values of U_N shown in Table 11–10. U_N varied in the low 4 percent range during the sixteen-year period prior to 1964, but since then it has risen sharply as a result of the growing up of the "baby boom" generation of the post-World War II years. Thus, by 1975, U_N was estimated at 5.5 percent of the labor force. Unemployment rates rose during the early 1970s as the Vietnam war cooled down (Table 11–7). There was much concern about appropriate policies to counteract overall unemployment, and there was particular concern about the high unemployment of youth. However, a comparison of Tables 11–7 and 11–10 suggests that despite rising unemployment for the six years following 1969, U_N was not surpassed by as much as one-half percentage point until 1975. As the population and the "baby boom" generation age, the procedure used to calculate U_N implies a declining full employment unemployment rate as labor market experience is acquired and knowledge of relevant job alternatives is acquired. There was

TABLE 11-10

"Full Employment" Unemployment

Year	$U_N(\%)$	Year	$U_N(\%)$
1948	4.5	1962	4.2
1949	4.4	1963	4.4
1950	4.3	1964	4.5
1952	4.2	1965	4.6
1953	4.1	1966	4.7
1954	4.0	1967	4.8
1955	3.9	1968	4.9
1956	4.0	1969	4.9
1957	4.0	1970	5.0
1958	4.0	1971	5.2
1959	4.0	1972	5.3
1960	4.1	1973	5.4
1961	4.2	1974	5.4
		1975	5.5
		1976	5.5
		1977	5.5

Source: Michael L. Wachter, "The Changing Cyclical Responsiveness of Wage Inflation," in Arthur M. Okun and George L. Perry, eds., *Brookings Papers on Economic Activity*, 1, 1976. © 1976 by the Brookings Institution; and personal communication.

heated debate during the mid-1970s about using government monetary, fiscal, and labor market policy (for example, designating the federal government as "employer of last resort") to force the unemployment rate down to a level of 4 percent, as stipulated in the so-called Humphrey-Hawkins bill. The values of U_N in Table 11-10 imply that such a target rate of unemployment would be extremely low in view of the normal behavior of the labor force and its current age distribution.

THE EFFECT OF UNEMPLOYMENT INSURANCE AND ELIGIBILITY ENFORCEMENT ON UNEMPLOYMENT

Changes in the age-sex composition of the labor force are not the only factor affecting the normal or "full employment" unemployment rate. Herbert Stein, a former chairman of the president's Council of Economic Advisors, has noted that several additional changes in the economy have probably caused the normal rate of unemployment to rise over time: (1) increases in the marginal tax rate faced by the average worker; (2) the proportion of the labor force covered by minimum wage legislation; (3) unemployment compensation level and availability of welfare; (4) new requirements that welfare recipients register for work; and (5) general affluence.[23] In this section, we focus on the first and third factors emphasized by Stein. A number of recent studies indicate that the unemployment compensation system and the income tax have interacted to cause a significant increase in the normal rate of unemployment over the years.[24]

The unemployment insurance framework in the United States affects the economy's unemployment rate through two channels. (1) Payments to the unemployed raise the level of household expenditures that can be maintained when one or more family members are not working. These payments reduce the economic pressure to find work immediately, encouraging a longer period of job search during which the unemployed worker hopes to find a more attractive job than might otherwise be offered. They also may reduce the intensity of search, encouraging those without work to use more of their time between jobs as "leisure" or to perform household tasks (for example, repairs and improvements) than would be the case without unemployment insurance payments. The impact of unemployment insurance on the individual's decision to search for or to accept a job is significantly magnified by the fact that unemployment benefits are not subject to federal or state income taxes or social security tax. (2) Although unemployment insurance payments are financed through a system of taxes levied on firms' payrolls and adjusted upward for firms that contribute more to unemployment with relatively high layoffs, the method of "experience rating" is incomplete. Firms that have the highest frequency of layoffs are not taxed as much per additional dollar of unemployment insurance paid to their laid-off workers as are firms with more stable employment. In this way, our present system of unemployment insurance and taxes subsidizes layoffs, thus contributing to higher unemployment than would otherwise exist.

The mechanism through which the unemployment insurance system (UI) raises the normal unemployment rate can be seen more clearly if it is studied with the aid of the analysis of search and layoff behavior developed earlier in this chapter. We first consider the impact of unemployment compensation on search behavior. In analyzing the impact of unemployment insurance on the worker's decision to accept a job or continue searching, it is crucial to recognize that UI payments are unavailable to most individuals who have not had recent work experience. As Table 11–1 shows, in 1975 two-thirds of unemployed individuals under twenty years of age were entering the labor force—over half of them for the first time. Over one-third of unemployed females over 19 fell into this category, as did approximately one-sixth of the men in this age group. Altogether labor force entrants and reentrants constituted almost 40 percent of total unemployment. The job search model

---

[23]"Full Employment at Last?" *The Wall Street Journal*, September 14, 1977.

[24]A fuller overview is contained in Daniel S. Hamermesh, *Jobless Pay and the Economy*, Policy Studies in Employment and Welfare No. 29 (Baltimore: Johns Hopkins University Press, 1977).

clearly applies to the labor force entrants, but since unemployment compensation is generally unavailable to them, it cannot affect their search behavior. Unemployment compensation is generally available to the remainder of unemployed workers who were laid off or quit their previous jobs, except that workers who were laid off for "misconduct" or who quit without "good cause" may be disqualified, depending on individual state laws. The degree to which unemployment compensation influences overall unemployment through search behavior, therefore, is limited by the proportion of the unemployed who qualify for benefits. However, not all workers who qualify for benefits should be classified as genuine job seekers. Many persons who are laid off because of cyclical, seasonal, or other reasons have such strong reason to believe they will be recalled soon that it does not pay them to search for a new job. In terms of the search model, the expected returns from any search fall short of the costs; time on layoff may be even viewed as a substitute for vacation time by such workers. The unemployment compensation system may have a significant impact on the willingness of firms and workers to use temporary layoffs as a means of allocating time between work and nonwork activities of employees and thus affect the unemployment rate through this means. For now, however, we will concentrate on the impact through actual search behavior.[25]

UI can alter search behavior through lowering the cost of search and perhaps providing financial resources that permit more efficient search and hence higher returns. The most likely channel would appear to be via lowering search costs. For purposes of our discussion, we will follow the most common assumption in empirical studies of search behavior and assume that the main component of job search costs consists of the best alternative use of time spent searching. While it might be tempting to assume that the value of search time to a laid-off worker is zero, this is clearly unlikely to be the case. The theory of labor supply, along with the fact that workers typically allocate some time to "leisure" activities, implies that the value of an additional hour of "leisure" when a job is held is equal to the market wage rate. It is hard to believe that time becomes valueless when a worker is laid off. Moreover, it is reasonable to suppose that many unemployed job searchers know of jobs they implicitly reject because of unsatisfactory wage or working conditions. Such jobs set a floor on the opportunity cost of search time. In the absence of UI, a worker would formulate a search strategy based on equating the marginal benefit and cost of search and behave accordingly. *When UI is available, the attractiveness of longer search is increased, because UI payments cease when a new job is begun.*

The effect of UI benefits on the relative attractiveness of continued

---

[25]Individuals may be classified as unemployed even though they are not actively seeking work if they are on layoff from their job. Moreover, a worker may satisfy the criterion of actively seeking work while engaging in only desultory search and establishing very stringent criteria for accepting a new job.

search for covered workers depends on the dollar amount of weekly payments and the number of weeks an unemployed worker is eligible to receive them. Both weekly benefits and the period of eligibility vary according to state laws, with the former generally depending on prior earnings of unemployed workers and the latter normally equal to twenty-six weeks.[26] During periods of prolonged high unemployment, extended benefit periods are usually made available. There are also significant differences among states in the stringency with which eligibility criteria are applied and the requirements that the recipient be actively seeking and available for work enforced. These differences in enforcement criteria also influence the impact of UI on the unemployment rate, as we will see below.

How large are unemployment benefits relative to earnings for a typical worker? It would be too complicated to provide all the necessary data here to answer this question in detail. However, it has been estimated that unemployment compensation replaces about 70 percent of lost after-tax earnings (unadjusted for fringe benefits) for male family heads with relatively low incomes, but only about 40 percent for those with higher earnings.[27] Martin Feldstein[28] provides an example for a worker in Massachusetts in 1975 whose before-tax earnings are $120 per week or $6,240 per year if he experiences no unemployment, and whose wife earns $80 per week or $4,160 per year for full-time work. They have two children. Suppose the husband is unemployed for ten weeks. After one week of waiting, he is eligible to receive a weekly benefit equal to one-half of his wage plus $6 weekly for each child. These nontaxable benefits amount to $648 after ten weeks of unemployment (9 × $72). At the same time, his *after-tax* wages (ignoring fringe benefits) fall by only $875, since he would have paid $194 in federal income tax, $71 in social security tax, and $60 in state tax had he been working. Thus, unemployment compensation amounts to $648/875 = 0.74$ of his net wage loss. Moreover, part of this income difference is offset by reduced expenses of transportation to work.

More relevant for the search decision, however, is the *marginal* tax on one additional week of unemployment. This is even higher, mainly because of the one-week waiting period before becoming eligible to receive benefits, which typically does not have to be repeated regardless of the number of unemployment *periods* per year. In Feldstein's example, an additional week of unemployment would cost $120 in gross earnings, but only $15.50 after being offset by tax reductions and UI benefits. Put the other way around, by accepting a job in the eleventh week identical to his former job, the husband would raise his family's net income by less than $0.40 per hour of work—an implied tax rate on wages of 87 percent. It would not be surprising

---

[26]See U.S. Department of Labor, *Comparison of State Unemployment Laws*, 1971.

[27]Council of Economic Advisers, *Economic Report of the President, 1975*.

[28]"The Unemployment Caused by Unemployment Insurance," *Proceedings of the Industrial Relations Research Association 28th Annual Winter Meetings*, 1975.

in view of these figures to learn that the frequency and length of unemployment periods are increased by UI availability.

Empirical Studies.   In the past few years, a number of empirical studies have lent support to the hypothesis that the generosity of UI benefits tends to increase unemployment. One study, by Ronald Ehrenberg and Ronald Oaxaca,[29] is based on four samples of 5,000 men age 45–59, 5,000 women age 30–44, and 5,000 (each) young men and women age 14–24 who experienced unemployment during the period 1966–71. Their study is based on the following model of search unemployment:

$$E(D) = f(c, n, s, r, d)$$
$$E(W) = g(c, n, s, r, d) \qquad (11\text{--}2)$$

where $E(D)$ is the expected duration of spells of unemployment, $E(W)$ is the expected postunemployment wage, c is the cost of search, s is the worker's skill level, n is the individual's time horizon (particularly time to retirement), r is the individual's discount rate, and d represents anything that influences the variance of expected wage offers. Increases in c and r are expected to reduce both $E(D)$ and $E(W)$; an increase in n is expected to increase both $E(D)$ and $E(W)$; an increase in s is expected to increase $E(W)$, but not necessarily $E(D)$. The authors do not deduce expected effects for d, although as we have seen, an increase in d should increase $E(D)$. Since direct measures of c, n, s, r, and d are not available, proxies were found among the variables on which information was available. Of particular interest is the proxy for c, which is measured by UI/W, where UI is the unemployed individual's weekly UI payment and W is his or her preunemployment weekly wage. The higher UI, the lower the proxy for the cost of search, given W.

Ehrenberg and Oaxaca used regression analysis to estimate the relationship between the logarithm of the duration of unemployment for unemployed persons and the change in wage rate that occurred, on the one hand, and the proxies for c, n, s, r, and d, on the other.[30] Not surprisingly, they found that UI appears to affect unemployment duration and wage change only for those unemployed persons who changed employers. In other words, those workers who were on layoff and were recalled by their previous employers do not appear to behave as if they were searching for new jobs, as our previous discussion suggested would be the case. In all four samples, the estimated impact of UI on the duration of unemployment is positive and statistically

---

[29]"Unemployment Insurance, Duration of Unemployment, and Subsequent Wage Gain," *American Economic Review*, 66 (December 1966); "Impacts of Unemployment Insurance on the Duration of Unemployment and the Post-Unemployment Wage," *Proceedings of the Industrial Relations Research Association, 28th Winter Meetings*, 1975. The *American Economic Review* paper gives references to other related studies.

[30]Although each sample contains about 5,000 observations, the number of persons who experienced unemployment was much smaller.

significant. Ehrenberg and Oxaca's results suggest that an increase in the ratio of UI/W by 0.1, from 0.4 to 0.5, increases the average duration of unemployment for men 45–59 by 1.5 weeks; women 30–44 by 0.3 weeks; young men, 0.2 weeks; and young women, 0.5 weeks. Only for the older men and women, however, does an increase in UI appear to help unemployed individuals achieve a higher postunemployment wage rate. For young men and women, the estimated impact of UI on the wage change from preunemployment to postunemployment job is positive, but statistically insignificant. This does not necessarily mean that these groups' job search is unproductive, although it is consistent with older persons' being more efficient in this activity. For example, young persons may use their search time to find jobs that offer greater OJT possibilities, resulting in higher future wages, but not higher current wages.[31]

One possible bias in Ehrenberg and Oaxaca's study should be borne in mind when interpreting their results.[32] Part of their sample of unemployed persons received no UI payments at all. Some received no benefits not because they were ineligible, but because they remained unemployed for less than the minimum period of time required to qualify for payments. For these individuals, causation runs from unemployment to UI benefits, rather than vice versa, as we (and Ehrenberg and Oaxaca) have hypothesized. Thus, their empirical results are biased in the direction of accepting the hypothesis. The magnitude of this bias is unknown, as Ehrenberg and Oaxaca provide no data on UI eligibility.

In another study using a different empirical approach based on aggregate average data for 48 states in 1971, Arlene Holen and Stanley Horowitz[33] also observed a significant impact of UI on unemployment. Their measure of UI generosity is similar to that of Ehrenberg and Oaxaca—namely, average weekly UI benefits per recipient in each state divided by average hourly wages in manufacturing. They estimate the effect of this measure of UI benefit liberality on statewide unemployment rates in a multiple regression framework. Their approach is novel in two respects: (1) they recognize that UI benefits may themselves be influenced by the economic and political environment in each state; and (2) they investigate the degree to which state differences in the stringency with which UI eligibility criteria are enforced affects the unemployment-UI relationship. The possibility of feedback from the economic and political environment to UI benefits leads to estimation of the regression equations by means of the simultaneous equations technique of two-stage least squares.

---

[31]Ehrenberg and Oaxaca find some evidence that UI benefits may induce young women to act as if they were unemployed rather than out of the labor force, which suggests that their (additional) search may well be unproductive.

[32]See Finis Welch, "What Have We Learned from Empirical Studies of Unemployment Insurance," *Industrial and Labor Relations Review*, 30 (July 1977).

[33]"The Effect of Unemployment Insurance and Eligibility Enforcement on Unemployment," *Journal of Law and Economics*, 12 (October 1976).

Holen and Horowitz find that a 1 percent increase in their measure of benefit liberality is associated, all other things being equal, with a 0.69 percent higher state unemployment rate on the average. That is, the elasticity of unemployment with respect to their index is 0.69. Of equal interest is their finding that the major contributor to the influence of benefit liberality on unemployment is the strictness with which UI eligibility criteria relating to job search and voluntary separation from last job are enforced. A doubling of the proportion of UI applications denied on these grounds would lower the unemployment rate by 1.4 percentage points, according to their estimates.

Additional studies support the hypothesis that UI benefits tend to prolong unemployment duration. A collection of papers reporting such findings is contained in the July 1977 issue of the *Industrial and Labor Relations Review*, and includes papers by Kathleen P. Classen and Arlene Holen. In the same issue, Finis Welch summarizes, evaluates, and criticizes these and related papers that report the results of studies of the effects of UI unemployment duration and subsequent wage gain. In a more recent study, Daniel Hamermesh[34] points out that there are theoretical reasons why UI may increase employment as well as unemployment. Since a period of work is required before an individual becomes eligible to receive UI benefits, UI provides positive as well as negative work incentives. One would expect such positive "entitlement" effects to be particularly pronounced among workers who are not typically the primary earners in a family—for example, married women (why?). Hamermesh found, for a large sample of married women in 1971, that both positive and negative UI work incentive effects exist and are fairly substantial in magnitude.

As noted above, there is another, subtle but probably quite important, way in which UI increases the economy's normal rate of unemployment. Firms with a high frequency of layoffs typically do not pay an unemployment insurance payroll tax sufficient to cover the payments received by their laid-off workers; that is, "experience rating" is not complete.[35] Consequently, the UI system subsidizes the use of temporary layoffs by firms rather than other devices to allocate labor between times of high and low production. We have already discussed the role of "income insurance" in implicit contracts between firms and employees regarding the tradeoff between wage rates and employment stability. Insofar as workers are risk-adverse and employers are less so, there are mutual gains to be obtained if employers implicitly agree to reduce workers' likelihood of being laid off due to seasonal, cyclical, and

---

[34]"Entitlement Effects, Unemployment Insurance, and Employment Decisions," *Economic Inquiry*, April 1979.

[35]For a detailed theoretical study of the influence of UI taxes on layoffs, see Frank Brechling, "The Incentive Effects of the U.S. Unemployment Insurance Tax, in R. Ehrenberg, ed., *Research in Labor Economics* (Greenwich, Conn.: JAI Press, 1977). Also, "Unemployment Insurance Taxes and Labor Turnover: Summary of Theoretical Findings," *Industrial and Labor Relations Review*, 30 (July 1977).

insofar as feasible, even structural fluctuations in demand in return for workers' accepting lower average rates of pay.

Insofar as the UI provides "free" compensation to workers when they are laid off (from the firm's point of view), the firm's incentive to smooth out unemployment fluctuations is reduced. The effect on wage rates and employment in industries prone to fluctuating labor demand is depicted in Figure 11–13. D represents the firm's demand for labor during periods of peak

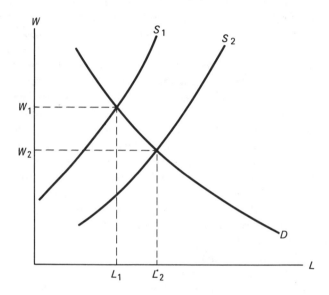

FIGURE 11–13. Effect of Subsidized UI on Wage Rates and Employment in Industries with Fluctuating Employment

demand and S_1 represents the supply curve of labor to such a firm when there is no UI subsidy to layoffs. In an extreme situation, where there is no cost to the firm of UI benefits, introduction of UI has no effect on the demand for labor, but the supply curve of labor is shifted to the right. Workers are willing to go to work for the firm at lower wages, given the probability of layoff, because they are assured of UI benefits when they are unemployed. This lowers the equilibrium wage rate and increases employment during periods of peak labor demand. Because lower wages induce lower production costs, the output of goods in industries characterized by volatile employment is increased relative to what it would be in the absence of subsidized UI. Moreover, because the gain to workers from steady employment has been reduced, firms have less incentive to reduce employment fluctuations through such means as producing goods with offsetting seasonal or cyclical demand fluctuations, providing worker protection from extreme weather conditions, and the like. All these changes tend to increase the number of workers who are laid off during periods of low demand. Such layoffs will typically be perceived by both workers and employers as temporary, and laid-off employees will have little incentive to seek new jobs, although they may give the appearance of doing so to satisfy UI eligibility requirements. They would usually be counted as unemployed for census purposes even without active search because they would be classified as on layoff.

Job layoffs, as opposed to permanent job losses, constitute an important cause of unemployment, and UI probably contributes to the frequency of layoffs in our economy. As Table 11–3 shows, job losses are a particularly important "cause" of unemployment among men and women 20 years of age and older. The importance of temporary layoffs in overall unemployment has been emphasized by Martin Feldstein,[36] and data from a recent study are shown in Table 11–11. For men aged 25–64, job loss accounted for the unemployment of 73 percent of unemployed persons. Among these, 40 percent were on temporary or indefinite layoff; in manufacturing, approximately one-half of job losers were on layoff. Feldstein notes that data from the National Longitudinal Surveys (the data used by Ehrenberg and Oaxaca) show that among men aged 45–59 in 1966, 61 percent of all those who experienced some unemployment between 1966 and 1971 did not change jobs.

The data suggest that workers on temporary layoffs are a sufficiently important component of overall unemployment so that the impact of UI through this channel could be significant. The quantitative impact, however, is not known. We do know that a substantial number—probably over one-half—of firms do not cause an increase in the UI payroll taxes they pay by increasing the number of workers they lay off.[37] Moreover, a study by Barry Chiswick of the effect of Special Unemployment Assistance (SUA) in agriculture during 1975 provides evidence of a significant impact on employment and unemployment in that industry.[38]

Agricultural wage and salary workers are typically not covered by UI legislation and therefore do not receive UI benefits, presumably because of the pronounced seasonal, and hence highly predictable, nature of agricultural unemployment. However, the Emergency Jobs and Unemployment Assistance Act which was signed into law on December 31, 1974, provided such coverage. The legislation provided for complete federal funding,

---

[36]"The Importance of Temporary Layoffs: An Empirical Analysis," *Brookings Papers on Economic Activity*, 3, 1975; also "Temporary Layoffs in the Theory of Unemployment."

[37]See Joseph Becker, *Experience Rating in Unemployment Insurance* (Baltimore: Johns Hopkins University Press, 1972). Reference is from Martin S. Feldstein, "The Unemployment Caused by Unemployment Insurance," *Proceedings of the Industrial Relations Research Association 28th Annual Winter Meetings*, 1975.

[38]"The Effect of Unemployment Compensation on a Seasonal Industry: Agriculture," *Journal of Political Economy*, 84 (June 1976).

TABLE 11-11

Characteristics of Job Losers by Selected Industries, Men Aged 25–64, March 1974

Characteristic	Industry				Total, All Industries
	Manufacturing	Trade, Finance, Business and Repair Services	Construction	Transportation and Public Utilities	
With job, on layoff					
fixed duration	21.5%	5.4%	10.4%	15.8%	13.0%
temporary duration	29.1	13.4	36.0	34.0	27.4
No job	47.5	79.4	52.6	47.7	58.1
New job to start within 30 days	1.9	1.8	1.0	2.5	1.5
	100.0%	100.0%	100.0%	100.0%	100.0%

Source: Martin Feldstein, "The Importance of Temporary Layoffs: An Empirical Analysis," in Arthur M. Okun and George L. Perry, eds., Brookings Papers on Economic Activity, 3, 1975, Table 3. © 1975 by the Brookings Institution.

meaning there was no experience rating. Thus, SUA provided a much greater subsidy than any previous UI legislation to firms' use of temporary layoffs as a part of their overall employment strategy.

Chiswick's study explored the effect of SUA on agricultural employment and unemployment using the simple analytical framework summarized in Figure 11–12. In particular, he hypothesized that SUA would result in an increase in the agricultural labor force, with a concomitant increase on on-season employment and off-season unemployment. Chiswick's procedure was as follows. He first set up "prediction equations" in which quarterly agricultural unemployment rates and employment for a period preceding the SUA legislation, 1948 through 1974 (unemployment) and 1950 through 1974 (employment), were each expressed as functions of a set of exogenous variables. Those exogenous variables are as follows: unemployment equation: the unemployment rate of males aged 20 and over, the unemployment rate of males aged 16–19, and trend variables; employment equation: an index of prices received by farmers, the wholesale price index for all industrial commodities, the unemployment rate of males 16–19, and trend variables. These equations were estimated by regression analysis, and the resulting regression coefficients were then used to "predict" unemployment and employment during the nine months following passage of the SUA legislation. Deviations from the predicted values are taken as measures of influence of SUA.

Chiswick's test, unfortunately, does not cover the entire off-season following the first on-season after SUA legislation, since his data end in September 1975. Thus, his study is not likely to pick up the full impact of SUA on off-season unemployment. Nevertheless, he found evidence that on-season employment was about 2.7 percent higher than it would have been in the absence of SUA, while off-season unemployment was increased by approximately two percentage points, or about one-fifth.

An Appraisal.   Economic analysis and a review of the evidence suggests that overall unemployment is increased by current unemployment insurance programs. The magnitude of the impact is much less certain than the direction, however. Feldstein "guesstimates" that the overall normal unemployment rate in the economy may be 1.25 percentage points higher than it would be in the absence of UI.[39] There are two reasons to be interested in this magnitude. One is to answer the question, does UI cause too much unemployment? UI does appear to raise the supply of workers to jobs with a high risk of layoff, raising the size of the high unemployment sector of the economy. In the process, implicit contracts between workers and firms are altered, so that the provision of "income insurance," reducing workers' exposure to the risk of layoff, is lessened.

In this way, UI probably causes an undesirable increase in unemployment.

---

[39]"The Unemployment Caused by Unemployment Insurance," p. 232.

On the other hand, the impact on unemployment through increasing the length of time genuine job searchers look for new jobs is more difficult to evaluate. From the point of view of human capital theory, UI may enable those individuals who face difficulties in financing human capital investment to invest in search to a point more closely approximating the social optimum—that is, to invest up to the point where the social cost of the last week spent searching equals the gain in increased labor market productivity that results from a better allocation of labor. Indeed, if this effect were sufficiently great, the economy's unemployment rate might ultimately be reduced as a result of better matching of workers and jobs. On the other hand, to the extent that UI merely subsidizes unproductive search or leisure, the unemployment rate is raised to an undesirably high level.

As with other government programs intitially intended to alleviate economic hardship, such as farm price supports, to the extent that receiving the payments depends not on being poor but rather on being "unemployed," unintended effects of UI legislation have emerged. Whether these program disadvantages outweigh the benefits of supporting those who suffer from genuinely low incomes because of unemployment or whether an alternative program would be able to furnish income maintenance as rapidly and as efficiently to intended recipients is unclear. One glaring gap in UI legislation is that there is no provision for payments to genuine searchers with no recent labor market experience. Although there are other "manpower" programs aimed at this important group, perhaps direct payments to all those who fall below a given income level ("poverty" level) would provide a more satisfactory means of alleviating the plight of individuals who suffer misfortune at the hands of the labor market.

One thing is clear: When evaluating employment policy against the criterion of the "full employment" unemployment rate, the influence of UI on the latter magnitude is ignored at the peril of risking dangerously destabilizing actions. (This assertion is supported in Chapter 12.) As the proportion of workers covered by UI has risen and as inflation and economic growth have pushed workers into higher and higher marginal tax brackets, the impact of UI on labor market unemployment has probably grown over the years. Suppose for the sake of argument that UI has caused a rise in unemployment of a half percentage point since 1955. Added to changes in the normal rate of unemployment attributable to demographic factors, the economy's employment rate if 1975 had been a year of full employment would have exceeded 6 percent instead of the 5 to 6 percent indicated in Table 11–11. Although this is not as high as the 7 percent suggested as a possibility by Stein,[40] it is much closer to that figure than to the 4 percent established as a national economic goal in the "Full Employment and Balanced Growth Act of 1977" (the Humphrey-Hawkins Act).

---

[40]"Full Employment at Last?"

Conclusion

We have examined the phenomenon of unemployment from various perspectives. We have tried to point out the diversity of unemployment experience. Although much unemployment arises because information is scarce and reflects search while an individual is unemployed, unemployment in other instances is more akin to temporary "leisure" than to a type of human capital investment. The latter type of unemployment also arises because of incomplete and imperfect labor market information, but is not a search phenomenon. Although firms may benefit in the form of lower labor costs from offering "income insurance" to their workers, it is uneconomic to offset completely the effects of uncertainty with a lower, but steady, stream of wage payments.

Because unemployment is caused by the basic economic problem of scarcity, it would be no more desirable to reduce unemployment to zero (without eliminating the root problem of scarce information) than to try to legislate that the prices of economic commodities be zero in order to make consumers better off. There exists a normal, or "full employment," unemployment rate that reflects the amount of search and income insurance the economy "produces." The normal unemployment rate will vary with the demographic composition of the labor force, the types of goods produced, the desire for income insurance, the efficiency of search activity, and so on. A reduction in unemployment may reflect an improvement in the operation of the labor market if, for example, it comes about because of reduced information costs (for instance, through improved transportation and communications systems). On the other hand, an increase in unemployment does not necessarily reflect a deterioration in labor market conditions; increased economic well-being may result in individuals' choosing to search more carefully before accepting a job just as they may also choose more schooling as their ability to fund human capital investments grows.

Exercises

1. The annual unemployment rate (U) is approximated by the relationship

$$U \cong (sn) \cdot 100$$

where

$s \equiv$ average duration of search (per worker) expressed as a fraction of a year

$n \equiv$ number of job seekers expressed as a fraction of the civilian labor force.

While an increase in either s or n (the other held constant) will increase U, it should also be obvious from the above equation that U, s, and n do not all have to "move together."

Obtain a recent *Economic Report of the President* and examine the data for U and s in the postwar era.

(a) When the unemployment rate is relatively high, is the average duration of search typically relatively long or relatively short?

(b) When U is relatively high, is n usually relatively large or relatively small?

(c) Of what practical importance (for economic policy) is the information you discovered in parts (a) and (b)?

(d) Name some governmental policy actions that influence s.

(e) Name some governmental policy actions that influence n.

*2. You are an employment counselor whose assignment is to advise college students seeking summer employment. You have the following information: (1) Firms are paying from $2 to $3 per hour. (2) Any wage offer between $2 and $3 is equally likely. (3) Unlike the more complex, sequential search process discussed earlier, students do not accept or decline wage offers until their search processes are completed. (4) Each job opening is for 40 hours per week and lasts for 10 weeks. (5) All firms are equidistant from campus, all students live on campus, and the sum of direct and indirect costs is $20 per search.

Your supervisor has instructed you to help students determine their economically optimal number of searches. Being an expert labor economist, you know that in the type of labor market situation just described, a student's wage offer is related to his or her number of searches by the equation $2 + [n/(n + 1)]$, where n is the number of searches.

(a) Calculate the marginal benefit of each of the first five searches.

(b) What is a student's economically optimal number of searches?

(c) Suppose the university decides to subsidize student's job-seeking activities at the rate of $5 per search. Explain what happens to a student's optimal number of searches.

(d) Suppose, instead, that job duration were extended by one week. What happens to a student's optimal number of searches?

3. Listed below are estimates for four local labor markets (for the month of May) from regressions of the form

$$U_t^A = \alpha + \beta_1 U_t^N + \beta_2 T$$

where

$U_t^A \equiv$ the labor market unemployment rate during time period t

---

*Indicates more difficult exercises

$U_t^N \equiv$ the national unemployment rate during time period t

$T \equiv$ time trend variable $(D, 1, 2, 3, \ldots)$

Labor Market	α	β_1	β_2
Altoona, Pa.	−1.212	2.015	−0.105
	(1.23)	(7.69)	(7.34)
Baton Rouge, La.	4.235	0.044	0.051
	(7.70)	(0.30)	(6.37)
Lowell, Mass.	−4.213	2.530	0.004
	(6.89)	(15.59)	(0.41)
Seattle, Wash.	−8.80	2.933	0.076
	(12.69)	(15.93)	(7.57)

Note: Absolute t values are in parens.

Source: Robert Fearn, Department of Economics, North Carolina State University.

(a) Which labor markets exhibit sensitivity to aggregate economic fluctuations?

(b) Which labor markets seem to be experiencing "structural" difficulties?

(c) For those labor markets experiencing structural difficulties, calculate the number of years before such difficulties increase the unemployment rate by one-half a percentage point.

(d) Suppose you are director of the labor market development agency for Altoona. Your agency will receive a large grant from the federal government if in five years Altoona's unemployment for May exceeds 7.5. Five years from now, the national unemployment rate is predicted to be 5 percent. Should you expect to receive the grant?

References

AZARIADAS, COSTAS, "Implicit Contracts and Underemployment Equilibria." *Journal of Political Economy*, 83, 6 (December 1975), 1183–45.

BAILY, MARTIN NEIL, "Wages and Employment under Uncertain Demand." *Review of Economic Studies*, 41, 1 (January 1974), 37–50.

BECKER, JOSEPH, *Experience Rating in Unemployment Insurance*. Baltimore: Johns Hopkins University Press, 1972.

BRECHLING, FRANK, "Unemployment Insurance Taxes and Labor Turnover: Summary of Theoretical Findings." *Industrial and Labor Relations Review*, 30, 4 (July 1977), 483–92.

———, "The Incentive Effects of the U.S. Unemployment Insurance Tax." In Ronald Ehrenberg, ed., *Research in Labor Economics*. Greenwich: Conn.: JAI Press, 1977.

CHISWICK, BARRY, "The Effect of Unemployment Compensation on a Seasonal Industry: Agriculture." *Journal of Political Economy*, 84, 3 (June 1976), 591–602.

Economic Report of the President, 1975.

EHRENBERG, RONALD G., and RONALD L. OAXACA, "Unemployment Insurance, Duration of Unemployment, and Subsequent Wage Gains." *American Economic Review*, 66, 5 (December 1976), 754–66.

Employment and Training Report of the President, 1976, pp. 171–72.

Employment and Training Report of the President, 1977, Tables A-1, A-15, A-21, A-29.

FELDSTEIN, MARTIN, "The Importance of Temporary Layoffs: An Empirical Analysis." In Arthur M. Okun and George L. Perry, eds., *Brookings Papers on Economic Activity*, 3, 1975.

————, "The Unemployment Caused by Unemployment Insurance." *Proceedings of the Twenty-eighth Annual Winter Meetings, Industrial Relations Research Association*, December 1975, pp. 225–33.

FRIEDMAN, SHELDON, DENNIS C. BERNSTEAD, and ROBERT J. LUND, "Inverse Seniority as an Aid to Disadvantaged Groups." *Monthly Labor Review*, 99, 4 (April 1976), 36–37.

GORDON, DONALD F., "A Neoclassical Theory of Keynesian Unemployment." *Economic Inquiry*, 12, 4 (December 1974), 431–59.

HAMERMESH, DANIEL S., *Jobless Pay and the Economy*, Policy Studies in Employment and Welfare No. 29. Baltimore: Johns Hopkins University Press, 1977.

HELLER, WALTER W., "The Administration's Fiscal Policy." In Arthur Ross, ed., *Unemployment and the American Economy*. New York: Wiley, 1964, pp. 93–115.

Historical Statistics of the United States, Series F1-5, P74-92.

HOLEN, ARLEEN, and STANLEY HOROWITZ, "The Effect of Unemployment Insurance and Eligibility Enforcement on Unemployment." *Journal of Law and Economics*, 12, 2 (October 1976), 403–31.

LIPPMAN, STEVEN A., and JOHN J. MCCALL, "The Economics of Job Search: A Survey." *Economic Inquiry*, 14, 2 (June 1976).

MARSTON, STEPHEN T., "Employment Instability and High Unemployment Rates." In Arthur M. Okun are George L. Perry, eds., *Brookings Papers on Economic Activity*, 1, 1976.

OI, WALTER Y., "Labor as a Quasi-Fixed Factor." *Journal of Political Economy*, 70, 6 (December 1962), 538–55.

PARSONS, DONALD O., "Specific Human Capital: An Application to Quit Rates and Layoff Rates." *Journal of Political Economy*, 80, 6 (November–December 1972), 1120–43.

REDER, MELVIN, "The Coming Demise of Unemployment." *Proceedings of the American Statistical Society*, 122, 3 (June 1978), 139–44.

REES, ALBERT, "The Meaning and Measurement of Full Employment." In *The Measurement and Behavior of Unemployment*. Princeton, N.J.: Princeton University Press, 1957, pp. 13–59.

ROSEN, SHERWIN, "Short-Run Employment Variation on Class I Railroads in the U.S., 1947–1963." *Econometrica*, 36, 3–4 (July–October 1968), 511–29.

Statistical Abstract of the United States, 1976, Tables 1267, 1300.

STEIN, HERBERT, "Full Employment at Last?" *Wall Street Journal*, September 14, 1977.

STIGLER, GEORGE J., "Information in the Labor Market." *Journal of Political Economy*, 70, 5, part 2 (October 1962), 94–105.

U.S. Census of Housing, 1970, Vol. 2, Table 1.

U.S. Census of Population, 1960, Vol. I, "Characteristics of the Population," Part 6, p. 218, Part 40, p. 275, and Part 23, p. 119.

U.S. Census of Population, 1970, PC(1)-D1, Tables 349, 354.

U.S. Department of Labor, *Comparison of State Unemployment Laws, 1971*.

U.S. Department of Labor, Bureau of Labor Statistics, "The Structure of Unemployment in Areas of Substantial Labor Surplus," *Study Paper No. 23*, 1960.

U.S. Department of Labor, Bureau of Labor Statistics, Bulletin No. 1310-4, No. 1312-4.

U.S. Department of Labor, Bureau of Labor Statistics, *Employment and Earnings*, Bulletin 1370-3, 4.

U.S. Department of Labor, Bureau of Labor Statistics, *Employment and Earnings*, *States and Areas, 1939–1974*, Bulletin No. 1370–11.

U.S. Department of Labor, *Manpower Report of the President, 1967*.

U.S. Department of Labor, *Manpower Report of the President, 1970*.

U.S. Department of Labor, *Manpower Report of the President, 1976*.

WACHTER, MICHAEL, "The Changing Cyclical Responsiveness of Wage Inflation." In Arthur M. Okun and George L. Perry, eds., *Brookings Papers on Economic Activity*, 1, 1976.

————, "What Have We Learned from Empirical Studies of Unemployment Insurance?" *Industrial and Labor Relations Review*, 30, 4 (July 1977), 451–61.

CHAPTER 12

Unemployment, Money Wages, and Inflation

A. Educational Objectives
1. Connect unemployment behavior with changes in the level of prices and wages
2. Show that the normal level of unemployment is independent of the rate of inflation

B. Search Behavior and Inflation
1. When there is unanticipated inflation, the rate of unemployment will temporarily decline
2. When inflation is fully anticipated, the rate of unemployment will tend towards its normal level

C. Inflation and the Firm's Employment Strategy: "Waiting" Unemployment is also Negatively Correlated with Unanticipated Inflation

D. Evidence on Inflation and Unemployment
1. The Phillips "Curve"
*2. Statistical analysis of the relationship between wage inflation, unemployment, and price inflation

---

*Represents more advanced material

The main purpose of this chapter is to extend the analysis of unemployment developed in Chapter 11 to make the connection between the theories of job search and the firm's wage-employment strategy with the behavior of the general level of money wages and prices. Up to this point we have considered only the determinants of real and relative wage rates. But important questions of economic policy also deal with the rate at which money wages and prices are growing and how these growth rates are related to the level of unemployment. The average growth rate of prices is, of course, the rate of inflation in the economy, and this is closely connected with the rate of growth of the general level of wages both through firms' profit-maximizing behavior and workers' attempts to achieve the highest real wages obtainable subject to the constraint of the demand for labor. Thus, the questions treated in this chapter center on the relationship between unemployment and inflation.

Search Behavior and Inflation

One important means by which inflationary pressures are transmitted to changes in labor market variables is through the search behavior analyzed in Chapter 11. The theory of search is based on the same kind of wealth-maximization assumptions used in the theory of human capital. Resources are spent on search up to the point where the marginal benefit (in present value terms) no longer exceeds the marginal cost. The wealth-maximizing sequential search strategy developed in Chapter 11 involves the worker's setting an acceptance wage and continuing to search until he or she is offered it, but no longer. Using a numerical example, we showed that the acceptance wage is positively related to the expected duration and negatively related to the cost of search. A decline in the cost of search results in an increase in the wealth-maximizing reservation wage and the expected number of search periods.

We now use the theory of search to show how inflation and search unemployment are intertwined. Figure 12–1 depicts a distribution of expected money wage offers, $f(W)$ for a typical job searcher during a period of general wage and price stability. Since the price level of goods and services is assumed constant, $f(W)$ also represents the distribution of *real* wage rates. This is so because we can derive the real wage rate, W/P from W simply by dividing by the consumer price index, P. Figure 12–1 can be applied equally well to the case in which the expected rate of inflation is zero as to the case in which the expected rate of inflation is not zero, but known with relative certainty. If both W and P are known to the job searcher, then inflationary rightward shifts in $f(W)$ can be related to the distribution of real wage offers through knowledge of changes in the consumer price index. To begin with, the individual searcher selects a wealth-maximizing acceptance wage W^*,

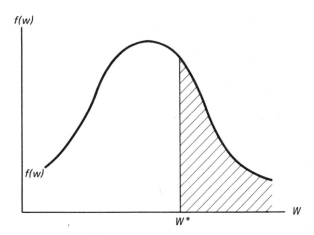

FIGURE 12–1. The Distribution of Expected Wage Offers and The Acceptance Wage

as in the example of Chapter 11. The shaded area to the right of W^* in Figure 12–1 represents the probability of receiving a job offer with wage equal to or greater than W^* in any given time period; hence it is inversely proportional to the expected length of time the searcher will remain unemployed. The farther to the right $f(W)$ lies, given W^*, the larger is the shaded area to the right of W^* and the shorter is the expected duration of unemployment.

Suppose now that expansionary governmental monetary policy generates inflationary pressure in the economy, and the rate of change of both money wages and prices increase by the same amount. In a world of perfect knowledge about the future—one, in other words, in which information were not a scarce commodity—a typical job searcher would have no difficulty forecasting the change in the real wage rates he or she would be offered. It would be zero, the increase in prices offsetting the increase in money wage rates. He or she would know that the whole $f(W)$ curve was about to shift to the right and adjust the search strategy accordingly by adopting a new, proportionately higher acceptance wage rate. In a world of scarce information, however, searchers will not be able to forecast the future perfectly accurately; indeed, in general it would not pay to devote sufficient resources to be able to make such forecasts. Thus, when there is unanticipated inflation, the actual distribution of wage offers will shift to the right before individual searchers recognize there has been a change in the rate at which wages and prices are rising. The searcher will be temporarily deceived into thinking real wage offers have improved, and may be "fooled" into accepting a job that would be rejected if he or she possessed accurate knowledge of the rate of inflation.

The effect of unanticipated inflation on search behavior is depicted in

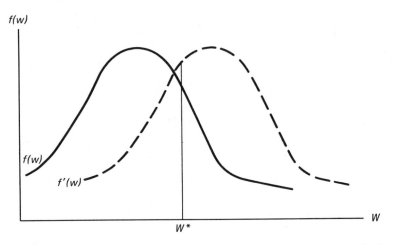

FIGURE 12–2. When There Is Unanticipated Inflation, the Perceived Wage Offer Distribution Lies to the Left of the True Distribution

Figure 12–2. The unforeseen increase in the rate of inflation has caused the true distribution of money wage offers to shift from $f(W)$ to $f'(W)$. Because they do not immediately forecast the future accurately, job seekers continue to formulate their search strategy on the assumption that $f(W)$ is the true distribution; thus, the acceptance wage remains unchanged at W^*. It is easy to see in Figure 12–2 that this ignorance results in a greater proportion of job offers exceeding W^* and a reduced duration of unemployment for the typical job seeker, since the area to the right of W^* on curve $f'(W)$ is greater than that on curve $f(W)$.

As workers and job seekers gradually perceive that there has been an increase in the rate of inflation, they will adapt their labor market behavior accordingly. To continue our example, suppose that the rightward shift of $f(W)$ to $f'(W)$ in Figure 12–2 is due to an increase in the rate of inflation from zero to 10 percent per year. After reaching a rate of 10 percent, wage rates and prices continue to rise at this rate every year and are expected to do so indefinitely. By observing the rate at which wage offers (one's own and those of other workers) are rising and noticing that prices are now rising as well, job searchers gradually become aware that W^* is no longer the wealth-maximizing acceptance wage. It, too, has shifted to the right. With no other change in the economy besides the upward movement in the "permanent" rate of inflation from zero to 10 percent, the acceptance wage will also rise by 10 percent per year when searchers have learned of the new rate of inflation. Although the acceptance wage rises 10 percent in *nominal*, or dollar terms, it does not change in *real* terms, since the numerator and denominator of W/P both rise by the same proportion. Thus, the acceptance wage will ultimately assume the relationship to the distribution of wage offers that it held when the rate of inflation was zero.

Figure 12–3 depicts the rightward 10 percent shift of the acceptance wage that eventually follows the increase in the rate of inflation from zero to 10 percent. As you can see, the area to the right of $W*'$ under the distribution $f'(W)$ is the same as the area to the right of $W*$ under distribution $f(W)$. *Once searchers have learned that the rate of inflation has changed, the expected duration of unemployment for the typical worker rises to the level that existed when the rate of inflation was zero.* The amount of search unemployment in the economy, which fell when the rate of inflation initially shifted upward, also rises once workers adapt to the new rate.

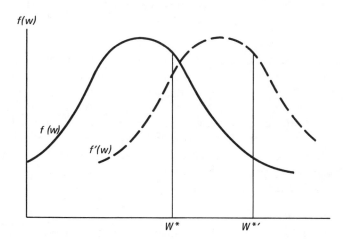

FIGURE 12–3. When $f(W)$ Shifts to $f'(W)$, $W*$ Eventually Shifts to $W*'$

The process in which job searchers lag in their perception of the true rate of inflation generates the relationship between search unemployment and the percentage rate of change of money wage rates ($\dot{W}$) shown in Figure 12–4. When the rate of inflation was zero, the amount of search unemploment in the economy was represented by the "normal" search unemployment rate $U*$ (point A). During the period before the labor market adapted to the new 10 percent rate of inflation per year, the amount of search unemployment declined, so that the search unemployment rate fell to a lower level, U' (point B). However, when searchers increased their acceptance wages to match the new rate of inflation, the unemployment rate rose, regaining its old value of $U*$ (point C).

A similar scenario would characterize the labor market response to a

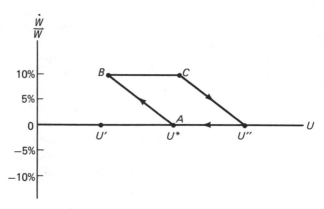

FIGURE 12–4. The Short-Run and Long-Run Relationship between $\dot{W}$ and Search Unemployment

reduction in the rate of inflation. If the government adopted a restrictive monetary policy that reduced the rate of inflation to zero, search unemployment would initially rise to an abnormally high level such as U'', but as workers became convinced that the distribution of wage offers had permanently shifted to the left, unemployment would gradually approach its normal rate, U^*.[1] Unfortunately, in an economy that has become accustomed to long-term inflation, the length of time it takes for unemployment to fall from a "temporarily" high level such as U'' to its normal level U^* may be discouragingly long.

Inflation, the Firm's Employment Strategy, and "Waiting"[2]

Not all unemployed workers are actively seeking new jobs. As we have seen, the firm's employment strategy (its decisions to lay off and hire workers) can best be understood if we recognize the importance of the need to anticipate future events in reaching current wage and employment decisions. The future affects the firm's present demand for labor for two interrelated

---

[1]The position that "real" economic magnitudes, such as the unemployment rate and the real value of the acceptance wage, are ultimately determined by *correct* perceptions of prices and wages has been most rigorously propounded by supporters of the "rational expectations" view of the way individuals make decisions. See, for example, Robert E. Lucas, Jr., "Econometric Testing of the Natural Rate Hypothesis," in Otto Eckstein, ed., *Econometrics of Price Determination*. Papers from a conference held October 30–31, 1970, in Washington, D.C., by the Federal Reserve Board of Governors and the Social Science Research Council.

[2]The discussion in this section draws heavily on Donald F. Gordon, "A Neoclassical Theory of Keynesian Unemployment," *Economic Inquiry*, 12 (December 1974).

reasons: (1) most workers receive firm-specific OJT that raises future productivity in return for expenditures of the worker's effort and other resources during the initial years on the job; and (2) workers are usually willing to accept a lower average rate of pay in return for "income insurance"—the assurance that the worker will not be asked to accept a reduced wage rate or be laid off except under conditions of an extraordinary decline in VMP. To the extent that firms and workers share in the cost and returns to firm-specific OJT investment, this act in itself provides a form of insurance to both sides (see Chapter 9). VMP may fall considerably before even a short-sighted profit-maximizing firm would lay off a worker in which the firm had invested in OJT. Moreover, the wage rate obtainable in the worker's best alternative job would have to rise considerably before a worker would quit his or her present job, since the OJT investment process would have to begin anew.

Implicit income insurance agreements would provide an additional cushion for both firm and worker to protect each side against short-term fluctuations in VMP. The worker would "pay" for this insurance, as we have said, by accepting a somewhat lower average rate of pay as well as by "agreeing" not to take advantage of short-term opportunities to earn a higher rate of pay when business conditions are especially prosperous. The firm on its part retains workers whose VMP has temporarily fallen below their wage by a greater amount or for a longer period of time than it would were there no implicit income insurance agreement. It is reasonable that the amount of income insurance provided increases with a worker's tenure, or seniority, along with the shared returns to firm-specific OJT. These actions mutually reinforce each other. The worker hesitates to take advantage of short-term opportunities to earn a higher rate of pay, because his or her new firm would not be expected in general to provide the same degree of protection against layoff when prosperity lessens as a firm with whom a great deal of seniority had accumulated. The firm hesitates to lay off an experienced worker because the worker might not be available for rehire when the firm wishes to increase its employment when business conditions improve.

Firms and workers both have an incentive to honor their implicit long-term commitments to each other, since both benefit from being recognized as "good" employers and employees, respectively. Under these circumstances, a worker who is laid off will have an incentive to remain available for recall, since the wage rate on the old job will be higher than that he or she could obtain elsewhere without further investment in OJT, and knowledge of the former firm's "fairness" makes the old job more attractive than an alternative job offering an equal wage. That is, laid-off workers have a much smaller incentive to search for new jobs than individuals who are unemployed because they are entering or reentering the labor force, "fired" from their last job, or who quit because of job dissatisfaction. It is useful to categorize laid-off workers who are awaiting recall as "waiters," in contrast to other unemployed workers ("searchers") who find it rewarding to engage in an active job search.[3]

How does "waiting" unemployment relate to the rate of inflation? Should we expect to observe, as with search unemployment, a negative short-term correlation between waiting unemployment and inflation that disappears when employers and workers fully anticipate the future course of inflation in the economy?

Suppose, as in our description of the relationship between inflation and search unemployment, that the government has engaged in expansionary monetary and fiscal policies which will raise the economy's long-term rate of inflation from zero to 10 percent. Individual firms will notice that sales are rising faster than expected, but it will be some time before they realize that a period of economywide inflation has begun. Even though we hypothesized an initial state in which there is no inflation and what might be called "full employment," some firms and industries at any moment in time have recently experienced slack demand for thir product, while others have experienced unusually prosperous times. Firms in the former category will find it relatively easy to expand output as demand increases by simply recalling laid-off workers who have been waiting to return to their old jobs. These workers have already been trained, and output can be increased relatively easily without increasing unit production costs. Other firms that have been experiencing relatively strong demand for thier products will not find it quite so easy to expand output. They will probably initially ask their existing labor force to work overtime at premium wage rates, raising production costs. The increase in unit production costs coupled with strong sales will tempt these relatively more prosperous firms to raise prices.

As the number of experienced unemployed workers falls, firms face only three options if they wish to continue to increase their labor forces: (1) Hire the experienced unemployed whose prior employment was with another firm. Such workers will require some training, raising production costs. (2) Hire new employees from the pool of relatively inexperienced individuals who are searching for employment. This also will force the firm to invest in considerable training expense. (3) A third option is to hire employed workers away from other firms by offering them higher wage rates. In a world where firms offer implicit long-term contracts to workers, none of these three options will be undertaken until the firm has become convinced that the increase in demand is going to persist for a considerable length of time. Option 3 is particularly costly, because it would be difficult to maintain employee morale if wages paid to newcomers rose above the pay of a

---

[3]Once again, it should be emphasized that this theory of the firm's (and worker's) employment strategy is consistent with but by no means requires the existence of collective bargaining agreements which deal with wage and layoff policies.

firm's older employees. Thus, firms will be forced to raise the wages of all employees in order to maintain "parity" between old and new employees performing the same tasks. "Maintaining employee morale" should not be thought of as simply a charitable act on the part of an employer. During a period of tight labor markets, employers will wish to reduce quits in order to maintain and expand employment. Raising wage rates in an obvious means of accomplishing this goal. Clearly, all the options open to the firm that wishes to expand employment when its pool of experienced unemployed workers has been depleted will tend to transform the increased demand for output into rising wages, costs, and prices.

We have described how an increase in aggregate demand reduces waiting unemployment as well as search unemployment and creates inflationary pressures, in part by causing firms to increase unit labor costs. Moreover, a general increase in demand will also eventually cause the prices the firms pay for inputs to rise. As costs increase, firms will not only try to raise prices commensurately, but will also find it less attractive to maintain production above normal, or "full employment," levels. The higher prices firms are able to obtain for their output will be offset by rising prices of inputs. Thus, as the economy reaches the new 10 percent rate of inflation—which we have assumed is to be maintained by government actions—production and desired employment fall to their former levels. Some recently hired workers will be laid off and firms will cease trying to raid the labor forces of their competitors. The unemployment rate will rise back to its normal level, but the rate of inflation will continue at its new rate—10 percent per year.

As the economy's rate of inflation increases toward 10 percent, firms may not initially need to increase the pay of all workers at an equal rate. The speed with which a firm increases the wage rates of experienced employees, who are already earning more than they would in other firms because of their investments in firm-specific OJT, will depend on implicit long-term "contracts" covering layoffs, quits, and the degree to which unanticipated increases in prosperity or the rate of inflation are to be "shared" with senior employees in the form of higher rates of increase in wages. Eventually, however, such contracts will require that if the "real" environment has not changed as measured by the firm's profitability in real terms, then real wages must be maintained. When workers and firms have decided that the long-term rate of inflation has become 10 percent, then the wages of experienced employees will be adjusted upward by the same annual amount, over and above increases that would have been called for at a zero rate of inflation. Ultimately, *real* wage rates will be unaffected by the rate of inflation.

The relationship between the rate of inflation and waiting unemployment is qualitatively similar to that depicted in Figure 12–4 between inflation and search unemployment. An increase in aggregate demand causes firms and workers to adjust in ways they would not choose if they immediately perceived the new long-term rate of inflation. Ultimately the unemployment rate is unaffected by the rate of inflation, although a negative relationship is observed between the two variables before the rate of inflation is fully anticipated by firms and workers.

The length of time that elapses before the rate of unemployment returns to its normal level—point C in Figure 12–4—depends on the speed with which the inflationary pressures are transmitted through the economy and on how rapidly anticipations adjust. The adjustment of workers' and firms' expectations regarding the future course of prices will be conditioned by the past. If history has been inflation-prone, expectations will probably adjust upward rather rapidly if excess demand increases, and the period during which there is a "gain" from inflation in the form of reduced unemployment may be quite short. Conversely, if the government wishes to eliminate inflation, the reverse process, in which aggregate demand declines, sales and production fall, layoffs increase, and unemployment rises, may persist for a politically and economically uncomfortable length of time after the rate of increase of prices begins to slow.

Suppose now that the government alters its aggregate economic policy in order to reduce the rate of inflation after employers and workers have come to believe that an annual inflation of 10 percent is the normal state of affairs. As demand for output falls, firms will first lay off those workers in whom they have invested least in OJT. These workers will typically be those with the least claim to income insurance. Searchers will find it increasingly difficult to find employment. Employed workers who are unhappy with their current jobs will encounter considerable difficulty moving to new jobs as employers sharply reduce new hires as well as recalls from among the experienced unemployed. Thus, employed workers will quit their jobs much less frequently, adding to firms' difficulties in reducing their labor forces downward. Insofar as firms and workers have come to expect a 10 percent annual inflation, long-term implicit contracts between firms and those employees who are not laid off—these are the employees in whom firms have the greatest long-term interest—mitigate against reducing wage rates immediately in response to the growing excess supply of labor. Thus, the rising pool of job searchers and laid-off workers is not likely to be accompanied by a quick decline in the rate of wage or price inflation.

Eventually, excess supplies of manufactured goods and raw materials will create irresistible downward pressure on prices, and the rate of price inflation will begin to decline. Job searchers will adjust their acceptance wage rates downward in order to gain employment. After a longer lag, implicit labor contracts with employed workers will be adjusted to allow a slower rate of increase in wage rates paid. Ultimately, the downward trend in the rate of wage and price inflation will offset the initial negative impact of the rate of aggregate demand on output and employment. The government's effort to restore the rate of inflation to zero will succeed if the political party in power can withstand the immense pressure to readopt inflationary policies while unemployment rises above its normal rate. It is this *political* diffi-culty—the short-term gain in the form of temporarily reduced unemploy-ment and the cost in terms of elevated unemployment—that makes the adoption of inflationary policies attractive and their elimination so difficult in most of the world's economies.

Evidence on Inflation and Unemployment

Our lengthy analysis of the relationship between inflation and unemploy-ment explains what is commonly known as the **Phillips curve**,[4] named after the economist who popularized the short-term negative relationship between unemployment and inflation we have described. The use of the word "curve" is unfortunate, since it connotes a stable relationship between unemploy-ment and inflation—perhaps akin to a supply curve or even a kind of budget constraint that describes the economy's available choices between unem-ployment and inflation. This is misleading because our analysis of the rela-tionship between unemployment and inflation implies that over the long term, the economy cannot choose between low unemployment and a high rate of inflation on the one hand or higher unemployment and price stability on the other. Rather, our long-term choice lies only between different rates of inflation, since unemployment will always tend toward U^* in Figure 12–4. Just think of it—a stable Phillips curve would mean that we could perma-nently reduce scarcity simply by adopting sufficiently expansionary mone-tary and fiscal policies. Failure to recognize the fallacy of a stable long-term Phillips curve not only exposes us to the risk of ever-increasing inflation and the attendant real costs of increased uncertainty in the economy, but also to the even greater danger that, frustrated in its efforts to overcome inflation through contractionary monetary and fiscal policies, the government will ultimately resort to "incomes policies," direct and rigid wage and price controls, and eventually to interference with the free market at all levels. Political as well as economic freedom are at risk under such extreme forms of intervention.

Evidence on the relationship between unemployment and inflation is contained in dozens of empirical studies, and we could not possibly sum-marize them all here. Figure 12–5 shows graphically the relationship be-tween the annual percentage change in wages (average hourly earnings in the total private nonfarm sector) and unemployment for the United States between 1957 and 1977. The arrows should help you see how the inflationary period of the late 1960s only *temporarily* reduced unemployment. The "big

---

[4]A. W. Phillips, "The Relationship between Unemployment and the Rate of Change of Money Wage Rates in the United Kingdom, 1861–1957," *Economica*, 25 (November 1958), 283–99.

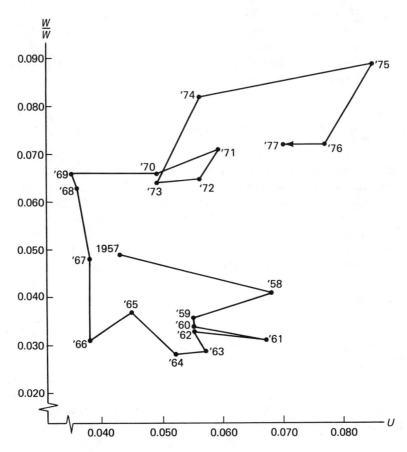

FIGURE 12–5. A Phillips Curve for the United States Economy, 1957–1977

Source: Employment and Earning Report of the President 1977, Tables A-1, C-11.

picture" shows unemployment revolving around an average rate that evidently has tended to rise over time (as we have seen).[5] One recent study that serves to illustrate more rigorously both the short-term relationship between unemployment and inflation as well as the tendency of the unemployment rate to return to its normal level, and which also addresses the difficulty of

---

[5]The clockwise motion shown by the arrows in Figure 12–5 is consistent with the stylized relationship between unemployment and inflation depicted in Figure 12–4. It is characteristic of the American and British economies since World War II. Before World War II, counterclockwise "cycles" were noted. See Herschel I. Grossman, "The Cyclical Pattern of Unemployment and Wage Inflation," *Economica*, November 1974, for a discussion of these patterns.

measuring normal unemployment, is that of Michael Wachter, discussed in Chapter 11.[6]

Wachter examined the relationship between the quarterly percentage change in the average hourly earnings of private nonsupervisory workers ($\dot{W}$), a measure of the deviation of unemployment from the "full employment" level ($UGAP$), and the quarterly percentage change in a broad index of market prices ($\dot{P}$). Wachter's basic wage equation is of the form

$$\dot{W}_t = \alpha_0 + \sum_{i=0}^{m} \beta_i UGAP_{t-i} + \sum_{i=1}^{n} \gamma_i \dot{P}_{t-i} \tag{12-1}$$

The subscripts indicate that the percentage change in the wage measure is expected to "respond" to lagged, or previous, values of the unemployment measure and the measure of price inflation. The i subscripts indicate that the lagged effects of unemployment and price inflation may continue for more than one quarter—that is, values of $UGAP$ and $\dot{P}$ for quarters $t - 1$, $t - 2, t - 3, \ldots t - m$, and $t - n$, respectively, may be included when estimating equation (12–1) by means of regression analysis. When lagged values are included, the *total* effect of the lagged variable on $\dot{W}$ is represented by the sum of the regression coefficients on all the lagged values of the variable ($\Sigma \beta_i$ and $\Sigma \gamma_i$). If you find this difficult to understand, suppose for example that $\dot{P}$ rose to a new level, $\dot{P}^*$, in quarter $t - n$ and remained *constant* for n quarters, through quarter $t - 1$. The ultimate effect on $\dot{W}_t$ would equal $\gamma_{t-1} \dot{P}^* + \gamma_{t-2} \dot{P}^* + \ldots + \gamma_{t-n} \dot{P}^* \equiv \sum_{i=1}^{n} \gamma_i \dot{P}^*$.

The unemployment variable $UGAP$ is defined as $(U_N/U)C$, where U_N is the "normalized rate of unemployment," or "full-employment" unemployment rate, average annual values of which are shown in Chapter 11, Table 11–10; U is the measured unemployment rate, and C is a constant, included to facilitate comparison of Wachter's empirical results with other studies. Since $UGAP$ varies inversely with the deviation of measured unemployment from "normal" unemployment, the expected short-run association with $\dot{W}$ is positive. That is, $\sum_{i=0}^{m} \beta_i$ should be positive and statistically significant.

The theory of the Phillips curve presented above implies that over the long term, higher $\dot{W}$ cannot be traded off against a lower rate of unemployment. Equation (12–1) allows us to test for this possibility. In order to see this, it must first be recognized that equation (12–1) is really only part of a

---

[6]Michael L. Wachter, "The Changing Cyclical Responsiveness of Wage Inflation," *Brookings Papers on Economic Activity*, 1, 1976.

Robert E. Lucas, Jr., has pointed out that the numerous studies which draw inferences regarding the independence of unemployment and the rate of inflation on the basis of regression estimates of relationships such as equation (12–1) are not rigorously derived from the "rational expectations" theory. See his "Econometric Testing of the Natural Rate Hypothesis."

two-equation model of the wage-unemployment-price level relationship. The missing equation represents the feedback from $\dot{W}$ to $\dot{P}$. In a stable economy with no inflation, $\dot{W}$ would not necessarily equal zero. Economic growth due to improvements in technology and consequent increases in the marginal product of labor would allow $\dot{W}$ to exceed zero with no inflationary impact on $\dot{P}$. Inflationary increases in $\dot{W}$—rises in money wage rates in excess of increases in the productivity of labor—will, with a lag, cause the prices of goods and services to increase. $\dot{P}$ will eventually equal the excess of $\dot{W}$ over productivity growth. This price inflation itself feeds wage inflation, as described verbally in our preceding analysis of the Phillips curve and as represented mathematically in equation (12–1). This "accelerationist" view of the Phillips curve bears a definite implication for $\Sigma \gamma_i$, the cofficient of $\dot{P}_{t-i}$ in equation (12–1). To see this, assume for simplicity that labor productivity, $UGAP$, and $\dot{P}$ are constant, and rewrite equation (12–1) as

$$\dot{W} = \alpha_0 + \beta^* \, UGAP + \gamma^* \, \dot{P} \tag{12–2}$$

where β^* and γ^* represent $\sum_{i=0}^{m} \beta_i$ and $\sum_{i=1}^{n} \gamma_i$, respectively. After full feedback from $\dot{W}$ to $\dot{P}$ occurs, $\dot{W} = \dot{P}$, and (12–2) may be rewritten as

$$\dot{W}^* = \alpha_0 + \beta^* \, UGAP + \gamma^* \, \dot{W}^* \tag{12–3}$$

or

$$\dot{W}^*(1 - \gamma^*) = \alpha_0 + \beta^* \, UGAP \tag{12–4}$$

Solving for $\dot{W}^*$, we obtain the long-term relationship between unemployment and inflation, after all wage-price-wage feedbacks are accounted for. This long-term relationship is

$$W^* = \frac{\alpha_0}{1 - \gamma^*} + \frac{\beta^*}{1 - \gamma^*} \, UGAP \tag{12–5}$$

Our theory of the Phillips curve implies that price inflation is eventually fully reflected in wage rates; hence $\gamma^* = 1$. But as γ^* nears a value of 1, $\beta^*/(1 - \gamma^*)$ becomes very large (approaches infinity). Stated formally,

$$\lim_{\gamma^* \to 1} \frac{\beta^*}{1 - \gamma^*} = \infty \tag{12–6}$$

The accelerationist view is that the long-term impact of a permanent reduction in unemployment from its normal level is to induce infinite inflation! Conversely, if it is desired to reduce U permanently below U^*, it is not sufficient to adopt a permanently higher rate of inflation. U will gradually move upward again toward U^* as depicted in Figure 12–4. It will be necessary to *accelerate* the rate of inflation continuously if $U < U^*$ is to be maintained. Eventually employers and employees will come to anticipate $(d\dot{P}/dt)$, the rate of increase of the rate of increase in the price level, and so on, until runaway hyperinflation occurs. A test of this view of the unemployment-inflation relationship is whether $\gamma^* = 1$. If $0 < \gamma^* < 1$, some feedback from wages-prices-wages occurs, but perhaps not enough to support the accelerationist position.

Wachter estimated equation (12–1) in a variety of ways with different lags on *UGAP* and $\dot{P}$, and allowing β^* and γ^* to shift over time. The period covered was from the first quarter of 1954 through the second quarter of 1975. His estimates of β^* range between about 2.0 during the early part of this period through about 4.0 toward the end. These estimates are statistically significant. This implies that if there were no price-wage feedback, a one percentage point decrease in measured unemployment, from 7 percent to 6 percent, when $\beta^* = 3$ and U_N equals 5.5 percent, could be "bought" for the apparently modest price of an increase in the *annual* rate of inflation of 0.39 percentage points.[7] A further reduction to 5 percent would "cost" more—an additional 0.55 percentage points of annual inflation. However, the estimates of γ^* are all close to unity when more than one period lagged values of *UGAP* and $\dot{P}$ are used to estimate equation (12–1). The difference between the estimated value of γ^* and unity is never larger than 1.25 standard deviations, which is statistically insignificant. The long-term relationship between unemployment and the rate of inflation allows for no "tradeoff." In Figure 12–4, the long-term relationship can be depicted by a vertical line through U^*.[8]

Conclusion

In this chapter we related the behavior of unemployment to the process of inflation. The main point bears on the difficulties we have encountered in the United States in controlling the inflation that has troubled our economy throughout the past decade. Casual observation of macroeconomic events during this period has led many observers to conclude that efforts to hold inflation to a "reasonable" level (say, below 5 percent per year) are futile unless we are willing to pay for relative price-level stability by tolerating extraordinarily high unemployment. It is true that once inflationary expectations become entrenched, a period of severe excess supply in both goods and labor markets may be required if inflation is to be quickly reduced. "Incomes policies" in their various forms of formal or "voluntary" limits on wage and price increases, "jaw boning,"appeals to patriotism, and the like

---

[7] $\dfrac{3 \times 5.5}{6} - \dfrac{3 \times 5.5}{7} = 0.39.$

[8] Remember that U_N is Wachter's estimate of the theoretical concept, U^*.

can be viewed as attempts to soften the impact on unemployment of reducing inflation.

Our analysis of the inflationary process allows us to see how incomes policies *might* be effective. By altering expectations of future inflation, an incomes policy might succeed in inducing workers and firms to use "restraint" in seeking wage and price increases, thus softening the impact of restrictive monetary and fiscal policies on unemployment. The difficulty in obtaining such cooperation, however, is a fundamental principle of economics. No *individual* worker or firm will reap the benefit of a reduced rate of inflation unless *all* workers and *all* firms act as if they expect the rate of inflation to decline. Thus, each individual, acting in his or her own best interest, has a strong incentive to ignore appeals to cooperate in anti-inflation efforts. Voluntary incomes policies are therefore almost certainly doomed to failure, and governments are frequently tempted to impose mandatory wage and price controls when they are afraid to face the political difficulties of controlling inflation through more effective means.

Since the cure for inflation is almost inevitably difficult, prevention would definitely seem to be in order. Once again the root problem of scarcity must be recognized and respected if inflation is to be avoided. If government attempts to deceive the public into believing that wars can be fought, defense maintained, and social programs continued and enlarged without reducing private consumption expenditures, then the tax of inflation is sure to result.

Exercises

1. Consider two countries that are identical except for the fact that in one the consumer price index is kept a secret and in the other it is published in the daily newspaper. Using the tools developed in this chapter, discuss the long-run and short-run relationships between $\dot{W}$ and the unemployment rate in the two countries. Specifically, are they alike and how should they differ? What is the implication of this for economic policy?

2. Suppose that society dislikes both inflation and unemployment (both are social "bads"). Draw a set of social indifference curves reflecting this fact. Be sure to explain carefully the economic meaning of their slopes and positioning. Draw the long-run Phillips curve suggested by the theoretical analysis of this section. Using the above set of indifference curves and the Phillips curve, indicate and discuss society's optimal combination of unemployment and inflation.

*3. Suppose that the economy's wage movements are determined by the linear relation

$$\dot{W} = \alpha_0 + \alpha_1 U + \alpha_2 \dot{Z} + \alpha_3 \dot{P}*$$

---

*Indicates more difficult exercises

and that its price movements an determined by the linear relation

$$\dot{P} = \beta_0 + \beta_1 \dot{Z} + \beta_2 \dot{W}$$

where

$\dot{W} \equiv$ rate of change of money wage rates

$U \equiv$ unemployment rate

$\dot{Z} \equiv$ rate of change of labor productivity

$\dot{P}* \equiv$ expected rate of change of product prices

$\dot{P} \equiv$ (actual) rate of change of product prices.

By definition, wage increase are fully reflected in final prices in the long run, and the expected rate of change of product prices is consistent with the actual rate of change in the long run.

(a) Show that this implies a long-run rate of money wage growth and price inflation of

$$\dot{W}_L = \frac{\alpha_0 + \alpha_3 \beta_0}{1 - \alpha_3} + \frac{\alpha_1}{1 - \alpha_3} U + \frac{\alpha_2 + \alpha_3 \beta_1}{1 - \alpha_3} \dot{Z}$$

$$\dot{P}_L = \frac{\alpha_0 + \beta_0}{1 - \alpha_3} + \frac{\alpha_1}{1 - \alpha_3} U + \frac{\beta_1 + \alpha_2}{1 - \alpha_3} \dot{Z},$$

where the subscript L denotes long run value.

(b) Under what circumstance(s) will the economy experience a long-run vertical Phillips curve?

(c) Show that if the long-run Phillips curve is vertical, the natural rate of unemployment ($U*$) is

$$U* = \frac{-\beta_0 - \alpha_0 - (\alpha_2 + \beta_1)\dot{Z}}{\alpha_1}.$$

References

GORDON, DONALD F., "A Neoclassical Theory of Keynesian Unemployment." *Economic Inquiry*, 12, 4 (December 1974), 431–59.

GROSSMAN, HERSCHEL I., "The Cyclical Pattern of Unemployment and Wage Inflation." *Economica* (November 1974).

LUCAS, ROBERT E., JR., "Econometric Testing of the Natural Rate Hypothesis." In Otto Eckstein, ed., *The Econometrics of Price Determination*. Collection of papers from a conference held October 30–31, 1970, in Washington, D.C., by the Federal Reserve Board of Governors and the Social Science Research Council.

PHILLIPS, A. W., "The Relationship between Unemployment and the Rate of Change of Money Wage Rates in the United Kingdom, 1861–1957." *Economica*, 25 (November 1958), 283–99.

WACHTER, MICHAEL L., "The Changing Cyclical Responsiveness of Wage Inflation." *Brookings Papers on Economic Activity*, 1 (1976), 115–67.

Index